No Separate Refuge

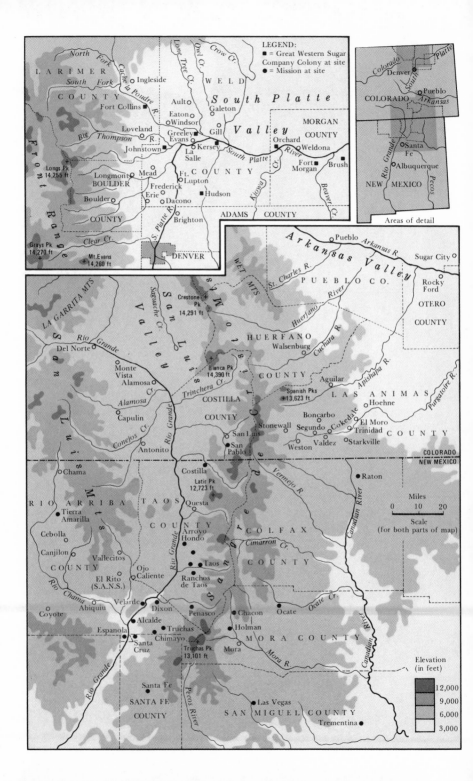

No Separate Refuge

Culture, Class, and Gender
on an Anglo-Hispanic Frontier
in the American Southwest,
1880–1940

SARAH DEUTSCH

OXFORD UNIVERSITY PRESS
New York   Oxford

Oxford University Press

Oxford   New York   Toronto
Delhi   Bombay   Calcutta   Madras   Karachi
Petaling Jaya   Singapore   Hong Kong   Tokyo
Nairobi   Dar es Salaam   Cape Town
Melbourne   Auckland

and associated companies in
Beirut   Berlin   Ibadan   Nicosia

First published in 1987 by Oxford University Press, Inc.,
198 Madison Avenue, New York, New York 10016-4314

First issued as an Oxford University Press paperback, 1989.

Oxford is a registered trademark of Oxford University Press

Library of Congress Cataloging-in-Publication Data
Deutsch, Sarah.
No separate refuge.
Bibliography: p.
Includes index.
1. Mexican Americans—Colorado—Social conditions.
2. Mexican Americans—Colorado—Economic conditions.
3. Mexican Americans—New Mexico—Social conditions.
4. Mexican Americans—New Mexico—Economic conditions.
5. Colorado—Social conditions.   6. Colorado—
Economic conditions.   7. New Mexico—Social conditions.
8. New Mexico—Economic conditions.   I. Title.
F785.M5D48   1987   978.8'0046872   86-32421
ISBN 0-19-504421-5
ISBN 0-19-506073-3 ppbk.

10 9 8 7
Printed in the United States of America

Acknowledgments

Without the generous assistance I have received from my colleagues, professors, and advisors, from archivists and institutions, and from helpful, if scattered, relatives, I could not have written this book. Without the support of a Woodrow Wilson Women's Studies Research Grant and an American Association of University Women Fellowship, the research on the site would have been greatly curtailed. Martha Graves at the Greeley Municipal Museum, Mariann Gallegos at Greeley's Catholic Community Services, and Professor Reyes Ramos at the University of Colorado, in addition to providing moral support and affirmation, made possible a series of vital interviews and oral histories. Cassandra Volpe and Beth Ann Berliner at the Western Historical Collections, Collette at the Colorado Historical Society, Sherry Smith-Gonzalez and Stan Hordes at the New Mexico State Records Center and Archives, Fred Heusen at the Presbyterian Historical Society, and the women who staff the YWCA in Denver and the Menaul Historical Library of the Southwest in Albuquerque performed the feat of making archives a warm and human place and research a less lonely task. John Brennan, Richard Rudisill, Orlando Romero, Margarita Mackenzie, and Tom Chaves were also generous with their time, and the staff of the Denver Public Library, the special collections at the University of New Mexico, at Adams State College, and at the National Archives were particularly helpful in seeking and retrieving obscure documents. I would also like to thank Charles Briggs, Eric Margolis, Esther Stineman, Suzanne de Bourgheyi-Forrest, Velma Garcia, Betty Naster, Karen Anderson, and Rosalinda Gonzales for sharing material and for warm encouragement. John Blum, Albert Camarillo, Pauline Maier, and particularly Nell Irvin Painter and William Cronon also gave generous and helpful critiques of the style and structure of the manuscript. Stephanie Sakson-Ford at Oxford University Press helped me say what I meant more clearly.

I owe a very special debt also to the men and women who were kind enough to share their experiences with me, to make a historically invisible people that much more visible, and to provide inspiration. For them I have the greatest respect as well as gratitude. For the sake of their privacy, I have changed most of their names here. But they lived difficult lives well, and should be proud.

I would particularly like to thank Nancy Cott, David Montgomery, and Howard Lamar for being a wonderful dissertation committee, for providing morale, balance, and challenges, for being willing to keep pace with me as I galloped through my dissertation, and for intellectual generosity, for contributing and stimulating ideas, revealing flaws, and yet leaving me free to benefit or to differ, and to create my own work. And I must thank my husband, Kimball Smith, for daily support—material, moral, and editorial—and daily laughter.

Cambridge, Massachusetts   S. D.
December 1986

A Brief Note on Terminology

This field of research is new and heavily politicized. As such, there seems to be little consensus on the terms used. While most people agree on "Anglo" as a convenient if occasionally inaccurate way to group non-Chicanos, "Chicano" is more controversial. "Chicano" apparently originated as a pejorative term, an abbreviation of "Mexicano," though there are other explanations. It tends now to be used much as "La Raza" used to be, to emphasize the Mexican and Indian heritage over the Spanish-imperialist one, and to stress the common experience of all Spanish-speaking, Spanish-heritage, or Spanish-surnamed people. Among non-activists and non-academics, different terms prevail in different areas. In Colorado and New Mexico, the preferred terms on the part of Spanish-heritage people whose ancestors settled before 1900 in what is now the United States are "Hispanic" and "Spanish American," and have been since at least as early as the turn of the century. Partly in reaction to anti-Mexican sentiment in the United States at various periods, these preferred terms are designed to distance these earlier people from more recent Mexican immigrants and to deny their common experience. In deference to the people this book describes, I use for the most part the terms of self-reference; but from a desire to have their common experience recognized, I use the term "Chicano" to incorporate both Spanish Americans and more recent Mexican immigrants.

Contents

Introduction 3

1. Strategies of Power and Community Survival:
   The Expanding Chicano Frontier and
   the Regional Community, 1880–1914 13

2. At the Center: Hispanic Village Women, 1900–1914 41

3. Invading Arcadia: Women Missionaries and
   Women Villagers, 1900–1914 63

4. Redefining Community: Hispanics in the Coal Fields
   of Southern Colorado, 1900–1914 87

5. "First-Class Labor, But No. 2 Men": The Impact
   of World War I and Mexican Migration
   on the Regional Community 107

6. On the Margins: Chicano Community Building
   in Northern Colorado, the 1920s 127

7. The Depression, Government Intervention,
   and the Survival of the Regional Community 162

   Conclusion 200

   Abbreviations Used in Notes and Bibliography 211

   Notes 213

   Bibliography 307

   Index 345

No Separate Refuge

Introduction

The houses of northern New Mexico blend into the land. Often they lie hidden behind or atop mesas, but even in plain sight, by their color and shape, they merge with their surroundings. Their plaster façades bear the same pastel earth and vegetable tones as the hills, and the dramatic rises and falls, light and shadows of New Mexico's arid north dwarf the one-story adobe structures.

Perhaps it is this posture on the land, so unlike the aggressive skyscrapers of Anglo cities, that rooted the perennial stereotype of a passive and fatalistic Hispanic culture in so many American minds. Certainly the stereotype measured not simply biased perceptions but cultural conflict. It marked a struggle between societies. For here Hispanics and Anglos met and still meet not simply in a political or even economic contest, but in a larger cultural competition.

What happens when two cultures meet is, in its broadest sense, the topic of this book. At its heart lies the dynamic of intercultural relations across time and space, and the essential role gender plays in that dynamic. Examining the strategies of Hispanics and Anglos who forged this particular intercultural frontier in Colorado and northern New Mexico from 1880 to 1940 illuminates both the specific local picture and the larger picture of cultural interactions.

Properly speaking, this was not a bicultural but a multi-cultural frontier. An increasing body of literature demonstrates the interweaving of Hispanic, Native American, and Anglo history in northern New Mexico and southern Colorado. And in the adaptation of these groups to each other and to the site, the environment, the lay of the land and its declin-

3

ing fertility, also played a crucial role. Both these strands of history need and are receiving further attention.[1] But the focus here is on the development of a specific migratory pattern linking northern Colorado, southern Colorado, and northern New Mexico and linking local political, economic, and social strategies with national ones. In this nexus, it is Anglo-Hispanic relations which take center stage. Native Americans and environmental factors enter only where they directly impinge on this set of Anglo and Hispanic strategies.

Traditionally the home of intercultural or ethnic history in the United States has been the field of immigrant studies. Chicanos have in large part been left out of this field, yet an examination of their position shows important similarities between Chicanos and non-Chicano immigrants. It is true that in Colorado and New Mexico immigrants formed only part of the Chicano population. And their experience differed from other immigrant groups in the proximity of their homeland and its vulnerability to economic forces in the United States. Nonetheless, the shift of Chicanos between their own cultural areas, including Hispanic rural villages within the United States, and Anglo-dominated industrial towns, mining camps, and commercial agriculture, mirrored the European immigrant experience in its shifts back and forth across the Atlantic.[2] Proximity of homeland never prevented permanent Chicano relocation in Anglo centers and the gradual expansion of the Chicano frontier from southern Colorado to Denver, the beetfields of the north, and beyond. In fact, from the building of the first railroads in New Mexico in the 1880s to the displacement of Chicanos by "Okies" in the 1930s, the Chicanos in Colorado and New Mexico provide a paradigmatic case of intercultural relations.

In addition, their story echoes that of race relations in the southeastern United States, colonial dynamics in Africa, and peasant-industrial contacts in China, Africa, and Latin America; the sequence of events almost anywhere people of one culture find themselves by force or choice integrated, at least economically, into an economy dominated by another culture. Not to recognize these larger similarities is to add imperialism's saltwater fallacy—that is, if salt water is not crossed, aggression and domination are not imperialistic—to theories of American exceptionalism and impose them as blinkers on the study of American race and ethnicity.

Few historians have written of the Spanish Americans of northern New Mexico, and fewer about those of Colorado, but since at least the 1930s sociologists and anthropologists from eastern universities, as well as from the Southwest, have studied them as the "peasant" within our borders. Their reflections, relatively unchallenged, have gained a remarkably tenacious hold on public opinion, for they loaned their authority to older stereotypes echoing those that dominators held about subordinates elsewhere.[3] The researchers largely agreed on what political scientist Jack Holmes refers to as a "Procrustean synthesis," that is, a sweeping if arbitrary depiction of Hispanic values.[4] These "values" include blind loyalty to and dependence on ethnic leaders (or "patrons"), a dislike of competition and personal initiative—the former feared as a threat to a communal life and the latter dismissed as useless because life is determined by fate or forces beyond the individual's control—and a resistance to social change.[5] Hispanics were supposed to be isolated, static, inflexible, paternalistic, and passive.

Nearly all these traits were perceived as threats to democracy, capitalism, and progress. Hispanic culture, thus defined, was conveniently the antithesis of all that was meant by "American," and provided at once a target for those who saw it as dangerous, and a foil and refuge for those critical of the predominant norms of the modern United States. Departures from the assumed Hispanic attributes were easily explained as "Americanization," as an abandonment of rather than an extension of traditional roles.[6] Like the "culture of poverty" theory, the view had its uses for those who needed to explain away continued impoverishment and marginalization.[7] Hispanics were generally seen as victims, but of their own heritage—their Catholicism, their environment, and their own elite.

The enduring and pervasive nature of this stereotype is revealed by the variety of its proponents. It is hardly surprising when such early organs of Anglo enterprise as Colorado Fuel and Iron's *Camp and Plant* and the Presbyterian *Home Mission Monthly* depict a primitive, isolated, fatalistic Hispanic society.[8] It is more surprising when George Sanchez, a perceptive observer whose *Forgotten People* has stood as a landmark in the recognition of New Mexico's Hispanic population, writes in the 1940s of the New Mexico villager, "he became self-sufficient in his crude way, having little trust in innovations and no notion of a changing civilization."[9] According to Sanchez, village economy "did not provide for major changes and did not anticipate the effects of new culture contacts and conflicts." Apparently the Hispanic villagers had learned nothing from their centuries of contact with the Indians and their trading relations with polyglot fur traders and mining camps. In a doctoral study of Anglo-Spanish relations completed in 1944 and reprinted in 1974, Carolyn Zeleny concurs that "political organizations, religious control and economic conditions in colonial New Mexico combined to create an atmosphere stifling to independence of thought and action, which left the Spanish Americans peculiarly ill-fitted to cope with Anglo-American culture," although in the northern villages colonial government had been conspicuous by its absence and priests visited only three or four times each year.[10]

This belief in the inflexibility and stolidity of Hispanic culture, despite contrary evidence, still had its purveyors in the 1970s, when even a new interest in Hispanic resistance movements failed to drown the old stereotype of passivity. In 1971 Andrew Schlesinger gave a fascinating and detailed account of the fence cutting and labor regulating "Gorras Blancas," but, evidently untroubled by the seeming contradiction with his study and by an absolute lack of evidence, he inserted that the Spanish American had "learned how to accept and resign himself to his fate. . . . He did not worry about the future, as he did not regret the past."[11] Positing a conservative peasant revolution, Schlesinger continued in the same vein, portraying the typical Hispanic who "sitting on the precarious edge of existence, . . . suspected that innovation, changing what had worked for so long, was a dangerous risk. So things did not change, and he learned how to avoid making decisions, to postpone what made no difference now." Even the Hispanic editor of one of the first books to discuss Spanish Americans in Colorado, *The Hispanic Contribution to the State of Colorado* (1976), described Hispanic culture as isolated, patient, and resigned.[12]

Though created from a patchwork of hazy impressions and fantasies, such stereotypes long made it difficult to conceptualize Anglo-Hispanic contact in a way that endowed both parties with initiative. Finally, in the 1980s, although the prevailing view remains the traditional one, the balance is beginning to shift.[13] As historians of immigration have moved beyond notions of "uprooting" to notions of "transplanting," so too have historians of the Chicano experience moved to theories of cultural interaction rather than victimization. They emphasize cultural continuity rather than disorganization, acculturation rather than assimilation, and continuous movement rather than a simple crossing of the border.

New interaction models eliminate the necessity of equating the geographical "host" culture with the dominant culture, a questionable equation in the context of the southwestern United States. After all, it was the Chicanos of New Mexico, Texas, California, and Colorado who first played host to the incoming Anglos, and it was the Anglos who displayed characteristic immigrant patterns of organization: clustering, voluntary associations, establishing a foreign-language press.[14] When the roles reversed, and Anglo capitalists dominated the region's economy, what Chicanos had in common with European immigrants of the same era was less a geographic phenomenon than an economic one. They found themselves partially incorporated into an increasingly powerful national and international capitalist economy controlled by an alien culture. When Chicanos sought work in Anglo-dominated spheres, they "immigrated" to a new economy, an Anglo world whose very structure was, to an extent, formed by and dependent on their presence as laborers.

Interaction models also transform the very developments once seen as evidence of victimization, disorganization, and enforced isolation— such as perpetual migration or the formation of ethnic "ghettos" and "barrios"—into evidence of initiative, enterprise, and autonomy. For European immigrants, Frank Thistlethwaite postulates, migration was less an act of desperation or evidence of cultural breakdown than a geographic expression of social mobility, the fulfillment of the economic requirements of one society by temporary entry into another.[15] Similarly, Ricardo Romo sees the high degree of spatial mobility in the East Los Angeles barrio as evidence that Chicanos refused to be "stuck" in the low-paying, seasonal jobs available to them there, and refused to be mired in the area's discrimination.[16]

The barrio itself and its organizations, according to Romo, Arnoldo De León, and Richard Griswold del Castillo, marked a creative and constructive response to changing circumstances. Chicanos chose to live in the barrio because its familiar language, kinship, and folk customs provided a sense of identity with the homeland and a place where they could socialize and even Americanize on their own terms.[17] Ethnic organizations fostered group identification rather than assimilation, adapting organizational styles and functions as the needs of the group changed from religious and social to political and cultural. The associations and the barrios signified reorganization rather than disorganization, and provided a tangible intermediary with the larger society.[18]

While the new emphasis on interaction and Chicano initiative offers a desperately needed corrective to the previously distorted view of Anglo-Chicano relations and dispels the image of lethargy, it risks, also, fostering a new imbalance. In depicting the barrio, for example, as an arena of autonomy and choice, harsh barriers of occupational discrimination and residential segregation can fade to a shadowy backdrop. Arnoldo De Leon demonstrates an extreme example of the risks involved. In an excellent and thorough study of Tejano culture, he lauds the "psychic prowess" of the Tejanos—Mexican settlers of Texas— which allowed them, in a hostile environment, to define their own identity. But he goes too far when he asks, "what did it matter that Mexican Americans did not experience upward mobility at the rate of the white population? . . . The point is that they provided for themselves and ministered to their own in common and familiar terms." In his claim that "while racism and oppression made the great majority of them politically powerless and financially poor, neither impinged upon the Tejanos' cultural world," he has separated too sharply the realms of society, economy, politics, and culture.[19]

In order to understand intercultural relations in the Southwest, and the Chicano experience in particular, these realms all must be examined together. Albert Camarillo, for example, challenges scholars who see the tensions after 1848 as the product of solely a cultural clash. More important in his depiction of the Mexican-American experience in southern California was the Anglo dominance of the growing capitalist economic system there, which by 1880 had locked most Chicanos into unskilled and semiskilled work.[20] And Mario Barrera sees political and economic powerlessness as the key to the continued subordination of Chicanos throughout the Southwest. To him, the barrio, far from being a Chicano asset, is an American colony whose inhabitants lack control over institutions within the barrio as well as outside it.[21]

There is a middle ground between these views. Chicanos and Anglos both tried to control the interaction on this frontier, and both discovered the limits of the control they achieved. By focusing on the relationship between their strategies, a new vision of the Anglo-Hispanic frontier emerges. Essential to that vision is the nature of Anglo-Hispanic relations across space as well as across time.

The spatial mobility of Chicanos has long been recognized, and yet few if any have tried to study them along their whole route.[22] On the contrary, the inhabitants of village and barrio have usually been seen as distinct, if not antagonistic, groups.[23] And the focus of late has been on the barrio. New studies of Chicano communities in San Antonio, Los Angeles, El Paso, and Santa Barbara have deepened and altered our understanding of the Chicano experience and of intercultural dynamics. They have detailed changes in labor patterns as the Anglo economy and industry increased its presence; they have chronicled the enclavement

of a once dominant urban population, and they have explored the limited options open to more recently arriving Mexicans in these cities.[24]
    But a group with as large a migratory element as Chicanos calls out for a study that will go beyond the bounds of a single geographically defined community, a study that will link, as the migrants themselves did, the disparate sites of Chicano experience: the home village, the city, the fields, and the mining camps. Even many urban Chicanos—since 1930 the majority of the Chicano population in the United States—lived not wholly or even most significantly in the city. Their family networks and strategies were not encompassed by the city line. For these Chicanos the region is their community, and questions of cultural and familial survival or breakdown, initiative or adaptation, can be understood only through a regional focus.[25] To focus on any single community, any single site—Denver, Albuquerque, a mining camp, a village—distorts not only the picture of Chicano experience in the region, but even the Chicano experience at that site. The Chicano experiences inside and outside the barrio are mutually illuminating, and taken together they reveal more completely the dynamics of the Chicano experience in the southwest, the parameters of autonomy and of subordination.

The northern New Mexico Hispanic villagers before the conquest had a culture like many other frontier cultures: dynamic and adaptable, flexible in economy and sexual structure. They exploited a variety of sources for income and added seasonal migration to expand their repertoire. This Hispanic frontier did not collapse with the American conquest. As will become apparent in succeeding chapters, Hispanic expansion and initiative continued afterward, marked both by continuity in patterns and by changes in means as the interlocking Anglo frontier brought new opportunities and constraints. From at least the 1850s the villages of northern New Mexico continually if gradually expanded, sending out runners to Colorado, north and south. They created a regional community bound by ties of kinship as well as economy. As a student of these Spanish Americans marveled, "It is remarkable to see a culture in conflict with a conquering culture yet still able to, in effect, colonize a new area in competition with the expanding conquering culture."[26]
    In this "regional community," individual Hispanics would not identify themselves as members of a region. In Greeley or Denver, they would not say, "I am from the Southwest," but "I am from Canjilon"

or "I am from Capulin." They would claim membership in a Hispanic village, even if they had lived in the Anglo north for decades. It was the dozens of such attenuated communities, one representing each village, which in aggregate made the area a region. "Regional community" thus describes the mutual dependency of migrants and villagers and the extended village that dependency created. It describes both a strategy and a geographical area, a migrant system and the routes those migrants traveled.[27]

"Strategy" here bears no connotation of conspiracy or of voting in popular assembly, though villagers did make collective choices regarding land use and schooling. For the most part it implies, rather, a pattern of private choices, an aggregate choice. And both the region and the choices continually evolved, as externally and internally initiated changes required new responses and adaptations.

The Hispanic communities stretching across Colorado and New Mexico, linked by common migrating participants and by kinship, created at once a single, expanded community and a multitude of cultural frontiers. Historians surrendered long ago the Turnerian notion of the frontier as a line between "savagery and civilization." Most recognize that "frontier" better describes both a zone and a process, an interaction between two or more different cultures.[28] The Anglo-Hispanic frontier in Colorado and New Mexico, which continued long after 1848, was no finely delineated line, but a range of situations, a spectrum.[29] In the frontier zone, Anglos and Hispanics settled in different densities at different locations, from the Hispanic heartland of the northern New Mexico villages to the Anglo north of Denver and the northern beetfields. The nature of their contact, and the distribution of power and autonomy between them, varied with location and time.

Moreover, conditions at one site affected other sites. This was not a series of distinct frontiers—villages, mining camps, cities, and commercial agricultural sites—but a continuous frontier, a single region, where patterns of contact at these different types of sites were interwoven.

The regional community emerges as a vital framework for the Hispanic side of the Anglo-Hispanic frontier, but it is only a shell. Strategies adopted by Anglos and Hispanics, including that of the regional community, embroiled concepts of gender as well as changes in actual behavior. As I conducted my research, I found my basic hypothesis—that Hispanic women, subordinated at home, found the move north a liberating experience—being undermined. Written history of female minorities or "ethnics" is rare, that of Chicanas or Hispanic women rarer though increasing, and of Chicanas or Hispanic women in Colorado virtually non-existent. The history of women in the American West, an exciting field in its own right, has focused more on gender patterns within the dominant groups than on minorities or women's roles in intercultural relations, with the exception of an increasing literature on fur-trade women.[30] Partly as a result of this gap in the literature, I had fallen into the common trap of accepting conventional wisdom, the received version of Hispanic women's village experience.[31] As I discovered my error, I began to look further afield for confirmation of my ideas, in particular to sociological and anthropological studies of women in similar economies across the globe and across history. The resulting revision, however, changed not only the picture of Hispanic women's experience, but the entire picture of the Hispanic-Anglo contact, the strategies and the possibilities for each party.

Middle-class Anglo women and men, social workers, educators, churchgoers, and farmers' wives, focused their missionary and Americanizing efforts—and their hostility—on working class Chicanas as they did on women of other minorities.[32] And Chicana work patterns became, as did those of women from other ethnic groups, an intimate part of the group's survival strategy.[33] The reliance of the debate regarding change and continuity on old male-oriented models of intercultural relations has distracted historians from changes occurring within female activities, even when the forms seem most stable. Furthermore, those older models have hidden the impact of changes in women's activities on the group as a whole, an impact crucial to the interaction of the group with Anglo society.

The aspect of this study which is women's history, which uses gender as a category of analysis, is not isolated from the rest of the study but causally linked to it. Chicanas experienced the Anglo and even the village world differently from Chicanos, but their experience vitally affected the Chicanos' experience. The male experience can neither be understood in isolation nor can it represent the experience of the entire population. Using Hispanic women in Colorado and northern New Mexico as a case study, this book reassesses the role of women in the process of cultural interaction. By tracing the transformation of work, family, and community roles of Chicanas from 1880 to 1940 through patterns of migration, organization, and interaction, it reveals the nexus of culture, class, and gender in a new light. It provides for an ethnic history that encompasses the experiences of both men and women as well as the interaction between them.

Using the regional community as a framework, this book examines this intersection of culture, class, and gender at disparate sites on the Anglo-Hispanic frontier: the villages or Hispanic center of the upper Rio Grande Valley; the mining towns of southern Colorado's Las Animas and Huerfano Counties where the two groups for a time shared equal numbers; and northern Colorado's Denver, Weld, Larimer, and neighboring beet-growing counties, an Anglo center. Only by recognizing the differences in interaction across the region, as Anglos and Hispanics met in the various settings, and by examining how those settings were related, can the nature of Anglo-Hispanic interaction and its ramifications for both groups be understood. Individual Hispanics still identified their community as the village, but what was being created on the peripheries of this region was as central to village survival as the village itself.

After laying the foundations of the regional community in Chapter One, and examining in Chapter Two the dynamics of the villages and women's place in them as the regional community becomes increasingly important, in Chapters Three, Four, and Six, I examine Hispanic-Anglo relations at specific parts of the cross-cultural frontier. These chapters focus on the dynamics peculiar to each site and on the continual change and adaptation that occurred within a particular political, social, and economic framework. Chapters Five and Seven cover moments—World War I and the Depression of the 1930s—when larger economic trends impinged on local adaptation and interchange and altered the game plan by changing the rules.

This study thus traces the rise and decline of the regional community from 1880 to 1940, and the crucial impact of Anglo contact and policies and of the regional community itself on women's place in the villages, in southern Colorado mining towns, and in northern Colorado beet-growing areas. In so doing it helps explain how households could bridge a gap across cultural and production systems, could remain culturally aloof from Anglos by supplementing the village economy without supplanting it, and also how and why Hispanic women, at the center of village life, found themselves, when on the edges of the regional community, when in Anglo towns and on Anglo farms, isolated and peripheral for the first time. Together these findings provide us with essential clues to the dynamics of contemporary as well as past Chicano communities.

1

Strategies of Power and Community Survival: The Expanding Chicano Frontier and the Regional Community, 1880–1914

When U.S. Colonel Stephen Watts Kearney marched into Mexican Santa Fe in 1846, his work was quick and nearly bloodless. He annexed New Mexico without firing a shot. But that was only the official victory. Achieving domination and cultural conquest took far longer. Even after the uprising of the following year failed, Hispanics had the advantage of numbers and an entrenched society and economy. And in the years following 1848 they thrived and even expanded their frontiers, settling new villages in southern Colorado and exploring new trade routes to gold fields. By 1880 the Hispanic frontier and the Anglo one interlocked rather than merely met. It was at this joint frontier that the Anglos arrived in force in the 1880s, with railroads, lumber mills, coal mines, and commercial agriculture and stock enterprises. This renewed Anglo assault posed an even greater challenge to the territory's Hispanics.

As they vied for survival and power, both Anglos and Hispanics formulated new strategies. The developments of these years, from 1880 to 1914, set for at least the next four decades the basic lines of contact and

13

conflict in the region. They also exposed the enduring tensions between
Anglo aims for both the land and its inhabitants, and Hispanic villagers'
own visions.

At the center of Hispanic strategies on this intercultural frontier was
the northern New Mexican heritage of communal villages, multi-source
income, and expansion of settlement. Of these three, the communal villages seemed most alien to the Anglos of the 1880s, and most fundamental to the Hispanics. By looking first at the Hispanic villages on the
eve of this enhanced Anglo activity, then at the nature of the new Anglo
activity, and finally at the choices available to Hispanics and the strategies villagers developed in response to their changing circumstances,
the implications for future cultural relations become clear.

To encourage the settlement of their vast arid frontier and to buffer the
empire against the depredations of Indians and other ambitious rival
powers, the Spanish and later the Mexican government had bestowed
communal grants on groups petitioning for land in northern New Mexico. The government subsidized the settlements not only through these
land grants, but through patronage of local church and government
services, and by taxing only the products of the land and not the land
itself. Furthermore, for the cash-poor villagers, taxes were payable in
kind. By the mid-nineteenth century, although the population seemed
thinly scattered on the land, Hispanics filled the arable river beds and
slopes and grazed their cattle on the grassy plateaus. Relatively short
distances separated settlements, and the settlers exploited the land,
through a mixed economy, to the maximum feasible extent.[1]

Village size and society varied depending on access to grazing lands,
ease of irrigation, and the proximity of trade routes, but the communal
mountain villages had more in common than not. In most villages, each
settler owned a small agricultural lot, a house, and the land immediately
surrounding the house. The rest of the grant, the pasturage and water,
was held and managed communally, much as in early New England
towns. Elected boards assigned grazing rights and delegated maintenance work, usually on the basis of acreage farmed, which, in turn,
tended to reflect family size.[2]

Villagers pooled resources in labor as well as in land. Women plastered houses, baked bread, spun wool, and stuffed mattresses in groups,
while men, sometimes with the aid of women and children, plowed,
harrowed, hoed, harvested, and threshed together, and herded and
sheared their sheep cooperatively. In some areas selected elders supervised the distribution of grain, weighing "the ownership of the land, the

amount of labor and time devoted to production, as well as the needs of the individual," and those unable to labor received their portions all the same.[3]

Each family, as on most frontiers, survived by varied production. Even village artisans and craftsmen usually farmed small tracts of land near their shops. Most families owned at least a few sheep also, and in this non-monetary economy, wool became an important medium of exchange, whether raw or woven.[4]

As on most frontiers, also, the villagers' economy depended on the labor of each family member. Women's work, in particular, and the flexibility of the sexual division of labor were essential elements in allowing seasonal migration by men to herd or to trade. While the husband selected the crops for other fields, the wife had exclusive control over the garden plot which produced most of the food for the family table, and which she tended with the help of the entire family. When men were away on seasonal absences, women irrigated the land. If the garden was as large as the fields, both sexes helped plant and harvest each.[5]

As a reflection of the crucial nature of women's contribution, daughters usually inherited land equally with sons, although in some villages they received livestock, furniture, and household goods in lieu of land.[6] This inheritance custom, their position as heads of households during men's absences, and the tradition that a woman retained her right to whatever property she had when she entered marriage, as well as her right to "community property" (property she shared with her husband), gave women a degree of independence, an ability to act on their own which would prove significant as more and more men left the village for longer periods.[7]

Status differences did exist, but the differences were greatest between generations. Sons, even sons of the relatively well-to-do, hired out as shepherds, goatherds, or farm laborers, to their own fathers or to other farmers and stockholders to earn the resources to establish their own households or launch their own careers.[8] Geography, climate, and village structure helped minimize differences between families. With small private plots and diversified land, large-scale mono-cropping was impossible. With communal grazing lands, none could monopolize this vital resource for his or her own cattle or sheep. And with fully occupied families, a rainfall inconsistent at best, and a communal ethos, there was not much room for a single family to gain a lasting dominant position by using village resources.

Still, it was a communal system with ambiguities, and the delicate balance between private and communal property in these villages was particularly opaque to most Anglos. Men and women held their private land individually while they also shared in the larger communal property. Private land played a key role in the membership of individuals in the community and in their sustenance and autonomy. No written law governed its disposal; theoretically the owner had complete discretion. It could, then, have threatened communalism and fostered individualism. But village mores militated against selling the land to an outsider, and such a sale was likely to result in the ostracism of seller and buyer. Privately held land gave room to individualism within the community, but at the same time the community limited that room in the interests of its own survival.

Unusual wealth, like privately held land, had the power to disrupt the sense of egalitarian mutuality on which the village depended. Yet there were "ricos." These wealthy merchants of northern New Mexico, however, were minor compared to those on the haciendas of the south or on the cattle ranches of the state's grazing areas. In mountainous northern New Mexico, the ricos' wealth tended to come from links to the world outside the village, and was subject to extreme fluctuations in the constantly evolving economy of the region. Nonetheless, the difference in wealth was sufficient to keep the ricos from attending public dances and public schools and from joining such village organizations as the Penitentes. And these ricos had servants and retainers—usually Indian *captivos*—and attended private Catholic academies where they learned English and acquired a taste for Anglo food, politics, and status.[9]

Despite their new Anglo ways, ricos remained, by their own definition, adamantly Hispanic and interested in "helping their people."[10] The villagers, however, saw them as occupying a world apart, different in its tastes, customs, and values.[11] There was, in a sense, mutual dependency. The ricos looked to the villagers for labor and later votes, and supplied them with jobs and sometimes credit. But this was a mutualism hierarchical in nature. The exclusion of the rich from village communal activities was a mutual decision. By externalizing the rich despite their obvious ties to the villagers, the villagers maintained an ethos of egalitarian communalism.

In so defining itself, the village walked a fine line. For the village was not self-sufficient, and trade played a crucial role in its economy. There were few barriers to trade, and most families owned the necessary team and wagon. The villagers produced small amounts of hay, wheat, onions, chilis, cabbage, sheep, and wool—products from the women's garden as often as from the men's fields—for sale in such regional centers as Española, Taos, and Santa Fe. Individual enterprise was more often channeled even farther outside the village.[12] Villagers traded at first with the Utes to the northwest and with St. Louis and Mexico.[13] After the Mexican-American War stifled the Mexican market for New Mexico sheep, New Mexicans shifted their trade targets to take advantage of new opportunities. They drove their sheep to the California and Colorado gold fields, to Denver, and occasionally to Kansas and Nevada.[14] To the Colorado gold fields also went provisions from Mora and Rio Arriba counties and the newly settled San Luis Valley.[15]

Family labor thus produced a sort of venture capital for the men, but that capital sought external markets. Village communalism was not incompatible with the individual commercial endeavors necessary for village survival. By profiting modestly from outsiders rather than from other villagers, by being capitalists abroad but villagers at home, these villagers, unlike the ricos, posed little threat to village harmony, and to the communal nature of village economy. They remained recognized and active participants of the village.

As families could not survive solely on the profits of such trade, when villages became crowded or grazing land depleted, small groups from the parent village would form a new settlement, again much as villagers in colonial New England did. In the 1840s and 1850s, for example, families from Abiquiu in Rio Arriba County settled Guadalupe in southern Colorado, families from El Rito settled Rincones, and Taos families settled San Luis.[16] From these settlements family groups would later form their own placitas such as Lucero Plaza and Los Valdezes.

Ironically, the United States conquest increased such expansion. Families set out to occupy new sites on their old grants, moved onto Indian grants or even to the California gold fields not only because of over-grazing and diminishing land at home, but also to seek better trade conditions and to escape the increasing Anglo influence, in particular the now Anglo-dominated Catholic church's new stand against the villagers' Penitente brotherhoods.[17] Some of this expansion was, in fact, made possible only by the expanding Anglo frontier, by the protection that Anglo forts afforded to Hispanic settlers, and the trade opportunities Anglo settlements provided.

The Anglo conquest and control over land had still barely begun to impinge on Hispanic movement and livelihood in the 1870s. The railroad had not reached New Mexico and had only just reached southern Colorado. At this point, its Anglo towns provided new outlets for trade rather than threats to old ones. Anglos entered New Mexico and southern Colorado with improved livestock, but in small numbers, so that the 300,000 sheep shipped out of Raton each year from 1876 to 1878 still largely belonged to Hispanics, and the boom in sheep brought attractive if ephemeral profits and prosperity to the villagers.[18] Land grants were finding their way into Anglo hands, but were seldom fenced or Anglo-colonized so the loss held little tangible threat.

The impact of such Anglo initiatives on traditional Hispanic strategies can be seen in the case of Elfido Lopez's father. In Colorado in 1871 Mr. Lopez and eleven other men went from Trinidad to Red Rock to file on homesteads, but only six of the twelve could afford to buy the shovels necessary to dig the irrigation ditch. They planted three or four acres of wheat each and harvested communally. Obviously, Mr. Lopez could not subsist on these holdings, even combined with his ten or fifteen cows. In 1876 he went to Las Animas, Colorado, to the southern end of the railroad line, and in company with several hundred men worked on the line while his son herded the town cows for a dollar per head per month and sold milk. In 1878 the family returned to the homestead with more cows, now thirty to forty head which Elfido still herded, and opened a small store.[19]

Railroad work, not farm produce and not permanent wage work, provided the capital for Mr. Lopez to make a success of his homesteading. This newly available episodic wage labor allowed a continued Chicano expansion even into a territory governed by an Anglo system where neither agricultural land nor pasturage was free. Such an expansion demonstrated one of the essential patterns of communal Hispanic village life which had survived beyond the conquest although through new means, as the Anglo and Hispanic frontiers interwove.

Villagers still had de facto free communal pasture at home, the possibility of physical expansion through groups settling grants or homesteads, and access to outside income via seasonal labor and trade. Village survival depended neither on isolation nor on refusal to change. On the contrary, through trade, migration, and expansion, the villagers proved the flexibility of the village system which had evolved on this frontier, and proved their ability to adapt to shifting circumstances. Up to this point, the Anglo conquest had more positive than negative ramifications for the Hispanic villagers. For every resource it diminished, it provided commensurate opportunities.

Ultimately, however, the same Anglo frontier that stimulated expansion became a major obstacle. While northern New Mexicans continued to homestead and settle on grants, and traders sometimes moved permanently to the Anglo enclaves where they traded, Anglo cattlemen, Mormon farmers, and Anglo railroadmen, land speculators, and merchants formed an increasingly complete circle around the expanding Hispanics.[20]

In the 1880s the changing pattern became clear. For the first time, Hispanic migrants from New Mexico to Colorado were matched by Anglos migrating from Missouri, Pennsylvania, Ohio, and Illinois. With each succeeding decade, while the number from New Mexico stood roughly the same, more and more states sent more and more people.[21] In the 1880s, also, the railroad arrived in New Mexico, and brought increasing numbers of Anglos there as well. Before the 1880s, because of their relatively small numbers, Anglos in the region had found it to their advantage to adopt Hispanic customs, language, and wives. Now their increasingly complete community in the West rendered superfluous earlier Anglo assimilation of Hispanic ways, and their increasing numbers enabled them to impose their desire for and attitude toward land and business more effectively on the local scene.

For Hispanics, barriers to trade rose on all sides. Licenses were required to trade with the Indians, and agents were inclined to favor Anglos over Hispanics. They believed "the average Mexican is too much like the Indian," and therefore trade between them would not perform its designated function of transforming Indian culture; would not, in the parlance of the day, Americanize the Indians.[23] Other trade moved away from old Hispanic villages to new Anglo railroad towns, and Hispanic freighters who had carried the majority of business could not compete on hauls covered by railroads.[24] In the past, these Hispanic traders and freighters had supplied essential income to their villages. Now they found their operations threatened because they lacked the capital required to gain access to the new means of trade.[25] On the most basic level, it takes a lot more capital to buy a railroad than to buy a wagon. And although a few Spanish Americans operated small stores and dance halls in the villages, most were thrown back on farming and sheep raising for their subsistence, a combination which had never completely met their needs.[26]

The new Anglo threat went even beyond the loss of trading income. The communal village land itself was at stake as Anglo attitudes toward land and economy, so different from Hispanic villagers', triumphed.

Anglo capitalists who came to New Mexico in this period took for granted private property, commercial use, and a monetary economy. The structures they created to settle land disputes, support the state, and manage the state's resources all assumed the validity of those propositions, not merely as something specific to their culture or environment, but as part of human nature and universal progress. To the Anglo, land not visibly occupied or, worse, not producing a profit, was wasted and vacant. In line with this philosophy, most Hispanic land grants, as confirmed by Congress, included only the home lots and the irrigated fields. Much of what had been the villagers' common land went to the public domain and in turn to railroads, Anglo homesteaders, and national forests.[27] Without pasture, the land remaining in villagers' hands was often insufficient to sustain their pastoral economy.[28]

Hardly quiescent, Hispanics filed suit after suit, but theirs was not the legal system. After forty years of turmoil, Congress established the Court of Private Land Claims in 1891 to depoliticize the land issue. But the court only increased the loss of land by Hispanics. Of 35,491,020 acres at stake, the court confirmed to Hispanic claimants in New Mexico, Arizona, and Colorado 2,051,526 acres.[29] The judges interpreted the law rigidly, rejecting even grants which were over one hundred years old and without previous dispute.[30] And the procedure was not free. Hispanics who won their case could lose land to their lawyers. From 1891 to 1910 every lawyer in the area had at least one land grant case at any time. As the villagers usually had no cash—even the payment of new Anglo taxes required selling essential land—lawyers accepted payment either in land or, if the decision was for partition and sale as the most "practical" remedy, proceeds from the land. Some lawyers received as much as half the grant.[31]

In the relatively small Anglo community, these court-appointed commissioners, the new claimants, the judges, and the lawyers of both sides were often friends, if not partners. Thomas Catron, for example, had come to New Mexico with two wagons of flour in 1866. He joined a college friend in a law practice, and was attorney general of the territory by 1869. Aided by this position and by his other legal and political connections, Catron had amassed, by 1894, nearly two million acres of land and held part ownership or represented the owners of four million more. Catron and other such speculators, both Anglo and the occasional Hispanic collaborator, often acquired title from as many of the communal grantees as possible, destroyed deeds given to them for safekeeping, and then claimed absolute right to the common lands and fenced them.[32] Alternatively, a single heir to a communal grant could, as did a financially desperate David Martinez, Jr., at Velarde, in Rio Arriba County, dispossess all other heirs by using an Anglo legal system which allowed, until 1913, any heir to petition for partition of the grant on the theory that the common land was "simply the aggregate of a large number of individual possessions."[33] The strategies varied, but the results, like the players, were almost always the same: the communal villages lost essential land.

Even for Hispanic villagers who did not lose title to their land, Anglo "progress" could spell disaster. Mine operators at Torres, Colorado, acquired right-of-way across Madrid Plaza in 1901 and used the land as a refuse site for mine tailings. The dumping caused erosion, leading to decreased agricultural productivity and the eventual abandonment of the plaza town—incidentally, making labor available for the mine.[34] In addition, the once free range was limited by the government's removal of over six million acres of New Mexico's land for national forests and by new homesteaders who, as early as 1900, claimed nearly one million acres in New Mexico.[35]

By 1900 most Spanish American villagers both in Colorado and in New Mexico found available range limited by Anglo settlement and corporations, and the range to which they did have access—whether by leasing privately held land or buying grazing permits for national forests—now cost them hard cash, if they could afford it at all.[36] This set of circumstances changed the structure of the sheep industry in this region in the same way the railroads changed the structure of trade, and thus changed the structure of the villages themselves.

In 1880, Rio Arriba County's sheepmen had grazed 21 sheep per square mile, one of the densest populations in the state. By 1900, 100 to 120 sheep roamed each mile of the county, an increase of approximately 500 percent. By opening new markets, the railroad had brought a boom in sheep. At first it might have seemed to Hispanics as though the increased income from the expanding market for sheep would make up for the loss of trade outlets, but by the 1880s those commercial sheep operators which had been glimpsed in the 1870s had poured into the Southwest with capital and improved livestock. The Spanish Americans lacked the Anglos' better breeds as well as their ample financial backing, and another facet of the Hispanics' life as capitalists had come under seige.[37]

As the number of Anglo-owned livestock companies increased and the market became more competitive, pressure on the land also increased. Land rose in value, and land transfers accelerated. Public domain became an object of exclusive control as stock growers acquired title, if not to large acreage, to essential watering places. By controlling access to water, stock growers controlled the utility of the surrounding range. Railroads in New Mexico, as elsewhere in the trans-Mississippi West, had received vast land grants of their own. In their own freighting interests, when granting leases they tended to favor Anglo commercial users over Hispanic small-scale operators. The Hispanic village system of stock farming based on ownership of sheep rather than land was rapidly becoming obsolete.[38]

Both Hispanics and Anglos enlarged their herds, but gradually the balance of ownership shifted and not solely because of shifts in control of land. The development is perhaps nowhere better illustrated than in the story of Frank Bond. In 1883 Bond and his brother, young Canadians, borrowed money from home and opened a mercantile business in Española, in northern New Mexico's Rio Arriba County. The business combined a general store with middleman operations in sheep and wool.[39] As virtually no Anglos lived in the county, the small-scale Hispanic mixed pastoralists constituted the bulk of the Bonds' custom.

The lack of a money economy in the region made credit extension an essential part of the business, if business was to be conducted at all. By the end of 1890 the Bonds had extended $10,265.68 in credit, by 1898, $54,685.18. The Bonds extended these sums on the basis of expected returns from their patrons' sheep, which the Bonds usually handled. And by 1893, the Bonds were buying all the wool in the area as well.[40]

This extension of credit brought the villagers directly into the national economy and made them vulnerable to its convulsions. In the depression years of the 1890s and in 1907 when debts were recalled, or at other times when the sheep men could not meet their accounts because of grazing fees or other expenses, many of the sheep farmers lost their flocks. They became "partidarios," or sheep sharecroppers, with the very herds which the Bonds had acquired from them.[41]

Unlike the traditional "partido" agreement, wherein owner and renter had shared both profit and loss, in the new arrangement the renter alone bore all the loss. What had started as a way for sons to establish their own herds became a self-perpetuating system to provide pastoral labor for consolidated and rationalized sheep farming and a way to assure the Bonds a steady flow of sheep and wool for market.

The Bonds rapidly acquired 25,000 sheep and handled 100,000 to 200,000 each year, as well as half a million pounds of wool.[42] Credit extension had provided the Bonds with entrée to the local economy and with the means to control it. By 1905 the Bonds were using their profits from Española to expand their business dealings in New Mexico and to carry them into southern Colorado, investing in land and sheep there as well.[43] What had been the scant trade resources of the Hispanic villagers were now providing the capital instead for Anglo expansion, while the Hispanics themselves were gradually losing control over their own means of production.

By 1900, one-quarter to one-half of all New Mexico's sheep were under partido contracts.[44] Many villages shared the experience of Tierra Amarilla, which, between loss of common land and credit relations with the Bonds and their ilk, had gone from a village of farmers with a few ranch hands in 1880 to a village of workers for wages.[45] In 1880 in Rio Arriba county, to be a sheepherder was to be a youth, a subordinate member of a household. In 1900, roughly half the greatly increased number of shepherds and day laborers were heads of households. Sons could no longer expect to move from being a laborer to an owner. Instead they went from their parents' or grandparents' ranches to work for other owners as buyers, foremen, or, most often, as herders at fifteen or sixteen dollars a month with board.[46]

This revolution in the local sheep industry also revolutionized villagers' relations with the outside world, for it meant that, deprived of their long-distance trade and of their sheep—their major sources of capital—the vast majority of Hispanic villagers would enter the Anglo economy as laborers only, whereas once almost all had been both laborers and capitalists. Moreover, as the growing commercial livestock industry, railroads, and national forests consumed more and more land, Hispanics, like Indians, found themselves on a land base increasingly inadequate to their needs.[47] Crowding was not new to the Hispanic villages. The decreasing land base became a problem only when traditional avenues of expansion (colonization and trading) had been cut off by Anglo incursions onto the Hispanics' economic base. Faced with a truncated frontier and an increasingly intrusive conquering economy and culture, the Hispanics could not retreat. They had to find new modes of expansion, had to choose how to adapt or to resist. They had to formulate new strategies in order to maintain the viability of their villages.

And it was not only loss of resources that Hispanics confronted after

the renewed Anglo conquest. Social relations between Anglos and Hispanics also affected Hispanic choices of resistance or accommodation.
While intermarriage and mingling for business purposes continued to
occur at elite levels, albeit in declining numbers, they were rare among
the villagers, and the generalized interracial experience was probably
most articulately expressed by John Lawrence, a rancher married to a
Hispanic woman in southern Colorado. In his diary, Lawrence recorded
his reactions to Anglo behavior on two separate occasions, in 1902 and
in 1904.[48] On the first occasion, a jury had delivered a verdict of not
guilty for the accused Anglo murderer of a Spanish American sheep
man. Lawrence claimed that

> this was expected by me, as it was race prejudice, for in the nearly 36 years
> of the county . . . there never has been a case where . . . the American com-
> mitted a crime against a Mexican but what the American has gone clear, and
> for the same time there has only been one case where an American has
> accused a Mexican of a crime . . . but what the Mexican has been found guilty
> and sent to the penitentiary.

The second incident occured during a flu epidemic. Lawrence mis-
trusted the care of the Anglo doctor when the daughter of Hispanic
friends died:

> And here I want to say, that it looks to me as though the doctors have no
> more care or sympathy for the sick than a coyote has for a rabbit, if they are
> rich, the drs. will do everything for the money, but if they are poor, a dead
> Mexican is as good as a live one to them. The county or town pay them, and
> it all goes in the bill dead or alive.

Socially as well as economically marginalized by the new order, the economic and social foundations of their culture threatened by new Anglo
institutions of industry, government, and education, many Hispanics
organized along ethnic lines to resist the onslaught, control it, or even
turn it back.

Resistance coalesced particularly around the most tangible symbols of
the Anglo conquest and Hispanic loss—the railroads and fences. In the
1880s New Mexico's Hispanic small farmers, like other farmers across
the nation, resented the huge grants made to railroads, their control
over the leasing of those grants, and their monopoly of trade. Hispanics
also resented their power as employers and their exploitation of local
lumber resources. To Hispanics, the railroads were simply among the
largest of the Anglo land-grabbers. By the end of the decade, this hos-

tility toward the railroads and what they represented, as well as conflict over Anglo and Hispanic attempts to fence and control the range, burst into violence in San Miguel, Mora, and Rio Arriba counties in New Mexico, and in the San Luis Valley of Colorado. The best remembered of these organized resistance movements is the "Gorras Blancas," or "White Caps" of San Miguel County. At their peak, the secret organization claimed 1500 members, including respected officials of the villages; a good number of the local, largely Hispanic, Knights of Labor, including a district organizer; and a sprinkling of "quasi-bandits." They rode abroad, mainly at night, in groups of varying size, from 66 to 300 or more, and, for the most part, confined their activities to fence cutting and the defense of fence cutters. They cut the fences of Hispanics as well as of Anglos, and of the parish priest, and were not above using the general "disorder" to settle personal grudges. But they also attacked the railroads. They tore up tracks, burned bridges, ordered teamsters to strike, hacked nine thousand railroad ties in half, and tried to set standard prices for all wood cut and hauled. Their platform, which they nailed to the buildings of East Las Vegas one midnight in March 1890, claimed, "Our purpose is to protect the rights of the people in general and especially those of the helpless classes."[49]

In their platform, the Gorras Blancas cried out against land grabbers and "knavish" lawyers, against monopolizers of water, against bossism, and even against agitation on racial issues. They covered, in short, the whole scope of the Anglo impact, and they enjoyed the support of almost the entire Hispanic, and for a time even some of the Anglo community. In December 1889, when alleged fence cutters were released from jail in Las Vegas, they paraded down the street led by women waving the American flag and singing, "John Brown's Body," and were followed by "a squad of little girls." "These people," a mystified local editor, Russel A. Kistler, wrote, "in some way regard themselves as martyrs."[50] The Gorras Blancas and their supporters did not see a necessary connection between living under the American flag, enjoying the liberties it promised, and living under a particular economic system. After a town meeting the following August, Governor Prince complained that nearly four-fifths of the audience, including many of the "best citizens," had expressed sympathy for the fence cutters.[51]

With the development of the local People's Party in 1890, which incorporated many of the leaders of the Gorras Blancas and channeled their energies in more institutionalized directions, and with the estab-

lishment of the Court of Private Land Claims in 1891, incidents of organized violence in San Miguel County declined. But the "Manos Negras"
or "Black Hands" rode on in Rio Arriba County through the 1890s, and
both organizations continued to ride, cutting fences and burning barns
sporadically through at least the 1920s.[52]

The Gorras Blancas met with some success. The People's Party won
at the local polls in 1890; the railroad bought its ties elsewhere (a mixed
blessing as the preserved lumber resources cost the county's inhabitants
an estimated $100,000 in revenue); and settlement by Anglos of the Las
Vegas grant slowed to a virtual halt until 1906.[53] But in general, the tide
could not be turned back, and for Hispanic villagers, organized violence
required time, money for lawyers' fees, and great personal risk for questionable rewards. Most Hispanics turned to other means, both outside
and within the Anglo system, to resist Anglo incursions and dominance.
They turned to other strategies, both organized and individual.

In the more remote villages, even local Penitente societies shifted
focus and became politically active, some evolving into political
machines.[54] Elsewhere, in villages suddenly surrounded by Anglo-controlled mining or railroad towns and among Hispanic trackworkers,
"mutualistas" (mutual aid organizations) sprang up; seventeen formed
in New Mexico between 1885 and 1912, and eight branches of a single
Colorado organization, the "Sociedad Protección Mutua de Trabajadores Unidos" (S.P.M.D.T.U.) took root.[55] The S.P.M.D.T.U., like
mutual aid societies of other ethnic groups, developed an insurance program, but it had begun with a different aim. It originated during the
1900 election as an attempt to mobilize Spanish Americans against discrimination.[56] As villages became ethnic enclaves, Hispanics drew on
village precursors, like the Penitentes, and recast them in more urban
and political modes. Sharing the newer aims of the Gorras Blancas, such
organizations stood against bossism and political corruption, and for
mutual protection and an active role in determining the new hierarchy.[57] Like the more violent groups, they were part of a broadly based
attempt to retain or achieve some control over the confrontation with
Anglos, but unlike those organizations, they were adapted to a situation
of daily coexistence.

Hispanics as a group did retain some leverage in electoral politics.
The numerical superiority of Hispanics in New Mexico until the 1920s
and in parts of Colorado ensured that politicians of either ethnic group
would ignore the accusation that courting the Hispanic vote was "fan-
ning the race issue." The People's Party victories had proved the effi-

cacy of the ethnic vote, and in New Mexico, Spanish Americans long had a majority in the House of Representatives.[58] Predictably, however, working through Anglo institutions brought only limited success. In territorial New Mexico, San Miguel County's People's Party found that too many key positions were appointive for them to be able to effect their pledges. And networks of patronage erected in territorial days, extending from Anglo politicos in the capital to Hispanic villagers, continued to foster division on party lines among Hispanics long after the achievement of statehood in 1912.[59] Hispanics never succeeded in attaining sufficient political unity, despite the exhortations of the Spanish-language press, to dominate New Mexico's government. And while Hispanic grantees continued to sue, even victorious court cases rarely retained for grant residents the right to use the grant for commercial purposes; such villagers still had to look elsewhere for the capital necessary to pay their taxes and fees, to look elsewhere in defense of their interests.[60]

Many Spanish Americans eagerly sought to acquire Anglo skills, believing these would allow them to succeed in the new economic order. A county school superintendent reported that rural Hispanics "especially . . . seem to be realizing the fact that, if their children are to compete successfully in the struggle for existence . . . the new generation must be educated and trained according to modern standards."[61] In counties such as Taos and Rio Arriba, where poverty kept the few public schools poorly staffed and open for only one to three months, Hispanics flocked to Catholic boarding schools if they could afford them, or to inexpensive Anglo-run and -staffed nine-month Protestant, usually Presbyterian, mission schools. Impoverished parents drove a hundred miles with their children, and mothers moved into town for the winter to send their children to these Protestant schools despite dire warnings by priests and the missions' package deal of Anglo skills wrapped in Anglo culture.[62]

All this activity was a welcome development to many Anglos, who had seen in such groups as the Gorras Blancas a threat to the Anglo way of life and who felt much the same about Catholicism and communalism.[63] In their drive for a Protestant citizenship, these Anglos rejoiced at the apparent Hispanic disposition "to break away from their priestley [sic] bondage and superstition" and at what seemed to Anglos an inseparable "readiness to adopt our political ideas and our social customs and institutions."[64] Actually, Hispanics never converted in impressive numbers regardless of how many attended the schools, but the shortlived Presbyterian College of the Southwest did turn out eight ordained ministers, nine teachers, ten evangelists, four editors, four ministers' wives, three merchants, one lawyer, and one government employee, all Hispanic.[65] The Presbyterian education produced an elite corps of Hispanics who succeeded in the Anglo context, but at a price. Strictures regarding clothing, smoking, drinking, and sabbath observance help explain the pattern of twin Hispanic villages in southern Colorado, split along religious lines.[66] The new religion could distance its adherents from old neighbors as well as old customs. And yet the new power of the Presbyterian graduates was in some ways illusory. To a degree they had simply been co-opted, kept in a marginal position and brought under Anglo control. Through Anglo control of local and national presbyteries, which provided funds and assignments, Anglos retained control even of local Spanish-speaking churches.[67] Furthermore, as Anglo communities grew, previously mixed congregations were segregated into "first" (Anglo) and "second" (Hispanic) churches.[68] The aim may have been to "Americanize" the Spanish Americans, but it was not necessarily to integrate them.

There were other ways for Hispanics to achieve elite status through collaboration or contact with Anglos, ways that may have failed for the group as a whole but brought success to certain individuals. Spanish Americans who held vast individual land grants on the plains were independent of communal lands. They had already built up large herds of sheep and had accumulated capital. These ricos benefited most evidently and rapidly from the growing traffic and its cash nexus. But even in mountain villages, minor differences could become greater. A few small-scale commercial sheep farmers and merchants gained access to Anglo markets and creditors and became channels of the same for their compatriots of increasingly modest means. And new patrons arose whose very position, and not just contacts, resulted from the new Anglo system. The new patron could be the local party official who recommended men and women for postmasterships, or the newly elected justice of the peace, or the president of the school district who dispensed contracts for fuel, janitorial services, and teaching. He might be a labor recruiter or someone who leased land from the railroad, and re-leased it to other villagers. Most important, he came nearest to controlling access to credit in the village.[69] These "ricos," new and old, could, in turn, provide Anglo contacts with political support, implemented through their economic influence over increasingly dependent fellow

Hispanics. As mediators, they hoped to secure their own status in the new regime.[70]

By 1880, the connection between the "ricos," commercial sheep farming, and politics was clear, as was the small size of the Hispanic group who gained through the triad. In that year three-quarters of New Mexico's sheep belonged to just twenty families, four-fifths of them natives of New Mexico. The Spanish Americans in the legislature belonged to "no more than 26 prominent families."[71] It was not a strategy even accessible to the majority of Hispanics.

The increased stratification and the dependence of ricos on Anglos meant that accommodation often took forms that served the interest of only the upper 5 percent of Spanish Americans. For example, property in livestock was uniformly underestimated by large-scale ranchers of both ethnic groups. One reporter in 1903 claimed that while owners of 2000 head of sheep would report only 200, "where a poor man has only four or five hundred sheep the assessor puts them all in, and thus those who should pay the bulk of the taxes get out of it and the small property and stockowners pay them."[72] To many Anglos, this sort of behavior on the part of the ricos was proof of assimilability. Congratulating the wealthy rancher Miguel A. Otero (whose mother, incidentally, was an Anglo), on his appointment as New Mexico's first Hispanic governor, an Anglo fan in Washington, D.C., wrote in 1901:

> You are looked upon as the leader of an advanced movement among the Native race in New Mexico and had you been struck down it would have been notice to the world that the Native race was not in favor of the new order of things. The hardest thing I have to combat is that the 'Mexicans,' as the native race is termed, is [sic] not in harmony with American ideas.[73]

These elite collaborators may have begun a steady decline in power by the end of the nineteenth century relative to Anglos, but at the state level they continued to dominate Hispanic politics.

In the northern New Mexican villages, on the other hand, local dynamics limited the power of patrons. The egalitarian traditions there were inhospitable soil in which to root a new power structure. In the lower Chama Valley, villagers called community leaders "tatas," or "grandfathers," not "patrons." "Don" was a form of address relegated to the absent or the dead.[74] Less wealthy than the plains ricos, village ricos shared much the same comforts and housing as their neighbors. And despite all stereotypes, political scientist Jack Holmes asserts, "no personal or party monopolies of power existed in the typical Hispanic community." Generations of experience in electing irrigation supervisors, Penitente officers, and land grant managers, in mediating disputes over water rights and joint ventures in trading and herding, saw to that.[75] In addition, their position as cultural mediaries forced conflicts of interest upon these elites.

When villagers saw their patrons and ricos cooperating with newcomers in ways that damaged rather than aided the villagers, a common ethnicity could not save the ricos from retaliations such as Gorras Blancas raids.[76]

But more inhibiting than village traditions was the rise of even newer Anglo landowners, merchants, employers, and company towns. These Anglo competitors, unlike the Hispanic ricos, acknowledged few reciprocal obligations with their tenants, customers, or laborers. They relied for survival only on external capital and credit. But they nonetheless provided alternate and larger sources of credit and livelihood for the villagers. Hispanic village merchants could not compete, for example, with the Rockefellers' Colorado Fuel and Iron Company.[77]

Collaboration had benefited few and proved for many an ephemeral way to retain capitalist status in the new Anglo economy. It had granted them only temporary benefits in power, income, and recognition. None of these forms of resistance to Anglo domination, from those furthest outside the Anglo system to those attempting to turn its fundamental institutions to the Hispanics' benefit, succeeded in effectively safeguarding Hispanic control of the cultural confrontation while still allowing room for the expansion necessary to Hispanic village survival.

Most Hispanic villagers had not even the choice of trying to survive and accommodate the new order as capitalists. An observer in 1902 pointed to villagers who "live on credit all year at the store and then, when the harvest is gathered, many times find that the debt amounts to more than the value of their crops."[78] These villagers had to seek other modes of subsistence and expansion, other strategies. Among the options offered, seasonal wage labor proved the most attractive. It provided a form of livelihood which allowed the villagers to retain certain cultural traits, and to do so within old patterns. Seasonal wage labor permitted them to perpetuate a multi-source income (protection against disaster in any single field), a flexible sexual division of labor, a communal village, and seasonal migration into a cash economy as an outlet for individual enterprise. In it they beheld a new mode of expansion, one that allowed increased density on the land, and one that kept them from poverty without requiring either a permanent departure from their own culture or a permanent entry into Anglo culture.

Homesteading may have seemed a more attractive alternative than wage labor to the uninitiated, and many Hispanics did take out homesteads in this period. But homesteads carried with them substantial costs, both monetary and social. The filing fee on a 160-acre tract was three dollars, the patent fee ten, the recording fee one dollar, and surveying costs also had to be met. The claim itself had to be filed at a land office, which was often a long and therefore costly journey away. As a result, just as Elfido Lopez had done in the 1870s, even those who filed homesteads had to find wage labor, and it had to be seasonal labor as the homesteader had to establish a residency of six months each year.[79]

Homesteading suffered from other flaws as a strategy. The land available was usually suited to commercial dry farming only, not the irrigated subsistence farming typical of most Hispanic villages. It required new technology and consistent rainfall. It also required dispersed settlement. The loss of the plaza structure would mean the immediate loss of all the social services—church, school, recreation, and economic support—of the village; and all lost for a new system that had proved risky at best. It was not that Spanish Americans would not or could not change. The search for wage labor was itself change. But homesteading required greater change, even abandonment. It required permanent, not episodic, entry into a world and a culture alien to the Hispanics' own. Even landless or nearly landless villagers preferred wage labor.[80] In this context, there was some truth to the remark of a later observer that what was important to the Spanish American was that "the village was independent not the individual."[81] Wage labor formed a more effective strategy for the retention of group autonomy than did homesteading.

The railroads provided some of the earliest and most convenient opportunities for Hispanic wage laborers. In 1880 tracks reached Albuquerque and Santa Fe. In the next two years, the Denver and Rio Grande built two narrow-gauge lines through the heart of Hispanic southern Colorado and northern New Mexico, and the growth of railroad mileage in New Mexico did not slow until 1912.[82] Although Chicanos in the United States were confined to track maintenance or section work—usually under American or European foremen—and other full- or part-time unskilled labor, even the sectionman's wage of one dollar for a twelve-hour day or about $25 per month compared favorably to shepherd's wages.[83] It attracted mountain villagers who lived twenty and more miles from the nearest tracks. In 1900 entirely Hispanic Chimayo, a northern New Mexico mountain village, had, in addition to its 83 farm laborers and 16 shepherds, 18 railroad workers.[84] Hand in hand with the railroad in the creation of both a new Anglo economic framework and new opportunities for Hispanic wage labor came the exploitation of the coal deposits in southern Colorado. The railroad needed coal to run and provided the means to market it or ship it to steel plants. As the railroad arrived in southern Colorado in the 1870s, the first mines opened at Engleville and Starkville and, like the railroads, they expanded rapidly in the first years of the new century. The coal mines, too, were conveniently close at hand for Hispanic villagers needing seasonal wage labor. While not entirely seasonal, coal production increased in the winter months as demands for fuel rose, meshing well with the villagers' agricultural schedules. The number and proportion of Hispanic mine workers varied from camp to camp, but in 1905, 11.5 percent of all Colorado Fuel and Iron's mine workers were Hispanic. By 1914 the figure had risen to 17.37 percent, and 92.59 percent of its 540 lumber workers were also Hispanic. Piece rates were standard, but Hispanics did tend to receive poorer "rooms" in the mines, and so as in railroad work where there was wage as well as occupational discrimination, Hispanics made less money than Anglos. Even so, Hispanic miners could earn up to twice the monthly income of Hispanic track laborers.[85]

Whether they lived near the mines or not, Hispanic miners integrated their forays into this Anglo enterprise with their own cultural economy, as they did with their railroad work. In 1908, government investigator Victor Clark explained that "most of the Mexican laborers in this district are American born, and though more intelligent, are less steady than laborers from Old Mexico. . . . The local Mexican laborers of Colorado and New Mexico usually own a cabin and a small piece of land within walking distance of the camp or within a day's journey, and therefore are more independent of regular wages."[86] Mine work was no more full-time employment than railroad labor was. Along with the railroad, the mines allowed the Spanish-American villages to survive long after the erosion of their economic base began, while the village agriculture and livestock, in turn, spared the villagers from total dependence on what opportunities they might grasp or be allowed to grasp in the Anglo economy. It was on this basis that wherever Anglo development created wage jobs, in sawmills and smelters, railroads and mines, Hispanics arrived to take advantage of the new opportunities.[87]

In new railroad towns, lumber and mining camps, and military forts plunked down amidst the older Hispanic villages, Hispanic village women, too, found opportunities for employment. In 1880 the new railroad town of Chama was filled with wives and daughters of laborers and with female heads of households who were seamstresses and washerwomen.[88] Village widows who would have supported themselves with their ranches or farms in earlier days, but had suffered the same deprivation of land as the men, worked for wages instead. They worked not only in sewing and laundry trades, but as cooks, boarding-house and hotel keepers, and domestic servants, and even occasionally as bakers, nurses, midwives, postmistresses, and prostitutes.[89] In 1900 in Embudo, New Mexico, a town of 169 households and only 20 Anglo individuals, 42 Hispanic women worked for wages. They formed over one-sixth of all Hispanic wage workers in the town. In other villages, women went to the new camps to sell their produce and their poultry.[90] In line with their tradition of flexible sexual division of labor, economic autonomy, and a family economy, and with depletions in the land base affecting their purview as it had the men's, the women, too, quickly took advantage of new opportunities for cash income.

The turn of the century brought yet another seasonal wage occupation into being: sugar-beet labor. In the 1890s would-be sugar-beet growers had, with local capital, put companies together all over Colorado. By the end of 1901 at least four processing factories had been built, covering each of the areas that was to become a major producer: the Arkansas River in southern Colorado, the South Platte River in the north, and the Western Slope. By 1907 there were fifteen factories, the South Platte area had become the largest producer, and the Sugar Trust had stepped in and rationalized the business.[91] The Spanish Americans, who often juggled their new wage-earning jobs, began to abandon railroad work during rushed times in the beetfields, or to spend one season on the tracks, the next in the mines, and the next in beets.[92]

In May 1900, when a sugar company first brought two groups of "Mexicans," as Spanish Americans were known locally, to Rocky Ford, Colorado, as beetworkers, the Anglo residents drove them from the town. By 1903, however, the dearth of Anglos eager for seasonal stoop labor reconciled the farmers and workingmen to the presence of Hispanics. That year the National Sugar Company "imported" 100 Hispanics from Las Vegas, New Mexico. At the same time, northern Colorado sugar companies brought 275 "Mexicans" from Dry Creek and Trinidad, Colorado, to show the German-Russian farmer-laborers their dispensability.[93] Three years later, the north's Great Western Sugar Company had a Spanish American recruiting agent, a Mr. N. P. Martinez, who brought whole families from Pueblo and Huerfano in southern Colorado and from New Mexico to Timnath, in northern Colorado.[94] By 1909, the 1,002 Hispanics in the north and the 1,630 in the south provided almost one-quarter of Colorado's beet labor.

At first, the vast majority of these Hispanic beet hands were male migrant laborers, hired in gangs. About 1910, however, a shift in hiring strategies began.[95] As early as 1908, one southern Colorado district had erected an "adobe village" to try "to hold the Mexicans as permanent settlers." And after 1910, the Great Western Sugar Company, by far the largest of its kind in the state, made a policy of recruiting only family labor. Both Hispanics and the beet-growing areas felt the impact of the shift. Hispanic children began to appear in northern Colorado school districts in 1909, though their families seldom stayed in one town for more than a year.[96] Denver social service organizations began holding mother's meetings in the winter for "Mexican" women who worked beets in the summer.[97] And schools in Pueblo began to complain of large numbers of late-entering "Mexicans," beetworkers from the Rocky Ford district.

Beet labor, unlike railroad and mine labor, was now family labor, and unlike railroad and mine labor, it required absence from home during the harvest season. While hoeing, planting, and harvesting were hardly new to Hispanic women and children, the families could not simultaneously tend the plot at home in New Mexico and the beetfields in northern Colorado. Some families did continue to migrate seasonally, but others sold their lots in their increasingly crowded villages to their siblings, and came north to colonies, to homesteads, or simply to rented housing. They hoped, usually in vain, to make enough money to buy enough land to resettle in the village. They would visit home once or twice a year, but they would winter in the northern cities, seeking employment for themselves and schooling for their children.[98]

Beet labor, in particular beet labor where colonies had been built, though onerous and a departure in some ways from older patterns, afforded yet another mode of physical expansion and cultural survival for the Hispanic villagers. As in the folk expansion of the previous century, families often came north in clusters and never severed their ties with their parent village. These pioneering Chicanos often sent money back to relatives in their villages who, in turn, sometimes sent produce north. In the northern cities, on the isolated northern farms, these extended kinship links retained for the otherwise bereft migrants a sense of community.

The interplay of Anglo and Hispanic strategies had, by 1914, resulted in this regional community, this extension of community links, village by village, like runners from a plant, to encompass an entire region. No longer could the village exist or be understood apart from its laboring migrants, and the migrants, too, had inseparable and essential links to the village. The railroads, the mines, the beetfields were all in place, and the people were moving. Northern New Mexico's Rio Arriba County remained over 90 percent Hispanic. Only ten school districts had as many as five Anglo school children, but the people of the county were on the move. By 1908, 59.3 percent of Hispanic marriages in the county involved people not hailing from the same site. In 1912, Prudence Clark, the Presbyterian mission school teacher in Chimayo, noted that not only did five or six times as many people now weave for market as formerly had, but many went to Colorado to find work. In 1907, Victor Clark, the government investigator, found seventy men absent from one small village.[99] In Las Animas County, southern Colorado, the changes were even more striking, coupled as they were with the Anglo invasion and the New Mexico village migrants. In 1900, Colorado had 10,222 residents who had been born in New Mexico; most lived around the mines, in Las Animas County. In the same year, in the same county only nine of 114, or 7.8 percent, of the Hispanic marriages were between people of different towns, and only three Hispanic-Anglo marriages occurred. By 1916, 39.2 percent of Hispanic marriages in the county were between Hispanics of different towns, while eleven, or 8.4 percent, were mixed.[100] As Victor Clark explained in 1908, "The New Mexican no longer is village shy, averse to leaving the neighborhood where he was born and where he can always find shelter and food among his friends. He makes seasonal migrations to distant parts of the west in search of work, often leaving his family behind him to attend to the crop in his absence."[101] Migration had become an essential and integral part of life for the Hispanic villagers.

Neither assimilation nor acculturation, uprooting or transplanting—the common terms used in such cases—seem adequate to describe what was happening in this particular cultural interaction. With the development of a regional community, Hispanics took another tack in adapting to an increasing Anglo presence.

In a regional economy, the goods and services tie the area together as they are transported from place to place. In a regional community, it is the people who are the bonds. They make use of the opportunities throughout the region for the benefit of a single community, their village. They tie the village, through themselves, to other economies, just as they themselves are bound to the village. In the sense that villagers actively chose this pattern over other alternatives, not in concert, but in aggregate, migration and the form of community it created had become the dominant Hispanic strategy on the intercultural frontier. This strategy of strictly limited entry into the Anglo world carried vital implications for intercultural dynamics. For the new strategy had arisen not merely as a result of economic necessity and opportunities offered. Anglo attitudes toward land, business, and work had placed under siege not only Hispanic sources of livelihood, but Hispanics' ability to define their own culture and values. The resulting Hispanic strategy was not merely an economic but a cultural choice. Hispanic and Anglo frontiers interlocked, and so did their strategies.

To many Anglos, the new pattern of labor and migration, this new Hispanic strategy, seemed to stem from flaws in the Hispanic character. Victor Clark called these "Mexicans" the "scavengers of the mining industry, picking up the positions left by other classes of workers, and supplanting the least skilled and reliable Europeans and Asiatic."[102] In this and other fields, Clark found them lacking in thrift, ambition, and strength, and filled only with listlessness, unsteadiness, and indolence. Clark did acknowledge the role of institutionalized discrimination, of "a line drawn in accordance with nationality rather than competency" in keeping Hispanics subordinate to Anglo workers on the railroads in contributing thus to their seeming "lack of ambition," but allowed it only a partial contribution. The rest, it seemed, was inherent in the race. With these handicaps, the Hispanic workers would never be able to break out of their migratory pattern and their poverty. Clark complained, "They are not permanent, do not acquire land or establish themselves in little cabin homesteads, but remain nomadic and outside of American civilization."[103]

Clark also realized, however, that these very "flaws" served a purpose in the Anglo economy. "The Mexicans," he quoted one mine superintendent as remarking, "make good reserve labor." Clark himself concluded that "the thriftless laborer is a good man for emergencies— a short job pleases him as well as a long one—and he will work cheap," and also posited that "if he were active and ambitious, he would be less tractable and would cost more. His strongest point is his willingness to work for a low wage." To the Anglos, then, the migratory pattern in and out of the industrial economy was a pathology, a failure on the part of the Hispanics, but a useful one to the success of Anglo interests. Most Anglos placed no more blame for the new pattern on their own development than they gave credit to the Hispanics for developing strategies to keep themselves "outside of American civilization." To these Anglos, the developers had created a world more perfect than the scattered pastoral and relatively unproductive hamlets, and one where the thrifty, enterprising, and American—the good—were welcome. They saw their discrimination as much a result of Hispanic maladjustment to the labor market as of their own rational calculation of Anglo interests.[104]

The antagonism of Anglo culture toward the villagers' more communal modes did not limit itself to a critique of Hispanic behavior at the mining camps and in the cities. Critics struck, too, at the village itself.[105] To the Anglos, the Hispanic villages were pretty, but they were also full of filth and decadence. The Anglos deplored the undisciplined character of the place: the chaotic streets, the irregular hours, and, most of all, the patterns of mutual support that robbed the villagers of "emulative influences" and "the sense of individual economic responsibility." Victor Clark admitted that "there is a comfortable condition of equality among all members of the community," but this clearly did not compensate for the lack of progress caused by a mutual dependence where "the lazy man and the man out of work live off their relatives and neighbors," and which destroyed both the surplus of the industrious and the incentive to accumulate that surplus.[106]

With neither the incentive to accumulate nor the constant threat of destitution, there was nothing to bind the worker to his job or to increase his consumption of industrial goods. In a classic example of what historian Herbert Gutman has described as the confrontation of the old agricultural and the new industrial cultures, Anglos attacked every aspect of Hispanic culture, from the language to the food. In the 1930s, New Mexico writer Ruth Barker called the original suppression of native customs and crafts "the law and order code of subduing a hostile territory," while two decades earlier Victor Clark had seen in the creation of new desires for Anglo goods not only a new market, but a means to infiltrate and erode village communalism.[107] Despite the utility of the Hispanic villagers to the Anglos as a reserve labor force, their relative or seeming independence of the Anglo labor market and their communal traditions, perceived as inherently antagonistic to an efficient industrial state, remained a blot and an anomaly in the Anglo vision.

Hispanics were not blind to the antagonism of Anglo culture. Even had they not ventured out to the mining camps and cities, merchants and missionaries brought the message to the village. Confronted not merely by a different, but by a hostile culture, the Spanish Americans had found migration and the regional community the best defense. "Social enclavement," Morton Fried explained in 1957, "is the self-protective reaction of a small ethnic group which feels that its way of life is threatened by acculturative pressures."[108] Never totally self-sufficient and never static, the village could better control the cultural confrontation by this pattern than by direct and permanent entry into the conquering culture and economy.

The villagers could, to a certain extent at least, select those facets of Anglo culture they desired and bring them back to the villages. They had a long history of such cultural borrowing on the Spanish frontier, and in the late nineteenth century in Colorado had learned to make beer and potato pancakes from German ex-soldiers near Fort Garland.[109] Now they "improved" their homes with iron beds, steel ranges, glazed windows, sewing machines, and oilcloth tablecloths. Where they could, they also bought agricultural machinery, as at Cundiyo in Rio Arriba County, which increased both the yield and the variety of their produce to such an extent that they no longer had to buy feed for their livestock.[110]

The Anglo item most often listed in early accounts both by Anglos and by Hispanics was the kitchen range. In 1907, one merchant sold an average of one a month to Hispanics in a community of only five hundred. As early as the 1880s, as Luisa Torres of Guadalupita, New Mexico, remembered, "those who were a little better off bought cookstoves."[111] The cookstoves, sewing machines, and clothing that the Spanish American villagers bought in these years were female-centered items and simultaneously items of priority. Victor Clark claimed that "these new standards of style and ostensible comfort are set by the women rather than by the men," and that the women "appear to be the spenders, or the ones for whom money is first chiefly spent."[112]

This consumption pattern arose from a situation in which, except for beetwork, the men's new wage work dissociated their economic function from the family. Whereas women had processed the wool from the sheep that men had raised, and even helped tend them when they were pastured close to home, women had little contact with the railroad or the mine and their products. This dissociation is typical of the shift from an agro-pastoral family economy to an industrial one, but the Spanish Americans had not made a complete shift. Often the women and sometimes even the men were still agricultural producers, at least part-time. In any case, the bringing of Anglo technology into the home not only provided recognition of the continuing importance of the woman's economic role in the family, but also provided a way to integrate her into the man's new economic function in his occasional forays into the new system, as well as to integrate those forays in a tangible way into the life of the village and the home.

Where the Anglos tended to confuse material culture with larger social interrelations, the Hispanic villagers did not. The new technology and industrial objects the Hispanics adopted did not represent fundamental cultural changes. There may have been a consensus on the benefits of technological advance, but there was not one on forms of ownership and social relations of the community.[113] The Hispanic villagers who bought stoves and sewing machines were not buying "American" culture. Through their selective acculturation, which the Anglos recognized and resented, the villagers succeeded in retaining a remarkable degree of control over the development of their own culture, despite their decreasing opportunities in commercial and political spheres.

Carolyn Zeleny explains accommodation as "the process by which conflicts between the two groups are regulated while their essential differences remain. Through it the hostile elements in the relationship are not eliminated, but sufficiently controlled so that a *modus vivendi* may be established in a common society."[114] The essential question for the villagers was who would control those hostile elements. By 1914, Hispanics in Colorado and New Mexico had largely lost control over developments affecting the region as a whole, but, through their strategy of work and migration patterns, they retained their control over their own enclaves, retained for themselves a homeland—both a refuge and a base for expansion without loss of cultural identity.

Hispanics had made "a unitary system," of the two disparate, fairly closed social systems, using the migrants as "living links" to the goods, services, and cash of the Anglo economy.[115] With prejudice and discrimination prevalent outside the villages, there was little incentive to substitute frayed social ties to Anglo settlements for effective links to the home village. For the Hispanics, even when they settled permanently on the margins of Anglo cities and farms, face-to-face relations with the home village remained the primary relationship, and emigrating family members in New Mexico were "kept track of forever."[116] It was as though the village had expanded its bounds to follow its members and embrace the region.

Migration for wage work was not, then, a pathology, aberrant behavior to be ignored in studying the village, but an essential strategy for survival, a part of the village without which the village could not have continued to exist. Furthermore, the pattern of work and migration was not a departure from but a logical extension of the pattern of work and expansion followed by Chicanos in northern New Mexico from the eighteenth century. When the traditional pastorally based expansion of settlement was made impossible through federal land appropriations and Anglo incursions, migration for wage work was substituted as a new solution to the problem of increasing population density. Permanent migration did at times accompany wage work in a continuation of the expanding frontier, but Hispanics rarely migrated as farmowners, and they always maintained close connections with the home village. That this strategy of migration also served Anglo needs did not, as yet, render it less effective as a Hispanic strategy of cultural autonomy in the face of a hostile and powerful rival. Hispanics did not abandon other strategies. They continued to seek Anglo education, to form organizations, and to enter politics. For the largest number, however, migratory labor was the strategy best adapted to their aims and interests.

The regional community had arisen between 1880 and 1914 as a strategy of autonomy and expansion interwoven with Anglo strategies and development. It had arisen, in short, from the changing dynamics of the intercultural frontier. The tradition of a multi-source income, family economy, communal village, and seasonal absence of men was proving a highly adaptable system. The villages, with their "living links," were not isolated and static, however unchanged their structure may have seemed. That very seeming continuity paid tribute to the early success of their efforts to control and limit the impact of the Anglo confrontation while still expanding their community to embrace both Colorado and New Mexico.

2

At the Center: Hispanic Village Women, 1900–1914

Looking back on a New Mexico village of the early twentieth century, Luisa Torres recalled:

> I watched my maternal grandparents a lot. . . . On the day that my grandmother was seventy, I saw her open the doors of her little adobe house. It was a spring day and there were millions of orange and black butterflies around the corn plants; my grandmother ran towards the butterflies and gathered so many of them in her apron that she flew up in the air, while she laughed contentedly. I wanted to know all that my grandmother knew.

Like many grandmothers of the time, Luisa's grandmother knew particularly about medicinal plants, "remedios."[1] But in wanting to know all that her grandmother knew, Luisa was expressing more than a desire to share in the knowledge of herbal medicine. At the southern end of the regional community, in the Hispanic heartland's communal villages, women had their own world. They had realms of expertise which served the entire village, and a society and economy that coexisted with those areas they shared with men and areas men held alone.

Nestled between mountain peaks, arid and relatively inaccessible, the villages seemed to many observers changeless and idyllic. Yet the rise of the regional community and the increasing migration of men affected relations even here. To understand the resilience of the villages, how they survived that migration and how they faced an Anglo presence not only at the edge of the region but in the villages themselves, requires a deeper understanding of village dynamics, the social organizations there, and, in particular, the activities of women. For as the men migrated, the women's world and the world of the village began to merge.

This world of village women has scarcely appeared in the historical literature of Chicanos except as overgeneralized and stereotyped images of submissive, cloistered, and powerless women. The focus has been on a rigidly patriarchal ideology, articulated only by those peripheral to or outside this world, by the Hispanic elite or Anglo observers of the time, or by later authors imposing views derived from other sites and times. Their vision and the concentration on ideology have not only distorted our view of village life, but marred our understanding of the dynamics of intercultural relations. Recently, authors have cast doubt on these stereotypes, exposing their roots. But the work of historical reconstruction for the period covered here is only beginning.[2]

It is against a more concrete village background that the developments of the regional community must be seen, and that the Chicanas' and Chicanos' experiences as they moved into Anglo enclaves and cities must be judged. Only by examining this world and the gender structure of the village as it was lived, in the family, the neighborhood, religion, and work, can the impact of cross-cultural relations in the village and outside it be understood.

At the center of the family stood Hispanic women, and they dared not move beyond it, or so runs the common wisdom. According to this wisdom, sexual divisions and the separate women's world served to keep women subordinate, cloistered, and protected within the family. But the family was more complex than a woman's kingdom or her prison. An examination of village women's lives as daughters, wives, mothers, and widows reveals more subtle nuances regarding their status, even within the realm of family.

At age eight or nine, the separate women's world began. Before that, villagers expected boys and girls to behave in much the same way and share the same chores.[3] But after their first Communion, they could dance at "bailes" and learn adult tasks. By age sixteen, girls had received enough training from their mothers or grandmothers to be ready for marriage.[4] At this crucial stage, the village insisted on monitoring male/female relations. Unmarried males as well as females found that "almost the only recognized means of contact" outside their own homes and away from their families was the informal ritual of the village dance.[5] Adolescent girls went out always accompanied, whether by mother, aunt, little sister, grandmother, or, later, a number of girlfriends.[6] So between fiestas and weddings, the young men used their earnings to sponsor dances in the hope of finding a mate.[7]

At dances, women and children seated themselves on benches around the walls, and men stood outside the dance hall except when requesting a dance or dancing. Conversation was theoretically forbidden between unmarried partners, but acquaintance from a dance could lead to a courtship conducted through furtive letters if the parties were literate, by studiously fortuitous visits with the family, or by communication through siblings. Sometimes secret engagements resulted.[8] Even for adolescents, the distance between theory and reality permitted a degree of autonomy.

Village girls more often than boys were the targets of warning stories which depicted the dire and often supernatural consequences of walking out with mysterious strangers.[9] But these stories did not simply reflect a double standard. They told of village mores: the young man was never a local village youth, the girl was always in her grandmother's care. The tales reveal as much about expectations for village boys and the trials of elderly widowed grandmothers raising none-too-submissive young girls, as they reveal about definitions of female virtue. And reality was often more lenient. Of the family and the village, it was only Jesusita Aragon's grandmother who never forgave her the two illegitimate children Jesusita had while under her roof. The children's father escaped equal shame only because Jesusita, who did not want to marry him, refused to identify him.[10] Marriage might, in a sense, have liberated Jesusita. After marriage, a woman might "act as she pleases," and some went to dances and traveled without their husbands, but before marriage ritualized meetings were designed to minimize potential complications and unresolvable conflicts within the village.[11]

When a village youth decided to make a public offer of marriage, he required the consensual participation of a panoply of villagers, male and female. He had his father, or occasionally his mother, and a godparent visit the girl's parents and leave a written offer.[12] The girl's father and mother discussed the matter and sent for the "madrina," the godmother. The madrina acted as an intermediary between the parents and the girl, who was "at liberty to accept or refuse." Women within the family were acknowledged to have a mind of their own, and not socially forbidden to exercise it. Both the boy and the girl communicated through their parents and grandparents. Age determined one's actions more than sex.

The groom or his family provided the wedding, trousseau, and reception, which helps to explain why males tended to marry later than females.[13] But this was not a purchase of the bride by the groom's family. The bride often brought property into the marriage; the new couple was equally likely to live with the bride's as with the groom's parents, and after the wedding ceremony the "entregada de los novios" symbolized the giving of the groom to the bride's family and the bride to the groom's.[14] The marriage created not just binary ties, but networks.

In a rigidly patriarchal society, one would expect consistent and sizable age differences between spouses, but in the villages there were no strong norms as to age difference in first marriage. Women tended to marry between the ages of 15 and 21, men between 19 and 26.[15] But every village had women who had married younger men as well as the occasional woman married to a man twenty years older than she.

Lack of strict norms regarding age at marriage, of course, is hardly proof that marriages were not rigidly patriarchal. But there is other evidence. In the northern New Mexico and southern Colorado villages, molestation of women and wife-whipping were considered punishable crimes and cause for divorce. In 1903, for example, a Hispanic man in a Hispanic southern Colorado county was arrested merely for quarreling with his wife. Arbitrary male behavior was considered deviant; decisions, particularly major ones such as moving for work or school, or regarding the marriage of a child, were made jointly by husband and wife.[16]

Even child-rearing, even of daughters, did not fall solely to the mother or to women. The whole family—father, mother, aunts, uncles, and grandparents—participated in bringing up the children.[17] Fathers and grandfathers dealt with girls as well as boys not merely to discipline them, but to teach them about such things as farming and horseback riding, to tease them and tell stories, and to take them to school and town. "My grandfather," recalled Patricia Luna, "always spoke to me as a strong person, capable of doing just about anything." Living on his farm with her uncles, she said, she "used to do everything they did, work in the fields, whatever. If there was something I didn't know how to do, they wouldn't do it for me, they'd teach me."[18] Girls growing up in this cooperative atmosphere looked forward to companionable and not rigidly hierarchical marriages.

Property relations in marriage testified to this lack of rigid stratification. That husband and wife shared rights in property acquired during marriage was the rule for Hispanic families long before it became so for Anglos, as was equal inheritance by sons and daughters.[19] Unlike early agricultural settlers in the eastern United States, at death Hispanic men tended to leave the bulk of their property to their wives rather than to their daughters or sons. This pattern created a number of widowed females in almost every village who were more than titular heads of household. These women were listed in the census as general farmers who owned their own land and used the labor of their married and unmarried children, or planted the land themselves.[20] This inheritance norm was strong enough for a Señora Martinez in southern Colorado to contest the disposition of her husband's estate even though in this case all the property had been in his name. She claimed a right to half the property "because," she explained in 1900, "all know that I worked as much as my husband and spent less than he and our son. My husband always told me that for my work half was for me, that it was not owed me except that I had earned it."[21] Women who pulled their own weight economically in these Hispanic families expected the fact to be acknowledged in tangible as well as intangible ways.

When women did enter marriage with their own property, particularly women who were better-off than average, they often quite consciously kept the property separate from their husband's and managed it themselves. John Lawrence's Hispanic wife let her sheep out on partido contracts separately from his sheep, and Cleofas Jaramillo noted that her "husband had borrowed the money from [her] and had never paid it back" when he died unexpectedly.[22] Less wealthy women joined their husbands in taking out mortgages and partido contracts, but affixed their name separately. These women also participated, with or without their husbands, as heirs in land-grant litigation. And one woman, "of her own separate means," added a few hogs and chickens valued at $150 to an estate the total value of which was only $700.[23] A married couple's identity of interest was a desirable but not always assumed state in these Hispanic villages.

Even an unhappily married Hispanic woman, however, when asked why she had married, responded, "Where else could I have gone?"[24] The norm in the villages was a household headed by a married couple.[25] Women, even propertied women, would not want to grow old in the village alone. Marriage provided a means to integrate the individual once more into the group and to perpetuate that integration through children. In villages as interdependent for labor and subsistence as the Hispanic communal villages of New Mexico, such reinforced networking was crucial to ensure mutuality and harmony. Whether male or female, the individual found that multiplying the ties to the group increased his or her security, and remarriage after widowhood was common for both sexes.[26]

Widowed women nonetheless engaged actively in business enterprises and defended their interests in court beyond the traditional geographic bounds of Hispanic women's activities, the village. They bought, homesteaded, or rented land, or entered and continued business on their own or with their children.[27] As widows, their role as head of the family made the enlarged scope legitimate. Since these women had often retained the management of their own property throughout their marriage—unlike, for example, the colonial New England farm wives described by Laurel Ulrich—what was new was less the nature of the activities than their occasional location outside the village.[28]

Widows were not the only women who broke the bounds of women's usual behavior with impunity. So, too, did midwives. Indisputably in the women's realm alone was childbirth. And the partera, the midwife, stood at the apex of the community of women, and at the same time transcended it. As a key figure in the community she had no male equivalent and was not bound by many of the strictures which applied to male/female interactions. When the men came to fetch the partera for childbirth, none cast aspersions on her for traveling alone with a man even for thirty miles. The midwives themselves recognized a danger "because," as Jesusita Aragon admitted, "sometimes you go out when you don't know the guy who comes to get you, and you don't know if you can trust him or not. But," she concluded, "you have to go, and any hour night or day."[29] Both men and women realized the village relied on children to perpetuate itself, and that in the partera's hands lay the well-being of mother and child.

Any adult woman could become a midwife, but relatively few did so, and they were never, in this period, entirely self-selecting. They tended to be middle-aged or older women, women who did not have young children to mind, who could come day or night, and whose family could take care of their other work while they were gone. And they could be gone for some time. Midwives were called when labor began and stayed until the mother was settled after the birth, which might take two or three days.[30]

Expectant women selected parteras and their selection created parteras from neighbors. The process usually began simply by a sequence of village women asking a particular neighbor for help in childbirth. They asked a woman known to be somewhat altruistic, one who did not seek the post too actively, who was trustworthy, strong, fearless, and intelligent—all considered female as well as male virtues—and, most important, who had great experience and success with childbirth.[31]

Because of the responsibility for life involved, because of the heavy demands on one's time, and because it was never, until at least the 1920s, a full-time profession, women tended to be diffident toward the opportunity to become midwives.[32] As they gradually realized, however, that they had been chosen—and a call to assist in childbirth could be refused only in case of physical disablement, and would be answered "regardless of time, weather, distance, and the parents' economic, marital, or religious status"—these women set about apprenticing themselves informally to other midwives, eager to learn all they could to alleviate the uncertainty and lighten the responsibility.[33]

This was strictly a female apprenticeship, women passing knowledge to women; just as childbirth itself was restricted to the women's community, the knowledge and the personnel were defined and controlled by women alone. Older midwives were happy to pass on the responsibility, if not the authority, to the next generation. Jesusita Aragon found that the three midwives in Trujillo "were glad when I started because they were getting old. . . . And they talk to me, how to do this and how to do that."[34]

The mode and ritual of payment were also significant and reinforced communal values. In contrast to the set fees of Anglo male doctors, the compensations "were called gifts, because they were free-will offerings," a WPA investigator discovered in the 1930s.[35] Like curanderas (herbal healers), when the patient "asked how much was owed her—they knew she would not charge them—she would reply that it was nothing, 'just what you want to give me.'"[36] As neither curanderas nor parteras could refuse to treat destitute villagers, the recompense varied from a value of fifty cents to a maximum of ten dollars, and was almost always in kind.[37] The villagers never lost sight of the personal nature, the community aspect, of midwifery and health care, and except among rich and Anglicized families, the busy, impersonal, non-communicative, and very expensive doctors could not compete.[38] As midwife Susana Archuleta explained, "you can't look at midwifery in terms of dollar signs. You have to be sympathetic." Rejecting the ability of men to make good midwives, she insisted, "delivering a baby is not just a business. It's a personal thing, a very personal thing. It's a woman-to-woman experience."[39]

The midwife's specialized knowledge and vital function gave her a respected place in the community as a whole. It was not just that her calling exempted her from certain mores. According to one observer:

> The midwife was the only type of leader in a village community except for the men who were politically inclined, and, of course, except for the religious teachers. People would go to the midwife because there was no other leader.[40]

For women, the midwife became "a general counselor."[41] But the men, too, recognized her importance and took pains to assure her contentedness in the village. Mothers and fathers often chose the partera as godmother to the children she delivered, creating a multitude of connections to bind her to village families. In a communal society where illiteracy was common, respect depended on knowledge, character, and function. Parteras combined the three in high order, and although their authority had its base in the community of women, it was not limited to that community.[42]

For almost all women, relations between sexes within the family were characterized not by rigidity and hierarchy, but by flexibility, cooperation, and a degree of autonomy. Important family decisions were made jointly, parteras' families and widows filled in for those absent, and wives managed their own property and created and perpetuated the all-important partera system. Yet family was only one facet of women's lives. Female experience even here varied according to age, marital status, and calling. If the calling of midwife could so affect the status of parteras in the larger society, it is clearly worth looking beyond family life to discover women's village experience and, inseparable from it, the village's social organization and dynamics.

In addition to the community of family, women shared in the larger community of the village. This wider world displayed many of the same patterns that characterized relations between the sexes in the more intimate realm of the home. As mothers, wives, and daughters, women bound the community with ties of kinship. They also, however, entered the community as women and as individuals, unmediated by family, particularly in religion and production. Indeed, women not only shared in the community, they were instrumental in creating it, socially and physically, and in sustaining it.

As girls played "comadres," or co-mothers, in the dusty soil near the house, promising to choose each other as "madrina" or godmother for their children, they pledged, as one woman recalled, "not to quarrel, or be selfish with each other."[43] Between Hispanic women, the comadre relationship was among the most significant of relations. The natural mother and the comadre, natural father and copadre, shared the parenting, but co-parents' ideas on child-raising prevailed in any dispute. They named the child, sponsored the christening, acted as surrogate chaperones, consulted on the choice of a mate for the child, and were the only witnesses at the child's wedding. The parents usually asked the wife's parents to be co-parents for the first child, and the husband's for the second, and then other relatives and friends.[44] In this way, the comadre relationship created a dense network of care and obligations in the village.

Besides reinforcing close relations and fostering a special relationship between grandmother and granddaughter, the madrina relationship provided insurance. The grandmother/madrina frequently ended up raising her godchild, sometimes because the mother had died and the widowed father had married a woman who did not want the extra child, or, as one Anglo observer put it, because "the grandparents must have some children to be with and work for them in old age."[45] From their grandmothers these girls learned such skills as healing and midwifery, and in turn they provided lifelong care and devotion. Sometimes the girls were their grandmothers' only companions. The madrina system worked to ensure companionship, to prevent isolation, and to provide care.

The clustered settlement pattern so chaotic to Anglo eyes further fostered the sense of neighborhood created by networks of co-parents and other relatives. It encouraged cooperative labor and aid in difficulties such as illness, and provided mutual benefits and responsibilities which "neighborhood" implied. Many married children built houses on their parents' land, often attached to their parents' house. Occasionally entire plazas or village squares were enclosed. Butchering, house raising, harvesting, and funerals became community-wide social events for both men and women.

As in other agricultural communities, however, women had more of a hand in creating the neighborhood than men did.[46] Their daily visiting, sustaining social networks, far exceeded that of the men. Observers in one village home counted as many as fourteen different visitors in a single afternoon.[47] Women also maintained the links with kin in other villages; wives went on visits for weeks at a time, traveling sometimes with the whole family, other times alone.[48]

These neighborhood and kin networks provided temporary or permanent care for children whose own parents could not support the extra mouths. They provided farm labor in case of old age, illness, or widowhood; employment (in exchange for food and services) for widowed mothers or their children, or children living with destitute grandparents; and temporary homes for children in villages with schools. In maintaining community ties, women ensured the cohesiveness of the village as well as the welfare of themselves and their families.[49]

Women maintained the community through their participation in religion, also, although the most visible sign of Hispanic Catholicism in northern New Mexico was the widespread male religious society known as the Penitentes. The Penitentes, with their mutual benefit aspects and flagellant practices, involved the entire village, members and nonmembers, in their Holy Week rituals.[50] While it was not their show, women were not entirely excluded from Penitente rituals. Some women performed physical penance privately or at separate times. Other women, members of Penitente auxiliaries, made Lenten meals, cleaned the moradas or chapter chapels, and cared for sick members.[51] A third way in which women participated was in the village-wide aspects of the Holy Week's events: preparing feasts, participating in church services, and following in procession the image of Mary carried out of the church by women to meet the image of Jesus carried into the village by the Penitentes for a ritual embrace.[52]

In Penitente functions, women acted mainly as auxiliaries, but they had their own answer to the male-dominated Holy Week. They had the month of May, which was devoted to Mary. During the month many women met daily for prayer meetings, and in some villages they gathered twice daily. Women led a procession carrying an image of Mary from house to house and conducting prayers. One Hispanic convert tried to explain to his fellow Protestants the importance of Mary among the villagers: "They need and they deeply seem to feel that need of merely a human justified and glorified person to plead their cause before God, as they dare not approach him by any other means."[53]

The importance these Hispanics attributed to Mary provided a basis and legitimation for woman's role in what has often seemed a male-dominated church. Where the tangible symbol of that male dominance, the priest, appeared monthly at best, there was little to enforce a subordinate role for women. Indeed, in many villages a local woman, usually an older woman or one prominent for some other reason, led services in the weeks between priestly visits. Most of the villagers, male and female, attended.[54] Religion in the Hispanic villages was clearly the property of both sexes.[55] While the men led the Penitente Holy Week services in the morada and Penitentes performed special funeral services for members, the women's activities sustained the ongoing, year-round church.[56]

Women had a prominent, distinct, and organized role in religion. Their church services, their month of May, and their auxiliary functions did not set them apart from the community of men but rather provided an integrating force for the community, just as their building of networks based on kinship did. In both religion and the neighborhood, women functioned as community builders and sustainers, using the family at times, but not bound by it, and creating a central place for themselves in the community as they built it.

In their productive work, as in religion and in the family, women achieved an autonomous base and, simultaneously, integration into the village. Both mutuality and parallelism characterized the sexual division of labor here as well. Moreover, work and religion were not entirely separate. That most vital of village work, agriculture, demanded religious faith for success. In turn, such faith manifested itself through active participation in production, helping other producers, and placing God's will above one's own desires, for women as well as for men.[57] Village religion fostered a communal ethos in production, and women played a vital role in sustaining both.

Perhaps the most fundamental work of women, the one most obviously allied to maintenance, centered around food in all its stages: production, processing, provision, and exchange. Hispanic women were responsible for the garden, a plot of irrigated land usually close to the house. As loss of land led to a decline in livestock, the garden grew in significance. Women controlled this land, and planted, weeded, irrigated, and harvested such items as melons, chili, onions, garlic, native tobacco, sweet corn, green beans, radishes, and pumpkins with or without the help of men.[58] Often a widow who had no other land survived on the produce of her garden.[59] Where families owned a few goats and chickens, these too fell under the care of the women or the children under their supervision, and produced eggs and milk from which women made cheese.[60] The garden provided Hispanic women with an autonomous base, a source of subsistence independent of but not in competition with men. In addition, women's participation in the essential production phase of food—though they also helped process men's crops and livestock—legitimized their participation in ownership and minimized status differences between sexes.[61]

Sometimes there was little to harvest. As two anthropologists cogently explain, "During years when late frosts killed spring blossoms people didn't eat fruit. During years when insects or other causes diminished the crops or decimated the herds, people didn't eat much of anything."[62] The uncertainty of harvest underlined the actual as well as the ritual significance of produce for the villagers and the vital role of its distribution in ensuring village harmony.

The effort and time involved in processing, the vagaries of the harvest, and the love of the land which had produced it for generations, as well as its life-giving properties, imbued food at times with a symbolic significance. Cooking was usually simple. Once the foods were all milled or dried, a single pot of beans, vegetables, and occasionally meat would be put on the fire and would serve as the day's meals. On special occasions, the women gathered to bake bread.[63] It was not the cooking itself, but what women did with the food after it was cooked that mattered. During Holy Week in particular, when the women were preparing feasts, "little girls had to carry the trays of food to many houses and bring others back before they could eat their dinner."[64] Observer Olen Leonard found it was "a day when homemakers vie with one another in the preparation and exchange of food."[65] But this was no mere rivalry in housewifely tasks. Sociologist Antonio Goubaud-Carrera revealed that "exchange, borrowing, and sharing of food among members of the extended family and friends is a definite and important means making for the integration of the society."[66] The significance went even further than village integration, however, and involved the definition of female virtue, as is best revealed by a Hispanic midwife's story.

The midwife had come to deliver a child and found the labor lasting an unusually long time. Exhausted, she went to borrow something from a neighbor and there discovered the apparent reason for the difficult birth. It seemed the woman ate her meals standing in her doorway, but gave nothing away. Children who were hungry asked for bread and stood watching her eat, but to no avail. The midwife concluded that the mother was so stingy the child did not want to be born to her, so the midwife took the woman's wheat flour (considered a luxury and kept for feast days) and made a large number of tortillas. Then she had the mother-to-be call in all the children she could find and dispense the tortillas with her own hands. The child was finally born, and the woman became very generous.[67]

Food was a woman's own product, the disposal of which she controlled, and her treatment of it defined her character both as a woman (one worthy to be a mother) and as a member of a communal village. Men could and did share their butchered meat with their neighbors, and their field produce with those who helped harvest and with those in need.[68] As individual participants in the same community, women and men shared a set of values in regard to production and distribution, and female as well as male virtue required this generosity and degree of selflessness. Women did not enter the community simply as wives whose place there depended on the behavior of their husbands. They entered as producers, and it was in part through the distribution of their own produce that they held a place in their own right.

This definition of virtue did not preclude either the men or the women from producing food for exchange. One woman "sold" her cheese "to the village people who did not have cows or goats of their own." She sold it within an informal women's network; mothers sent their children for it and bought it "not for money, but traded" for "flour, cornmeal, and sometimes a bar of home made soap."[69] In addition, women paid church dues with hens and, when they could, children's school fees with their produce.[70] Trading for cash, however—outside the village almost by definition and certainly outside a woman's network—usually remained in the hands of either married men or widows.

The allocation of dealing with outsiders to men was at least in part a legacy of bad roads, inadequate transportation, and women needing to stay near their children in the village. Just as women processed some of men's produce, men sold some of women's cash crops, such as chili peppers or goat kids.[71] But food remained distinct from other products, and there were separate requirements for its legitimate sale. It was more like village land, whose preferred buyers were always relatives, than like, for example, weavings or sheep. A woman from Cordova rejected the opportunity to sell her homemade ice cream through a local merchant. "It would be dishonest to sell food you make in your home for profit at a store," she explained, and her husband concurred, "she is right, because to make food is part of our life as a family and to start selling that is to say that we have nothing that is *ours* . . . better to have less money and feel we own ourselves, than more and feel at the mercy of so many strangers."[72] Exchange for trade, even sale for cash by the producer, retained the intimate connection between producer and subsistence-product and retained the producer's control over that product, but by introducing a middleman, one lost control of one's virtue. Women's production of food, like women's creation of neighborhood, was thus both imbued with the communalism of the village, and vital to it.

Women had a hand more literally, also, in the construction of the community. While men made adobes and built the basic structure of the houses, women plastered them each fall, inside and out, with plaster made by mixing burnt and ground rock with water, and they built their own fireplaces and outdoor ovens. Plastering was usually a communal event, both for individual homes and for community structures. In 1911 at Embudo, New Mexico, forty women joined together to plaster the new school and build two fireplaces. In 1901 at San Pablo, Colorado, the village women working on the church divided their services among child care, kitchen work, and plastering.[73] This was not work strictly within the home, nor work strictly for their own family. Plastering involved women as members in their own right of a larger community, in a service which required work both inside and outside the home, and it allowed them a share in shaping the village environment.

Much of this women's economy of production and exchange has remained invisible to historians, made so less by its unsalaried and often informal nature than by male recorders and census takers. It is highly significant that in the 1910 census for Rio Arriba County, whereas male or Anglo female enumerators listed ten females with occupations for every one hundred males in communities they covered, Sophie Archuleta, a public school teacher in Truchas whose father was a general farmer, whose mother was a seamstress, and whose sister and brother performed labor on the home farm, listed seventy-nine females with occupations for every one hundred males.[74] To Hispanic women, their own work was highly visible and, in terms of value, on a par with that of the men.

But even the basic outlines of acceptable women's work had always depended more on the composition of the family than on sexual norms. Anthropologists Paul Kutsche and John Van Ness noted that within the household, tasks were divided by sex and age "in a marked but not rigid fashion," adding that "the division of labor is not absolute. If age and sex distribution in a family, or illness, or jobs away from home, makes it inconvenient to go by custom, then anyone does anything without stigma."[75] Men could wash, cook, and iron; women could build fences, hoe corn, plant fields, and herd and shear sheep.[76] In Chimayo, the men usually did the carding of wool, the women spun, and both wove. Prudence Clark recalled visiting a house in Chimayo in 1903 where, while twelve women sat spinning, in the adjoining room the men smoked, gossiped, and looked after "the little people." The women, too, would stop occasionally "and have a smoke."[77] As men increasingly migrated for labor, both women's work and the traditional, flexible sexual division of labor were increasingly exploited, and their prior existence eased the transition to a migratory community whether or not the norms changed.

Both Anglos and Hispanics noted the relatively rapid spread of "bedsteads, tables, chairs, sewing machines, and cooking stoves" into Hispanic homes between 1880 and 1900, and that the men's newly available wage labor paid for it.[78] They noted the technological cross-cultural contact, but gave less notice to the concommitant extension of women's work. Not the new technology but the patterns of the regional community it signified, extended the women's world and strained its usual patterns and mores in ways both similar to and different from the strains placed on the migrating men.

That women often enjoyed the new technology, in particular the cookstoves, is not in dispute. In 1901, two women were sufficiently attached to a single cookstove to bring the case to court.[79] But the alterations in women's labor were not limited to their work within the home. In most villages, the women's gardens lay closer to the home than the men's grain fields did, so that the women could tend the children and the garden at one time. When the men left the village for wage labor each spring, gathering at the local store with their families and bedding and departing "moist-eyed" for the railroad station, the women were left with the care of the men's crops. In the 1930s, Cordova resident Lorin Brown reflected back on this "new order":

> There was no abandonment of the land; rather a new order saw the women taking charge of the planting of crops aided in part by their children and men too old to seek work outside the valley. . . . During the long summers, the women tended their gardens and fields with perhaps more care than even their menfolk might have done.

When the men returned with the summer's wages, they found they needed to purchase only sugar, coffee, salt, and possibly some white flour and clothing.[80] Women were moving from a shared position at the village center as village producer, to sole tenancy of that position.

Not everyone found that ends met easily. In an increasingly cash-dependent economy, some women found the new pattern required them to go even further afield, beyond adopting the men's farm work. Whether because of declining fertility of home fields, an early or late frost, loss of land, or other reasons, wives and daughters even of farmers found themselves working as seamstresses and laundresses away from home. Their cash income supplemented whatever the men's crops brought. In isolated Truchas, many of the nine out of sixteen laundresses who worked away from home were daughters and wives of landowning farmers. To an even greater degree did the wives of those wage earners (usually sawmill, railroad, or farm laborers) who had moved off the land permanently and now lived in rented housing in the villages, perform wage labor either in or away from the home.[81]

The women who had not only joined their husbands in the new wage sector, but had moved off the land, whether from desire to live with their husbands year-round or from inability to keep up the farm alone, found their community status altered. In their new home they lived divorced from their traditionally intimate relationship with the land and what they produced on it, and often from the village itself.

Still, in all of these scenarios, though the sexual structure of work was altered, men and women retained a mutuality of production without either sex's activities becoming more critical than the other to the survival of the family and community. And, in many cases the altered patterns could be seen as perpetual "emergencies," which, like the lack of male children, legitimized departures from the norm at the same time they produced strains.[82] In this way, new facets of women's work could alter women's place within the community while affecting their relations within marriage to a lesser degree.

Within the villages, subtle shifts occurred in the nature of women's work. For the most part plastering had been performed for exchange or as community service, though it was acknowledged as a skill if not an art. By 1910, however, census records show that some women had become professionals, making their living by plastering. Similar trends emerged in sewing, weaving, and later, mattress-making. By 1910, Chimayo held fourteen men and twenty women whose primary occupation was weaving; none had been so listed in 1880.[83] Women were crossing the fine line between the traditional provision of labor for others for the maintenance of community and the newer trend of providing the same services within the community for maintenance of self.

There were other departures from the communal norm which did not necessarily originate with the renewed Anglo activity of the 1880s but were exacerbated by it. For example, between 1895 and 1905, Hispanic men brought seven divorce cases and Hispanic women brought six into Rio Arriba County's district court; from 1905 to 1910, the men brought seven and the women thirteen, more than keeping pace with the increase in population.[84] By 1913, in the court's June term alone there were fourteen Hispanic divorces; eight of them brought by men.[85]

For both men and women, desertion was the most common reason for divorce, although at least two women brought charges of cruel and inhuman treatment, and three men of adultery.[86] Countersuits appeared occasionally. One man in Rio Arriba County hotly denied that he had mistreated his wife, and in retaliation accused her of adultery. In Santa Fe County, another man countered his wife's claims of abandonment with his own complaints that she "continually and shrewishly quarrelled with him" and "told him that she did not care or wish to live with him any longer and that he must leave the house."[87] Whoever brought the suit tended to get custody of the children, but only the father—as the one with more lucrative options in the wage sector—paid child support, and regardless of who brought suit, the husband usually paid the court costs.

According to the census records almost every village had at least one Hispanic divorced person, usually female, and there were frequently more. In 1910, for example, Chimayo had one divorced man and four divorced women, Coyote had four divorcées and Truchas had two divorced men and five divorced women. In rare cases, a divorced woman would live with her parents. Usually these women lived alone as heads of households with their children and occasionally a widowed mother or grandmother.[88] The pattern did not vary remarkably for divorced men.

Sometimes the divorced women owned property. If it were a farm, and they had grown sons, life could continue more or less in its old patterns. But if it were only a house, which was far more often the case, and particularly if the children were young, the women had to enter the cash sector, which usually meant work as poorly paid washerwomen inside or outside the home.[89] Widows and single women who had become heads of households usually had done so as property owners, with adult male wage-earners or farm labor in the house. They remained within the mutually essential sexual structure of family labor. In contrast, propertyless divorced women with young children, as limited wage earners without a land base, found themselves struggling to keep afloat in a lopsided household.[90]

Divorce and separation were thus acceptable when either partner deviated from the norms of mutual support and respect, but such disruptions in the network of village life could not be encouraged. One woman who left an abusive husband and eventually moved to Cordova became "Tia Lupe" (Aunt Lupe), to the whole village, providing healing and counseling services and receiving fuel and other compensation, but she lived there alone.[91] Divorced women and men may not have been shunned by the community, but neither were they fully reincorporated through, for example, a return to their landowning parents. Many parents lacked the resources to maintain the enlarged household. Instead, incorporation and survival in the community for the divorced often came to rest on wage labor or monetary relations with fellow villagers or outsiders, rather than on the communal exchange of produce and services. The plight of these families underscored the essential nature of the integration of men's and women's labor, village and cash economies, neighborhood and migration, for the survival of the Hispanic communities.

In these less than perfectly harmonious communal villages, also, lived single women with illegitimate children.[92] In the late 1930s, Daniel Valdez commented, "this is common throughout the Valley. Every year brings a score of illegitimate babies with it. This is no more common now than it was a generation past."[93] Illegitimacy was not the product of cultural breakdown or of a new modernism, but a long-term phenomenon of an agricultural society. But length of tradition did not necessarily mean smooth acceptance, and the increasingly dominant cash economy placed extra burdens on unwed mothers. While Ruth Barker claimed that "even the illegitimate child inherits no town censure. . . . the unmarried mother . . . [is] treated with kindness, leaving social errors to the wisdom of the confessional," there is no evidence that unwed mothers had an easier life than divorced or separated mothers. While most illegitimate children seem to have been accepted by the community, there were husbands who refused to recognize them, and mothers whose washing work could not support them or who fostered them to couples who abused them.[94] Perhaps these are the children who fell through the social net of the northern Hispanic villages and landed in St. Vincent's Orphans' Home for girls in Sante Fe, which had forty-seven Hispanic girls in 1909, and 116 (at least 23 from Rio Arriba County alone) in 1913.[95] Of the fifty-nine Hispanic women in the New Mexico State Penitentiary between 1884 and 1917, nine were separated wives, three were single women, and two were widows. Forty-two had been charged with sexually related crimes, including thirty-seven cases of adultery. Of the forty-two women charged, ten were laundresses, seven seamstresses, seven servants, two laborers, and one was a farmer. It is a measure of the difficulty of these women's lives that of the eight who gave reasons for their "crime," two listed desertion by husband, five claimed "necessity," and only one claimed "love."[96]

There was another set of women who found no comfortable place in village society. These were the "brujas" or witches. Egalitarianism and communalism do not necessarily exist at the expense of individuality. Rather a broad-minded tolerance may characterize such a group, limited only by perceived threats to the village's existence.[97] For the Hispanic villagers, broken marriages and brujas provided such threats. Divorced people and witches existed not simply as eccentric individuals, but as individuals unattached and possibly even hostile to the dense and vital network of family relations that sustained the community.

Ironically, belief in witchcraft could operate to ensure tolerance of a certain degree of eccentricity. New Mexico's Writers' Project investigators in the 1930s found that "brujas were taken for granted by all. The men as well as the women believed in brujas, and were careful not to offend anyone they were not sure of."[98] Eccentric behavior in these cases was safest dealt with politely. As with witchcraft elsewhere, in New Mexico these beliefs also provided a forum for the relief of social tensions, as when Hispanics told Charles Briggs, "all *Indios* are witches."[99] Witches in New Mexico could be either male or female, but they were usually female, and in a classic juxtaposition of good woman/bad woman, the color blue, associated with Mary, was used to protect against witches, while "I go without God and without the Holy Virgin" was the incantation which allowed witches to fly.[100]

According to historian Marc Simmons, it was only after Hispanics realized that the United States courts would not hear witchcraft cases that vigilante-style reprisals occurred. In 1884, a woman near Chimayo "was taken from her lonely adobe hut by three roughs . . . and murdered," apparently for suspected dealings with the devil; and in 1882 a woman from Abiquiu was whipped until near death by the henchmen of her supposed victim.[101] Those suspected of witchcraft in the villages tended to be older women, usually of somewhat mysterious origins, women, whether widowed or never married, who lived alone with few if any kinship ties to the villagers.[102] The village women's fear of growing old alone which led them to adopt and foster small children thus had far more than economic or even affectional roots, and the loss of ties to the village had more than economic consequences.[103]

Some of these village tensions were less a sign of cultural breakdown or even of the adjustment to the new economic context than a witness to the perpetual distance between the ideal aspired to and the reality in any society, and to the perceived fragility of the corporate community. They represented the ways in which villagers had long dealt with elements that threatened the family economy and communal virtues, elements potentially too disharmonious to incorporate safely into their small mutually dependent society of one hundred to five hundred people. Into this pattern of dealing with village tensions they thrust the newer tensions, the potential problems, caused by the adaptation to the regional community and the Anglo-dominated larger economy: the professionalization of former services, the cash-dependent widows. As they held the disruptive elements of Anglo society at bay, beyond the village, the villagers also relegated their own disruptive elements, including witches and divorcées, to the village periphery if not beyond.

At the orderly center of the village, on the other hand, lay a closely knit community of women. It encompassed informal hierarchies of skill, age, knowledge, and spirituality, and it fostered communal virtues. Women's social existence was not cloistered, not limited to the home and family or even to the community of women, nor did they participate in the village solely as wives, mothers, and daughters. They performed communal labor and religious services for the entire village, work that took them out of the house, as well as autonomous labor in the garden and in the home. In the northern New Mexico and southern Colorado villages, the parallelism of Hispanic men's and women's work on the land, in religion, and in building was not competitive and stratified but mutually supporting.[104] Neither men nor women were as effective economically on their own as they were together. Yet neither was powerless or completely dependent.

The rise of the regional community had not placed women at the center of village life. They were already there. But it did create a situation where they held that spot increasingly alone. Others have commented on the autonomy and power of women in primarily subsistence economies with small-scale exchange. Anthropologist Alice Schlegel has explained, "each sex in any society has primary control over certain activities, and the rewards and power accruing to each sex depend upon the centrality of these activities to the society as a whole."[105] In a village increasingly divided into village women and migrant men, women's activities sustained the community physically and spiritually. The integrative function of women in the village grew in importance, and more frequently women provided the continuity for the village, as they did for the church during the absences of the priest. As women's work was not limited to hidden and reproductive work in the household, the work of both sexes remained visible and essential to subsistence itself. That the Hispanic village as a whole, not just the women, acknowledged the equally vital nature of men's and women's work was attested by property-holding and -use practices, marital and inheritance norms, and religious practices, which recognized and perpetuated women as autonomous beings.

The men's purview of external affairs included not just the cash sector and migrant labor, but Anglos, investigators or tourists, who came to the village.[106] Most likely it was this allocation of external affairs to men which led to the first distortions in depictions of village sexual structure. This division of labor meant that when Anglos dined at Hispanic village homes, they ate with the men while the women and children ate later, whereas when the family was alone they usually all ate together. It also meant that virtually all impressions of Hispanic society received by Anglos were received through Hispanic men, who naturally had a stake in creating an image for themselves acceptable to Anglo notions of gender and to whom, most likely, it would not occur to volunteer information about the women's world. This is brought out particularly in obvious gaps in some sociological literature. Olen Leonard, for example, places the labor of the woman firmly in the home, ignoring her garden duties, and insists that the father "is definitely the head," handling, for example, finances and provisions for the family. But what happens when, according to Leonard himself, the father is gone from six months to a year is a question Leonard does not tackle.[107]

The women made up the stable core of the village. The society and economy of women was inextricably linked to the ability of Hispanics to survive in their new cultural economic patterns, just as the lack of a rigid sexual division of labor allowed women to compensate for men's seasonal absences. Through their visiting, their sharing of food, plastering, childbearing, and, most important, their stability, production, and earnings as non-migrants, women provided for increasingly mobile villagers not only subsistence, but continuity and networks for community, health, and child care, for old age and emotional support. As leaders both within and outside the community of women, as churchwomen and parteras, willing to act independently and even combatively in legal struggles over property and marriage, and as property owners and producers in their own right, Hispanic village women were hardly, after all, cloistered, powerless, or even, necessarily, submissive. It was these women who would have a crucial role, not just in maintaining the larger structure of the regional community—that human network extending the ties of the village over hundreds of miles so that the village could survive—but in resisting whatever Anglo cultural threat manifested itself within the village.

3

Invading Arcadia: Women Missionaries and Women Villagers, 1900–1914

"Had I been set down upon some other planet," Harriet Benham marveled in 1900, "the country, the people and their customs would, probably, not have been stranger to me than those of New Mexico."[1] Foreign in language and dress, Catholic in heritage and fact, Hispanic New Mexico seemed to many Americans not harmlessly peculiar, but a threat to national unity and virtue. Such a threat created its own imperatives, demanded a second conquest. It was the Protestant churches who claimed the privilege.

By 1900, churches in the United States had come to think of mission fields as frontiers of Christian civilization and missionaries as a vanguard.[2] Anglo Protestants spoke in one breath of Americanizing and of "Christianizing" New Mexico, of conquering this frontier. Presbyterian minister George McAfee exulted biblically in 1903, "The whole land is before us. Shall we go up and possess it?"[3] Through church and school, the Protestants hoped for a more effective conquest, one that would bring the recalcitrant former Mexicans firmly into the English-speaking Protestant nation spiritually and culturally as well as geographically.

Church men like McAfee exhorted, but by and large it was women who went up and did the possessing. In New Mexico in 1900 nineteen of twenty-one mission schools were run by women.[4] Over two hundred mission women came to New Mexico and southern Colorado between 1900 and 1914 alone. These women, as Rev. Robert Craig explained in 1903, were "compelled in the prosecution of their work to invade a foreign speaking community and to overcome time honored prejudices."[5] The mission women were not always comfortable with their new role as invaders, but they recognized a moral imperative. Congregationalist Honora deBusk, after describing a "picturesque and quaint" New Mexico village scene with children's "happy voices ringing out in the clear cold air," continued, "if we did not know the awful sinfulness and the real soul hunger of the people . . . it would seem too bad for us to invade such an Arcadia."[6] Since these women felt they did "know so well the depravity of their [Hispanic] lives," the apparent idyllic nature of village life proved an inadequate defense for Hispanics on this women's frontier. Instead, Protestant Anglos concluded, "to the women, missionary guardians of the coming generations, sound the call."[7]

Representatives of this invading force often found themselves not just the only Anglo women, but the only Anglos at all in their Hispanic villages. There they were not merely the vanguard; they were the whole army. In the Hispanic heartland and the women's world of the northern New Mexico villages, the most direct intercultural contact was thus female. Examining the missionaries themselves as well as the contact reveals the significance of the female nature of this frontier, for the character of the assailants intimately affected the ways in which villagers were able to protect the village from the cultural threat within as they protected it in the larger context by the regional community and its migratory networks. While other Anglos determined the nature of cultural interaction elsewhere in the regional community, in the villages it was the missionaries whose backgrounds, attitudes, aims, and actions, in conjunction with those of the villagers, formed the pattern of relations.

The missionaries proclaimed a multiple purpose for their schools in New Mexico:

> to convince of a full and free salvation through the savior of the Cross; to make true American citizens, intelligent and enthusiastic supporters of our institutions, and to give a moral and technical education that will enable them to cope with the social temptations and problems of the twentieth century.[8]

Such a mission, frequently consolidated under the rubric of teaching Hispanics "what real living is," obviously went beyond the purely religious. To these missionaries, the task of creating "in a generation or two . . . good American citizens and loyal servants of Christ" required that they "change in every respect the homes and habits of these Mexicans." Like missionaries in other countries whose sweeping rejection of their host culture was accompanied by equally sweeping aims, the women who came to New Mexico drew no distinction between the religious and the secular facets of their message. During an Easter service geared to compete with a Penitente service in the same village, the mission leaders had their wall "fairly covered with our beautiful big [American] flag and Bible lesson pictures illustrating the life of Christ."[9]

And yet for all their enthusiastic evangelical patriotism, the missionaries recognized that many back east did not see their schools as true mission work. It seemed to these doubters that at least part of this multidimensional mission in New Mexico should have been performed by the public sector. The superintendent of the mission schools himself called for the "normal and effective development of the public school as the greatest agency of American civilization," while in 1907 New Mexico's Assistant Superintendent of Public Instruction, A. M. Sanchez, called the rural schools "our main stronghold in the work for the uplift and advancement of the main masses of our people."[10] The rhetoric of New Mexico's public school representatives, in fact, often differed little from that of the missionaries, and Grace DeNison concluded in the *New Mexico Journal of Education* that teaching Spanish Americans "places us in the capacity of missionaries."[11] Why, then, weren't the public schools succeeding? Why did most Hispanics, sixty years after conquest, still speak no English and missionaries feel justified in insisting on their own indispensability?

In 1912, the year of statehood, seven school districts in mountainous Rio Arriba County had no schools, and nine-tenths of the schools with teachers met for three months or less.[12] The county had no public high school until 1917. Unable to collect the requisite tax levy, cash-poor Rio Arriba lost matching state aid for education.[13] Other Hispanic counties of northern New Mexico enjoyed a similar dearth of facilities.

The attitude of teachers, too, was not uniformly constructive. Anglo teachers tended to regard "teaching Spanish American children . . . as a last resort," an educator revealed in 1915.[14] Some of these reluctant "missionaries" considered Hispanic children sadly lacking "that spirit

of liberty and that love of education . . . the ambition . . . courage and
determination," in short "the aspirations of the Pilgrims" that presumably came to Anglo children as their "birthright."[15] Such teachers,
according to another educator in 1912, led Spanish-American children
"to believe that they can not do as well as others."[16]

On the other hand, the resulting lack of qualified teachers did not
imbue villagers with great respect for public education. Children were
kept home from school by parents who relied on them for various agricultural and domestic chores such as herding goats, planting and harvesting, and doing the laundry.[17] One villager remembered with dev-
astating candor, "very few people would go to the public schools. They
just didn't learn, the teachers did not know how to teach, they were not
educated."[18] When Agnes Smedley got her first teaching post, near
Raton, New Mexico, she was, at sixteen, underage and had low marks
in math, grammar, and other subjects on the teachers' exam; by her own
admission, she learned as she went.[19] The Hispanics' well-grounded
skepticism reinforced an inadequate plant and teaching staff, most of
whose ability to speak English was heartily disputed, and ensured that
public schools would have a minimal impact on the community as an
external, Americanizing agency or, in fact, as any agency at all.

Beginning in 1909, an attempt was made to remedy the situation by
establishing a Spanish American Normal School. Poverty, lack of public
high schools in Hispanic counties, and discrimination had almost
entirely excluded all but the wealthiest Hispanics from higher education. Only seven of the eighty-seven people who graduated from New
Mexico's public high schools in 1913 were Hispanic.[20] The new school
at El Rito lay in the somewhat inaccessible heart of Hispanic northern
New Mexico, distant from railroad transport and dense settlement, in
buildings originally designed for a reform school, but it provided for
many inhabitants of Rio Arriba and Taos counties their first opportunity to attend beyond fourth grade.

For the modest sum of ten to fifteen dollars a month for room and
board—tuition was provided free—the school promised to train Hispanics as teachers and leaders for their home villages.[21] While it did
certify a steady trickle of teachers, it was plagued with problems from
the start. The miniscule appropriation of the first year was gradually
raised, but remained at one-third the state appropriation to each of New
Mexico's other normal schools.[22] And though the school made a special
effort to assuage the anxieties of parents who might hesitate to send ado-

lescent daughters to a coeducational boarding school, in 1913 only half as many females as males attended.[23]

In addition, the students were overage, undereducated, and sporadic in attendance. Four-fifths of the enrollment withdrew before the end of term for harvest duties. "The material that comes to us," one school official apologized bluntly in his report, "is crude."[24] In desperation, officials of this Spanish-American school started admitting Anglos and began to provide scholarships to Anglo as well as to Hispanic students, "so that English may be learned in the playgrounds as well as in the classroom."[25] With the one experiment geared specifically to remedy the educational flaws of Hispanic New Mexico so far from a raging success, the way lay open for the women missionaries.

By 1902, 1500 New Mexican children attended mission schools. That year, twelve requests for schools from unserved villages reached the Presbyterian Women's Board of Home Missions, by far the most active in the field.[26] But the impact of the schools reached beyond the sites and certainly beyond the approximately 1400 Hispanic converts.[27] Matilda Allison's Presbyterian school for Hispanic girls in Santa Fe had seventy-seven pupils from twenty-eight plazas and towns; only slightly over a third were Presbyterian.[28] Since many had the resources to attend for only a year, former pupils scattered over the landscape.[29] In plaza day schools, students were largely Catholic, but mission teachers who stayed in one village, as Sue Zuver did for nineteen years, found they had taught nearly the entire village.[30] In addition, graduates of Presbyterian schools, particularly the high schools, were in great demand. In 1909, mission teachers in Chimayo found that five of the public schools near them had former mission pupils as teachers, and of fifty-five teachers at the annual teachers' institute for Taos County three years later, fifty-one had attended Protestant mission schools.[31] The Anglo women missionaries represented a cultural contact at once diffuse and intense, one that penetrated deeply into the Hispanic hinterland and found few Anglo competitors for influence.

The mission schools, in their teaching force and organization, stood in direct contrast to the villages' school system. Hispanic schools were locally controlled and often staffed, through political patronage, with sons, daughters, wives, or widows of long-established families.[32] While Hispanic women occasionally served on county school boards after receiving school suffrage in 1912, and the feminization of the Hispanic teaching force proceeded with relative rapidity between 1912 and 1916, even in the latter year only 34 percent of Rio Arriba County's public school teachers were women.[33] The Presbyterian schools, in contrast, were controlled by the women of the Women's Board of Home Missions in distant New York. Approximately 80 percent of the teachers were single Anglo women in their twenties, most of whom came from the Midwest or Pennsylvania and spoke no Spanish on arrival in the villages.[34] The missionaries at once feminized and Anglicized the teaching force and education in general in northern New Mexico.[35]

The feminine nature of the mission force was no accident. "The teachers," declared the Presbyterians in 1905, "—faithful, gentle, persevering, brave, unfaltering ... are the power used to drive the wedge."[36] This was to be an invasion propelled by the "pedagogy of love," the "nurturant approach," which had gained favor with American educators elsewhere in the mid-nineteenth century accompanying the shift in emphasis from rote learning to moral inculcation. Only the American woman, as "the natural and appropriate guardian of the young ... who has those tender sympathies ... who has that conscientiousness and religious devotion," as reformer Catharine Beecher had put it, could inspire in the children the virtue "indispensable to the safety of a democratic government like ours."[37] This tradition of moralism and more personal pedagogy was clearly what the Presbyterians called forth when, recognizing that Hispanics were more eager for Anglo knowledge than Anglo religion, they insisted "that where the preacher can not go the teacher may, and with *her* loving service and ready sympathy win the love and confidence of the people."[38]

Teaching itself was already regarded as a highly respectable calling for women among Anglos, and missionaries cut a heroic figure on speaking tours throughout the United States. For girls imbued with both the optimistic, adventurous activism of the 1890s and a spirituality derived from missionary or ministerial relatives, or simply from the centrality of the church in the small-town social life of the midwest, the opportunity to become a missionary seemed a shimmering promise.[39] Missionary Louise Murray confessed, "I *lived* the church" and, like most, felt irresistibly called to mission work.[40]

Mission women found themselves living in adobe houses and "trying to cook on an open fireplace" in villages where infant mortality ranked among the highest in the nation, and typhoid, diphtheria, and malaria swept with depressing regularity.[41] The teachers' home in Truchas did not have running water or electricity until 1922, and the house in Holman lacked indoor plumbing until the late 1930s.[42] Yet the women seemed to glory in overcoming these difficulties, to glory in a strength that was not only spiritual. "My sister," wrote one missionary glowingly and in the hope they would be placed together on the mission field, "is a splendid *big* strong girl and you know me."[43] Olinda Meeker reported to her male supervisor, Rev. Craig, "I had hardly bargained for a carpenter's job when I accepted Raton but I knew enough of mission work to expect most anything."[44] They were proud of their ability as women to manage on their own. A change in financial organization in 1918 brought an angry protest from Mollie Clements, who had served for thirty-one years: "[C]andidly, Mr. Allaben, I do feel hurt and humiliated, by this new plan which seems to me to show a lack of confidence in our ability as responsible women to manage own own personal and private affairs."[45] Miss Clements had no intention of keeping receipts for each small item judged necessary to run her school so that she could account for it to her male superior.

These devout and independent invaders were also proud of their professionalism, for mission teaching was a "calling" in this sense as well. Most of these women had taught in public or in mission schools before coming to New Mexico, or had trained in normal schools. Even those women who had not trained as academic teachers, but as musicians or matrons, insisted their professional training be used and refused mission work outside it.[46] On the other hand, they viewed housework not as a task which, as women, they would naturally assume, but as a separate and additional occupation. When listing the multifaceted occupations demanded by plaza work, these women almost invariably included housekeeping in such ways as "going to housekeeping and teaching school in a Mexican plaza" or "I struggled along, teaching, keeping house, and nursing."[47] When they could, they hired an assistant or had the board hire one for them, or imported a sister or other companion.[48]

Their spirituality drove the missionaries to New Mexico, but other attributes equally influenced their impact there. Not just their independence and professionalism, but their pride in those characteristics shaped them as models of Anglo womanhood in the village. Whatever other contrary images they attempted to convey would suffer by comparison with their own vivid example.

When these professionals arrived on the field, they at first experienced certain difficulties in finding acceptance in the villages. Some problems were due to lack of preparation. In her first year at San Juan, Colorado, Mollie Clements was "thankful that I could smile . . . for not knowing the language, to smile was about all I could do!"[49] Other difficulties had their basis in moral and cultural concerns. In 1900 Anna McNair reported, "[W]hen our mission teachers visit the homes in some of the plazas they feel the stigma put upon them by the priests, through the frown that greets them, and the fingers held firmly in the form of the cross until they leave the house."[50] Slotted into the category of "witch," the missionaries found the villagers at new sites less than open. Eventually, however, villagers chose other slots for women missionaries to fill, and by the 1920s, if not before, the "witches" had become, in the words of the villagers, "Protestant nuns."[51] While the results of mission contact varied, by looking first at missionary attitudes which fostered tension and conflict, then at the interplay of mission and village strategies which mitigated the conflict, and finally at strategies which controlled the impact through integration, the larger pattern at this end of the cultural frontier becomes clear.

The ambivalence of many missionaries toward the village could have diluted their secular message. For them as for Honora deBusk and other Americans of the time, cultural-Christian expansionism, the faith in American industrial progress, warred with a back-to-nature, pluralist impulse expressed partly in President Roosevelt's "strenuousity" and partly in an aesthetic which found the quaint endearing and which admired primitive virtue and natural beauty.[52] In the majestic New Mexico mountains, one missionary exclaimed, "one cannot but feel the very heart-beat of the Creator."[53] Occasionally these women endowed the native Hispanics with some of the sanctified splendor of the terrain, referring to "quaintly-dressed natives" as part of the scenery, or describing "a people simple, ignorant and poor, but kind hearted."[54]

But the strangeness could also be frightening. Among the elements inhibiting integration, understanding, and cultural exchange were the missionaries' own fears, fantasies, and racial attitudes. In the strange beauty, they found something sinister, a dark side hidden behind the next mountain, the next black-shawled woman, or the plaza walls.[55] The deceptively idyllic beauty seemed to these missionaries, who sought truth and honored straightforwardness, almost a trap.

The missionaries not only noted what seemed to them the dark side of village life, they were fascinated by it. Given the vaunted stealth of the Penitentes and the emphatic disdain expressed by the missionaries, it is amazing how many of these women saw the Holy Week ceremonies, and to what lengths they went. Josephine Orton traveled two miles and "crouched among the bushes" to witness the spectacle. The element of voyeurism blended with the fascination of the exotic to give the women a dark adventure which would place them on a level with the foreign missionaries. Elizabeth Elliot, after making sure the reader knew New Mexico was "worse" than "Darkest Africa," related that on one "Good Friday we started out early, determined to see all that could be seen."[56] Most of the women missionaries who served in New Mexico had, on their applications, expressed a preference for a different field.[57] In the hierarchy of missionary adventure New Mexico seemed to hold a low place.[58] The darkness which so fascinated the missionaries provided their raison d'être. They were "bringing brightness to these spots of darkness and superstition."[59] The scene had to be dark, and not just beautiful, just as the New Mexican had to be childlike, or the missionary had no function.[60] The seductive simplicity of the people and spectacular scenery had to be resisted, to be kept at a distance, and exposed for the degenerate society the missionaries knew them to be.

In their anxiety to prove themselves as valid, courageous, and heroic as those missionaries in more remote stations, these women at times magnified their adventures for the audience back east. Some of these fantasies found an outlet in short pieces of fiction created for mission magazines, often by women with little actual experience on the field. In such stories, for example, women missionaries who lived alone in New Mexico faced stoning and death from the hostile villagers, although actually only two women missionaries were known to have had anything like such dangerous encounters in the eighty years these women served in New Mexico, and in both of these cases the perpetrators were outsiders to the village.[61] Other stories depicted an oppressive and barren life for Hispanics and an exaggeratedly humble gratitude for the mission presence.[62] The stories brought out the fundamental racism of the period, in which many of the women missionaries participated, enhanced by the mission need to emphasize the "otherness" or foreignness of their subjects at the same time they struggled to eliminate it.

Some of the missionaries had faith that Anglo settlement would in itself sufficiently improve the "natives." Josephine Orton wrote from Tierra Amarilla of a "general awakening on the part of the native population toward a bettering of their condition," apparently stimulated largely by the fact that "with the opening up of large tracts of land for settlement in this vicinity, there is a healthy influx of Americans and foreigners, a good working class, who have come here hoping to build up homes."[63] For other women, this conquest by "a good working class," taking over Hispanic lands and providing an "American" example, was not enough.[64] Some of the missionaries found "these hearts as sterile as the hills among which the people live. The physical nerve centers are paralyzed with nicotine, while the moral consciousness has been deadened with the opiate of Roman doctrine."[65]

This conviction of their own superiority often led to a self-imposed isolation and loneliness that not only impeded but precluded their cultural mission. Like other frontier women, separated by living styles so different that missionaries were convinced "no American could live as they do," these Anglo women resisted integration and found their most "trying ordeal was being shut off from associates of like interests."[66] "I confess to you," one missionary wrote the Board, "It is a dreadfully lonesome place."[67]

Anglo women, however, were more likely than men to overcome the popular images of Hispanics planted in their minds and to retain at least an ambivalence toward Hispanics and Hispanic culture marked by a like ambivalence toward their own.[68] Firmly rooted in America's Victorian ideology of domesticity, the women missionaries' vision was of a world more nurturing and less competitive than that outside the walls of middle-class homes. They had less of a stake than Anglo men in defining civilization and progress as cutthroat competition for commercial ends. While the men, including the men of the church, were more likely to note waste of New Mexico's "latent resources" and see in them a "Mexican" who lacked "a vista, an ambition," some of the women found their preconceptions modified by the universal "efforts at homemaking," the "clean white walls," and "carefully tended plants." In direct contrast to the men, at least one of these Anglo women missionaries concluded, "I believe the majority of the people have high aspirations."[69] The communal sharing of wages and other resources so criticized by the industrialist seemed to many women to be virtues. "They give their best to their guests, they treat strangers kindly, and to the poor they give freely," praised Harriet Benham. Some of these Anglo women were less than enchanted with "our exceedingly hygienic methods of living," with "Americans who have located in New Mexico with a view only of money-making," with, in short, "the merciless white man."[70] They could more easily than Anglo men admire an industriousness that did not hinge on industrialism or large-scale commercial agriculture. Ambivalent toward both their own and the Hispanic culture, they did not merely seek to perpetuate the civilization from which they had come, nor did they wish to leave unchanged what they found.

The women missionaries, in fact, determined to take over the direction of the entire village and to reshape it, in a brand of miniature empire building. If male empire builders evinced paternalism, then this was maternalism. "'She is the mother of us all,' is heard constantly on the lips of the people," Alice Blake revealed, "till one comes to feel one's self so much a necessity that it is hard to go away even for the needed vacation."[71] These women, often trapped by their sense of necessity and their divinely appointed mission, tried to deliver a female version of the imperial message. The female nature of this cross-cultural contact influenced both the particular targets chosen and the nature of the culture conveyed.

Mission boards recruited women by urging each "to respond to the plea of her sister who, 'suffering as a slave or beast, knows not the meaning of womanhood.'"[72] The New Mexico missionaries' perceptions of Hispanic women's lot lay firmly within the more general secular tendency to credit Christianity with "the elevated status of Western women" and to deplore "the depraved condition of women in heathen lands." Hostility to education for women, the loveless marriage, cruel, non-Protestant husbands, and tyrannical parents or parents-in-law became stock elements in missionary literature of such diverse fields as China, Africa, and New Mexico.[73]

According to popular stereotypes of the time, all but the most elite Hispanic women were voluptuous, poor, dirty, and morally lax. Hispanic men were lazy, filthy, stupid, cowardly, and conniving.[74] To mission women in New Mexico who had grown unaccustomed to women working outside the home, it did seem that Hispanic women were forced to do the men's work, while the men were not men enough to make sufficient provision for them to stay within doors.[75] Missionaries complained, too, that the tyranny of the mother-in-law, if not the other members of the family, made marriage "little more than slavery." A churchwoman of the time provided a near parody of these beliefs in her fictional story of "poor Manuela," recently deceased, the very type of Hispanic womanhood:

> From earliest childhood she had tended babies, carried water and helped her mother from daylight to dark. A wife at fourteen, mother at fifteen, the slave of a dissolute husband who had been killed in a drunken row a month before she looked old and worn now, and ready to lay down life's burden at the age

of 23. 'I am glad for her,' said Miss Raymond to her companion, the other mission school teacher.[76]

Given these stereotypes, however distorted, of drudgery and degradation, and given their own single, professional womanhood, it is not surprising that, when hearing of a broken engagement, one woman missionary "rejoiced in a few more years of freedom, perhaps, for her."[77]

Mission women determined to wrest control of child-rearing, in part, at least, so that they could remedy the perceived abuses of womanhood along with the other flaws in Hispanic culture. Some complained of brutal parents, others of Hispanics "disposed to be too lenient with their children."[78] It did not really matter. If the Hispanic child were to grow up to be "American," if the missionaries were to succeed in their mission, the children had to be trained by representatives of that culture, that is, by the Anglo women, and not by their own parents.

The obvious answer was the boarding school. It may have seemed to the Anglo women a natural choice and an easy adjustment, given the system of fostering which they at first perceived as resulting from parents "nearly devoid of a feeling of responsibility for their families, if only they can shift it onto someone else." They soon found, however, that parents were reluctant to leave their children at the schools.[79] Fostering was actually a far-from-perfunctory system of redistributing children within the village or family so as best to provide for the welfare of both the children, usually from large families of little means, and the childless villagers.[80] When missionary Melinda Conway, having paid for two of her plaza's girls to go to the Allison school, "decided that it might be unwise to allow the girls to come back under the doubtful influence of their homes" and placed them, without consulting their parents, in Anglo homes, the girls' parents were "furiously indignant." But Conway's discovery that these were foster parents led her to obtain authorization from the "true" parents and make it stick legally. The threats and the removal of children from her school left her unrepentant: "I was content. The elder people need to learn that Indian [i.e. Hispanic] customs must give way when they conflict with the laws of the United States, and the lesson was worth all it cost."[81]

Most mission women were not quite so autocratic, but cultural disputes over child-rearing methods placed the Anglo missionaries and the Hispanic mothers in direct conflict as teachers and, more particularly, as women.[82] Parents were naturally loathe not only to part with their children, but to leave them for the day or overnight in the hands of those whose teaching in both spiritual and secular matters would counter their own, and who would, if they could, usurp authority and control. Only the tremendous value placed on education and the opportunities it afforded both boys and girls kept the Presbyterian boarding schools full to overflowing and the Presbyterian day schools packed. By the constant instruction in religion and manner—aggression rather than reserve for both girls and boys—as the parents feared, and missionary Alice Hyson reported, "the child's mind in many cases is divided, because they must decide who is right, the mother or the teacher."[83] Hispanic parents and missionaries were simply fulfilling their socially assigned roles as cultural bearers and conveyors, but the cultures were in competition.

Women missionaries made special efforts to bring Hispanic girls into the day schools as well. They believed, at least in part, in the maxim, "Educate a man and you educate an individual; educate a woman and you educate a family."[84] In the 1880s, the Anglo women had found Hispanics reluctant to send their girls to school. The villagers had viewed education as unnecessary for the village-centered functions of the women and gazed askance at coeducational school rooms. By the turn of the century, however, parents had changed their minds. Missionaries had argued the need for female literacy to enable women to take their places in the modern world and to teach and provide nurses for the villages, and by 1900 the men and women villagers agreed.[85] One Hispanic woman moved into town with her daughters, telling, not asking, her husband. "I don't want them to be raised like tontitas [dummies]," she insisted. Another woman, who had at times been responsible for her own livelihood, wanted her girls educated in order to be independent.[86] By 1900 the villagers realized that the maintenance of the relatively egalitarian relations between the sexes demanded that both sexes "benefit from the more modern training."[87]

Although the missionaries emphasized the need for literacy and the training of independent women, the strongest message they broadcast, perhaps even stronger than the strictly spiritual message, was quite different. "The native girls need Christian help no less than the boys," wrote Judge William Pope in *Home Mission Monthly,* "that they may make homes for coming generations."[88] The Allison School gave a regular academic course, but the Home Mission Board's male superintendent, Mr. Allaben, insisted that the Allison School's "emphasis should be on home economics and general training for homemaking," which included the use of an adobe oven, that the girls might "be expert in native cooking if they are to prove equal to home demands." And when the Anglo women set out to educate Hispanic girls, what they, too, had in mind was education for domesticity. The future roles they allocated to Hispanic women were quite clear: "better housekeepers, more devoted mothers, and more intelligent and economical wives."[89]

Housekeeping, mothering, and wifehood encompassed a far more limited round of activities than the Hispanic women and certainly than the Anglo missionaries habitually enjoyed. But the Anglos blamed Hispanic poverty, at least in part, on the idleness and mismanagement of these village women and the laziness of their husbands.[90] In their schools, as they trained the girls in homemaking, the missionaries trained the boys to manage the traditional female fields of gardens and poultry. They spoke in this context of "Menaul training the young men, and Allison-James developing the young women among the Spanish Americans in Colorado and New Mexico for the manifold responsibilities of a Christian-American citizenship."[91] The key message of the missionaries, then, involved the Americanization of Hispanic gender roles, the replication in the plazas of Anglo gender patterns—women in the home, men outside it—in short, the cult of domesticity. This was the elevated status of women for which they held Christianity responsible.

While their reports were replete with the mention of the training, establishment, and impact of Hispanic girls as homemakers, it was quite clearly not the traditional Hispanic home they had in mind. The women missionaries demanded "the right sort" of homes, which alone would produce "the right sort of men and women."[92] Despite the fact that most observers regarded Hispanic women as house-proud, as "excellent housekeepers," many Anglo women missionaries saw their adobe houses as "cheerless homes" which produced "sad-eyed and spiritless," "idle, cigarette-smoking women."[93] Not content to meddle with or "Americanize" home life through the school, mission women attacked the home within. In some sense, they entered these homes only to change them. From homes so distressingly unlike their own, they concluded that "decency and true refinement are not found among the Mexican people." Agreeing with the China missionary who declared, "civilization is shown so clearly in the way one eats," the missionaries were appalled to see families who not only slept on the floor, but ate there from a common dish with tortillas for spoons. "We hope," wrote Alice Blake, "to be able to establish better habits in these matters."[94]

The missionaries were particulary concerned with the twin themes of respectability and refinement. They taught women to sew "respectable" dresses, and rejoiced when, through the influence of their schools, a "filthy, uncombed, unkempt, sad-eyed" Hispanic became "a frank, bright, clear-eyed, neatly-clothed and combed lady-like girl."[95] Much ink was spent here as elsewhere by these middle-class women with different notions of privacy, deploring, however neat the home, the customary "crowding of large families into one living and sleeping room" as "necessarily productive of much evil" and as "not at all favorable to the development of the true moral nature."[96]

The missionaries tended to count their moral victories by tables "set with American dishes," tablecloths, "cooking utensils and furniture." When filled with these new items, the homes at last would display "a general air of refinement."[97] "The evolution of the Mexican home," concluded Alice Blake triumphantly, "is now making toward Americanism."[98] Americanization was thus defined in terms of spreading material culture; "America" meant bedsteads and board floors, closed stoves and sewing machines. As did other interested Anglos, these women tended to confuse enthusiasm for cultural artifacts with enthusiasm for the entire cultural complex. They seemed to believe deeply in the power of material culture to recreate the entire culture which produced it.

They also firmly believed in the power of this reformed home to effect "the salvation of the Mexicans," and, inseparably, believed that flowers, curtains, the multitude of "things" and rooms of which the Hispanics "cannot seem to understand" the need were essential to that salvation.[99] Middle-class morality, taste, and gender patterns, Americanism, and Protestantism were all tightly bound together in mission teaching. As the missionaries pursued their efforts in the areas of childrearing, refinement, respectability, and the elevation of Hispanic women, as well as in homemaking, which encompassed all four, consciously or unconsciously they were not simply trying to turn Hispanics into Americans, but into Americans of a particular class. In so doing, they threatened the variety and relative autonomy of Hispanic women's activities and the survival patterns dependent on them.

Not just in the home but in the wider village, the mission woman threatened the integrity of village society. Simply her presence, as a representative of an alternative religion, disrupted patterns of hierarchy. Catholic priests, resident on less than half of the Protestant church sites in New Mexico and on an even smaller proportion of mission school sites, felt vulnerable.[100] The Presbyterians, while charging a minimal tuition fee payable in kind, provided free services for baptism, marriage, and burial, whereas the priests often demanded cash payments for each of these rites.[101] And although the ratio of Presbyterian ministers, Anglo or Hispanic, to Presbyterian Hispanic churches and schools was even lower than that of the Catholic clerics, the mission teachers carried the pastoral work between visits much the way the Catholic village women did for the priests.[102] By her presence, her education, and her prominent role in local church affairs, the woman missionary provided a rival authority to the nearest Catholic priest.[103]

The women missionaries not only threatened the power of the priests, they threatened the status of Hispanic women in religion. They condemned the "worship" of Mary and its related rituals. Ironically, the Protestants praised women as uniquely religious creatures through whom mankind could be brought to salvation, but were horrified at the attention paid to Mary in village churches. They lauded Juan G. Quintana's conclusion, on being taught that Mary could not intercede, "I resolved to stop prayer to any woman, whether she be Hebrew, Roman, or Greek."[104]

Converts like Quintana posed perhaps the most tangible threat to a village unity which depended at least in part on all inhabitants attending the same church, school, fiestas, and bailes. Missionary Alice Hyson "was disturbed by the rather riotous Sundays honoring the patron saint of Taos and Taos Pueblo."[105] Such fiestas involved dancing, drinking, racing, and gambling, all anathema to the missionaries. But according to anthropologist Wesley Hurt, the fiesta was "more than a religious ceremony.... It also tend[ed] to strengthen the community bond between the various inhabitants of the town."[106] The mission organizations had too limited a membership to replace the integrative and matchmaking functions of the fiesta and the accompanying dances, and yet some missionaries threatened converts attending dances with expulsion from the church.[107]

Even resettlement could not erase all the problems of a conversion so loaded with cultural meaning. Hispanic religious conversion was tantamount to a confession that Hispanic religion, at least, and the concomitant facets of Hispanic culture were not only inferior, but wrong.[108] Polita Padilla, a young Hispanic missionary in 1905, confessed a feeling of distance from and rejection of her own Hispanic culture as a result of mission school training: "I am a Mexican, born and brought up in New Mexico, but much of my life was spent in the Allison School where we had a different training, so that the Mexican way of living now seems strange to me." Her ambition was "to aid my people . . . as by God's grace I have been helped," that is, helped away from Hispanic culture.[109] For some girls, conversion meant at least temporarily "a disastrous breach in her closest family ties."[110] More common was a feeling of isolation on the part of the converts similar to that of the Anglo mission women.[111] Anglo women missionaries made an effort to provide for some of these young Hispanic women a network of their own. This informal system of protégées was an intense form of maternalism on the part of Anglo women who found the adults, once they had trained them, as acceptable as they found the "lovely adorable Spanish children."[112] Yet there were limits to the ability of mission patronnesses to help establish their protégés, male or female, in a new community. They could not, for example, overcome the segregation of the wider society. Not fully acceptable as equals to most Anglos, including most Anglo Presbyterians, labeled "extinguished lights" by their Catholic neighbors, and prohibited from participating in most village activities by their Protestant mentors, the Hispanic converts often found themselves caught in a perpetual marginality to both worlds, and neither Mary nor the women missionaries could provide for them an effective mediator.[113]

Having requested the mission presence for its educational benefits, however, the villagers did their best to prevent it from disrupting their society. They even resisted an attempt by Elizabeth Craig to introduce individual competition for prizes into the customarily communal production of food. Craig found that "our pupils seemed afraid to take it up in that way," though a number did plant gardens.[114] They particularly resisted the spiritual message and avoided, as one frustrated missionary noted, " conversation that will touch their special beliefs." "The great majority," reported Jeanette Smith, "are willing to accept social good times, medical aid, education, everything that the mission has to give, except its religion."[115] With equal determination Catholic and Protestant alike attended the same dances, participated in each others' services, and attended the same school.[116] There were tensions. Though some priests and Penitente leaders eventually modified or withdrew their opposition, in 1901, after a particularly virulent priest's sermon in Velarde, Elizabeth Rishel confessed, "It was hard to stand in the schoolroom and hear former pupils laugh, as they passed, and say loudly: 'Look at the heretics!'"[117] To the missionaries, disruption of the social fabric seemed unfortunate but necessary before it could be rewoven, and the efforts of the villagers to minimize the conflict only frustrated these women. But villagers had found few alternatives which so met their needs as their integrated village community. Even converts made compromises to remain part of their village, marrying Catholics in Catholic ceremonies, for example, and they usually discovered that "natural parental affection overcame religious opposition" within six months to three years.[118]

Hispanic definitions of village membership could, in fact, mitigate friction arising from the missionary presence. When two Anglo mission teachers at Velarde applied for the postmastership, the Hispanic county school superintendent responsible for passing on recommendations to Senator Catron was inclined to be indignant. Although Rio Arriba County did appoint women as postmistresses in this period, "[W]e consider, he informed Catron, that the teachers "are only temporary residents of the delivery of the P.O." Not only did these missionaries go back east during vacations, but they owned no real property in the village, had no commitment to it.[119] Slightly over half of the missionaries spent only three years or less on a single site in the Hispanic field. Both their intineracy and their ideas and aims could keep them, like brujas, divorcées, and converts, at the village margin. Anglos who wished to "change in every respect the homes and habits of these Mexicans" and who rejected the society around them without trying to understand, roused resentment on the part of the villagers and found themselves shut out from the villagers' life and from influence on the cultural direction it would take.[120]

New Mexico novelist Orlando Romero, however, has noted that the chain of social relations securing house to house in a plaza and thus encircling it could be broken by the settlement of an outsider in one of those houses.[121] Given the delicate nature of such a system, it was in the interest of the villagers, particularly when confronted with a more enduring and intrusive mission presence—many mission teachers stayed not three years, but five, ten, and even twenty—to find some way besides exclusion to defuse the threat mission teaching represented. At the same time, such missionaries, in the interest of the mission, made every effort to penetrate that dense social network.

As part of their mission to "get into the hearts of the families," missionaries made a point of visiting the homes.[122] Village fathers tended to visit the school, in keeping with their role of handling external relations. Mothers, however, could be reached most effectively at home. Politeness, and village mores of not offending witches, ensured a universal reception. This acquaintance helped to lower barriers raised by priests and other rival authorities, and led to a pattern of rapidly rising enrollments, with an increase of 700 percent not uncommon.[123]

Alice Hyson found visits to the homes "in times of affliction" particularly "effective." According to Miss Hyson, "they realize that you have no other motive than that of love when you try to relieve them."[124] The mission women adopted visiting as their strategy, and participation in critical life stages as a crucial part of their "pedagogy of love." They did not realize that village women also used visiting as a strategy, but as a strategy of integration rather than as one of cultural tutelage. Inadvertently, by participating in the normal functions of village women, the women missionaries had begun their own integration into the village on terms they neither fully understood nor controlled.

In much the same way, mission women participated in the customary pattern of mutual exchange of goods and services, with a few variations. Plaza teachers received an annual salary of approximately $350. By the standard of the national public school average, $485, it was small, but it easily outstripped that of local New Mexico teachers.[125] This relative wealth often proved insufficient for vacations, retirement, and luxuries, especially if the missionaries helped support other members of their families. But coupled with the fact that theirs was often the only cash income earned in the village, it gave the missionaries some patronage to dispense. They employed selected villagers, usually the elderly or children, on odd jobs, and sent children to school and even to boarding school at their own expense. Missionaries who had independent sources of income gave playground equipment or school buildings to the villagers.[126]

The largesse of the missionaries could have created a permanent sense of inequality and could have distanced them from the villagers. Once the lopsidedness of the exchange became equal, however, once the missionaries, too, became recipients, their status as elite outsiders diminished.[127] Missionaries found that those hired to do odd jobs were in return "always doing little things for us that we couldn't pay for."[128] One villager put his "conveyance" at the disposal of the missionaries; other villagers built new kitchens, cleaned house, and helped erect new teachers' houses by furnishing adobe bricks and hauling fence posts, all without charge. Sometimes the villagers even reversed the teacher-student roles, as when a dozen Chimayo women taught Jennie Clark to spin. "How it did please them," wrote her sister, "to find that there was something that her fingers could not do as well as theirs! . . . and how proud they were of her success."[129]

Most important, given the villagers' own valuation of it, was the donation of food by the villagers to the missionaries. "Many times," reported Victoria MacArthur from Truchas, "have we been invited to stay for supper, and been given a little bucket of beans, peas, potatoes or apples to bring home with us when we left."[130] Louise Conklin at Chacon realized such gifts represented a great sacrifice, but found the villagers "so eager to do something to prove their gratitude that I cannot refuse."[131] The missionaries interpreted the gifts as signs of affection, gratitude, and devotion, but to the villagers the gifts also initiated a set of actions designed to incorporate the mission women into the group as peers.

Perhaps the single most effective mission role giving these teachers access to village families was that of healer. The entry of Anglo women "medicas" could have led to competition and tension with Hispanic female practitioners. But the mores of the Hispanic healers placed as their first responsibility healing the patient and learning all they could, and demanded they accept any help that might aid in that end. Because of the exalted place of parteras and curanderas within the community of women and the village in general, and the distrust, cost, and scarcity of Anglo male doctors, the female missionaries' establishment of themselves as technologically superior resident medical advisers paved the way for their acceptance by the villagers beyond the confines of the classroom.[132] Leva Granger described how initial suspicion turned to trust because of the effectiveness of her medicine. Granger bent over a sick woman, trying to force medicine between the patient's teeth, when:

> the door opened suddenly, a woman, much excited, hurried in and pushed us aside so rudely that the cup was dashed to the floor.... For some time she refused to allow us to approach the sick woman, but, fortunately, the medicine began to act favorably, the friend at last realizing that we really wished to help and not harm, stood aside, and before we left even tried to assist.[133]

Granger fully recognized the cause for the woman's initial terror—"for were we not strangers and, above all else, Protestants?" But actions and results carried more weight with the bulk of the Hispanic population than the strictures of the priests, and once a healer had established herself, she had little further trouble. Unlike other mission territories where no model, in particular no female model, existed that allowed the natives to assimilate their would-be ministers, Hispanic Colorado and New Mexico had their curanderas and parteras, their maestras, and their female heads of households, as well, of course, as their nuns at convent boarding schools and their witches.[134] These pre-existing female models eased the way for the integration of women missionaries who desired a deeper involvement with the village. In a sense, they found their place awaiting them.

At the same time, mission women created new roles for themselves and new social forces within the villages. They tried to channel the integrative rituals of the community into forms not only acceptable to themselves, but which replicated their own society. After all, integration into village society without changing it did little to further mission aims. Reasoning that "our Protestant Mexicans are not yet far removed from their Romanist training, and love to have special days and special doings," missionaries held social gatherings in their schools.[135] They brought the Anglo import, Santa Claus, to the plazas and organized literary and Christian Endeavor societies, and, of course, women's missionary societies.[136] It was as though the villagers had suddenly acquired a social director. And the mission teachers were tempted to associate the high degree of attendance with success of their aims. Most, however, remained properly skeptical. One missionary acknowledged that church programs were always "packed" simply because "the mission school was the only place aside from the saloon for any recreation."[137] More mission functions complemented than competed with traditional gatherings; they coexisted, uneasily on the part of the missionaries, with saints' days and other fiestas.

In their varied roles as maestras, curanderas, and informal social directors, mission women had indeed assembled a formidable arsenal and achieved a strategic position for changing the Hispanic village into an American small town, or so it seemed. Mission workers pointed with pride to developments whose origins they attributed to themselves rather than to larger social and economic imperatives. They commented on increased male industry, migration for work, more fruit trees and vegetables, and an unspecified "decided improvement" among the young.[138] These mission women partook of the reform impulse of the progressive era in their desire to create a new world, and, unlike some missionaries elsewhere, they had access to both sexes to do it. And the mission women did indeed fulfill vital roles in the Hispanic villages. But their desire to use those roles to change the villages was matched by the villagers' desire to incorporate the missionaries on village terms. The enthusiastic village-wide welcome mission women received after an extended absence epitomized the conjunction of acculturative strategies. Like the exchange of food, it met the cultural needs of both missionaries and villagers. It legitimized the place of the missionaries as part of the village society in the same way the fiesta held each fall reincorporated the migratory male laborers. At the same time its rituals reinforced the mission women's own sense of how essential they were to the village.[139] Intercultural relations in the village took this confusing route of common experience diversely interpreted, though occasionally distilled through common values, as each group sought to channel the activities of the other into safe and constructive passages.

Elements in some missionaries' own backgrounds conspired to advance their integration into Hispanic society on Hispanic terms. Many of these women had grown up on or near farms. For them, the home was still a source of family production, and their experiences were, in that sense, closer to those of Hispanic women than to the experiences of the urban women who had witnessed, as historian Ann Douglas has described it, the "disestablishment" of the home and of the family as a productive unit.[140] In addition, most of these missionaries were single women with no children of their own. Not only did the strong Hispanic family appeal to them, but their incorporation into the village as generalized "mothers" provided them with surrogate families. This emphasis on the family gave the missionaries a common language to speak with their Hispanic villagers. Alice Hyson reconciled her plaza to the news that she was going home for the summer "only when I told them I had not seen my mother in three years."[141]

As the missionaries became heads of their own households, they converted their marginality as single women in Anglo society into centrality and a certain degree of power in the village. Many of these women had no relatives who could afford to keep them in case of illness or retirement. The mutuality of the village which encompassed them added to the contrast between their position in the village as honored member, and their position outside it as dependent relative.[142]

These missionaries did not always stop with a generalized "motherhood." They had a personal stake, beside their grander mission, in finding a place for themselves among the villagers. Relations with the villagers could become intense and intimate. One woman whom Mollie Clements attended at her deathbed, reached up "and, drawing me down to her, kissed me, saying, 'My mother! My mother!'" Another bereaved family asked Miss Leadingham to take charge of the funeral services for their daughter which included making and lining the coffin. Leadingham concluded, "[Y]ou can well see how dependent they had become on me, and how devoted and attached I had become to them." She had, she claimed, become "so buried in their interests and pleasures that I scarcely thought of anything in the outside world."[143] Long-serving missionaries including Prudence Clark, Alice Hyson, and Elizabeth and Lucy Craig lived on in their plazas after retirement.[144] And at least three Anglo women missionaries serving in New Mexico from 1900 to 1915 married Hispanic men.[145] Social distance for these women had been eliminated, but it was not at all clear whose culture had been absorbed by whom.

The strength of this communal, family-centered Hispanic culture appealed to single women disenchanted with the industrialization of America and its captains. Although desperately ill on the eve of World War I, Alice Hyson was glad she did not have to go "out in the world, as it were—it is enough to read about it in the newspapers, it makes one almost heart sick."[146] For some of the women missionaries, as for the villagers, the plazas provided more than a target; they provided a refuge, as well as a source of personal fulfillment. Antoinette Brengle insisted, after twenty-five years in the field, "I am quite sure that no other one thing could bring to me the pleasure that this work in NMex., has brought to me, and I count it a privilege to be here."[147]

Their mission gave these women missionaries the opportunity to try to shape a society. They had been sent by home mission boards to turn Hispanics into "Americans." Away from direct male supervision, or direct supervision at all, they had trouble fulfilling this function in the way anticipated by the mission boards. It was difficult if not impossible for a woman alone to convey an entire culture, particularly when women in the late nineteenth and early twentieth century seemed to have their own culture.[148] Not bound to the image of the Anglo world from which they came, they aimed for an improved version of that society, a more feminized version, with its emphasis on the power of the "Christian" female-created home to transform society.

Just as the role of social control and cultural bearer was allotted to the women missionaries, that of social integrator and cultural and community maintainer was the role adopted by the women villagers. Intercultural relations in the village thus took the form of a struggle, largely female, to integrate two peoples, each of whom tried to control and dominate the union, to bring it closer to their own culture. But the women missionaries had come so far, so alone, to reach the villages, that they had little chance. Those who did not retreat at the first opportunity founded an empire more personal than national. Those whose sense of racial and cultural superiority walled them off from the village community found the barrier worked both ways. Without some integration into the village to breach the defenses, the mission message remained, like these missionaries, isolated, unanchored, and ephemeral.

Even missionaries who partially abandoned the industrial definition of "American" could not always implement their own cultural program as intended. As female bearers of Anglo culture, they had sought most to replicate the women's world that they knew, with its language, family values, tablecloths, and tea services. The life these women promoted for the Hispanic women, however, bore little resemblance to the life the missionaries themselves led in the villages. Anglo women as cultural messengers could not help but convey a message ambiguous at best, as the very act of conveying it required transgressing the roles it relayed. Not only had they themselves ventured far from the domain of home and hearth, unmarried, but they disrupted Hispanic family life and community at their core, as rival authorities in child-rearing, education, and religion.

In turn, the recipients of this mixed message proved selective in the lessons they learned from the Americanizers in their midst, the "Protestant nuns." Language and technology they accepted, but separated these aspects from their over-arching culture as they had separated sewing machines and other Anglo material goods they acquired.[149] They selected those elements of an evolving Anglo culture best suited to their own evolving culture, and refused, for the most part, to receive the message in exactly the spirit it was given. Just as they slotted Anglo mission women into traditional Hispanic roles (curandera, maestra, nun), they interpreted their message and actions through the prism of their own female world of visiting, exchange, and labor.

A single set of events, a series of mission visits, for example, could seem a cultural victory to each group. But here, at the heart of the regional community, Hispanic mechanisms of integration and cultural control proved far stronger than the individual Anglo women who challenged them. Apart from the few Hispanic village women who achieved white collar status by replicating missionary roles, through teaching or through marrying evangelists, the village women for the most part continued, as before, to work outside the home as well as within it, in the fields or at wage labor. Traditional village rituals, dances, and mores encompassed both Protestant and Catholic and endured. It would require more than scattered and ambivalent emissaries in the Hispanic heartland to effect a cultural conquest.

4

Redefining Community: Hispanics in the Coal Fields of Southern Colorado, 1900–1914

In the coal-mining region of southern Colorado, an expanding Hispanic community met an Anglo advance more threatening than isolated women missionaries. "If you rode across the flat," recalled Agnes Smedley of her youth in southern Colorado, "to the Southeast lay soft rolling hills, and beyond those the world: first, an adobe Catholic church attended once a month by Mexicans. . . . Further on stood the saloon—the sign that Rockefeller civilization lay near. . . . Beyond the saloon stood the school house on the borders of Tercio, a Colorado Fuel & Iron Mining Camp."[1] Smedley's description, with its larger pastoral setting, its Hispanic church outside but near the camp, the saloon, school, and the camp itself, includes almost the full range of the symbols of this cross-cultural frontier and the structures it developed.

Colorado Fuel and Iron itself claimed that when Tercio came into existence, in late 1901, through "modern energy and science" it turned "a non-producing isolated mountain valley" full of sheep into "a scene of bustling industrial activity."[2] The company, its camps, and its workers moved onto a terrain dotted by Hispanic villages. At the turn of the century, these plazas resembled those of northern New Mexico in their social and economic structure. By 1914, however, the areas had marked differences, caused largely by the nature of this interlocking frontier. The average coal camp lasted only ten years, but its impact on the Hispanic community in and around it was permanent.[3] Not simply the development of the mines, but their importation of labor, their planned communities, and the capital involved changed the human as well as the physical landscape of what had been Hispanic southern Colorado.

The mining camps existed both outside and as part of the regional community. They were centers for migrants, tied to the village in a symbiotic relationship that protected a Hispanic cultural core, as well as being settlements for non-villagers and ex-villagers, Hispanics with a more permanent commitment to Anglo industrial labor. As such, the camps could have become more than an outpost of the village; by replicating the patterns of the original, they could have become a new core for further expansion. They did not. The examination of why they did not become a substitute for a village-centered regional community reveals the nature of this facet of the intercultural frontier, the limits of its newly defined communities, and the dynamics of the larger regional community.

The number of coal-mine workers in Colorado more than doubled between 1900 and 1910. Not only did many of northern New Mexico's small plazas send one or more of their men each winter into Colorado to mine coal, but over 11,000 New Mexicans, men and women, moved north permanently to work in the mines, raise food for the miners, or both.[4] Meeting and stimulating this expanding Hispanic frontier was an Anglo frontier financed largely by the Rockefellers. After the panic of 1893, their Colorado Fuel and Iron Company (CFI) acquired vast amounts of coal-mining land in southern Colorado, and their development of these holdings enabled them to become the largest producer of coal in the state by 1913, with Las Animas County providing the greatest output.[5]

A flood of Anglos in a multitude of nationalities followed the mines. According to CFI, by 1902 their mines held representatives of thirty-two nationalities who spoke twenty-seven different languages. Aguilar, in Las Animas County, Colorado, had been a tiny Hispanic village in the mid-nineteenth century. Fifty years later and surrounded by mines, it had quadrupled. Now only one-quarter of the population was Hispanic, and over half of these were either born in New Mexico or had parents born in New Mexico.[6] Despite their own increasing numbers, Hispanics had become a minority not simply of the mineworkers but of the area's rapidly changing population.[7] The large groups of Italian, and smaller groups of Slavic, Polish, Greek, Irish, Scots, English and other miners could not possibly be incorporated by the Hispanic villagers in the way one or two Anglo settlers or missionaries may have been.[8] They threatened the integrity of the Hispanic communities.

The nature of the work as well as the workers changed these Hispanic communities. Although relatively lucrative, work in coal mines was neither steady nor safe. Over half the miners in the United States lost three months' work in 1910, usually through cutbacks in production. And that year at least twenty-three Hispanic miners died in a single mine explosion at Delagua in Las Animas County.[9] Many Hispanics recognized that coal mining "offered little future." The scales that weighed a miner's output were often unbalanced, pay was in scrip, and the drawing of "rooms" where the miners worked was unfair. But miners around Trinidad worked more regularly than most, averaging over three hundred days a year in 1913, and at a time when farm labor received thirty dollars a month and board, native-born Hispanic labor in and around the mines usually made about twice that amount, or two dollars a day, and they or their families could often raise their own board.[10]

Whether or not they migrated seasonally, Hispanic miners tried to retain a symbiotic relationship with the traditional Hispanic economy. Although farming was no longer the principle occupation of the majority in Las Animas County, even outside the mining towns, in many areas more Hispanics engaged in farming than in either coal mining or railroad work.[11] Many coal miners were sons of farmers or ranchers and worked the mine only when not needed at home. One Hispanic miner noted that in the early days of the mining camp Primero he had, as a miner, made "enough money to feed my family and even help with the farming."[12] The higher pay drew Hispanics to the mine, but it did not uproot them from the soil when they had the choice.

Most of the miners, however, lived in mining camps or company towns of which CFI controlled more than did any other company.[13] Unlike the women missionaries, the companies had the capital to create the communities they wanted. The women missionaries had to work within the village framework in their efforts at social engineering even when, as some did, they would have preferred to replace it all. Colorado Fuel and Iron and the other coal companies in the southern fields could, and did, build their own communities the better to control them, to provide a "healthy" environment for their own operations. For example, at Tercio, having acquired the site by a land grant purchase, CFI declared the existing settlers "squatters." By denying the existence of legitimate prior settlement, the company could justify its erection of company "city-states," arguing that the "remoteness" of the sites from any real settlements necessitated their provision of all housing and community services.[14]

The company towns contrasted with earlier Hispanic communities. Many of the latter had taken the form of plazas, with adobe houses not only clustered but linked by walls surrounding an open square.[15] Adobe construction in general met with almost unalleviated praise, mainly for its qualities of insulation and thrift, but it met with no enthusiasm from the CFI. The company instead built towns on the grid pattern, with wide streets, individual frame houses centered on individual lots, and no central square. It conveniently classed adobe houses with shanties and determined to demolish all those within range as quickly as possible.[16] In so doing, it accomplished, quite literally, the destruction of the communally oriented plaza.

The company was fond of printing photos, side by side, of the old and new, with captions such as: "As the illustrations show, the house the miner is able to construct for himself is often inferior. For this reason the company has erected comfortable and convenient houses and rents them at a nominal price."[17] But the chief flaw of the Hispanic plazas, from the company's viewpoint, had been less in their construction than in that they lay beyond company control. On their winding paths and behind their communal walls one could never be sure what meetings were being held. Within the camp, Hispanic dance-hall owners could have their licenses revoked for allowing inappropriate meetings.[18]

In reaction to and defense against the threatening heterogeneity and company control, Hispanics and other ethnic groups became, according to their employers, clannish. Where they could, Hispanic settlers tended to cluster outside the town or camp in their own adobe houses, whether in the pre-existent settlements or, occasionally, on property leased from the company.[19] While moving them from the center to the margin of what had been their community, these clusters could maintain the constant informal visiting and social rituals which had been fostered and reinforced by the physical environment of the village, with its connected houses, kin next to kin. It was, after all, on such relations that the plaza inhabitants, particularly women, relied for interdependence and harmony.[20]

Inhabitants of these Hispanic enclaves, however, retained but a tenuous control over their livelihood. They sometimes owned goats which provided a supplementary and independent subsistence, and the company touted the ability to have a garden as an asset of its camps, but credit relations came to rest squarely in the company's hands.[21] The managers of the Colorado Supply Company, the company store chain, were all Anglos, and the Colorado Supply Company held a monopoly franchise at many of the camps.[22] Scrip, the currency of payment redeemable in goods at the company store, in 1901 was worth only ninety cents on the dollar outside the camp, and store managers were free to discriminate in the extension of credit. Spanish-American and Mexican credit was often poor. Commissary managers complained that they lost money through such patrons, and some store managers extended them no credit at all beyond the pay period. Accumulated charges at the company store coupled with charges for fuel whether or not used, for equipment, dues, and so forth, ate away at the miners' pay before they ever saw it. Miners often found their pay entirely gone to service the previous month's debt. In contrast, the Colorado Supply Company did well. Small mining companies in difficulties emulated the CFI system; they used store profits to offset mining losses.[23]

This loss of control over credit relations accompanied a loss of control over other institutions of village life. The CFI justified its control of the local schools, for example, on the slightly undemocratic grounds that "in as much as we pay at most of the camps the larger proportion of taxes, and in some cases nearly all, we feel that we may take the liberty. . . . " But despite CFI's claim of faithful tax paying, in 1914 the Executive Committee of the Justice League found that in one district alone Rockefeller interests "shirked" almost $8000 of school taxes. The company apparently preferred to lend the money to the school districts for the implementation of its suggested changes, rather than pay it in taxes.[24] The company enjoyed much the same relationship with churches which lay, unlike the Hispanic one at Tercio, within the bounds of its camps. The company subsidized both Catholic and Protestant churches indirectly, by renting space from them for club meetings, and directly, by helping to build them.[25] In the Hispanic village, the church was built, maintained, and informally run by the men and women of the village. The churches in the coal towns belonged to the external forces of the company and its polyglot workers, and its message of cooperation may have been quite different.

Villagers indeed were losing to CFI control of their crucial institutions along with their plazas. Their credit and social relations occurred increasingly in formal institutional settings beyond their power to manipulate. The company insisted that the work of providing a "healthy" social life for the camp "must be done by the great corporations controlling the coal fields, for they have the means and control the situation."[26] But critics called the company houses, company stores, company reading rooms, clubhouses, schools, and saloons the CFI's gift to itself, and Colorado's Senator Edward P. Costigan summed up the outcome in this way: "The motto of large industrial concerns, especially in Las Animas and Huerfano Counties, might be expressed in two words, 'We rule!' asserting ownership of land, courts, schools, houses [and] churches. . . . "[27] In the struggle over who would define the new types of community emerging on this frontier, Hispanics found their resources far outmatched.

By 1910 Hispanics in the company coal camps found the loss of control over issues such as credit and religion increasingly reflected in more intimate ways, reflected in changes at the family rather than simply the community level. The age structure, ratio of men to women, and age at marriage continued to resemble those of the Hispanic villages from which so many of the miners had come. Yet not only property ownership but family composition and the sexual division of labor changed. And these changes boded ill for the ability of these Hispanics to control cultural interaction, survival, and adaptation at this site on the Anglo-Hispanic frontier.

In the villages, almost every family owned land; in the new mining communities such as Segundo, only slightly more than half of the Hispanics owned even a house.[28] Households were simpler than in the villages. In Cebolla and Canjilon, New Mexico, over 17 percent of all households had members other than the husband, the wife, and their children. In Segundo, the figure was only 9 percent, and in two-thirds of these the extra members were boarders.[29]

These figures represent a departure from the village structure in several ways, most of which acted to curtail the scope of women's activities in the community. Complex households in the village often held elderly members who would tend young children while mothers worked in the garden or at income-producing occupations in the home or outside it. Without these child-tenders, and with houses increasingly separated from increasingly alien neighbors, women found themselves tied more closely to the home. Boarding, an occupation compatible with child-tending, came to provide the dominant income-earning occupation for married Hispanic women in the mining towns.

Boarding was a practice almost unknown in the northern New Mexico villages. Fostering and taking in relatives for schooling opportunities could be seen as informal boarding, but the practice was usually limited to relatives and was never a cash transaction. Boarding on a cash basis could operate successfully only outside the communal village or with boarders defined as outside that community, for community members' welfare would have been guaranteed by the reciprocal relations of the village, without monetary cost.[30] Boarding meant the intrusion of outsiders into the family, not the growth of communal bonding. This was no re-creation of the village community.

Only married women and a few men took in boarders.[31] Widows and single women did not. The restriction of boarding-house keeping to married women, combined with the lack of property ownership, limited the ability of female heads of household to survive in the camps. Even if a woman had a garden or took in boarders while her husband lived, when he died she could not make the cash rent on the property. Unlike a village widow with property who could survive on her garden, in the camp a widow could not remain unless she had cash-earning children. In the villages, female heads of household often relied on their children's labor, but not on their wage earnings. Cash-earning possibilities for boys or girls there were extremely limited. Such tasks as herding were often performed for one's own family or paid in kind. In the mining camps, however, female heads of household could and did tend to rely on their children's earnings as miners or occasionally as seamstresses or laundresses.[32] These women depended on their children for labor not performed for them directly, but for the company or for nonfamily members. They were dependents, not bosses. The structure of work and property holding as well as of wages thus decreased the authority of the head of the household and the immediacy of family mutuality. For many of these widowed female heads of household, what had in the villages been a position of true authority and some autonomy could easily, in the mining towns, become titular only. For village women, coal mining by male migrants had brought an increased productive role, but for women of the mining camps, it meant a role increasingly limited to consumer and reproducer with no guarantee of permanent residence. They were in an awkward position to begin creating, defining, and sustaining a larger community on their own terms.

It was within this framework of an externally controlled, institutionalized society and increasingly isolated and dependent women that intercultural relations and community formation occurred. Each group in the camps had its own identity and held its own dances, though not all had "their dances to themselves," as an elderly miner recalled of "the Mexicans," a term used at the time to denote both those born in the United States and the much smaller number of those born in Mexico.[33] In a few mines "Mexicans" were actually segregated, as were blacks, or not allowed work at all. There were also, however, areas of social mixing, particularly for the men. In most mines Hispanics worked alongside other races and nationalities, and in the saloons representatives of different groups drank together companionably. Their children learned each other's language in the streets and the school yards. And, as miners, they died together in mine explosions and accidents.[34] Although government investigator Victor Clark found in 1908 that marriage between Anglos and Hispanics was rare and "a subject for apology," it did happen. Of at least three such weddings in Las Animas County in 1900, two involved mining town residents, and in 1906, six of nine did.[35] Some mining town inhabitants later recalled little ethnic animosity at all, and numerous intergroup friendships.[36]

The ambiguity which characterized these ethnic relations is both explained and reflected in the relationship of Spanish Americans and Mexicans to organized labor. Both groups were often viewed with hostility by other miners as strike breakers and cheap labor, and the two groups held much the same view of each other.[37] Employers shared the view, if not the hostility, and exploited both the animosity and the Hispanics. They were as quick as Hispanic villagers to reap the benefits of a symbiosis between agro-pastoral and mining economies. As one employer's representative explained candidly: "Equally favorable to the operators in Colorado is the presence of the Mexican ... the native Mexican [i.e., Spanish American] acts as a buffer to the blows of the strikers." During strikes, managers gave Hispanics rooms in the mines that they could not get in quieter times, and the employers counted on their docile return to their farms when the strike ended.[38] They saw the local villagers outside the camps as an elastic labor supply which would work more cheaply and with less union interference than more dependent groups and would respond readily to changes in demand without striking in desperation.

This view of Hispanics as easily manipulated scabs, however, was incomplete at best. In the November 1903 strike, when 95 percent of the mine employees turned out, Hispanics played both roles, that of miner on strike and that of scab or strikebreaker. In addition, not all the scabs were Spanish-speaking; most were Slavs and "Austrians" sent out from West Virginia. Commenting on this strike, labor organizer Mother Jones declared, "No more loyal, courageous men could be found than those southern miners, scornfully referred to by 'citizens' alliances' as 'foreigners.' Italians and Mexicans endured to the end." Some Hispanics even held leadership posts in the union. The district union organizer who was beaten by a deputy sheriff in Trinidad in March 1903 and later jailed for thirty-one days without charges was a Hispanic, Julian Gomez.[39]

Yet six years later, according to one undercover company investigator, some of the Hispanic strikers felt they had been betrayed by the union. They claimed, "The officers of the union had sold out to the Companies" by settling in the northern Colorado fields, largely English-speaking, while the south remained on strike. The investigator dutifully added, "[W]hen an occasion like this presents itself to me, I lose no time in nursing this suspicion."[40] Such suspicions could prevent miners from uniting effectively across language and cultural barriers, and forming a community based on common interests rather than shared ethnicity. Those mine operators' agents who fostered hostility both used and furthered the isolation and ambiguous status of Hispanic mine labor. By doing so, they helped preserve a distinctively Hispanic element on this intercultural frontier, yet did not enhance Hispanics' control over their own future.

While many observers have blamed the CFI for fostering hostilities within this polyglot empire, the company in fact created a Sociological Department with the avowed duty of resolving these differences. The Department was to transform all miners into a community of ideal American miners.[41] Americanism, to this company as to others with like departments, meant the United States flag and homogenous unity as well as respect for the authority of corporate capitalism.[42] In their camps, among their miners, the company found this particular brand of patriotism lacking. The Sociological Department, as the designated agent of the major Anglo enterprise at this site on the intercultural frontier, promised to have a critical affect on the ability of those Hispanics who could not retreat to protected Hispanic villages to retain an autonomous cultural identity.

Some of the Sociological Department's campaigns now seem naïve. It created kindergartens "to inculcate the true democratic spirit—the spirit of sympathy, of unselfishness, and of equal rights."[43] Presumably, this "unselfishness" at an early age would help in the other, inseparable aims of the Department: to make them "better citizens and more contented with their work."[44] The miners had a distressing tendency, the Sociological Department confessed, to "regard their daily tasks, their lives and their environment as sordid and colorless, as monotonous and uninteresting." The rosy-eyed optimists at the Department devoted themselves and their magazine, *Camp and Plant,* to "helping men to see the joy in their work for its own sake. . . . to bring out the fact that in the environment of every coal miner, coke puller or steel worker there is much that is beautiful, piquant and of absorbing interest."[45] The Department found the 1903 strike, two and a half years after its establishment, a somewhat embarrassing proof of its failure to create a smiling and tractable, an "Americanized" and homogenous, work force. Nevertheless, it continued its work uninterrupted.[46]

In addition to the general problems the Department noted among the miners, it found several traits particularly unsatisfactory in the "Mexicans." The company view of Hispanics in the camp seemed to reflect perfectly the literary and popular stereotypes. One Department member labeled them "shiftless" and lacking ambition. *Camp and Plant* described them as fatalistic, patriarchal, presentist, oriental, subservient, irresponsible, improvident, and yet home-loving. The women, although highly moral, lived in a "primitive" fashion, and wore neither the hats, the corsets, "nor the other mysteries that go to make up the outline of the modern American woman."[47] Here again, as with the mission women, the critique came from a middle-class perspective, with middle-class notions of propriety and with complaints commonly made about working-class populations elsewhere in the nation. At issue was more than "Americanization"; yet the critics did not want to create middle-class miners. The aim was to create an "American" worker compatible with—not identical to—middle-class notions and dictates.

In Americanizing such a group to suit this definition of the term, R. W. Corwin, chief of the Sociological Department, saw his underlings as "in a true sense, social settlement workers." Yet the institutional context of the work seemed less human, and had definite roots in the scientific management of the industrial East. "Sociology is not a passing fancy or a matter of sentiment," Corwin explained; "It is a science and a necessity."[48] If the message of the Presbyterian missionaries who permeated the northern New Mexico villages sprang from a late nineteenth-century middle-class woman's culture, this Sociological Department's message and governing principles were distinctly industrial and male.

It is ironic, however, that even on a man's frontier, where the prom-

inent players were the male corporate managers who determined policy
and the male miners who worked for them, the work of cultural conquest and social control, regardless of the message, belonged to women.
Although the Department began with fourteen women and eighteen
men, the staff became increasingly female, until in 1905 it numbered
fifteen women and only six men.[49]

In part, the increasing number of women arose from the company's
strategy and the consequent increase in the number of kindergartens.
As Corwin explained, "It is difficult to change ways and manners of
adults . . . but not so is it with the young. Children are tractable, easily
managed . . . hence the importance of the kindergarten."[50] The company hoped, in addition, that the mothers' concern for their children in
the kindergartens would enable "the kindergartner [teacher] to get into
the home and win the confidence of the mother."[51] Like the missionaries, the company's agents tried to reach the parents through the children who, they hoped, would bring the lessons home.

In this strategy of converting first the more vulnerable future workers, the caretakers of the very young seemed more vital to the movement than did the men who sometimes ran the reading rooms and
men's clubs. These women workers, unlike the haphazardly prepared
women missionaries, were trained specifically for the task of teaching
kindergarten. They knew Spanish and Italian and met in Trinidad once
a month with their supervisor.[52]

Like the woman missionary, however, the kindergarten teacher was
to erect the social framework of a new community by being "the organizer and adviser in all the club work of the camp," even having influence over the "young men's club," in short, by forming "the soul of the
social life of the camp."[53] Her home, too, was to "serve as a model for
camp housekeepers," but where the missionaries emphasized coziness,
warmth, and modest curtains, these scientific homes, built and fur-
nished by the company, were "thoroughly practical and sanitary." "The
time has come," the Sociological Department revealed, "when dust-
catching curtains must come down forever, roller shades discarded,
tacked carpets replaced by rugs, and ornate furniture made plain."[54] The
women, both the teachers and the mothers, of the middle and the working class, were expected to compensate for the bleakness of life foisted
on them by their industrial environment. They were to create new
social organizations and effectively inviting homes, but the women of
neither class controlled the structure of that environment, or, it seemed,
even the ways in which that bleakness could be opposed.

Children of Hispanic as well as other ethnic and racial groups did

attend the kindergartens, those hopeful agencies of Americanization.
Sometimes they even came from outside the camp. In Segundo, children from the Hispanic plazas of Varos and Old Segundo traveled into
the mining town for kindergarten at the expense of the school board.[55]
There the children learned weaving, domestic science, basketry, and
manual training. This training may have seemed premature in kindergarten, but the Sociological Department pointed out "that most of these
children will be manual laborers or the wives of manual laborers, and
will find early need for all this practical industrial and manual
training."[56]

The boys would grow up to be miners, and the girls to be miners'
wives, which had well-defined characteristics for the company. In 1903,
Camp and Plant claimed that "the average man shrinks from the 'New
Woman,'" that such a man wanted instead "tenderness," "never failing
love," wanted a woman who would "have no interests apart from
him."[57] The early domestic science training, the mother's clubs, and
other activities would help create just such a woman and she in turn
would do what the company could not do, internalize the company's
work interests and bring that control into the home. In 1903 Corwin
insisted, "[N]o department is of more importance than that of domestic
science. The good accomplished through cooking and sewing is incal-
culable, and is thoroughly appreciated by the employees."[58] The "special stress . . . laid upon ethical and moral culture" was geared to make
mothers perform their work "because it is a duty to their families" and
to the company, not to themselves.[59]

The importance of domestic science rested in part on its presumed
ability to solve that "most difficult" of problems: liquor. "The need in
our coal fields is for better mothers and wives, better cooks and homemakers," wrote Corwin in a sentiment he and others of the time often
reiterated, "so that husbands will not be driven to the saloon for comfortable quarters or an appetizing meal."[60] Drinking lowered productivity and engendered absenteeism and costly accidents. Corwin complained that many miners "will drink and make any excuse for
drinking; small house, many children, cross wife, strikes, too long
hours, too little pay, too much pay, sickness, holidays and funerals; any
excuse, no excuse, but drink and lose time they will." The Sociological
Department wrestled with those excuses that did not interfere with
wage policies. They sought to recreate the homes and make them not
refuges from the industrial "American" world but collaborators in it.[61]

To the children of the camps, growing up in the coal towns with their ethnic mixture and company facilities could seem, as it had to one Hispanic woman, "a very beautiful experience."[62] It was these children who attended the kindergartens, and these "children of non-English speaking parents, especially Mexican and Italian" who came "freely" to the cooking clubs and classes, "but not their mothers," as the company itself confessed.[63] While "Mexican" women attended the sewing classes and "seemed particularly appreciative," they and other non-English-speaking people resisted interference with their diet and cooking. Yet their daughters went to the classes, "took the work into their own homes," and at times transformed them.[64] Cultural defense did not pass easily to a generation who received conflicting messages early in life from two different female authoritites. Anglo kindergartens in an Anglo-dominated area could create female generational rifts in Hispanic homes as well as breaches in Hispanic culture. And though their aim was to create a new "Americanized" community incorporating both generations, kindergarten teachers did not heal the rifts. They rarely stayed long in the camps. Only four of the thirty-five teachers and women workers between 1901 and 1906 stayed in the work as long as four years, and only two served on the same site for all four.[65] With such impermanence in a world as impermanent and filled with transients as a coal camp, even the most scientifically trained of teachers could neither help the company create a community from the series of buildings and institutions it erected nor thoroughly penetrate an existing community. They could only introduce new cultural tensions.

Outside the camps themselves, the Anglo invasion with its large-scale commercial mining had the greatest impact on the larger towns of the area. In the villages of the hinterland, while the number of renters and boarders increased, the basic social and economic structure, including the crucial sexual division of labor, remained more like the villages of New Mexico than like the mining camps. In Trinidad, Colorado, however, the nature of the Hispanic community departed dramatically both from the traditional villages and from the mining camps. In a sense, Trinidad was the complement to the camps, harboring those for whom the camps held no place.

As late as 1913, though rapidly becoming outnumbered, Hispanics in Trinidad, the county seat and largest town of Las Animas County, retained enough of a presence to cause one worried Protestant to claim, "[T]his is largely a Mexican papist town."[66] The Hispanics in Trinidad had two Spanish-language weeklies and a number of modest shops and saloons. The rate of property ownership was low (less than one-quarter owned property), and day and railroad labor predominated among the men, but the Hispanic population also included saloonkeepers, salesmen, clerks, stockraisers, an attorney, and other representatives of leading Hispanic families in the county.[67]

Hispanics presided over a distinct part of town, a community some saw as "neglected" by the Anglo population, and others simply as self-sufficient. The elite crossed the culture line and belonged to such predominantly Anglo organizations as the Knights of Columbus, the Humane Society, and the Trinidad Chamber of Commerce. They also founded their own ethnic societies such as Club Español and a branch of the Alianza Hispano Americana, and they immersed themselves in county politics.[68] These were Hispanic men and women so at home in the formalized institutional social life of the city that they could help to create it. They could cross cultural lines without surrendering their own cultural identity.

But it was not only in the stratified Hispanic society and the cross-cultural elite that Trindad departed from the Hispanic villages and the mining communities. Here, as in other southwestern cities, Hispanic women began to appear as heads of household, working for wages or not, in surprising numbers. In that section of Trinidad covered by the first ward in 1900, 35 percent of the Hispanic households were headed by women, just over half of them widows. In the second through fifth wards, over 50 percent of the Hispanic households were female-headed.[69] Among the most striking features of this situation was the substantial proportion of married women with absent husbands among the female heads, ten of twenty-eight in the first ward, for example.

It was certainly not property ownership that lured female heads of household to Trinidad or kept widows there. Over 85 percent of these women in Trinidad rented their housing, a rate more than 15 percent above that of the male heads of household in town. Nor does it seem to have been the opportunity to enter domestic service for the town's Anglo elite.[70] The demand for such workers was, in fact, quite high, but whether, as Victor Clark suggested, employers preferred not to have them, believing them incapable, or whether the job was too closely associated with Indian slaves in their own minds, few Hispanic women became domestic servants. Instead, in contrast to the camps, both female heads of household and married women with husbands present took in boarders; many others did laundering, and there were also a few prostitutes and unspecified day laborers.[71]

While the life of a female wage worker was not easy on any site, these women, who rarely spoke English, clearly found a better and perhaps more congenial market for their services in cities with large and diverse Hispanic populations than in polyglot mining towns or even the relatively impoverished and land-poor rural Hispanic villages. In the camps, the tendency of miners to move from mine to mine coupled with mining company pressures limited the possibilities of gradually erecting new mutually supportive neighborhoods and relatively autonomous communities. In the more articulated Hispanic community of Trinidad—with its own newspapers, shops, and elites—women could work outside the home but remain within the Hispanic community, a pattern more consonant with the village labor pattern of men working among aliens and women among villagers, in or out of the home.

The relative diversity as well as the relative self-sufficiency of this Hispanic community provided a basis for the greater opportunities working-class Hispanic women found in the city, but the presence of such a high proportion of female heads of household in Trinidad has other implications for this part of the regional community and for the migrant system. It suggests not only a geographically differentiated labor market, but an increasing disparity between the lives of men and women whether one or both migrated and whether they migrated permanently or seasonally. By migration for wage work, villagers could preserve the villages as a Hispanic core where Hispanics could control the development of their own culture. But the evolution of that culture was affected by the development of the migrant system itself. Members of that culture—migrant and non-migrant, male and female, mining camp, village, or urban resident—had less and less in common. The symbiosis between the different parts of the regional community was still there, but the growing differences in experience led Hispanics to try to redefine community, to create neighborhoods all along the way, despite opposing forces.

As an arena which transcended local geographic bounds, politics might have provided a means to unite and empower the increasingly disparate Hispanic population. Certainly for Hispanic women in the coal-mining region who found their power bases of garden production, religion, and property ownership eroding like their stability, participation in politics by voting could represent a new source of leverage. Susan Anthony had been inclined, in 1880, to blame the failure of her suffrage tour in Colorado on the "Mexican greasers," contrasting the "native born white men, temperance men, cultivated broad, generous, just men, men who think" who voted yes, with the "Mexicans who speak the Spanish language," but even she had admitted that "on the floor of the constitutional convention was a representative Mexican, intelligent, cultivated, chairman of the committee on suffrage, who signed the petition and was the first to speak in favor of woman suffrage."[72]

It was, nonetheless, the predominantly Hispanic Democratic counties of southern Colorado where the vote ran most heavily against suffrage. Although this vote has long served as proof of the rigidly patriarchal nature of Hispanic society, there were other factors. Suffragists in Colorado tended to stand not only for temperance and against dance halls, and thus in conflict with one marginal and one essential Hispanic cultural element, the suffragists also stood against Catholicism.[73] And yet Hispanic women were not indifferent to the vote. In June 1893, when Ellis Meredith reported to Anthony that the "Southern counties have not changed their spots nor their skins," she also noted, "a 'Greaser' Senator [probably Casimiro Barela] told our Press Chairman that all the women down there had sat up nights to discuss our bill and threatened to run him out of the county for voting against it."[74]

On gaining suffrage, Hispanic women in southern Colorado almost immediately entered politics at a number of levels and in a variety of roles, as election judges, candidates, campaigners, and even fraudulent voters.[75] Suffrage empowered them both within Hispanic society and in the larger cross-cultural society. When Mrs. Eutimia S. Mascarenas wanted J. U. Vigil's aid in securing a divorce from her absent husband in 1906, she was careful to ask the favor as "a woman poor and alone, though a firm Democrat."[76] And in the small town of Hoehne, Las Animas County, Hispanic women voted in greater numbers relative to Hispanic men than did Anglo women relative to Anglo men.[77]

It was not only the women who looked to the vote to recoup power lost in other areas. By the early 1890s the influx of largely Republican Anglos into the southern counties had undermined the power of traditionally Democratic Hispanics to the extent that session laws ceased to be printed in languages other than English, and Spanish disappeared from the common schools.[78] Hispanic voters had, nonetheless, retained a significance beyond their numbers not only because of their high turnout at elections, but because many of the newcomers to southern Colorado, notably the foreign-born miners, could not vote. They were noncitizens or non-residents. Citizenship made the Spanish Americans worth wooing, and many Hispanics exploited the situation.

As in New Mexico, politics provided a means to power and wealth for individual Hispanics, but offered poor solace as an ethnic strategy for the group. The patronage that Hispanics who stayed with the Democrats could offer (teaching positions, train passes, loans, and petty offices such as election judge), like the economic patronage these Hispanics could offer in their mercantile establishments, paled before the possibilities of steady employment and county-level positions that the Republican mining companies held out through their Hispanic and Anglo cooperators.[79] Any possibility of a solidly Democratic Hispanic vote, or a solid Hispanic vote at all, or even a solid Hispanic leadership broke down on impact, and Hispanics quickly found niches in the patronage systems of both parties, as they had in New Mexico.

The community tensions, social, political, and economic, created by the intrusion of the Anglo coal-mining industry into what had been Hispanic southern Colorado, reached a climax in 1913. The mining strike of that year and the massacre that occurred in the next illuminated the changing strategies of the miners and the Colorado Fuel and Iron Company for control of the community and its culture; it illuminated the dynamics of this now multicultural frontier. The conflict was among that most violent in this region, and was centered in an area contested by Anglos and Hispanics. The role that ethnicity did or did not play in the conflict serves as an indicator of the degree to which common interests had been redefined since CFI's arrival on the scene. It also reveals the degree to which there still existed in southern Colorado mining areas a distinctly Hispanic community, or whether Hispanics had redefined their allegiances.

The coal miners' strike had begun in the southern Colorado fields in August 1913 over wages, hours, unfair and illegal company labor practices, payment in scrip, checkweighmen (who ascertained the weight of the coal a miner produced, on which his wages depended), the company store monopoly, and other conditions in the camp that reflected company control of the community. When the company further exercised that control by evicting the strikers from the camps, the strikers erected thirteen tent colonies at strategic locations, commanding the entrances to the mines. These colonies formed in themselves a picket line of sorts.[80] Friction with the local militia led to the entrance of the National Guard in October, which set up bases in Trinidad and Walsenburg. By January 1914 the United Mine Workers union was supporting 21,508 men, women, and children.[81] Along with the physical removal from the

Colorado Fuel and Iron dominion, the workers had removed themselves economically.

The tent colonies were large and multiethnic. The one at Aguilar had approximately two thousand houses and tents and almost as many ethnic groups as miners, including Mexicans, Spanish Americans, Italians, Greeks, Poles, Slavs, and many others. One organizer recalled that although the colony inhabitants behaved "like one family," it was a struggle to keep them together.[82] Embarked on a common class enterprise, the strikers continued to organize themselves on an ethnic basis. But the ethnic barrier had become permeable. There were Hispanics among the elected union delegates from Tollerburg, Valdez, and Ramsey mines, none of which was solidly Hispanic, and Hispanic committeemen served at Pryor and at the tent colony of Ludlow.[83] Quite without the aid of the Sociological Department, the miners had, at least to some degree, proved capable of working together across ethnic lines.

Within ethnic groups, however, divisiveness ruled. The company shipped in at least forty Mexican-born miners as scabs and, illegally, failed to inform them that a strike was in progress. Some of the Mexicans learned of the strike from other workers, and some refused the jobs; but others left only when the company failed to keep promises of payment.[84] Union organizers and Spanish American strikers carefully distinguished between U.S.-born and Mexican-born, but that did not signify a neat distinction between striker and strike breaker. Spanish Americans played both parts, too. When, at the behest of the coal companies' attorney, the city marshall of Santa Fe arrived on the scene with fifteen Spanish American comrades, "the men refused to further participate in the strike as deputy sheriffs." Many local Spanish Americans had fewer scruples.[85] The notoriously corrupt Sheriff Farr of Huerfano County also recruited deputies to protect the coal companies' property; 16 to 43 percent of them at any given time were Hispanics, many of them local farmers and sheepmen. Other Hispanics stayed in the mine as bosses.[86] Local Hispanics also joined the National Guard contingent under the infamous Lt. Linderfelt, although they were "gradually eliminated, and Americans took their places" before the battle of Ludlow, according to a National Guard Captain of the time.[87] These Hispanic guardsmen, who had known the Hispanic miners, now received threats from them and acted as informants for the National Guard. Their later removal seems to have stemmed more from Anglo doubts as to where Hispanic loyalty lay than from Hispanic reluctance to serve.

These lines of division within the Spanish-American community failed to follow strict class or even occupational lines. A Spanish-American deputy sheriff of Las Animas County living on his farm in Weston had mined coal in his youth, retained union membership, and was "the man that owns this little coal mine up here where the union gets some of its coal." He had his guns confiscated during the strike without a receipt.[88] Farmers who had coal-mining sons or had mined coal themselves lined up against farmers and farmworkers who joined the National Guard. In these tangled lines of conflict, a unified community was difficult to locate among pre-existing categories.

Yet the strikers were, in a sense, forming a new community on their own terms. The testimony of the Hispanic women from the tent colonies indicated cross-cultural contact among women. They visited frequently, for instance, both among themselves and among the other ethnic groups.[89] When state Senator Helen Ring Robinson investigated the colonies, she "found a friendliness among the women of all nationalities—22 at least," and she concluded. "I saw the true melting pot set up at Ludlow."[90] The tent colonies survived by cooperation and mutuality, and away from the company structures and institutionalized life, different, older processes of community formation appeared.

Conflict now was not between Anglo and Hispanic but between the company and the strikers. Hispanics in mining towns had been subsumed in other categories. And the community that strikers were erecting was as threatening to the company as ever a Hispanic plaza had been. The Ludlow tent colony had approximately 200 tents and 1000 inhabitants. On April 20, 1914, National Guard soldiers began firing on the tent colony. It was not the first time shots had been fired at the striking families, and they were prepared. They had dug cellars beneath the tent floors in which the women and children now hid while the men ran off into the hills to draw the fire. But this time was different. The guns remained trained on the colony, and the tents were set afire. Among the eighteen victims of the fire alone, nine were Chicanos, five of them children. The colony was destroyed.[91] If the company could not control the community, the community would not exist.

The Colorado Fuel and Iron Company had institutionalized the social life of southern Colorado's Hispanic miners by ridding itself of the plaza, which encouraged informal contact, and setting up instead company saloons, halls, and individual houses, on a grid. This pattern made community action more visible and control from the top easier. Some of the women missionaries to Hispanic plazas would also have liked to create such an ordered, controlled existence, but they lacked the numbers and, more important, the economic resources. Even if they convinced the villagers to build on "blocks and streets," they could not then provide and control their economic livelihood. At this site on the intercultural frontier, the CFI succeeded in dominating the economy of southern Colorado, in destroying the framework of village life, and in preventing the miners from rebuilding it on their own terms.

At the same time, however, the CFI failed to resurrect from these ashes a community made to its own specifications. Historian Robert Kern cites among the causes of continual unrest in the coal-mining towns of New Mexico and Colorado between 1913 and 1935 not only the lack of a substantial mediating class between worker and manager in the coal camps, but the loss of a community-oriented system and the heterogeneity of the work force.[92] Even with the resources of the Rockefellers behind them, the women to whom the task was assigned fared no better at community control, at altering behavior patterns and values, at imposing a unified "American" culture, than had the isolated and meagerly provisioned women missionaries. The institutionalized framework itself, as well as the polyglot nature of the camps, required a generalized approach and distanced these women from the very women they hoped to reach in much the way it distanced these latter women from each other. As creators of community and bearers of culture both groups of women were hampered. Neither the Anglo social workers nor the Hispanic women enjoyed in the camps the centrality they had in the villages. In the coal camps, the economic functions of gardening and food processing were not central to perpetuating the community. The mines could continue without them. And the marginality of women on a man's frontier could not be overcome by social workers whose message merely reinforced that the duty of each woman was to her husband and children alone.

For Hispanics whose villages had been replaced by the camps, the alternatives were stark indeed. They might migrate from camp to camp, but they were trapped in this stalemate between Anglo and Hispanic strategies. As new sites of settlement, the mining towns offered little autonomy; the formation of the community lay so far beyond Hispanic control. Because of these conditions, Hispanic women and men continued, if they were able, to look beyond mining for community and for broader opportunities. These Hispanics looked instead to the villages outside the camps, to cities and towns, and to the network of kin that connected them. They looked, in short, to their regional community.

5

"First-Class Labor, But No. 2 Men": The Impact of World War I and Mexican Migration on the Regional Community

The coming of war stood on its head one basic premise of the regional community. Government indifference, at least for the moment, vanished. The government now needed to make soldiers and loyal citizens of the villagers. In addition, producers in the region demanded seasonal labor on a new scale. Just as elsewhere producers drew southern blacks and rural folk to the cities to replace a European immigration cut off by the war, in New Mexico and Colorado they drew Hispanics from the villages and added to them Mexicans from south of the border. From 1914 to 1921, the resulting massive migration movements and unprecedented federal interference threw competing cultures and groups into a new intimacy; it gave a new twist to the dynamics of intercultural contact on the Anglo-Hispanic frontier.

The new pressures threatened the delicate balance of opportunity and isolation on which the regional community depended. Not only was there a sudden surge of Mexican aliens with whom, in Anglo eyes, Hispanics were identified, but the sudden entry and withdrawal of federal funds, personnel, and the draft affected the regional community at

107

its very core, the Hispanic villages. By the time the dust of all the mobilization settled, and federal interference with the regional community receded, the picture of that community had changed, in some ways, permanently.

Mexican immigration to the United States had begun well before 1914. The war with Mexico in the 1840s barely interrupted Mexican migration to the north, despite the fact that the area now lay under the United States' instead of the Mexican flag. Mexican laborers manned the region's mines, railroads, and commercial farms, and homesteaded occasionally. Some formed a regional community similar in many of its patterns, its interdependent networks of kin, economy, and routes, to that of Hispanics in Colorado and northern New Mexico.[1] Between the mid-nineteenth century and 1910, Anglo migrants from the East, Midwest, and Europe overwhelmed this relatively modest Mexican migration. Then, in 1910, the Mexican revolution began. As civil war raged through Mexico year after year, increasing numbers of Mexicans—a few political refugees, others with a heritage of seasonal migration, and many others mobilized only by Carranza's decree in January 1915 liberating them from peonage—fled the war's chaos and its destruction of life and land.[2]

The Southwest's employers generally welcomed these new immigrants in the same way they welcomed Hispanics—as cheap labor. The war in the Balkans, home of many railroad laborers, had forced western railroads to rely increasingly on Mexican labor.[3] Small farmers along the new irrigation developments also looked to this labor as they continued to expand their acreage in sugar beets and cotton despite the declining profitability caused by the general economic slump in 1913 and the threat of gradual removal of all tariff protection on sugar. In fact, the ever-rising Mexican immigration coupled with the slump created a southwestern farmer, according to one labor recruiter, "satisfied by the thought that he can hunt up some Mexican any time."[4]

In just a few years, however, the situation changed drastically. With the onset of a wider conflict in Europe came an unparalleled increase in industrial and agricultural activity throughout the United States to meet European belligerants' demands. The slump was gone and so was the abundant cheap labor. The specter of a free market in sugar receded as United States producers eagerly strove to fill the gap created by the withdrawal of central Europe's beet sugar from circulation.[5] The corresponding disappearance of European labor from United States markets meant that new employers began to recruit actively and vie for Mexican and Spanish-American labor, formerly their labor of last resort. It was in 1916 that the Great Western Sugar Company of northern Colorado, on behalf of the small farmers whose beets it needed, began for the first time not simply hiring but recruiting Hispanic workers in southern Colorado and New Mexico.[6] As cotton and beet growers in California, Arizona, and Texas and railroad and mining enterprises increased the competition for this labor, increasing numbers of recruiting agencies, processing companies, and farmers' associations sought labor directly from Mexico.[7]

So it happened that, although the new Immigration Act of 1917 seemed to the Commissioner-General of Immigration "an eminently satisfactory piece of legislation . . . of great benefit to the country," the act provoked, in the Commissioner's own assessment, "no little hysteria" on the part of southwestern employers.[8] The law contained a literacy test as well as a doubled head tax. It threatened to halt the immigration of impoverished and largely illiterate Mexicans, at a time when southwesterners planted record sugar and cotton crops and when resident Mexicans fled the United States in droves, spurred by threats of conscription.[9] Beet-sugar companies warned of lost harvests, while railroad employers claimed that with half their summer construction workers barred, disrepair of tracks could endanger troop and supply movements.[10]

In response to such employer agitation, a series of administrative decrees temporarily exempted, in theoretically regulated numbers, Mexican agricultural labor from the head tax and literacy test and even from much older contract labor provisions. Local federal officials set the number of exempted laborers based on their estimate of the amount of labor already available on the site. Employers guaranteed to match prevailing wage rates and to return the exempted labor to Mexico within the year. The plan rapidly expanded to include railroad and certain coal labor, and later included laborers in government construction. As the time limit metamorphosed from a matter of months to the duration of the war, and then, for agricultural workers, to a season or two beyond that, the exemptions looked less and less temporary and limited.[11]

From the start, the exemptions converted Mexican immigration from a regional to a national issue. As interest increased, such widely distributed publications as the *New York Times* and the *Literary Digest* devoted more space to the issue. In this arena, Spanish Americans became dangerously entangled with Mexicans as older stereotypes combined with the issues of recent United States relations with Mexico, labor unrest in the Southwest, and rising nativism to create a more negative response to both Mexicans and Spanish Americans than that of southwestern employers.

Relations with Mexico since the revolution began were less than cordial, and the portrayal of the Mexican revolution in the United States did little to erase popular pictures of Mexicans as lawless, short-sighted, treacherous bandits.[12] Businessmen worried over the sanctity of their one and a half billion dollars' worth of investments in Mexico; Senator Albert Fall demanded an invasion; and the President ordered the occupation of Veracruz in 1914, and Pershing's massive "punitive expedition" in 1916 in response to Pancho Villa's raids.[13] Just as it seemed that little more was needed to convince the United States public that Mexicans were enemies, whether by virtue of United States aggression or their own, on March 1, 1917, less than two months after Pershing's withdrawal from Mexico, the newspapers, printed the famous "Zimmerman telegram." Sent by the German foreign secretary to his ambassador in Mexico, the telegram proposed that Mexico join Germany in a war against the United States to gain back the "lost territory" of the Southwest.[14] Setting the seal to the distrust, the telegram raised the specter of a possible fifth column: the stubbornly persistent Spanish-speaking community of that same Southwest.

Chicano labor unrest gave body to this specter of a fifth column. In June and July of 1917, large strikes broke out in the mines of both Arizona and New Mexico. In June, at Bisbee, Arizona, where a Western Federation of Miners organizer had recorded "a great deal of discontent" back in 1915, the strike was led by that bugbear of World War I nativism and antiradicalism, the Industrial Workers of the World. The county sheriff and two thousand armed men "deported" to Columbus, New Mexico, over 1200 strikers, one-quarter to one-third of whom were Mexicans.[15] In July at Gallup, New Mexico, it was the relatively safe United Mine Workers, with a large Hispanic contingent, who struck. Nonetheless, similar "deportations," imported gunmen who boasted of the numbers they had killed at Ludlow, and a new, entirely Anglo and instantly unpopular local Council of Defense revealed a population undisposed to work toward reconciliation.[16] By the end of 1917, the Mexican newspaper, *El Excelsior,* charged that four thousand Mexican strikers were imprisoned in Arizona and New Mexico.[17]

The violence of these mining strikes and of United States-Mexican relations made Mexicans and Spanish Americans in the United States vulnerable to the same repressive nativistic trends as enemy aliens were. Discontent was defined as disloyalty and alienation, and the cure for alienation, of course, lay in Americanization. As it did elsewhere in the United States and for other ethnic groups, Americanization became intimately tied to the war effort, and "100 percent Americanism" became the only way to prove loyalty and ensure national security.[18] Presbyterian mission administrator Robert McLean relayed, in 1918, "a cry . . . from the Southwest, from the thin line there on guard: come and help us to redeem the Mexico within our borders, that America may be made safe!"[19]

"Redeeming" this internal Mexico clearly required turning its inhabitants into Americans, unhyphenated. That "Spanish-Americans" were "terribly insulted if called Mexicans" did not remove them as alien targets of the new nativism. The majority of Americanizers were unable or unwilling to draw the distinction. Despite Hispanic service records and repeated testimonials to the loyalty of the Spanish Americans, church woman Katharine Bennett was not alone in her thoughts that "in this day when hyphenated Americans are unpopular it is a curious fact that here in the Southwest the form Spanish-American is constantly used."[20] *Literary Digest* declared the "hyphenate issue" the most vital of the day, and Woodrow Wilson, who had made Americanism an issue in his re-election campaign, later proclaimed, "Any man who carries a hyphen about with him carries a dagger that he is ready to plunge into the vitals of this Republic."[21] In this context, the retention of not only a hyphen but the Spanish language and a distinct culture as well seemed to Anglos evidence of divided loyalty on the part of United States–born Hispanics, evidence of a continued inability "to forget the wrong which they consider the United States inflicted on their country" in 1848. The Spanish American became more firmly tied than ever to the Mexican in the Anglo mind.[22] Mexican and Spanish American seemed to the Anglos more alike than not: equally alien, dangerous, and candidates for Americanization.

In a nation at war and with a President wedded to "Americanism," Americanization rapidly found not only increased popular support but official federal government support.[23] The goverment organized "Loyalty Leaguers" in Hispanic communities, selected "Four Minute Men" who spoke on behalf of the war in their local towns and plazas, and stimulated local, state, and county Councils of Defense.[24] Councils of Defense in heavily Hispanic southern Colorado pledged "to promote the establishment of the English language in the country." And in keep-

ing with the mix of "voluntarism" and direct federal intervention that
obtained throughout the war effort, Protestant missionaries in New
Mexico, in the interests of instilling "better patriotism," proclaimed,
"[T]he tongue of the state is Spanish, and we do not want one flag, one
country, and two languages, but 'one flag, one country, and one language.' "[25] Reinforced in this way, Americanization came to play an
increasing, though not a new role in missionary endeavors, dampening
whatever fires of pluralism may have glowed before the war. In this
way, too, the Americanization movement suddenly, if briefly, transformed missions from impoverished and isolated outposts of Christian
Americanism into mobilized agencies of the government's war effort.[26]

If the war brought the federal government to Hispanic villages through
an increased Americanizing fervor, it also came in less rhetorical ways.
The government needed these hyphenated citizens to act. The government had to call upon them for food and for fighting men. In the process
of this call, the government reached into every village, plaza, and town,
"bringing the war home" to the non-migrants.

The darkest way in which the war reached into Hispanic enclaves
was conscription. While little boys in these villages as elsewhere played
soldier, approximately 10,000 of their older brothers, making up 65 percent of New Mexico's contingent, served in the war.[27] Spanish Americans in southern Colorado also volunteered in numbers, one Anglo resident recalled, "much greater in proportion than any other class of
volunteers."[28] Almost every New Mexican village was tapped, and the
call seemed to reach in particular the few relatively well educated, the
graduates of mission schools and the teachers. Chimayo, a village of 129
households in 1910, sent forty-one men into the services; Embudo,
where Famy Mills thought it "beautiful to see the Americanism manifested by our Spanish-speaking (not hyphenated) Americans," sent
thirty-six, eighteen of whom went overseas and five of whom died.[29]

As the nation discovered, however, there were immediate difficulties,
in the government's attempt to call on village resources, even on its
manpower. Not only had some villages never heard the Pledge of Allegiance; in the first conscription of 1917 thirty-eight of forty-six draftees
from Taos and Mora counties, New Mexico, could not understand
"enough English to attempt to drill." Moreover, closer investigation
revealed this situation was no passing phase in the Hispanic hinterland.[30] For some Spanish Americans, conscription provided their first
contact with the United States government. A few, in good faith,

claimed exemption on the grounds of non-citizenship.[31] Their parents sometimes found the call even harder to comprehend.[32] It was not simply a question of divided loyalties and hyphens. In villages impoverished in terms of both cash and government services, reactions to the war itself, according to contemporary observers, ranged from people "much opposed" on whom the food regulations worked real hardship, to "great indifference" among others who seemed focused on "how to avoid going or allowing others to go into the service."[33]

Forays into the villages for the promotion of war bonds revealed other problems. Although William McAdoo had created Liberty Bonds to provide a relatively inexpensive way to finance the war, he also wanted them accessible to people of modest means, as a way of going directly to the people and making the war a popular movement.[34] It is a measure not simply of how poor Hispanics were, but of how far villagers remained outside the Anglo economy, that even when Hispanic villagers figured out what "Liberty Bonds" were, few could pay the necessary fifty dollars in cash. In Chimayo, New Mexico, a village of 536 people in 1910, only three men were able to purchase the bonds outright, and women limited their contributions to nonfinancial help.[35]

The most obvious way to combat Hispanic indifference, resistance, or alienation was to integrate Hispanics into the war effort at every level. When Governor Lindsey of New Mexico appointed his war committee, he included six Anglos and six Hispanics; the Women's Committee, less thoroughly integrated, had one or two Hispanics at all times.[36] The state's United War Work Campaign, a 1918 coalition of civilian organizations in New Mexico, targeted particularly the "Spanish Speaking Communities."[37] Colorado counties used much the same strategy. In Las Animas County, the Anglo-dominated Council of Defense appointed a Spanish Speaking Committee to canvass farming communities for the third Liberty Loan, and held a series of "Spanish American mass meetings" in mining camps and Hispanic villages for the fourth.[38] Despite the rhetoric of 100 percent Americanism, these organizers found that recognition of Hispanic cultural distinction proved a more effective integrating force than attempts to eradicate it did.

At the same time, the revelations gleaned in the war effort spurred government action and brought new Anglo attention and services to the villages. Government-aided studies exposed to many Anglos for the first time the conditions in Hispanic villages. As the investigators, usually women, found "the death rate appallingly high," they brought the villages a new allotment of health services.[39] Similarly, in Hispanic villages the lack of commercial farming meant that stimulating agricultural production there often had more in common with welfare work than it did on more profitable and usually Anglo acreages. The government's desire for increased food production opened new horizons to besieged Hispanics. To compensate for the previous year's poor grain crop and the unpromising spring, New Mexico encouraged lessees to plant crops on state land, offered seed at cost or on mortgage, and, with the help of newly enlarged federal appropriations, vastly expanded its agricultural extension and home demonstration services to include Hispanic as well as Anglo agents who would disseminate new technology and methods in the plazas.[40]

For Hispanics previously alienated from the Anglo United States, the new services, recognition, and above all their actual experience or their sons' experience in arms, as active and solicited participants in a common cause, could instill a new identification with the United States.[41] But the extent to which Anglos accepted that identification beyond the needs of the war showed in the war experience of Hispanic soldiers. Life in encampment could lead to a new camaraderie and even closeness with Anglo peers. One Anglo soldier would not tell his story without telling "that of my 'bunkie,' Adolfo Ortiz, who left Santa Fe with me and shared all my hardships and joys with me."[42] But camaraderie also sometimes gave way to condescension as in another soldier's eulogy to Jose Maria Peña, "the best type of Spanish-American," sober, educated in the public schools, and faithful to his employer. And condescension, in turn, could, and sometimes did, slip into outright discrimination on the part of officers at stateside training camps.[43] Even war service would not suffice to Americanize Hispanics or to reconcile Anglos to the differences.

Draftees and volunteer soldiers were not the only Hispanics to leave the villages in the war years. Hispanic farmers in many villages could not reap the benefits of the more than doubled price of wheat and corn or the boom in livestock prices that resulted from war-torn Europe's rising demand for United States foodstuffs. A two-year drought so severe that it, rather than the events of the war, became the marker for that time dessicated much of northern New Mexico. By the end of 1917, one missionary reported, "There is nothing to feed the chickens. . . . There are no eggs, no milk and no fresh meat."[44] Many commercial farmers and stockraisers lost their land. They and the erstwhile semi-subsistence farmers found themselves forced to buy food at the newly inflated prices. In addition, the opening of the public domain to home-steading in 1916 deprived many Hispanics of grazing land, while the drought rendered most of the homesteading unsuccessful. The new government services to the villages helped, but could not match the scale of dislocation. Zoe Ellsworth explained the results of these conditions at Chimayo in 1918: "[I]n addition to the many men who have been called to the war," she observed, "others, because of existing high prices, have gone to mines and smelters that they may earn enough money to keep the wolf from the door."[45]

As the economic base of the village dwindled still further, these hungry migrants swelled the number of those who already traveled the paths of the regional community. Like rural migrants across the country, they found the increased wages for common labor during the war an additional drawing factor. Beetwork wages, for example, rose by 50 percent. Some villages which had sent five or ten migrants north before the war now lost up to 60 percent of their population, at least seasonally.[46] Most of the migrants followed the old routes, some now crowded also with Mexicans. Some went to the coal region of southern Colorado, doubling the Hispanic population and moving from mine to mine.[47] Other migrants, in increasing numbers, traveled to northern Colorado's beetfields, and a few went as far afield as San Francisco for the duration of the war.[48] The increase in the number of the migrants, however, signified more than an increase in scale of participation in the regional community with its economic networks and human links. It signaled an increased dependence by the village on its members outside the core of the village itself, and on their ability to achieve a degree of economic success at the terminals of the network, whether or not they returned physically to the village.

Hispanic women in the villages, like women elsewhere during World War I and as they always had, took over the men's tasks on the farms or filled jobs left empty by male recruits and migrants. Young bilingual Spanish American women increasingly found employment as clerks, stenographers, and teachers. In 1916 only 20 percent of all teachers and 26 percent of Hispanic teachers in Rio Arriba County had been Hispanic women, but by the 1918/19 academic year, Hispanic women provided over 30 percent of all teachers and over 40 percent of Hispanic teachers.[49] With a dwindling land base, Hispanic women, like the men, sought a livelihood from the Anglicized aspects of the economy, but they did so within the villages instead of outside them.

Despite the continuing overall pattern of village women and migrant men, a significant minority of the villagers ceased their peregrinations and began, in new parts of Colorado, to form an increasingly persistent contingent, a series of more permanent outposts on the Chicano frontier. Sugar-beet companies anxious to cut recruiting costs erected more labor colonies as Hispanics increasingly dominated the state's sugar-beet labor force. By 1920 even in northern Colorado, Chicanos, half from New Mexico and southern Colorado and half from Mexico, formed 40 percent of the hand labor and 90 percent of the migrant labor. Although the Great Western Sugar Company in northern Colorado did not begin building beet colonies until the mid-1920s, the number of Hispanic families who stayed year after year on the same site in both mining and beet areas in northern Colorado grew to about one-quarter of the Chicano laborers, again half Mexicans and half Spanish Americans.[50] In Vollmer, for example, the number of resident Hispanic families with school-age children gradually rose from none in 1911 to one in 1912, four in 1915, and finally eleven in 1920. Six of these families had by that date lived in the district over three years.[51] The number of Hispanic marriages also rose, from five, or 2 percent of marriages in Weld County in 1913, to twenty-three, or over 5.5 percent in 1919.[52] And Hispanics numbered, if not prominently, at least consistently among northern Colorado draft registrants.[53]

There were limits, however, to the degree of community integration achieved by these new settlers. The American Beet Sugar Company had planned its thirty-two colonies "where the residence of Mexican people would be least objectionable to people prejudiced against them."[54] And beet laborers residing on farms may not have been isolated from Anglos, but they were not integrated on equal terms. One laborer retorted to his farmer, "[O]h yes, you are good to your labor, you spend $2500 for a house for your horses and $100 for a house for your beet workers." Housing was often located in cattle-feeding corrals or consisted of shacks as cold inside as out, where temperatures could drop to thirteen degrees below zero. The scant water supply was often six or seven miles distant, and there were frequently no toilet facilities.[55] In addition, some farmers tended to be less than clear when explaining wage withholding provisions in written contracts to laborers who could not read English; some merchants overcharged them; and company agents at times recruited migratory labor, despite government regulations, at less than the prevailing wage for resident labor.[56]

In part as a result of this lower wage rate, Chicanos more than other laborers needed winter employment. Even colony residents could not survive well without it. The colonies had not been built as self-sufficient communities. That would have defeated the purpose of settling the labor. Although the American Beet Sugar Company's 549 families boasted 2,565 chickens, 44 cattle, 413 hogs, 6 sheep, and 6 goats, they had only 139 gardens.[57] Some Chicanos found winter work as laborers in factories or mines, or on railroads, but, as investigators concluded in 1920, "little or no work [was] to be had." Some Mexicans and Spanish Americans unable to return south made their appearance on the poor relief rolls of the northern counties in the war years, and their numbers there rose and fell as a barometer of general economic conditions.[58] This scarcity of winter work as much as any other factor limited the growth of permanent Chicano communities.

A Children's Bureau study shortly after the war concluded that neither the Spanish Americans nor the Mexicans in northern Colorado had "been assimilated by the communities to which they have flocked." None of those in the study had become farmers, or even tenants, in contrast to the sprinkling of Chicanos who had come north before the war.[59] The beet companies may have wanted to keep a permanent supply of Mexican laborers on hand, but the farmers and tenants among whom those laborers lived were decidedly less enthusiastic, and the increasing numbers of Chicanos did not necessarily reflect the growth of links and ties and wider associations that would supplant their ties to the village.

The end of the war brought many Hispanic veterans home to their villages and northern settlements. They brought with them a desire for modern facilities, from gymnasiums to bathrooms.[60] But as the veterans brought home their dreams of improvement, the federal services and support that had in wartime finally begun to reach the villages quietly slipped away. In two or three northern New Mexico Hispanic communities a few domestic science and agricultural courses resulted from new funding for vocational education, but the agricultural extension service's outreach program, with its touring demonstrators, literature, equipment, and a drastically reduced staff, retreated to its former Anglo focus until the 1930s.[61] Red Cross nurses also vanished from the scene, as had the funds which supported them. At the same time the Medical Association of New Mexico secured a legislative act requiring certification of anyone providing medical services, including parteras, despite the "quite outspoken denunciation . . . of the law" by many villagers.[62] The villagers' moment in the spotlight was over almost before it had begun, and the Protestant missionaries who remained found themselves once more at impoverished and isolated outposts. The World War had exacted a heavy price from the villagers in money and in educated youths. It had left them with few lasting benefits, and with little sense of continuous participation in a larger American community.

After the war some Anglo club women continued to believe that Americanization numbered among "the great problems of the day."[63] Others, by 1920, were disillusioned. Their disillusionment brought further withdrawal of resources devoted to the cause. The president of the Colorado State Federation of Women's Clubs confessed:

> [W]e took up the work of Americanizing the foreigner with much enthusiasm and were brought after some discouraging experiences to realize that Americanization is not a plan of instruction which can be worked out systematically and concisely but it is a state of mind which, like Charity, must begin at home.[64]

These women, across the nation convinced of the failure of Americanization because of the enduring difference and cultural strength of immigrant and migrant groups, turned their attention instead to "citizenship" among their own ethnic groups, community service, and a "thrift" movement.

Neither had that other war, the suffrage campaign, succeeded in smoothing over ethnic differences among women at any but the most elite levels.[65] The campaign finally gained momentum in New Mexico in 1917, three years after that state became the only western state without woman suffrage. In an effort to reach the Hispanic population of the state, the suffragists printed leaflets in Spanish and cultivated Spanish American speakers and leaders, including Aurora Lucero and Adelina Otero-Warren, both members of families well entrenched in the social and political elite. But the vast majority, approximately 90 percent, of the organized movement in the state remained Anglo.[66]

At elite levels among women as among men, the war and its aftermath witnessed a continued alliance between Spanish Americans and Anglos based on mutual respect for ethnic difference. But on less than elite levels, suspicion and distrust prevailed. Alice Corbin Henderson's picture of "the English, Spanish and Indian women who met over the canning kettle, or across the Red Cross table where a common impulse moved them and a common purpose obviated the need of an interpreter," was charming but inaccurate. On the contrary, mobilization agencies in the state had found that "it is not possible to combine demonstrations for English and Spanish-speaking people even when they can all be reached by one language," because, as one county agent revealed, "the Spanish-speaking people will not come to a meeting called for both."[67]

In 1919, when asked why Santa Fe was so much an alien city, an elderly Hispanic businessman of Santa Fe reputedly said, "[W]hat would we gain by adopting your American civilization?"[68] In New Mexico as elsewhere it seemed, the wartime willingness to endure rampant and sweeping "Americanization," by 1919 gave way to what historian John Higham labeled "a long-suppressed resentment." The war emergency in New Mexico and Colorado had led to the currying of Hispanic favor. As this courtship faded and Anglos continued to define Spanish Americans as aliens, Hispanic resentment took the form of cultural reassertion. To one Anglo contemporary, New Mexico's Mexican-born Governor, Octaviano Larrazolo, was "a real American," one who "zealously preached an orthodox Americanism and has taught respect for and urged allegiance to the American flag . . . has extolled the ideals of Christianity and the virtues of the Christian home." Yet this Governor demanded of New Mexico's educators, "wouldn't it be well for every English-speaking child also to know Spanish?"[69] He further suggested that children in largely Hispanic villages be taught for the first four years in Spanish, and that Spanish be a required language in all the grammar schools of the state.[70] Some Hispanics, at least, were insisting that their culture, too, formed a legitimate part of the United States.

Bereft of the comforting belief in inevitable Americanization, Anglo fears regarding a large Hispanic population in their midst intensified just as that population became an increasingly evident factor. While the new Anglo intrusion into the villages had largely ended with the war, the augmented movement out of the villages continued, both seasonally and permanently. Economic forces initiated in the nineteenth century and intensified by the drought from 1916 to 1918 and the postwar depression in agricultural prices, pushed still more villagers into the Anglo economy to earn the cash necessary to survive. But equally important was the persistent and increasing demand for labor for commercial farms, mines, railroads, and smelters in Colorado. In the 1920/21 season, for example, the area served by Great Western Sugar Company's factories planted a record acreage in beets, one-half again as large as the previous year and approximately three times the acreage planted in 1914/15.[71] By April 1920, the company had twenty labor recruiters operating in fifteen states, each employing additional local recruiters and distributing advertisements and booklets in Spanish and other languages promoting work in the beetfields.[72]

Not only did the increased Spanish American migration continue, so did Mexican immigration. Employers of Mexican labor had justified the wartime immigration exemptions by pointing to new global demands for the cotton, wheat, fruit, and sugar of the southern, southwestern, and midwestern states. They labeled the measures strictly a wartime expediency. But the demand for labor, like Mexican immigration, had emerged before the United States became directly involved in the conflict, and it, like the exemptions, continued after the conflict ended. Many employers had come to rely increasingly on this supplementary Mexican labor. Arguing that the beet-sugar industry was "the creation of Government propaganda, conceived in the interest of the people of the United States," the beet-sugar companies together with Arizona, California, and Texas cotton growers prevailed upon the government to extend exemptions for Mexican agricultural labor beyond the armistice.[73]

In fact, the number of Mexicans entering under the exemptions for agricultural labor increased over 100 percent in the first year after the war, and continued to grow. The Great Western Sugar Company, for example, turned to Mexican labor only in 1919, requesting 700 laborers that year and projecting a need for several times that number for the following year. By 1920, the estimated number of Mexican laborers needed for sugar beets was 14,200, a not overwhelming but vital 20 percent of the crop's hand labor. The number of Mexicans headed for Colorado that year under the exemptions had more than tripled. The demand for imported labor increased faster than the acreage planted, which implies that it was Mexican labor, indeed, that provided the margin that made sugar-beet and other agricultural expansion possible.[74]

Even during the war, the regulations governing this vital labor had operated haphazardly. The situation did not change afterward. Not only was illegal recruiting commonplace, but legally recruited labor easily "escaped" the confining terms of its contract. At the end of 1920, of the 50,852 Mexicans legally admitted under the exemptions in the previous three years, at least 10,691 had disappeared from official view. Only 17,186 had returned to Mexico.[75]

The Mexican-born population of Colorado had increased nearly fivefold, and that of New Mexico nearly doubled. The figures, 11,037 Mexicans in Colorado, and 20,272 in New Mexico, were still small relative to the populations of these states, but it was the change in scale that struck the Anglos most forcibly. In Weld County, Colorado, the number of Mexican-born inhabitants had increased over 700 percent in ten years, from 90 to 756, and these were accompanied by an even larger number of Spanish Americans in this formerly almost entirely Anglo county.[76] Anglos no longer spoke, as they had ten years earlier, of an Anglo invasion of the Southwest. Instead they voiced fears of "this invasion of aliens."[77]

This "invasion" spelled danger to observers who ignored the long history of a Hispanic presence and warned "that the creation of a distinct nationality of another speech within our borders may constitute as real a menace as that which we hope has been over-thrown by the war with Germany."[78] Anglos whose heads still rang with the importance of "100 percent Americanism" saw the immigration as a threat to whatever fragile unity they had found during the war, a threat against which they stood exposed and disarmed by the removal of wartime federal support and controls. These anxious patriots saw evidence of corruption, degradation, and anarchy on all sides. The renaissance of the Penitentes, continued state support for Catholic charitable institutions, fiestas in Santa Fe, and, of course, Larrazolo's educational proposals were "but illustrations of the bondage to ignorance and superstitution" of the New Mexicans.[79] In addition, in a year of unprecedented labor uprisings in the United States, labor struggles involving Chicanos returned to Gallup, New Mexico, and led to the imposition of martial law in November 1919. "We must remember that the only government of which they have any knowledge," reported a *New York Times* correspondent, "is one of license and misrule."[80] And even the American Federation of Labor opposed Mexican immigration, accusing employers of using "the importation of Mexican laborers in an effort to beat down wage standards in sugarbeet raising states" by encouraging this relatively cheap labor "to accept employment in different lines of effort," such as railroad and coal-mine work.[81]

The debate over Mexican immigration culminated in the hearings before the House Committee on Immigration and Naturalization and the Senate Committee on Immigration in 1920. These hearings bore witness to the gradual ascendancy of racism in the United States over the more ethnically based nativism of the war. Increasingly Americans decided that biological factors would or should permanently prevent the assimilation of certain groups, among whom they included Mexicans and, inseparably, Spanish Americans. Men on these congressional committees called "race-mingling" "the greatest of all our problems"

and, as disciples of Madison Grant and his *The Passing of a Great Race,*
labeled Mexican "intermixture or intermarriage . . . a mistake, a crime,
and a damage to whatever population it touches," and even "an absolute tragedy" because "the product is a Mexican." They did not hear
with sympathy witnesses who queried, "[W]hat objection, if he is a
serviceable man, is there to assimilating him[?]"; or with credulity
claims of his childlike and tractable nature.[82] And by 1920, an Americanization movement relying on such feeble claims for success as "the
work of Americanization has gone on so swiftly that the Mexican children are able to sing 'Twinkle, Twinkle Little Star'" provided small
reassurance and seemed inadequate evidence of ideological
conformity.[83]

Most Anglos seemed to feel, with Secretary of Labor Wilson, that
"we have all the race problems in the United States that it is advisable
for us to undertake at the present time."[84] Particularly dangerous was
exactly this sort of immigration to farm and rural regions where "there
are not enough people," experts declared, "to keep up good social institutions unless all the people are of one race so that there are no impass-
able social barriers."[85] Even advocates of continued exemptions, such
as Representative Claude Hudspeth of Texas, hastily assured the committee, "If I believed by bringing these people in you were going to permanently increase the Mexican population down there, I would say to
keep them out."[86]

It was this impermanence and marginality that had justified the
exemptions, and it was here that advocates of continued Mexican
immigration took their strongest stand. Despite the evidence of an
increased resident Mexican population in the United States, the American Federation of Labor's complaints of 1919, the use of Mexicans as
scabs in the steel strikes of the same year in the Southwest and elsewhere, and evidence of increasing numbers of Hispanics in Colorado's
coal mines, a congressional investigating committee in 1920 found the
number of Mexicans displacing "white" labor "negligible."[87] "Our
investigation proves beyond a reasonable doubt," reported the committee, "that white men are averse to accepting, and refuse to accept (as
they have the right to do), employment as unskilled or common laborers, except, perhaps, where that employment is within the limits of
towns or cities."

The committee implied that Mexicans did not displace white labor
because they had a limited and defined role in the American economy:
rural manual and stoop labor, labor Anglos did not want. Despite the

fact that this assertion was more ideology than reality, it mingled with the traditional ideology of the farmer's role in America in the hearings on Mexican immigration of 1920. And through this conjunction, the congressional committees and the employers of Mexican labor struggled to find a compromise between the fears of recreating the racial problems and poverty of the South and the desire for an inexpensive and apparently inexhaustible labor reserve.

In arguing for continued unrestricted Mexican immigration, John Davis of Laredo, Texas, told the House committee, "I really think we can not get a more desirable citizen to occupy the place that he can occupy." When the alert chairman asked, "That is, a No. 2 place?" Davis reponded, "I would modify that by saying, to occupy the place that somebody must occupy."[88] It seemed to be growing increasingly difficult in rural America to move up the agricultural ladder from laborer to tenant to owner.[89] With the positions on the ladder fixed, some group had to be found to occupy the lower rungs permanently. In addition, Theodore Roosevelt's Country Life Commission had exposed the gap in the standard of living between the farm and the city. As migration from the farms to the cities continued to rise, efforts had been made to increase the comfort and perfect the economy of the small farm, to save the nation's backbone, the yeoman farmer. But the new conveniences demanded in the modern home had made "the American home an expensive proposition," according to the president of the National Sugar Company.[90] "It means," he continued, "a little automobile for the farmer; it means running water in the house and victrola for the wife . . . and it means the ambition of the parents for the children that they shall have their education and equal opportunity to advance in the world as far as any other citizen of the United States."

Advancing in the world did not mean common labor. "We have got beyond soiling our hands," Texas cotton farmer John Davis explained, "and we want somebody else to do the real work." "Do any of you," Davis challenged his unresponsive audience, "want to give up your places as members of this committee and go back and soil your hands in the dirt, cultivating cotton, picking cotton to make the clothes we have got to wear, or do you want to shear the sheep or slaughter the beef?"[91] Raising the standard of living on the farm to match that of the towns required, to these southwestern small farmers with their marginally profitable land, cheap labor. Common labor had become for them a threat to hold over schoolboys to make them study, while education, in turn, ruined a man for common labor. Even the black man, Davis asserted, had been educated "beyond his capacity to serve the land and he wants to live in town," and it was possible that resident Hispanics would eventually be so educated.

Many of the German-Russians who had provided beet labor in the earliest days had moved on to land ownership, and their farms and influence ensured their still laboring co-ethnics a chance to do the same. But the perpetually migrant Mexican would form a permanent underclass, with Mexico, as committee member John Raker baldly put it, "the breeding ground for more second-class cotton pickers and beet diggers, hoers, and toppers."[92] "This is not work the white man cannot do," admitted W. B. Mandeville regarding Colorado beetwork, but, he also asserted, "we have made an absolute class distinction in labor."[93] It seemed they were willing to make it a caste distinction as well. In another century, as historian Edmund Morgan has explained, early Virginian commercial farmers relied on the labor of a separate race, a visibly distinct common laboring force, to preserve a relative equality and a safe democracy among whites. In much the same way, these twentieth-century southwestern employers, although without legislated slavery, would use a radically distinct permanent laboring force to minimize the differences in living standards among Anglo participants in American democracy. A system of perpetually cheap migrant labor would boost the income and diminish the manual labor of the farmer and his family, at the same time it would exclude the poorest class in the vicinity from the Anglo comity.

By early 1921 the war boom had finally ended. Unemployment reached the highest level in United States history. At least one hundred fifty thousand Mexicans returned home.[94] In Colorado, the Great Western Sugar Company reaped, in a glutted market, the disaster of its postwar expansion. Denver, according to one news headline, was "Crowded with Mexicans Who Are Near Starving." The deputy city attorney estimated that "70 percent of the 5,000 Mexicans now in the city are without means of support and must be fed by charity." Hundreds of these Chicano beetworkers were jailed on vagrancy charges, and officials accused them of having "squandered their summer earnings," and being "a menace to the peace of the community."[95] In March, the Secretary of Labor finally rescinded the immigration exemption orders and called upon the importers "to return to Mexico all such aliens then in their employ" while federal officials tracked and deported those they could find of the 21,400 deserters.[96]

The marginality and vulnerability of the newly augmented Mexican and Spanish American labor force was harshly illuminated for this brief season as workers moved across the border, in and out of the villages, at the convenience of Anglo employers and the government which represented them, presaging the events of the greater depression in the 1930s. But this earlier depression proved only an ill-fitting prelude to the economic expansion of the 1920s. The renewed expansion would not be hindered by the lack of overt government sanction for the importation of Mexican labor. The government had withdrawn the exemptions that had permitted virtually unrestricted immigration, but had failed to appropriate money to restore the border patrol. Without this border patrol, the supervising inspector on the Mexican border had warned in 1920, "practically any alien desirous of entering the United States and possessed of ordinary intelligence and persistence could readily find the means of doing so without fear of detection."[97] By 1923, Mexican immigration, largely illegal now, surpassed its wartime rate, and the numbers of Mexicans and Spanish Americans in Colorado's mines and beetfields and on its railroad crews again began to rise.[98]

While the war years do not represent a watershed in the provision of social services or labor opportunities for Hispanics in New Mexico and Colorado, or even in Hispanic assimilation into Anglo culture, these years had witnessed the establishment of Mexican labor as a permanent and significant factor on the Anglo-Hispanic frontier and in the United States as a whole.[99] During the war, the Chicano migratory pattern, already essential for village survival, had become equally essential in the eyes of many Anglos to the maintenance of the Anglo small farmer's standard of living. Between 1914 and 1921, the federal government had played an unprecedented role in this regional system. It had reached into the villages as well as across borders, not only in terms of interference with migratory patterns, but in terms of technology, Americanization, and health. Federal mobilization had helped bring Mexicans and Spanish Americans into the public eye, and then had abandoned them there until the 1930s. The new services, the wartime clubs, the Hispanic demonstration agents, and the federal funds which had begun to integrate Hispanic villagers into the larger American polity disappeared.

Ironically, it was the "birds of passage," the migrant laborers, who had the more lasting effect, changing not the villages, but the world into which the villagers could move. That effect was to narrow the boundary of possibilities that the regional community held for its Spanish American participants. Before the war it was still possible that Hispanics moving within the regional community could become integrated with Anglo communities at the local level, could establish effective nodes of settlement through homesteading and property ownership, beyond New Mexico and the southern Colorado villages.[100] By the end of the war, the increased scale of migration, the introduction of large numbers of Mexicans into the same jobs and patterns, the labor imperatives of new irrigated farming developments, and the general nativistic and racist trends among Anglos conspired to ensure that such integration became a virtual impossibility.

It was ironic, also, that the language of "invasion" was reversed, that Anglos complained of a "Mexican invasion," just as drought, depression, and war measures lessened the Hispanics' ability to control even the timing of their migratory patterns. The regional community, the migratory networks, might still allow Hispanics to retain some cultural autonomy in New Mexico and southern Colorado, but its perimeters as a strategy of autonomy and control were increasingly rigid. It could no longer offer hope for an expansion of that autonomy or power into the new areas of settlement.

The unarticulated compromise which had emerged from the 1920 hearings lay in the blind eye of the immigration officials, in the admission, however illegally, of permanently marginal laborers. Though those admitted were Mexican, the racial ideology demanded the identification of all Hispanics, of whatever citizenship, as "Mexican," while the determination to avoid the re-creation of the racial problems of the South demanded the myth that all these "Mexicans" disappeared below the border each year and were no part of the United States polity. The 1920 hearings had made clear that what the Anglo employers now wanted, as the chairman of the House committee summarized it for them, was "first class labor, but No. 2 men." The small farmers who employed Hispanic labor had joined an ideology of agricultural class and caste to the Hispanics' regional community, and the regional community's core, its village heartland, was increasingly becoming merely a dependent colony.[101] And it did not augur well for the new Hispanic frontier, that a Colorado congressman expressed his determination to make "this country . . . as much as I can help to make it so . . . a white man's country."[102]

6

On the Margins:
Chicano Community Building
in Northern Colorado,
the 1920s

It was early spring when they began to arrive. In the lingering chill twenty thousand Chicanos settled over the beetfields, five here, ten there. To house them, farmers rousted the hens from the chicken coops and took the last of the grain out of the storage shacks. Most of the shacks had only one or two rooms to shelter the large families—families had to be large to make a living working beets—and throughout the twenties, most shacks provided "utterly inadequate" shelter at that. Investigators continually testified that they found shacks located "with no attention to adequate sanitation, toilet facilities, sleeping room, or water supply." Without shade, the shacks became hotter than the fields; often they had no screens. The surroundings were dirty barnyards and corrals.

If they worked on the western edge of the South Platte Valley, due north of Denver, Spanish Americans could look up from the five miles of rows they tended per acre (each averaged ten acres per season) and, looking across the plain, be soothed by the sun setting over the mountains, a reminder of home. But if they worked in the long stretch of the valley to the east, there was nothing to relieve the eye from the endless rows and level terrain; they were alone on the plain, alone in the Anglo north, with nothing to remind them of the mountains, the villages, the relatives, the gardens, and the churches of home. This frontier demanded from them a new life, a new way of living. To understand their life as it evolved in the 1920s, it is necessary first to set it in the context of the regional community, then to examine the factors that conspired to make the creation of a stable community in the north difficult—including the impact of the migration on Chicanas, the community builders—and finally to analyze new strategies as they emerged in the north.

With spiraling intensity, old and new factors combined in northern New Mexico to deprive Hispanics of land and livelihood, to drive them into increased dependency on the networks and settlements, and the success, of the regional community. Each new disaster of the 1920s, natural or man-made, meant reduced resources to meet the next. Hispanic vigilante groups like the Manos Negras continued to cut fences that blocked access to traditionally communal pasture and to burn barns of Rio Arriba County's Anglo and Hispanic commercial farmers, but such efforts to resist the trend had little impact. There also continued a depressed cattle market; limited access to Anglo-controlled credit; equal division of dwindling holdings among heirs, which left each with smaller and smaller parcels of land; and an average crop failure in some parts of northern New Mexico reaching 59 percent. In addition to these older factors, a 1924 Pueblo Lands Act resulted in the eviction of nearly three thousand Hispanics and Anglos. At the same time, Texans and Oklahomans with enough capital to stake a homestead invaded the region. They disrupted the Hispanic villages and demanded services such as moving a high school from a Hispanic settlement to their own settlement or building expensive irrigation projects that would increase the tax burden on the financially strapped Hispanics just when a 1926 state tax law made land that had been tax-delinquent for three years subject to foreclosure and sale for back taxes.[1]

These events ensured that a rapidly escalating proportion of Hispanic village families increased their reliance on wage labor or, like farm folk all over the country, left the villages altogether. Many headed for such larger towns of New Mexico as Grants and Albuquerque. Others departed for the state's coal-mining areas, Gallup and Raton, and for railroad shops and Colorado's coal mines. But the largest contingent set out for the beetfields, where push and pull came together.

Colorado's sugar-beet industry provided approximately 20,000 jobs each season, while the state's railroads employed only about 5000 Chicanos for maintenance of way, and its coal mines just over 3000. Moreover, to ensure an ample labor supply, Great Western Sugar Company, Colorado's largest, spent lavishly on recruitment campaigns throughout the decade, as much as ninety dollars per family recruited, or $250,000 in a single year. The company focused with particular intensity on the already vulnerable areas of southern Colorado and New Mexico, until the two states' share of the recruited Chicano labor rose from approximately 65 percent in 1923 to approximately 85 percent in 1927.[2]

According to one ex-villager, recruiters claimed "you'd rake in the money," and they distributed brochures that led Hispanics to expect a garden plot for each family, decent housing, a water supply, and a friendly employer who might provide milk and eggs at cost.[3] While it is true that a few of the Chicano beet-labor houses, more of them toward the end of the decade, were sturdy and weatherproof, that some farm owners and tenants had houses and sanitation little better than their labor did, and that farm labor conditions in other parts of the nation, notably in the South, were little if any better than those in Colorado, nonetheless, for the majority of Chicanos in the 1920s, life in Colorado's beetfields did not fulfill recruiters' promises. A simple description of conditions and attitudes there reads like a harangue against the agricultural system of the time.

Most of the farmers seemed to agree with Americanization teacher Alfred White, that "the peon has always lived like a pig and he will continue to do so." National Child Labor Committee investigator Charles Gibbons found that "the local people . . . feel they are giving the Mexican all he deserves; in fact one frequently finds the opinion that they (residents) are performing an act of charity in allowing the Mexican to work for them, and therefore any kind of a house will do for them to live in." Most growers and even investigators were convinced that whatever the conditions in Colorado, they represented an improvement over Hispanic and Mexican villages.[4]

Most Chicanos, on the other hand, saw little if any improvement. They had come north, to the margins of the Hispanic regional community, to better their condition. Though often bitterly disappointed in what they found, many could not afford to turn back. An exasperated Chicana living in a one-room shack with her family of twelve demanded, "How can you expect folks to live decently when given a place like that?" The Chicanas tried desperately to turn these shacks into homes, despite their long hours in the fields and the meager furnishings they could bring with them. The migrants used boxes as tables and cupboards, and often slept on the floor. Mary Vela remembered that her mother stayed up all night to clean when they moved. Another mother made her own paste and pasted a two-room shack with newspapers for decoration and warmth; her daughter remembered, "[W]e would lay there and read all the news there was in the newspapers."[5]

As to the work itself, there were some Anglo school children and a few Anglo women who, not needing to provide their entire support from the beets, contracted small acreages, an amount easily managed in workdays of reasonable length. A local lawyer assured investigators that "children are in much better conditions in the open fields and the open air than they would be in their homes. In general," he asserted, "this summer outing is looked upon by the children as a frolic." But Mary Vela recalled beetwork as "backbreaking and heavy. During the harvest we'd work 18-hour days." At least one Spanish-speaking woman lost two sons to a kidney disease exacerbated by long hours of stooping over the fields. Thinning the beets in the early summer required crawling, and topping them during the harvest required stooping, and it was all, according to investigator Paul Taylor, "disagreeable ... dirty ... monotonous and repetitive." Even C. V. Maddux, labor commissioner at Great Western Sugar Company in the 1920s, warned that "a man who is highly-strung could never work beets, because there are five miles of row to every acre. . . . He could not see the end."[6]

Great Western Sugar remained the recruiter and not the direct employer of beet labor, but it taught its agricultural fieldmen Spanish, retained files on each of the laborers it recruited, and mediated in grower-labor disputes. As the roving villagers created new and reinforced old paths connecting the village economy to the larger one, Great Western Sugar, by centralizing and expanding its recruiting and labor services, increased its control over the labor and the labor market on the Anglo-Chicano frontier, and so its power in the regional community.

The sugar companies together with the growers set the wages of beet labor, a crucial factor not only for Hispanic life in the north but for the possibilities of the regional community. Yet the laborers' cost of living did not enter into the companies' calculations. They simply promised to procure beet labor at the farmers' agreed rate per acre. Under the set rates, a Chicano beetworker earned only about $250 each season. Meanwhile, the cost of living in Denver for a family, according to the Colorado Industrial Commission, was $1,197.78 per year at minimum comfort.[7] For Chicanos wintering in rural areas, the cost may have been slightly less, but not 75 percent less. Chicanos quickly came to see in the family system of labor not the promise of vastly increased wealth, but simply survival.[8]

And even survival was questionable. "Families" under this system sometimes included distant cousins, neighbors from the home village, or even subcontractors. With more than six working members, at least four of them adult men, such a family could contract as many as 60 to 80 acres and make between $1500 and $2100 per season. But there were few such families, fewer, in fact, than 5 percent of the whole. Investigating the South Platte area in 1924, Sara Brown found earnings from beets for over half the contract families with children amounted to less than $900. Forty percent of Brown's families earned less than $700 for the season.[9] In other beet-producing areas of Colorado, beet-labor families earned even less.[10] Having promised to provide cheap labor to the growers, sugar companies had indeed fostered a family system where, according to one pair of investigators, "instead of paying one laborer a bare subsistence wage, the labor of father and several children is secured at this rate."[11] But family earnings of seven hundred dollars did not provide even subsistence, except, perhaps, during the months of labor.

Clearly such low wages demanded some kind of supplement, and it was here that the village strategy of migration and the beet industry's labor strategy intersected. Credit, relief, or the beet laborer's own farm in southern Colorado, New Mexico, or Mexico could supplement beet wages in the absence of winter work. Each of these alternatives informally subsidized the beet industry by making the low wages possible, but in some ways, perpetual migration seemed the most desirable to all parties. In much the way South African labor reserves function, migration placed the burden of inadequate wages on the laborers themselves. Having at the end of the beet season an average of approximately $150, "plenty to get them out of the country," as one farmer observed, and spending approximately two-thirds of it on returning to the village, a beet-labor family would have fifty dollars to pay taxes on the farm and supply cash needs throughout the winter.[12] In turn, the farm that could not support the family year round might provide the missing six months' subsistence. This semi-autonomous cultural retreat fit the mythological image of the vanishing "Mexican" whose "homing instinct" saved the Southwest from "the terrible mistakes which have been made in the southern states . . . a civilization of masters and servants." In Colorado, growers sent the "servants" home when they were not wanted, in an extended echo of a day work system rather than live-in help. This migratory pattern permitted members of each culture to deny their membership in and responsibility for the other, and allowed farmers to keep the doors to Mexican reserve labor open.[13]

The number of Chicanos who either lacked the farm to which to return or lacked the means to get there belied the comforting myth.[14] Mexican nationals in particular, unlike most Spanish Americans, tended to come from landless families. But both groups settled in the north in greater numbers than during the war.[15] The resident Chicano population of northeastern Colorado more than doubled relative to the total population and more than tripled in absolute numbers between 1920 and 1927 alone. Approximately one-third wintered in the open fields and the rest in towns. In Denver their number grew from approximately two thousand to over eight thousand. Expanding earlier settlements in Denver, Spanish Americans clustered west of the city center, in the vicinity of West Colfax between the Platte River and Cherry Creek, and also to the north along the east coast of the river. To the northeast of this latter area were the Mexicans, perhaps a fifth of the total Chicano population in the city. These were poor parts of the city, multi-ethnic, with rooming houses, the unemployed, and the transient. Among these last, Denver's Chicanos fit well. Over three-quarters of the families from each section left Denver each spring for seasonal labor. By 1929, such Chicano clusters, however transient, made it clear that the "Mexicans" disappearing from the fields after harvest had not moved very far.[16]

Outside Denver, the distribution of these Chicano settlers was by no means uniform. In some sugar-beet districts, as in Denver, the Chicano population exploded during the 1920s; at Fort Collins the number of Chicano families resident year-round grew from 10 in 1921 to 248 in 1927. Around the area's coal mines, as at Columbine, Puritan, and Frederick in Weld County, approximately one-third of the 1000 to 1400 men employed during the 1920s were Chicanos, half of whom were Spanish Americans and half Mexicans. Yet in other districts the permanent Chicano population remained relatively static. Some districts had no Chicanos at all.[17] Growers there simply rejected the "Mexicans" entirely or restricted them to seasonal residence. Paul Taylor, investigating in 1927, explained, "some communities dependent upon seasonal labor are eager for the laborers to move in when they are needed, and almost equally eager for them to move out when they are no longer needed," and since the farmers controlled the beet-labor housing, the beet labor moved on.[18] The unevenness of Chicano settlement allowed some Anglos to ignore the new settlers, but magnified for others the changing ethnic composition of the area, the changing shape of the Anglo-Hispanic frontier. Threatened with a potential loss of local dominance at a time of generally constricting opportunity, these Anglos reacted in ways that, combined with structural changes in the area's economy, defused the threat. They made it particularly difficult for Hispanics to achieve a stable base in the north.

Hispanics found the traditional agricultural ladder to ownership full of broken rungs. Landowners hesitated to lease farms to Hispanics. One who did complained, "People around here blame me for leasing to Mexicans and so displacing the whites."[19] But even a lease proved at best a rickety, inadequate vehicle. Few Chicanos would follow their predecessors, the German-Russian immigrants, to farm ownership. Chicanos arrived with smaller families than the German-Russians, and with an unwillingness to keep the women and children in the fields for the same long hours. Moreover, they came at a time when land values had escalated while beet-labor wages had not and when the move to ownership had generally dwindled.[20] It was, in fact, only the lack of movement between tenancy and ownership that reconciled Anglos to Chicano lessees at all. As one farmer's wife explained, "There is no danger from the Mexicans. They won't save enough to buy land."[21] Without land ownership it would be difficult for Hispanics to convert the periphery of one Chicano regional community, the outermost edge of the network system, into the center of another, the node of a new set of networks.

What year-round residences Chicanos could buy consisted of town lots and even these were not easily acquired. "Dealers in real estate," Paul Taylor revealed, "carry out the policy of separating Mexicans in northeastern Colorado." And even a modest $250 mortgage on a lot in a Chicano enclave, with the family paying only twelve dollars a year, outran beetworker resources.[22] One former beetworker remembered an Anglo realtor in Greeley in the late 1920s who "was working the Spanish real good, he *lived* off the Spanish," providing loans and repossessing partially paid-up houses. A reluctant Anglo host society joined with the dynamics of the beet industry to keep most Chicanos transient and hovering on the margins of society.[23]

Nor did the Great Western Sugar Company's compromise of company-financed colonies impinge markedly on this system. Faced with increasing recruiting costs, the company, unlike the farmers, wanted a larger resident population. In colonies they provided land lots Chicanos could buy as house sites. While the colonies did allow a number of Chicano families to winter in the north each year, the high turnover and lapsed payments proved them not much more affordable for Chicanos than non-company housing. In addition, the company colonies themselves emblemized the system which kept the Chicanos safely (for the Anglos) marginal and had as its aim the preservation in Chicanos of a perpetual and distinct laboring force. Their one- or two-room distinctive adobe structures stood on lots devoid of shade or farmland, a mile or two outside of Anglo towns or literally across the tracks.[24]

For those Chicanos who did succeed in purchasing such a home, it offered a measure of stability and avoided a winter in the often leaky, overcrowded, and unsanitary farm buildings and Denver shacks. But it offered scant if any aid to gaining subsistence or even acceptance into Anglo society. It had little in common with owning land in the village. For Chicanos, ownership of a home on the periphery of an Anglo community and unaccompanied by ownership of productive land could mark not upward mobility, but confinement to a seasonal laboring class.[25]

When these Chicano colonists and settlers no longer disappeared each winter below some imaginary border, the Anglo townspeople erected their own borders. They used the burning crosses of the Ku Klux Klan, so popular elsewhere in Colorado in the 1920s, to mark the edges of the adobe colonies, and used signs in restaurants, barbershops, and movie theaters bearing such inscriptions as "White Trade Only" and "No Mexican Trade Wanted," which made it impossible for Hispanics in towns like Greeley and Brighton to buy so much as a hamburger.[26] The rhetoric of a "Mexican invasion" continued virtually unabated both in the national popular press and in Colorado. And Hispanic colonists remembered vividly nearly sixty years later the indignity of having an Anglo doctor arrive unannounced to take blood samples for Wasserman tests to detect syphilis. "That's how bad they wanted to get rid of us," recalled one. Spanish Americans had difficulty registering to vote, and local Anglos continued to "wish the Mexicans were not there."[27]

It was ironic that the local growers simultaneously protested the invasion of their neighborhoods by "Mexicans" and petitioned Congress to retain unrestricted Mexican immigration. It was ironic, also, that at the same time Great Western Sugar was erecting its colonies, its representative vigorously contended that "the Mexican eventually returns south of the Rio Grande," having "ebbed and flowed into agriculture and industry as needed for the past fifteen years, with good results to all interests concerned." Colorado's Congressman, Charles Timberlake, even denied that the company had built any houses for Mexican labor.[28] The public and the private face of the industry, its social and its economic needs, had become increasingly disparate under the strain of reinforcing the myths which perpetuated the labor system.

Local Anglos and sugar company officials came up with new myths, or applied old ones, to justify the developments. Although the local Anglos gave the colonies unattractive names—the one in Eaton was called "Ragtown"—the vice president of Holly Sugar Company informed a Senate committee that "Mexicans" were "content to conduct their own community life apart from other races," and Robert McLean claimed that segregation was "due quite as much to the clannishness of the Mexican, as to the opposition of the American."[29] Mexican segregation, it was implied, was by their own choice. When the Fort Collins hospital relegated its Hispanics to the basement, "there were always some real good reasons why they did it," remembered Arthur Maes, "'more at home' . . . 'we can serve them better' . . . 'they can talk to each other in the same language.'"[30]

Many Chicanos—not consumers of the myths—resented the implications of such segregation. Some Hispanics remembered that people were considered "better" if they lived outside the colony, and that the colonies' lack of modern sanitary facilities helped give some colonists the attitude of "If I ever get a chance, I'll move out of this place." But the isolation from Anglo life, the Anglo prejudices, and the low wages reinforced each other and created, as one investigating team expressed it, "a vicious circle." "From this circle," they concluded, "few can escape through their own efforts."[31]

For during winter it was not only the housing situation that created an unstable life for Hispanics. As a rule, the majority of beetwork families who wintered in the north found no work at all between beet seasons. And those whose family members did find jobs, including mothers who did laundry and domestic service, averaged less than $300 in earnings for the winter. Most earned less than $200.[32] The sugar company itself admitted that in northern Colorado "the growers, generally speaking, have been less inclined with the Mexican than with the German-Russian to afford opportunities for extra work." As with those reluctant to lease land to Chicanos, these growers hesitated to displace regular Anglo winter farm labor.[33] In the area's small industrial sector, too, it seemed to some Chicanos that unless jobs were so temporary or

so bad that Anglos did not want them, Hispanics could not get them.
The Mexican Welfare Committee of the Colorado State Council of the
Knights of Columbus concurred, reporting in 1928 that only about 150
of the 7,000 men in northern Colorado employed in industry outside
the mines and railroads were "Mexicans," and these, the Committee
revealed, "were on rockpiles and at work no other laborer [would]
do."[34] Some Chicanos left their families in the north and migrated for
winter work, becoming sheepherders in Colorado or Wyoming or going
to coal mines or to Pueblo's steel mill.[35] But in this way, they were not
replicating the migrant patterns and village systems as much as extending them, since their life in the north centered not on a stable village
core, but on a transient migrant settlement, marginal to both Anglo and
Hispanic worlds.

Even the number of summer field-labor jobs fluctuated, offering no
security for the resident laborer. The beet acreage harvested in a single
sugar factory district could go up or down by as much as 75 percent
from one year to the next.[36] The beetgrower a Chicano family had
worked for one summer may not have been in beets the next. And even
if the grower stayed in beets, he might choose newly recruited labor over
resident labor, or Mexican over Spanish American. Mexican immigration provided only one-quarter of beetfield labor, but it provided the
valve which allowed sporadic large increases in beet acreage, and thus
in demand for labor without commensurately increased wages.[37]

The use of Mexican labor affected Hispanic community-building in
the north even beyond the lowered wage rates. According to Taylor, the
sugar company often brought the labor north a month early to avoid
the increasingly strident competition among recruiters as summer
approached, and tried to place the recruits on spring railroad work to
allow them to support themselves until beetwork began. This employment service brought the two groups, resident and migrant Chicanos,
into direct competition even before the beet season.[38] With Mexicans
posing the most immediate and visible threat to the Spanish Americans,
the latter did all in their power to dissociate themselves from the former
and to assert their prior claims to services and employment as citizens
and particularly as veterans.[39] One Spanish American told investigator
B. F. Coen that Mexicans "aren't any good. You'll only find one out of
every 100 that's a 'sitter' [citizen] and I don't think it's right." Spanish
Americans also blamed the Mexicans for the new restrictions posted in
barber and other shops. Living under the same conditions, Spanish
Americans and Mexicans usually resided in separate colonies, rejected

each other's company, and fought when mixed. Enrique Lopez recalled of his youth in Denver, "the bitterest 'race riots' I have ever witnessed—and engaged in—were between the look-alike, talk-alike *surumatos* [Mexicans] and *manitos* [Spanish Americans]."[40]

Even a few Anglos made distinctions between the two groups, endowing Mexicans with a character more docile and less educated, and allowing Spanish Americans "more fiery blood in their veins" and more Anglo habits which made them "less passive in their attitudes toward social and civil rights."[41] On the whole, those who made such distinctions placed the Spanish Americans above the Mexicans, and the Spanish Americans certainly placed themselves there.[42] Some of the children of Mexican immigrants began to adopt the term "Spanish American" to describe themselves as well, but most of them heartily resented the condescending attitude of the Spanish-speaking from Colorado and New Mexico and labeled them "comprado," or "bought," for having remained in the United States after 1848 instead of leaving for Mexico. They taunted them with Anglo discriminations, calling them people without a country.[43]

Infuriatingly, most Anglos continued in daily practice to make no distinction among them at all. "During the war," complained one citizen of Anglo attitudes, "we were Spanish Americans; now we are just Mexicans."[44] Anglos referred to the "Mexican, or his cousin the Spanish-American" as people "who easily merge" on United States soil, and in one area officials expressed their chagrin that not one of the local "Mexicans" had showed up at citizenship classes, apparently unaware that the majority of local Hispanic residents were already citizens, by birth.[45] To most Anglos, as one investigating team discovered, both groups "are called 'Mexes' or 'Greasers' and are regarded as foreigners."[46] This amalgamation continued the trend begun at least during World War I of excluding Chicanos from the United States polity both as foreigners and as a separate "race."[47]

The economic vulnerability and social marginality of the Chicanos in northern Colorado led many of them to at least some degree of dependence on two systems fraught with their own kind of peril: credit and relief. With the meager wages of the previous summer, the lack of winter work, and the fact that families worked four to seven weeks in the beetfields before their first pay installment, by spring credit had become an almost universal necessity.[48]

Most Chicanos in the north had come from villages where cash played a distinctly peripheral role in the daily economy. They did not, as one observer realized, "come from a district where life, comfort, and health depend upon the possession of money."[49] They also expected the stores in northern Colorado to carry them when they were out of funds as had the stores back home. But everyone had known each other in the villages at home, and only if a Chicano beetworker stayed in one location long enough to become known to certain growers or merchants could he obtain local credit from them.[50] The sugar company itself extended a limited amount of credit to new recruits and some others, but in any case, the sums advanced were deducted from the beetworkers' wages before the workers received their pay. Workers living on credit often became the target of merchants who overcharged for groceries, druggists who sold unnecessary or useless drugs, and aggressive salesmen who offered "easy" installment terms. In its results, this credit system echoed those of Colorado's mining companies and the rural South. By the time the first pay came it might well have been spent, and the beetworker locked into an endless round of advances and seasonal labor.[51]

Most of the Chicanos were no more used to formal welfare than to formal credit structures. Although the Confidential exchange service of relief agencies in Denver did find some Chicanos receiving help simultaneously from different sources, many displayed a great reluctance to seek impersonal doles. Mrs. Clara Gard, president of Fairview School, said of the Chicanos in her district, "[A]lthough many of the families in our community are extremely poor they rarely make requests for help. . . . We have to watch very carefully in order to give them shoes and certain things they may need."[52] Despite their almost universal poverty, Chicanos in the South Platte Valley, according to Paul Taylor, constituted only as many charitable cases as their proportion of the community as a whole, not as many as their proprtion of the lower income groups.[53]

The Chicano's reluctance to seek relief was met by an equal reluctance on the part of some relief agencies and most of the public to give it to them. Welfare work among Chicanos in Denver had begun as early as 1913 with the Deaconess Mission, but not until the 1920s did attention truly focus on Mexicans and Spanish Americans. In 1922, Miss Kinney of the city's Bureau of Charities declared, "Of course the Mexicans are utterly demoralized. There is not a center for them. Their whole tone is low as possible. The community is not trying to do anything, and another thing, we cannot feed Mexicans. They come in hordes."[54] Five years later, after the launching of numerous welfare efforts, the president of the Denver Deanery of the National Council of Catholic Women still found the work of Chicano relief "heart-breakingly difficult, because we have not the whole-hearted co-operation of the community at large. The sublime indifference with which our pleas for help have been met is discouraging in the extreme."[55] This was one subsidy to the sugar-beet industry that the public was unwilling to pay Denver's Salvation Army commandant considered Chicanos "tricky and deceitful, taking advantage of the fact that they are not understood and do not understand, and that they are dangerous if you make them mad, for you cannot tell what will happen." Accordingly, the Salvation Army tried to clear all Anglo cases first.[56]

Not only their need for relief and credit but the difficulty with which they obtained them clarified Chicanos' marginal status on this northern edge of their frontier, the periphery of the human network that comprised the regional community. And neither relief nor credit offered a way out of their condition. On the contrary, Chicanos found themselves trapped, for the current generation at least, in an economic system incorporating seasonal wage labor at inadequate wages, permanent insecurity, and tenuous, impersonal, subsistence relief and credit.

As for immigrant groups and minorities elsewhere, education was supposed to provide the compensating factor. The Great Western Sugar Company touted educational benefits as lending "a humanitarian impulse" to their proposals that beetworkers remain over the winter.[57] Even economist Paul Taylor believed that "despite interrupted attendance, as good or better education advantages are offered in the beet area than in the places from which the workers came."[58] Certainly public education in Hispanic northern New Mexico continued in the 1920s to be plagued by lack of funds, short school terms, and underqualified teachers.[59] Of the Spanish American parents who moved north, approximately one-quarter were illiterate in any language, one-half in English, and one-third had had no schooling.[60] For their children, they wanted more. They kept fewer of their school-age children in the fields than the German-Russians did, though it meant they made less money, and when Hispanic mothers worked beets it was often so children could attend school. "They want me to go to school so that I won't have to work beets," explained a Spanish American boy, and one girl's parents promised her a better job if she went to college.[61]

Hispanic children, however, often remained skeptical of their future possibilities, "because," as the college-bound girl put it, "the Americans won't give me a chance." They had some reason for doubt. Teachers who said, "Oh, why don't you go back to the god-damned beet fields," did not instill confidence.[62] A more sympathetic teacher reported that the Anglo children, also, "feel as hostile to the Mexican children on the playground as they do toward Negros in Gary, Indiana."[63] And so did their parents. A school superintendent of Weld County insisted that "the respectable white people of Weld County do not want their children to sit alongside of dirty, filthy, disease-infested Mexicans in schools."[64] Chicano school children found that, indeed, Anglos would not sit next to them, taunted them with phrases like "dirty Mexicans" and "greaser, greaser, sitting on an ice-cream freezer," "wouldn't want us ever to touch them," and made fun of their food until the Hispanic children hid away to eat.[65] The state's constitution, written within recent memory of the Civil War, forbade segregation, but de facto segregation, particularly with the erection of company colonies at some distance from town and with the mid-term entrance and departure of beetworking children, was relatively easily achieved.[66] Northern schools may have been better equipped than those in Hispanic villages, but the atmosphere was definitely more hostile, and the degree to which Hispanics would benefit remained in doubt.

Even when schools welcomed Chicano children, or were at least neutral, the necessity of family labor kept many children from attending. The work of children under sixteen, according to one 1925 study, contributed nearly one-third of the total contract labor's seasonal beet earnings. Most children working in beets were between ten and fourteen years old, but even six-year-olds sometimes spent their days thinning beets.[67] Schooling for these children represented a substantial and sometimes impossible sacrifice for the whole family. A few Hispanic children managed to get through grammar school by asking for advance work each March and doing extra work all winter, but even for these children, high school, which demanded a set number of credits, was impossible.[68] Almost universally, parents cared about education, but sometimes the alternative to child labor was starvation; Margarita Garcia remembered of her parents, "There was not much they could do. I guess we were so close to them, we didn't insist."[69]

Missing approximately one-third of each school year, though regular in attendance once they enrolled, four-fifths of the Chicano children fell behind in school, almost two-thirds of them, by 1925, three years behind. Often they had lost interest in school activities and had little in common with their classmates.[70] As a result, Chicanos in the north stayed in school little longer than those who remained in Hispanic villages. Most left school before sixth grade, and while the number of more advanced students rose in the 1920s, still only a handful enrolled in high school.[71]

Faced with economic pressures and hostile neighbors, many Chicano families simply did not enroll their children in school. To many Anglos, this seemed the best solution to the educational dilemma, better than segregated schools or special classes. A former school board member asserted, "They're needed in the fields and the school don't do them any good anyway."[72] Officials in the South Platte Valley granted illegal school exemptions to Chicano beetworking children and tended to turn a blind eye to those not applying. One confessed, "[W]e never try to enforce the compulsory attendance laws on the Mexicans. We just wink at the law."[73] And Great Western Sugar, despite its claims for education, perpetrated myths that justified this denial of duty. The company claimed that "while beet children may be absent for several weeks each year from their classes in geography and spelling," they learned not only "industry and thrift," but "the craft of their fathers," a blessing for "people whose social and intellectual state may be below the standards of our ideals."[74]

Underneath the justification ran other concerns. "If every child has a high school education," sugar company representatives demanded, "who will labor?" If the Anglo farmer was to keep his own children in school, he had to hire someone else to do the work. "[I]t is believed that a cheap labor supply is necessary for this industry," reported investigators in the Arkansas Valley, "and that the Spanish-American or Mexican is the one to furnish it. Too regular school attendance would not be compatible with this."[75] The marginalization of Chicanos was no haphazard social development. Great Western Sugar's C. V. Maddux explained, "We no longer want settlers to occupy vacant land. . . . What we want is workers to work for the settlers who came before." Fred Cummings, a beetgrower from Fort Collins, elucidated, "[N]o man can accumulate anything in this world until by some means or device he is enabled to enjoy the benefit of some other man's labor." That Anglo farmers well understood the developing situation was revealed even further by one South Platte school official who feared, "[W]e are building up a caste system that inside of two generations will be worse than India ever dreamed of."[76] Far from liberating the next generation of Chicanos from their backbreaking toil, the educational system of the north, better endowed than that of the Hispanic villages, seemed for the majority geared only to perpetuate the Chicanos as marginal agricultural labor from generation to generation. As the decade progressed, the informal, caste-like structure of the war period became firmly embedded in the area's institutions.

Chicanas did not escape this structure of discrimination and marginalization. It altered their patterns of life within the Hispanic community and its contrast to village structures had enormous ramifications not only for the place they would hold in Anglo-dominated areas, but for the viability of an autonomous Chicano community in the north, for a new node in the regional system. By first looking briefly at the evolving place of women in the villages, and then at life in the north for Chicanas and the nature of the compensations it offered, the impact of the changes becomes clear.

The Hispanic villages of northern New Mexico and southern Colorado in the 1920s continued their flexible sexual division of labor and mutual decision making, along with their migratory element.[77] Village women—single, married, and widowed—continued to own property and govern its disposal, run dance halls, clean school houses, butcher livestock, dry fruit and vegetables, take in laundry, weave rugs, lead religious services, participate in communal plastering and whitewashing, and barter labor with their neighbors.[78] They also continued to plant, cultivate, and harvest gardens that provided an increasingly vital proportion of the families' subsistence; toward the end of the decade they came to the attention of at least one county agricultural extension agent who taught them to treat their seed with formaldehyde and to increase their yield in other ways.[79] In addition, much as Anglo farm wives of day laborers did, Hispanic wives of migrants managed their husbands' duties on the farms with the help of their children. In fact, so completely had village life come to devolve on these women that by the end of the 1920s, as one Hispanic male recalled, "when the men came back, they were kind of like guests."[80]

In cases where the men did not migrate and so could do the farm work, the women, in increasing numbers, performed wage work for Anglos by taking in laundry, "babysitting," or doing other domestic service, to provide the cash their households lacked.[81] The female wage workers, like the males, tended to view wage work as subordinate to their main object, the continuity of village life. As service to village welfare, the villagers accepted both the day work of the women and the sorties of girls to Santa Fe and Albuquerque with, as one male Chimayo inhabitant remembered, "a great pride."[82]

The cash that male and female migrants brought home paid taxes, provided such modern necessities as gable or corrugated iron roofs and school supplies, and permitted villages to survive despite depleted resources.[83] Some women who earned wages used their earnings to buy canned goods and sometimes even canning equipment, and many women in remote communities treasured their Montgomery Ward and Sears catalogs, continuing a selective adoption of Anglo culture.[84]

The villages, however, continued to suffer high infant mortality rates, epidemics, and a lack of government health or other services.[85] Some work in instructing midwives began with the allocation of the Sheppard-Towner funds, but only at the rate of one instructor for all of New Mexico, and one for the San Luis Valley. Because the price of Anglo doctors was prohibitive, sparsely scattered women missionaries still provided the major channel of modern health information and services, and Hispanic villagers in northern New Mexico and southern Colorado continued to rely most heavily on their "uninstructed" parteras.[86]

Village life was far from ideal, but it provided a framework in which women had a certain degree of independence, a variety of duties, a supportive community of other women and kin, and a central and powerful role in community life. Chicanas in northern Colorado found themselves lifted out of that network of relations and provided with pallid substitutes for the village features that had given them strength and support.

Hispanic women in northern Colorado planted gardens when they could, but with over half the women working in the beetfields, even in the relatively rare instances when they had suitable land and water, they did not have the time to tend vegetables, and so often planted flowers instead.[87] Less than 2 percent of Hispanic beet-labor families in northern Colorado produced even a major part of their food, and at least 33 percent had no gardens at all. As in the villages, when the family had property Hispanic women could inherit and control it. But in northern Colorado that property provided sustenance for neither the women nor their families.[88] Food had to be purchased; preparation was not shared among the community. In the Hispanic villages, women had often measured their value by their ability to provide and prepare food, both for their own and for neighboring families. As in other societies, food was more than sustenance; it carried emotional freight, bound villagers to one another, and defined their relations. Change in this arena would eventually shake all others.[89] Women would have to find new ways to measure their value. As with the men, their relationship to the land and to what it produced, a relationship which had provided the key to village membership, had changed. Membership in the community, like women's own value, would have to be defined in other ways.

Religion could not provide the missing link. Hispanic women in the north as in the south attended church more regularly than did the men, who had their Penitente chapters and moradas in Denver and other towns by the early 1930s. For most Hispanic women in the north, church groups remained their only formal affiliation. But less than half the beetworking families attended church with any regularity.[90] Hispanic civil marriages in the north continued to outnumber religious ones until the end of the decade.[91] In addition, distanced from their own church, many Hispanics converted to Protestant sects when they reached northern Colorado, and others had converted before they came. Only about half the Chicano colonists at Greeley, for example, were Catholic. While religious divisions did not necessarily lead to strife within the colonies, they did not encourage community spirit as village rituals had. The Catholic church was not the all-encompassing social institution it had been in the villages, and neither did it provide the same unity for Hispanics or the same status for even the leaders, male or female, of its societies.

Nor did religion provide a gate to a new interethnic, Anglo-Hispanic community.[92] The First Presbyterian Church in Fort Collins allowed Hispanic members to meet in their building, but only in the basement, and Greeley's Catholic church reserved one row especially for Hispanics. "Even religion," concluded Paul Taylor, "does not obliterate the line of social cleavage."[93] Within the church, as in the larger community, Hispanics endured a marginal position.

Other areas proved equally flawed as foundations for the re-creation of Hispanic women's central role. In New Mexico and southern Colorado, Hispanic women in heavily Hispanic areas were achieving a variety of elective political offices, from county school superintendent to secretary of state. But in northern Colorado, they, like the men, had trouble proving citizenship and establishing residence of sufficient length to register to vote. Once eligible, they tended to vote in the same proportion as Hispanic men, but neither had the numbers nor the cohesiveness to achieve office or even leverage.[94] And while parteras became itinerate politicians in New Mexico, they were simply one more sign of an increasingly tenuous female community in northern Colorado.[95] Midwives had come with the Chicano migrants—"you couldn't survive without them," recalled Arthur Maes—but in the perambulating world of the beetfields, there was no assurance the partera would always be within call. One Hispanic woman had two of her children with the help of a partera in Greeley, but by the time she had two others, the partera had returned to New Mexico.

Residence in northern Colorado brought no compensation for the loss of parteras in improved health services. Hispanic infants died at a rate as much as twice that of other beetworking ethnic groups.[96] And when, in the early 1930s, Hispanic women turned to Weld County's new free doctors they discovered a mixed blessing. The women found it "much better" during birth because they had ether for the pain, but found it harder afterwards. In New Mexico, relatives and neighbors had gathered round. All helped. In the north, remembered one mother, "[W]e didn't have nobody to do anything for us so we had to work up to the minute we had kids and then up immediately, no women around to help."[97]

There were rare stories of interethnic friendship and even intimacy among women. At least one Hispanic mother learned English in an informal group of beetworking women, including Japanese and German-Russian, which met in each other's kitchens and exchanged ways of cooking. She learned to make German bread and other German dishes, and cried when the German lady moved away. Maria Chavez remembered that "neighbors" never visited each other, but also that "white and brown" came to dances on the farms.[98] And Paul Taylor related an incident of a female farm operator who cared for her Spanish American beetworking family's baby for three months when the mother went to the hospital with blood poisoning. There were even a few intermarriages: five in Weld County in 1926, or 8.6 percent of Hispanic and almost 1 percent of all marriages in the county that year.[99]

For many Hispanic women, however, the loneliness and isolation experienced in a childbirth unattended by relatives permeated their lives. They remembered a life in New Mexico where families always got together, one night at one house, one night at another, and now they spent months on isolated farms, scattered across the valley.[100] Amelia Cordova's mother liked to melt the snow that piled in corners and wash her hair with it. When one night a chemical in the snow blinded her, Amelia had to quit school to take care of her mother. No women came to help.[101] No community of women had arisen to replace that left in New Mexico.

The rejection many Chicanas in northern Colorado experienced was not simply by Anglo society as a whole, but in particular by Anglo women and girls. "American girls," reported Paul Taylor, "particularly expressed a prejudice against social intercourse with Mexicans."[102] Margarita Garcia remembered that there were clubs in her school, but "they wouldn't even tell us about it." The Anglo mothers were little different. Taylor found it was the farmer's wives, not the farmers, who most adamantly opposed social mixing. Hispanic mothers like the one so determined to give her children an education that she had no "time to visit or do anything else except care for her family" and work in the fields, attended P.T.A. meetings where "The Americans made it so plain that they were unwelcome that they didn't come again." A superintendent even complained, "It is too much trouble to have Mexicans in the P.T.A."[103]

Without the communal and exchanged labor of the village, the companionship of women in childbirth, the power bases of the garden and the church and of the village itself, Hispanic women in northern Colorado found their place in society altered indeed. No longer at the ordered center of village life, they were increasingly unable to affect the institutions, the church, the school, or the midwives they had controlled or helped to control at home.

Thoroughly dependent on a money economy, Chicanas in northern Colorado did not find in wage labor, when they could get it, a satisfactory replacement for their gardens as a means, or for their villages as an end. Performing agricultural labor for wages, unlike the non-wage labor in the garden or the village fields, provided neither the status of ownership nor even necessarily the control of income produced. The farmer contracted with and paid the husband and not the wife for the family's labor.[104]

Moreover, there was little in the off-season jobs available to them that would advance the status of Hispanic women either in the Hispanic or the Anglo society. The winter occupations open to women were even more limited and poorly paid than those open to Hispanic men. Only about one-tenth of the Chicanos with winter wage work were mothers, and while the men with winter employment averaged sixty dollars a month income, the women averaged half of that.[105] Domestic service, the largest category of jobs open to Chicanas, paid as much as ten or twelve dollars per week in Denver, but Maria Chavez remembered cleaning houses for fifty cents a day in the beet areas of Wyoming.[106] And not all employers looked kindly on Chicana domestics, as one Spanish American girl, a United States citizen working her way through school, recalled. "A woman to whom I applied for work when I first came to x———— said, 'People of your nationality are just terrible; I can't stand them, they're so crude, lazy, and so uncultured.'"[107] Denver was filled with women of other ethnic groups, including Italians, Norwegians, Swedes, and Danes, who also looked to domestic service as their most likely employment.[108] Yet possibly as many as half the resident Chicano families had one female member who performed domestic service at some point, usually as part of a family earning strategy, and the practice of taking in laundry was almost universal among widows.[109]

It was to escape both beetwork and the necessity of seeking low-paying and onerous domestic work that young Chicanas sought education.[110] Girls ran into the same obstacles to education as affected all Chicano children, and received neither more nor less schooling than boys from kindergarten through high school, but advanced education was particularly important for girls.[111] As studies of other ethnic groups have shown, girls lacked access to apprenticeships for skilled manual trades that did not require more school. They aspired instead to teaching and clerical positions. Both positions had long provided an acceptable occupation for middle-class Hispanic women and a route to social mobility for Hispanic villagers, male and female. Clerks received at least twice the pay of domestics, and even rural elementary teachers in Colorado received $163 a month by the end of the decade.[112] But both of these professions required education beyond the eighth grade. Only 8 Chicanos and 7 Chicanas were in Denver's public junior and senior high schools in 1925, and although the number climbed rapidly, to a total of 95 boys and 79 girls by 1930, in that year only 5 percent of Colorado's gainfully employed Chicanas worked as teachers, clerks, or in other professional and managerial positions.[113]

Even Chicanas who managed to obtain teacher's certificates found the north an uncongenial environment for job seeking. One Anglo freshman told an aspiring Spanish American girl, "If I were you, I wouldn't waste my time here for they'll never permit girls of your race to teach in our American schools."[114] Chicanas in northern Colorado found that even Denver lacked the Hispanic infrastructure necessary to provide more than a handful of clerical jobs. In Greeley no Hispanic clerked in the stores until after World War II. And Weld County, at the end of the decade, had only one Hispanic teacher.[115] Neither Denver nor smaller towns in northern Colorado could provide the complement to the narrowed arena of the beetfields, as Trinidad had for the mining camps.

Neither would the efforts of Americanizers help much in broadening horizons or advancing the status or centrality of Chicanas in northern Colorado. While Santa Fe and Albuquerque schools began to place emphasis on achieving independence and office skills for Chicanas, Fairview School in Denver, according to its president, was "placing special emphasis in its work with Mexican girls on homecraft, domestic science, care of the home and etc."[116] The sentiment there seemed to echo the common wisdom of the time regarding minorities, that "the Mexicans show considerable aptitude for hand work of any kind," as one educator phrased it, and that "girls should be trained to become domestic servants, and to do various kinds of hand work."[117]

Handwork, not office work, was seen as suitable labor for Hispanic women, and early echoes of the nascent Anglo impetus in New Mexico to "revive" Hispanic crafts did reach northern Colorado.[118] The "distinct artistic value" of some pieces, along with the belief in genetic Chicana aptitudes prompted one welfare worker to aver that it all went "to prove that Mexicans are worth salvaging."[119]

The "Mexicans" themselves often proved less enthusiastic about handcrafts. "In the Campfire Group," reported Flora Leavitt of the Garfield Welfare Association in regard to Chicanas, "the young girls are especially restless. They are not ready to apply their energies to bead work, or even sewing, for more than a few moments at a time, but enter into groupwork in dancing and singing, with great enthusiasm."[120] As Chicanas in northern Colorado continued to suffer a relative, though possibly decreasing, deprivation of educational opportunities and a channeling of education into manual labor, and as they found few if any office and teaching posts available to them, the occupational structure of their labor force continued to reflect not their own aspirations, but the low-skilled and low-paying profile of Chicanas elsewhere in the Anglo southwest.[121]

As increasing numbers of women entered the labor force throughout the country, they experienced the same sort of segmentation of their labor market as had men. Different jobs held different status, and access to education coupled with discriminatory hiring practices could divide the female labor force along ethnic and racial lines.[122] Middle-class Anglo Americanizers in northern Colorado as elsewhere participated in this division by seeing Chicanas as they had for years seen "dependent" and other "inferior" females of any race, as the ideal solution to the "one phase of woman's work we seem incapable of handling, that of the large class of women, who, as domestic workers are in our homes."[123] These Americanizers, like social workers with other immigrant groups, displayed a desire to mold the behavior of women from another culture into standards acceptable to but not identical with their own middle-class, "American" standards and aspirations. They trained domestic servants and "mothers," not professionals. They continued to believe that in mothers they beheld "the channel through which to raise the standard of community along all lines."[124] And what better way to train Chicanas in "American" mothering than by encouraging them to meet the demand for domestic servants?[125]

Religious Americanization work also targeted mothers. It too, emphasized home care. But Protestants and Catholics focused more on the community than on the workplace, and strove actively to involve the women. In this largely woman-to-woman cross-cultural contact, Americanizers saw themselves as liberating Chicanas from their isolation. A Woman's Christian Temperance Union volunteer English teacher in Denver's Colfax area visited Chicano homes to reach "the mother of large families," a "slave and prisoner" in her home because she spoke no English.[126] Presbyterians established two or three "Houses of Neighborly Service" in northern Colorado which replicated many village mission patterns; residents visited "the Mexican women" and invited them for English language study.[127] Catholics, too, decided that women held the key, and the Mexican Welfare Committee of the Colorado Knights of Columbus gave rosaries "to women on their promise that they will gather two or three families into their homes at least one evening a week to recite it." In ignorance of the religious structure of the village, the committee claimed, "[W]e make them leaders."[128] In 1927, its first year of welfare work, the Denver Deanery of Catholic women also "decided to concentrate on Mexican Welfare," and set up a clinic and two "social centers" which resembled settlement houses. Striving to provide a community center, they sponsored boys' and girls' clubs, glee clubs, English lessons, and classes on sewing, household care, laundering, table service, sick care, wise spending, and physical culture.[129]

This Americanization, although still bound by a somewhat one-dimensional view of Hispanic womanhood, was at least softened by a new sensitivity. Even the fictionalized versions of Hispanic life that emerged from this effort more closely resembled the truth than those from New Mexico a decade and a half earlier.[130] Robert McLean, in charge of Spanish-speaking work for the Presbyterians, warned that "Mrs. Garcia resents it when a 'home visitor' comes to her little house, and makes friendly observations, however kindly, upon the subject of home-making, care of babies or personal hygiene!" But Mrs. Garcia, McLean continued, was eager to learn English and was willing to sit through domestic messages embedded in language lessons at the teacher's home.[131]

As it had in the Hispanic villages, the assumption that women functioned as cultural bearers, that "the mothers frequently furnish a key to the situation" and so determine cultural survival or acculturation, ensured women, both Anglo and Chicano, a central role in the sphere of Americanization. They would comprise both target and teacher. But what had Chicanas to gain from the interaction? Learning English in and of itself would neither change their position from marginal to central in Anglo society nor return them to the center of Hispanic society; and neither would improved domestic care. Just as it would take more than isolated women missionaries to Anglicize New Mexican village culture, so it would take more than isolated English, home, and health-care lessons to transform impoverished and transient women into an integrated, stable, multiethnic or even simply Hispanic community. The role of cultural transmitter remained, but it was a role on the margin of each culture, at the intersection between them, and so provided centrality in neither.[132]

As Hispanic women and men moved north permanently, the variety of occupations open to both was narrower than in the Hispanic south, and in this way both men and women suffered a narrowing of their territories.[133] Despite the common loss of opportunity, however, as with cross-cultural contacts elsewhere and involving other cultures, relations between cultural groups at this point of the regional community impinged on women's and men's possibilities differently.[134] In northern Colorado, Hispanic laboring men found some compensation for the loss of both their village functions and the variety of opportunities in the approximation of a subsistence wage. Moreover, their traditional but previously peripheral sphere of dealing with external groups and a cash economy was now paramount. The women, on the other hand, lost their economic autonomy.[135] The few jobs open to women paid far less than a subsistence wage. Without the neighborhood and kin relations of the village, and with the older children in school or at work, child care became elusive or expensive.[136] The centrality of the Chicanas' traditional realm, that of intra-village relations and continuity, the barter economy, and the church, had dissipated with the village.[137]

Both men and women suffered from narrowed opportunities, but the men's purview, in a permanent life on the Anglo frontier, had gained weight within the Chicano society, while the women's lost it. Contrary to what many sociologists and other observers believed, this marginality of women in the Chicano society was not something the Chicanos had carried with them from the villages, but was the result of adapting to life in a new, Anglo setting.[138] In a sense, this development was an Americanization of gender roles, one echoing the experience of United States women during nineteenth-century industrialization and that of immigrant groups at the turn of the century. The institutions of female authority—the church, the garden, non-wage work, and the family—became for Chicanas as they had become in Anglo society, increasingly peripheral to the main concerns of subsistence in a centralized, male-dominated cash economy.

While their relationship to Anglo society became an increasingly vital force in altering relations between the sexes within their own culture and society, it is less clear whether and how it altered roles within Hispanic marriages. Both partners still participated in decision making and voted in elections when eligible. Women still asserted their right to full knowledge and often mutual control of financial matters. Men and women continued to marry at the same ages they had in the Hispanic villages, and age differences between spouses were more, not less, concentrated at the lower end of the range, from zero to four years.[139] But the changes in the larger, less intimate social framework wrought by Chicano-Anglo relations threatened ultimately to penetrate these family bonds.

With Chicanas unable to recreate the stable village core that sustained social harmony in the villages, and with Chicanos marginal economically and socially to the Anglo community, it was unclear what sort of community Hispanics could create on the northern Colorado frontier. Indeed, Anglos tended to be pessimistic about the ability of Chicanos to adjust to life in northern Colorado at all. Inheriting a legacy of disdain for seasonal workers and migrant laborers, which labeled their relationship to farm labor as "excrescences upon its fair face," Anglos were disposed to agree with a Weld County sheriff that "a Mexican is a 'natural born liar, thief, and gambler.'"[140] Visions of lawless and irresponsible hordes, visions unanchored by statistics, floated in the public imagination.[141] The colonies were seen as potential dens of iniquity, where "the dancing girl and the wine-cup are star attractions."[142] Their inhabitants appeared in local papers almost solely in criminal context, with their ethnicity prominently featured.[143]

Chicanos did commit some crimes. Most involved petty theft—stealing from coal bins—or revolved around prohibition: moonshining and drinking and selling liquor, activities popular among Chicanos in both New Mexico and Colorado, but hardly peculiar to them.[144] Anglos, however, even those with the most direct contact with Hispanics, consistently and greatly distorted the scale of lawbreaking. The official line held that prosecution of Chicanos accounted for three-quarters of Weld County court cases. An investigation in 1924 revealed instead that even including appearances as plaintiffs, Chicanos accounted for only 6 percent of the total county court cases and 10 percent of the justice of the peace cases, a figure not disproportionate to their number in the county's population.[145] Conspicuous in their "otherness" and their poverty, Chicanos found themselves subject to these myths and to arrest, according to contemporary investigators, "without a clearly defined case or cause against them." Where a fee system ruled, constables and other officers whose income depended on fines and costs advised their victims to plead guilty.[146]

In terms of relief and family stability, fears had also exaggerated the reality. Hispanic divorces in Weld County occurred at a lower rate than either Anglo divorces in that county or Hispanic divorces in southern Colorado or New Mexico.[147] Few Hispanic children spent time in either the state home for dependent children or the state Industrial School for Girls.[148] And the proportion of relief accounted for by Hispanics, while slightly greater than their proportion of the population at large, remained well under 20 percent, less than the proportion of Hispanics among the lowest-income groups. On the whole, concluded one investigator, impoverished Anglos in northern Colorado "indicated a much poorer social adjustment proportionately than did the Spanish-speaking group."[149] It is possible that, after northern trauma, divorcées, single and deserted mothers, and delinquent children all fled back to the Hispanic homeland. It seems more consistent with the evidence, however, that despite frequent migration, low income, and severe discrimination, solidarity and not disorganization characterized Chicano families in the Anglo north. These families proved stronger than the forces which buffeted them on the edge of the regional community.

It may have been, in fact, the regional community which bolstered this strength. Most of the migrants retained close ties with their more southern villages or home towns. "Kinship webs," as economist Paul Walter called them, extended along the routes of migration. Almost half the Chicano miners in northern Colorado, whether born in New Mexico, Colorado, or Mexico, sent part of their pay to their parents back home in regular monthly installments.[150] And over one-quarter of the wives of married northern Colorado Chicano miners still resided in southern Colorado, New Mexico, or Mexico.[151]

As an instrument aiding them in their day-to-day interactions with the Anglo world, however, Chicanos found this regional community had certain limitations. Parteras, for example, operated best in person, not through correspondence. And while some Chicanos resident in the north continued to participate seasonally in the communality of the villages, for many others low wages, a journey of several days by wagon, and the poverty of their village kin put such a long-distance mutual sharing beyond their reach. A fairly high degree of illiteracy further encouraged the migrants, despite their homesickness and itineracy, to seek a substitute community in the north, and by the end of the decade many Chicanos spent consecutive winters in highly concentrated clusters or colonies.[152] There they started to erect for themselves a new community less dependent on their village ties, one consonant with their new situation, their lack of land holding and of females as food producers, and their wage dependency.

As the Hispanic presence became more established, the coal camps, the Hispanic section of Denver, and the beet colonies all became foci of Chicano communities whose inhabitants' social needs were met from within rather than from the villages of the regional community.[153] Of these, the Chicano enclaves in Denver, growing in size and becoming more stable during the 1920s, were among the largest and most articulated. When Arthur Maes's father died in 1927, the second winter after the family had come from New Mexico to northern Colorado to work beets, his mother was unable to survive in Fort Lupton. She took the family to Denver where they had spent the previous winter, as she "knew the community in the Bottoms," and it was the only place she had any friends.[154] Whereas other towns in the area had at most one Hispanic realtor or cleaner to represent the community in the business world, Denver had tamale shops, some family stores, and the occasional scion of an upper-class New Mexican, southern Colorado, or Mexican family.[155] Yet even Denver hardly compared in the scale of its Hispanic community to Trinidad, and the majority of its Hispanic residents were seasonal laborers.

Like many of the coal camps, the Chicano sections of Denver were distinctly unlovely. Robert McLean and Charles Thomson described one in 1924 as "a district which looks as if both God and Denver had forgotten it . . . the mongrel off-spring of a deserted village and a city slum" with "no paving, sidewalks, no sewers."[156] Nevertheless, the concentration of Chicanos made possible some early attempts at organization on ethnic lines, including not only the Anglo sponsored missions such as Jerome Park Mission and the First Spanish Methodist Church, but the Sociedad Protectora, a mutualista in the Lawrence Street area originating in 1921, the Cruz Azul for Mexicans, the Spanish-American Club—a cultural association whose president was a former Mexican consul—and the Spanish-American Citizens Association, the latest of these organizations and one which in 1931 intended to organize the estimated 15,000 Spanish American citizens in Denver and the vicinity for industrial, political, and social justice in all public affairs.[157]

Denver was not unique. Larger than other enclaves, its Hispanic communities garnered more elites and Anglo attention, but they shared many of the same strategies and problems as the colonies and barrios across northeastern Colorado. The nascent Chicano community in the north was not yet entirely centered on a single site, despite the hostility of the environs. And while many Hispanics in northern Colorado wintered in Denver, more lived outside it, and many moved from winter to winter among the towns, the company colonies, and the city and had, by the late 1920s, relatives scattered across the area.

First erected in 1924, the Great Western Sugar Company's beet-labor colonies soon became not only the more stable clusters the company desired, but, like Denver, centers of Hispanic community organizing. Unlike Colorado Fuel and Iron, the sugar company allowed its control to lie loosely on these colonies. It retained the right to dispossess undesirables as long as it held the leases, and it contributed to church and community buildings, but the colonies were not closed camps, not located at the workplace, and not polyglot. Within them, colonists bought not just houses, but the land on which they stood. And ironically, their very isolation from Anglo society helped foster their development as something more than transient labor camps.[158]

As with racial and immigrant enclaves elsewhere, the colonies' homogeneity relieved some of the pressure to assimilate. Residents had, as one investigator found, "their own favorite dishes," and no one encouraged them "to abandon their native language for American."[159] Though economically dependent on the Anglo world, they retained, as had the villages, some social and cultural autonomy. Here, perhaps, those who did remain year after year could re-create the regional community in truncated and more vulnerable form. The barrio could be a new core.

By the late 1920s, some colonies increasingly resembled the interrelated villages. Chicano couples met and courted there, among the "meticulously tended lawns, and the watered and swept earthen patios," that one colonist remembered. They held dances and even fiestas in the colonies.[160] The women, recalled one early settler, "had their own clubs," and sewing, cooking, mutual aid, and church groups, and in January 1930, it was their efforts, in part, which culminated in a new Pentecostal Assembly of God Church built by colonists in the Greeley colony.[161]

From this more cohesive base, colonists and other settlers began to shift to more aggressive strategies in intercultural matters. The regional community, with its migrant patterns, was in some sense a strategy of retreat, as was the high turnover that embodied Chicano protest at conditions in beetwork.[162] In the same vein, Mexicans consciously decided against citizenship, rejecting the second-class status they believed it would bring. A Mexican in the South Platte Valley declared, "To hell with the United States. We don't have to be slaves in Mexico."[163] But as retreat to the villages became increasingly impracticable and more stable communities evolved, direct protests occurred. At least one Chicano in Weld County filed a civil rights case in 1927 against Greeley restaurant proprietors who ejected him on the grounds that he was a Mexican.[164] World War I veterans among the colonists also early asserted the colonists' rights in the community at large in regard to voting and discrimination. Their membership in local American Legion branches provided virtually the only organized non-charitable social link between ethnic groups and bolstered their legitimacy as spokesmen in each.[165]

As the sense of neighborhood in the colonies grew, resistance began to take more collective forms. Chicano boycotts in Greeley and Johnstown led to the removal of discriminatory signs from the shop windows, at least temporarily, in 1927. Though less successful, a committee of Chicanos also protested the establishment of separate school rooms for Chicano children.[166] By the end of the decade, like Denver, the colonies and mining towns had their own Hispanic groups and mutualistas. Some accepted both Mexican and Spanish Americans, others only one or the other.[167] Some of the colonies even organized into self-governing bodies under commissioners of their own choosing. In 1928 the Greeley colony, for example, drew up "articles of association for the management of colony affairs," including police and sanitary regulations, and filed them with the county police.[168] This was, perhaps, the ultimate declaration of an autonomous community on the Anglo-Hispanic frontier. These Hispanics created room for themselves and committed themselves to permanent residence without committing themselves to assimilation.

It was, nonetheless, the coal-mining communities, as they struggled through the violent I.W.W. (Industrial Workers of the World) strike of 1927, that gave the spur to the first sizable collective organizing effort among Chicano settlers in northern Colorado. The limited occupations available to these Chicanos and the shared social position of the vast majority blurred the lines between organizing on an ethnic and on a class basis. This strike both integrated Hispanic miners more thoroughly into the mine workers' community and led to the formation of new Hispanic strategies and adaptations, much as the strike at Ludlow, Colorado, had done further south.

The roots of Hispanic participation in the strike lay in the coal industry depression of the early 1920s, which hit the older, less efficient coal mines of southern Colorado particularly hard. With conditions worsening, Hispanics headed for the newer coal mines of the northern part of the state, in particular, the still rapidly expanding Rocky Mountain Fuel Company's Columbine Mine in Weld County. As the decade progressed, the fact that northern miners could work more days in the year and suffered fewer fatalities than those of the south outweighed for many Chicanos the discomfort of smaller tunnels, greater seasonality, and the frustration of less occupational mobility. Chicanos continued to come to Columbine from coal mines in New Mexico, southern Colorado, and Mexico.[169]

Organized labor in the form of the A.F.L. (American Federation of Labor), and individual Anglo miners was less than enchanted with the migration. The *Colorado Labor Advocate* criticized the importation of Chicano labor and the A.F.L. worked to limit it. Chicano miners themselves, according to one Anglo ex-miner, "got beat [physically] so bad it's not even funny."[170] In this context it is not surprising that although miners recognized common interests across ethnic lines, and respect for the Chicano miner grew as he proved himself "a damn good union man," within the union miners organized, as the I.W.W. traditionally had, on ethnic lines.[171]

In 1927 in Colorado a miner with three children needed approximately $1,680 for a minimum standard of living. In Weld County he received an average of $1,251.60.[172] State laws regarding safety and determination of pay were not enforced, and the union not recognized.[173] In August 1927, eight years after they started organizing in the Colorado mines, the I.W.W. led a four-day statewide strike protesting the execution of Sacco and Vanzetti. The success of this strike encouraged them to undertake a new statewide effort in October under the same strike committee, composed of a Mexican, a "Spanish," a Greek, an Anglo-American, an Italian, and a Negro member.[174] By mid-November, one estimate had 10,000 of the state's approximately 12,500 miners out on strike.[175]

In regard to the southern fields, the press claimed of the I.W.W., "practically all of [them] were Mexicans."[176] In the northern fields, Chicanos participated in the strike on both sides, though less prominently. As at Ludlow, class and ethnic lines crossed and neither proved a consistent predictor of behavior. But here it was the aftermath, rather than the strike, that carried the greater significance. After violent clashes including law officers firing into an unarmed crowd at Columbine, in February 1928 the strikers voted to return to work.[177] Most miners gained a slight increase in wages as a result of the strike, but for Chicanos in northern Colorado, more importance lay in the strike's impact on beetworker organization and the recognition of a larger community of interests among Hispanic workers, something possible only in an increasingly stable community.

What followed the strike revealed the crucial role Chicanos in an industrial work force could play in the adaptation of the Chicano community to a new site where there were no Chicano small farmers, police officers, or elected officials, as there had been in southern Colorado and northern New Mexico, to mediate, lead, manipulate, or provide support.[178] As over half the Chicanos at Columbine worked beets in the summer, it is not surprising that the I.W.W. strikers at a Fort Lupton rally of nearly two thousand miners in November turned to the beetworkers for supportive action. Chicano farm laborers in the state had engaged in small individual actions before, and might have been receptive, but now they were scattered on the ranches and the harvest itself was almost over. They had neither the cohesion nor the leverage for effective action. It was thus also not surprising that at first little came of the pleas.[179]

The organizational effort among beetworkers met with more success, however, as Chicanos gathered in the towns and colonies for the winter. One I.W.W. organizer claimed in January 1928 that "numerous groups of beetworkers requested the I.W.W. to send organizers into the field," and thousands of copies of the organization's *Solidaridad* were distributed.[180] Simultaneously, in a part of Weld County further from the coal fields, Chicano beetworkers who vigorously denied affiliation with the radical I.W.W. formed groups of their own, demanding the right to organize to better the conditions and ensure the pay of beetworkers. They hired an Anglo attorney, and published demands in the Greeley paper. Their spokesman, Lauro Valdez, himself clearly the product of the growing Chicano community in the area, had a real estate office in Greeley and worked as an interpreter of the court.[181] By the end of January 1928, the I.W.W. claimed to have founded fourteen beet-labor locals in Weld, Larimer, and Boulder counties, with 1700 members, and the unaffiliated organizers claimed at least three additional groups within Weld County.[182] In these organizations, ethnic and class lines were merging.

Although disputes between growers and the company led to a reduced acreage and so a reduced need for beetworkers, making 1928 an inauspicious moment to inaugurate a labor organization, the beetworkers continued to organize. The A.F.L. joined the effort at the end of the year with its own experienced Spanish American organizer. Local beetworker unions springing up in Colorado, Wyoming, and Nebraska claimed over 10,000 members, and when they were brought together in 1929 as the Beet Workers Association, two hundred delegates of widely varying political philosophies attended the Ft. Lupton convention.[183]

As the decade came to a close, this infant umbrella organization, like the incipient Chicano organizations in California, was plagued by insufficient funds and by an ever-enlarging labor surplus, but it also provided a base of unity and experience that would prove most useful as the Great Depression wreaked its havoc on the regional community. In search of an effective alternative to the strategy of retreat to the villages, a means by which to pursue their interests individually and as a community on the Anglo frontier, Chicanos in northern Colorado in the 1920s, as they had a decade earlier in the southern Colorado mining camps, turned increasingly to class, with or without ethnicity, as an organizing principle. They turned to a strategy that relied less on retreat and ties to the village and more on ties within a newer community on the margin of the Chicano-Anglo frontier.

At the end of the 1920s, Colorado was still the outer sphere into which Hispanics moved but which they did not dominate.[184] The nature of this Anglo-Hispanic frontier was apparent from both sides. Churchman Vernon McCombs explained in 1925 that "since the real 'Border' is more racial than geographical, it is the line of racial contact rather than the Rio Grande which must be crossed to reach the Mexicans."[185] The Anglo-Hispanic frontier had not been limited to the international border set in the mid-nineteenth century, but had moved ever north with the continuing expansion of Hispanic settlement.

Anglos in the 1920s, however, tended to deny that Chicanos on this frontier of limited contact and social mobility were "true pioneers." "Our frontier builders," insisted McCombs, "worked much harder."[186] Unwilling to accept that their democratic West could be responsible for creating a permanently marginal class of citizens, Anglo investigators of every sort in the 1920s fought their own evidence and sought instead to explain the persistent marginality and low status of Chicanos in terms of culture and not economics.[187] Paul Taylor, for example, after revealing the changing economic structure of beetgrowing areas which had made it more difficult for Chicanos than it had been for German-Russians to buy farms, and after having uncovered discrimination and de facto segregation, low wages and the vulnerability of Chicano labor, concluded:

> but these explanations are wholly inadequate as a complete account of the disparity of economic progress of the three ["American," German-Russian, and "Mexican"] groups. The cultural gap to be bridged is greatest in the case of the Mexicans. They do not bring with them from their culture and class . . . the ambition for individual acquisition of property, and the foresight necessary for its accomplishment.[188]

Similarly, Theodore Rice, unsatisfied with his own conclusion that inadequate income had placed many Chicanos on relief, felt obliged to posit "a general tendency on the part of dependents to allow the charity of the community to make up for the adoptation [*sic*] to their needs rather than seeking to remedy this basic weakness from their own effort."[189] In its function as an explanation of persistent inequities, culture tended to be defined, like race, as virtually immutable, as a static and not a dynamic phenomenon. This line of thinking encouraged a brand of pluralism, manifested in differentiated educational plans and standards, that was stultifying and resigned to acceptance of the status quo.

Taylor's and Rice's analyses required the communal ethos of Hispanic villagers to share the blame for continued poverty with economic causes and discrimination. But in so doing they ignored the delicate balance of the villages, which had always provided room for individual property ownership—livestock, farmland, money—within a communal structure of jointly owned grazing land and water resources. Cultural strategies of the Hispanics may have played a role in their marginality, but that role was not lack of ambition and foresight. On the contrary, the migrant system of the regional community which, in its heyday, permitted Chicanos to move in and out of the Anglo economy at will, had proven attractive precisely because opportunities were so limited in the Anglo sector, as well as because the Anglo mix of private wealth and community responsibility appealed less than their own. Yet in part that very ambition for acquiring property was what sent villagers far afield on colonizing, trading, and laboring forays.

As Chicanos began to build their colonies and enclaves in northern Colorado, it was clear they had a different picture of the forces at work against them. While the Anglos placed renewed emphasis on cultural difference, Chicanos began to focus instead on their economic and social position. Within ten years of the end of the war, the migrants had begun, like immigrant groups elsewhere in the nation, to erect not a replica of village life nor a distorted reflection of Anglo society, but a Chicano community adapted to their own needs and marginal political, social, and economic position in their new environment.[190] They adapted their culture to their present circumstances. The organizing principles of the new communities came increasingly to include, in the late 1920s and early 1930s, not simply the kinship, church, and mutuality of the villages, but wage labor.

Yet an emphasis on wage labor within the community further diminished the centrality of Hispanic women. On the periphery of the regional community, economic realities had helped move Hispanic women to the margin of Hispanic society just as Anglo definitions of community placed Hispanics as a group at the margin of Anglo society. Anglo Americanizers, often unintentionally, helped reinforce this new marginality of women by steering them to low-paying jobs when they steered them to jobs at all, and emphasizing the duties of the home. As inferior wage-earners in an almost entirely cash economy, Chicanas found themselves in a world which to a greater and greater degree limited their role to the home and eroded their former power bases of garden, neighborhood, and church. Their dilemma mirrored that of a New Mexican woman who had grown up on her grandfather's farm, encouraged by him and her uncles "to do everything they did." She found that her father, who had worked in San Francisco during the war, had acquired Anglo ideas and a narrower vision of womanhood: "He wanted me to take home economics. God, I hated home economics. I wanted to take industrial arts. . . . But I couldn't take industrial arts. I had to take home ec."[191]

Anglo attitudes and economic structures helped keep Chicanas and Chicanos marginal and transient in the north as the benefit to Chicanos of remaining outside the Anglo economy rapidly diminished. In addition, with little compensation for the loss of their village power bases, Hispanic women in the north could not replicate the stable productive core of village life. Chicanos in the north thus had no local refuge; they had only the increasingly inadequate Hispanic village core or wage labor. This situation spurred them to seek new strategies, which resulted in a panoply of Hispanic organizations: unions, mutualistas, and political lobbying groups. This new community already differed greatly in its sexual and economic structures from the villages at the other end of the regional community. But the two were still connected. Their members together would generate new strategies of survival on the Anglo-Hispanic frontier to meet the turmoil of the 1930s.

7

The Depression,
Government Intervention,
and the Survival
of the Regional Community

A Great Western Sugar Company spokesman labelled 1929 the "worst year in beet history." Things would not get better for a long time. That year an early freeze cost some growers nearly all their crops and some laborers all their wages. Drought and the national Depression took over where the freeze left off. In 1930, Colorado harvested 242,000 acres of beets. Five years later, it harvested only 140,000.[1] Four-fifths of the beetgrowers in the Arkansas Valley had gone bankrupt, and beet farms on the South Platte were sold for taxes or were repossessed.[2] The demand for beet labor in Colorado fell more than 45 percent. Anglo growers tended their own beets, if they still had any, or hired newly eager Anglo laborers. The largest single source of employment in the villagers' regional system threatened to disappear.[3]

But even for those who had it, employment was no guarantee of survival. New contracts demanded that beetworkers bear more of the risk; employers defaulted on old contracts, and wages plummeted. Wages in northern Colorado beets fell from $27 an acre in 1930 to $12.37 in 1933.[4] In 1934, the median family earnings came to only $250 a year. The reduced cost of living absorbed only a small fraction of the decline.[5]

162

It still took about $1000 for a family of five to survive. Workers had to seek government or private relief even while they worked beets.[6]

Chicanos kept pace with the upward spiral of those unemployed and on relief in Colorado as it rose from 9,093 families on federal emergency unemployment relief in October 1932 to 56,461 the following February.[7] Even the Hispanic strategy of a multi-source income could not save them from the depredations of the Depression. Other agricultural wages fell, railroads let their maintenance slip, and the coal mines of both northern and southern Colorado hired fewer men for fewer days each year.[8] Those who had broken out of these traditional occupations found no refuge. Chicano construction workers, factory hands, truck drivers, waitresses, musicians, and even representatives of the few Chicano clerical workers in northern Colorado also suffered from unemployment.[9]

As the Depression attacked the nation and eliminated Hispanic jobs, it threw Hispanics back on the resources of the Hispanic village heartland or on the communities they had managed to erect on the northern edge of the Anglo-Hispanic frontier. It tested the vulnerability of Hispanic communities both in the villages and on the periphery, and it called into question the efficacy of the strategies Hispanics had evolved. The regional community could not survive such an onslaught unchanged.

As Anglos and Hispanics struggled to control developments and relations on the Anglo-Hispanic frontier, they generated new forces, new strategies, and new adaptations. By analyzing first the breakdown of the regional community strategy and of the village as refuge, and then turning to new strategies emerging in Hispanic communities, and finally examining the impact of government policies on job and sexual structures and on Hispanic culture itself, the way in which the intersection of these often competing strategies and cultures shaped the future of the cross-cultural region becomes clear.

"People on the farm were better off than downtown," remembered a Hispanic woman who lived in northern Colorado during the Depression; "we had our gardens." In contrast, she remembered "an aunt in Fort Collins, they were living on the soup line; we could hardly visit them because they barely had enough for themselves. . . . [W]e would go after meals. They felt bad."[10] The few farmers who still hired Chicanos rarely let them winter on the farm. As a result, more than half of northern Colorado's Chicano beetworkers joined the unemployed Chicanos wintering in towns and cities. Almost none had cash or gardens, and all had to pay rent.[11]

Relief seemed the only hope of obtaining the income essential to the survival of the local Chicano communities and the larger regional community linked to them. It was far from perfect. Private agencies often collapsed under the relief load. And even after the federal government stepped in, its Works Progress Administration never absorbed all the unemployed. Moreover, its relief appropriations tended to provide only a portion, often less than half, of what people needed for subsistence.[12]

As opportunities for subsistence evaporated, the north became an ineffective part of the regional community. Fear of losing their resident status and so losing any relief benefits immobilized some Chicano families, but individuals and families with fewer children or with land to the south sought refuge from unemployment and new competition by retreating to the Hispanic villages of southern Colorado and northern New Mexico. Most of them would not venture north again for nearly a decade.[13]

The Depression disrupted migration patterns and strategies Hispanics had followed for ten, fifteen, and even twenty-five years. Only the skeleton of the regional migratory pattern survived. Villagers continued to visit relatives established at the perimeters of the regional community. A few men still managed to find work herding sheep or working beets in Colorado or Wyoming, and their wives, like one woman near Embudo, New Mexico, were considered "fairly well off."[14] But it was not enough. In the 1920s the 14,000 Hispanic families in northern New Mexico's Upper Rio Grande Valley sent seven to ten thousand individuals north for work each year. In the early 1930s, they sent only two thousand.[15] Those sent earned only about one-third as much as they had before. Persistence led to disaster for Hispanics who exhausted their credit on job-seeking in the north and found no jobs.[16] With such reduced participation, the framework of the regional community could survive, but the original function of the regional community, Hispanic village survival and autonomy, was less secure.

Two actions in particular reinforced the retreat to the villages and underscored the loss of Chicano control over the dynamics of the regional community: the repatriations in the early 1930s and the 1936 Colorado border closing. In 1929, the federal government attempted to increase its control over Mexican immigration. It enhanced penalties for illegal immigration, enlarged the Immigration and Naturalization Service Border Patrol, and adopted "administrative restriction": the more rigorous enforcement of existing laws. But pressure for legislated restriction continued unabated, like the Depression; three Mexican-quota bills appeared before the House Committee on Immigration in the spring of 1930.[17] As economic conditions further deteriorated, destitute and stranded Chicanos became increasingly visible on relief rolls. Impatient local social-service agencies took matters into their own hands. From 1930 to 1935, with and without the aid of local Mexican consulates and Mexican funds, relief agencies in Colorado engineered the departure of approximately 20,000 Mexicans and their often United States-born children. Across the Mid- and Southwest similar actions sent approximately 400,000 Chicanos to Mexico, "repatriating" them.

Whether the majority left "absolutely voluntarily," the victims only of "homesickness" and unemployment, or whether they felt the force of "polite coercion" via threats of removal from welfare or even deportation—both views documented and held by contemporary observers and historians—whole communities disappeared from Colorado and elsewhere. The movement south stood in stark contrast, at its peak in May 1932, to the years of a healthy regional community, when each May had witnessed the greatest number of Chicano arrivals.[18]

Much to the chagrin of the relief agencies and county commissioners, Chicanos continued to appear and reappear on county relief rolls in northern Colorado. "It was agreed and understood that these people were to remain in Mexico," complained the Weld County Board of Commissioners to the Commissioner-General of Immigration. But, contrary to the promises of the labor importers in the 1910s and 1920s, the Chicanos refused to disappear when unwanted.[19]

The solutions offered by taxpayers and politicians became more extreme as sugar, sheep, and railroad companies continued to recruit Hispanic labor in New Mexico, despite the growing number of Chicanos on relief. By March 1935, Governor Johnson of Colorado was proposing to round up all aliens in the state and deport them himself if federal immigration officials would not. Two months later, he ordered alien beetworkers out of the state and had local sheriffs in southern Colorado turn them back at the New Mexico border. Despite a protest from the Mexican Ambassador and the blatant illegality of his actions, Johnson merely increased the effectiveness of his policy. The following April he called out the National Guard and declared martial law along Colorado's southern border.

United States citizenship afforded Chicanos no protection from Johnson's blockade against "aliens." Spanish Americans as well as

Mexicans found themselves under arrest, as a group at Colorado Springs did—even one hundred miles inside the state—and they numbered among the over five hundred would-be laborers turned back by troops in the next ten days. Twelve Spanish Americans from northern New Mexico's Abiquiu and Peñasco were taken from a train, loaded in trucks and dumped out on the prairie at the New Mexico line. Hispanic reactions at the border, according to an Albuquerque newspaper report, "ranged from tears to indignation."[20] The regional community had been cut in half.

Other states had closed their borders to block Anglo dustbowl migrants, but both those who favored and those who opposed Colorado's action labored under no illusion as to the targets. "We are right behind you," wrote a Mr. and Mrs. Williams to the Governor, "in your move to keep the Mexican race out of our state." Anglo employers beseeched the governor to end the blockade, as it kept out the "Mexicans from New Mexico" on whom they relied for herding, lambing, harvesting, and section maintenance.[21]

Before the blockade, Spanish Americans had asked the governor for protection against the importation of alien labor. They favored deportation and voiced resentment over the presence of Mexican aliens on relief rolls.[22] The actual blockade, however, was another story. While Governor Johnson's administration insisted that the blockade protected "the Colorado Spanish-American working class as well as all of Colorado labor" by reducing the labor supply, Spanish American loyalties were not bound by state lines.[23] As the blockade continued, and stories of Spanish Americans suffering harassment surfaced, more conservative Hispanic groups and individuals in New Mexico and Colorado joined the radical Spanish Speaking Workers League in protest. They had wanted to shut out aliens, but they resented having "citizens of this government turned back and refused entry to the state of Colorado merely because they were of Spanish descent." They resented both this denial of Spanish American membership in the United States polity, and the arbitrary fragmentation of the region. Even the Beet Workers Union, local no. 20,190 of Greeley, whose Anglo vice president had spoken at first in favor of the blockade, joined the opposition.[24]

Spanish American outrage in Colorado and New Mexico helped end the blockade, but Hispanics were powerless to repair the migrant webs. The blockade had been an effective if illegal symbol of a more permanent problem. Few Spanish Americans tried again to cross the border even after the departure of the National Guard. In terms of demography and economy, the regional community had become more its parts than their sum.

The Hispanic beetworkers who participated in what contemporary observers called "a wholesale retreat . . . to the villages and their land," knew that their four or five acres of irrigated land held the promise of only an inadequate livelihood, but they also believed that these acres held "a house and a garden spot that would help cushion the shock from the collapse of practically all demand for their labor."[25] In the event, the cushion proved none too soft. The winter of 1931/32 brought to northern New Mexico unprecedented snows that left livestock marooned, frozen, or starved to death. The melted snow provided welcome moisture, and optimistic farmers planted accordingly, but hailstorms and grasshoppers destroyed much of the crop. Then began a prolonged drought, the worst the area had ever suffered, according to one agricultural extension agent.[26] Renewed vigilance on behalf of the Pueblo Indians led, in addition, to the transfer of some range land from villages to Pueblos and to increased stringency regarding pasturage quotas for other Indian land previously used as free range.[27] Clearly a retreat to purely pastoral activities would not suffice.

In those areas of northern New Mexico less affected by the drought and less dependent on livestock, returning migrants increased their cash crops and began selling their produce directly. During a peak month in 1930, joint trucking ventures and roadside booths brought a total of three thousand dollars to Rio Arriba County farmers. All too soon, however, the market for their chief commercial crops, chili and apples, collapsed from increased competition.[28] As state relief agents reported families in the county "verging on starvation," Rev. Julian Duran concluded, "None of the products our people have to sell are worth very much." As one resource after another failed the villagers, Duran trenchantly observed, "[T]here is a heaven and a hell to economics, as most of us have found out since 1929."[29]

The failure of cash-earning alternatives within the villages intensified the impact of the regional community's collapse. Before the Depression, village migrants had earned two million dollars a year. In 1935 they earned only about $350,000.[30] By mid-decade, 60 percent of the Spanish Americans in northern New Mexico villages were receiving government aid. In some villages every family appeared on the relief roll.[31] Tax delinquency rose from 32.4 percent of the levy in 1928 to 65 percent in 1932.[32] As more Anglos from Texas and Oklahoma drifted into the villages in the early 1930s, they brought with them the specter of Hispanic dispossession.[33]

The villages had proven unequal to their role as refuge. Returning migrants found themselves in much the same straits as those who had settled permanently in the north. Only the larger economy of the regional community had sustained the villages as a viable retreat for Hispanics. With no demand for their labor, the villagers could not retain control over their interactions with the larger, Anglo-dominated economy. Family networks had not disappeared. They still aided their members through adoption of children and exchange of produce, and passed on information about jobs and relief. But the demands of a cash economy exposed the limits of networks dependent entirely on what were now non-cash-earning families.[34] Relief proved as poor a substitute in the villages as it did in northern Colorado. Agencies, both public and private, ran out of funds. The Red Cross stepped in only in cases of crop failure, not of monetary shortage, and where many land-owning villagers at a single site claimed need, relief agents tended to view them with great suspicion.[35] Villagers adamantly asserted their rights. They held mass meetings to protest ethnic discrimination and planned to march on the bank when threatened with foreclosure. They protected their core as best they could, and neither mortgaged nor sold vital, irrigated lands and gardens.[36] But the Depression severely curtailed their power to assert, protect, and control. Like the Hispanics in the north, they would have to find new strategies of autonomy and survival to replace the regional community.

Chicanos in New Mexico and Colorado, stranded when the high tide of 1920s' prosperity ebbed, headed for cities and towns. They joined the seasonal laborers evicted by farmers for the winter, but they stayed in the city year round. In Denver, for example, the number of Chicanos trebled during the 1930s while other groups remained static.[37] These urban Chicanos retained village mores, much to the exasperation of welfare workers. They shared what relief they received among kin and other community networks, and Hispanic stores that grew up within these communities came to rely, as had those in the villages, on the relief orders of their clientele. Church membership and participation rose, accompanied by a proliferation of sects that reached into the villages.[38]

The new, relatively sedentary population in Denver and on the edges of rural towns reinforced the stable core emerging in northern Colorado's Chicano settlements in the 1920s and as lines to the villages frayed spurred an increasing sense of local community. These communities, like the ones in the southern Colorado coal camps and the 1920s beet colonies, were different from the villages. They were even more vulnerable to tides of the larger economy because they lacked a separate economic base, however insufficient. But they served other functions, provided other kinds of support and collectivity, as the shared relief and church membership implied.

Stability, though not necessarily entirely the product of choice, had benefits. Despite reports throughout the region that Chicanos lacked sufficient clothing, shoes, paper, and pencils, and despite the need for children's labor to provide additional income or child care for working mothers, increased stability led to increased Chicano enrollments in schools not only in northern Colorado, but in southern Colorado and northern New Mexico. As in other parts of the nation among similar groups, lack of wage-earning alternatives for the children, free school lunches, and the warmth of school buildings may all have played a role in greater enrollment. More children throughout the country went past the fifth and even the eighth grades for the first time. The proportion of enrolled Chicanos who were in Denver's senior high school, for example, rose from less than 2 percent in 1930 to over 5 percent seven years later. In Rio Arriba County, New Mexico, the Spanish American high-school enrollment almost doubled between 1933 and 1935 alone.[39] For Chicanos, however, the greater school enrollments and persistence did more than reflect greater stability. They meshed with a determination to gain broader opportunities within the Anglo society and economy as the retreat to the Hispanic world of the villages became less and less beneficial or even possible.

This determination together with the increased size and stability of urban settlements also intensified the 1920s' trend toward a more formally organized, assertive Chicano community in northern Colorado. Mutualistas, lobbying groups, and unions grew.[40] Whereas in the 1920s a lone individual had initiated a civil rights suit, during the 1930s an organization was formed to file lawsuits against public discrimination. And the Spanish American Citizens Association now had branches throughout southern and northern Colorado. It endorsed and bargained with political candidates, cooperated with organized labor, held mass meetings, and defended the rights of Chicano workers. In 1933 its Denver membership totaled 1100, and in 1934, its annual convention hosted one hundred delegates.[41] Adapting to the fragmentation of the regional community, Chicanos reorganized along lines suited to their new economic, social, and political dilemma.

Even non-labor organizations usually had some connection with labor or saw their interests as allied, but as in Texas and California, Chicano labor organizations particularly grew, both in membership and in activity. Communists—who adopted a resolution late in 1930 to form local Agricultural Workers Unions across racial lines—and the A.F.L. worked to organize and stimulate the grass-roots upheaval among beetworkers that had resulted, in part, from the disruption of the regional community and from Anglo attempts to manipulate movements within that community. Together, they built on the beetworker unions formed in the late 1920s and made the agricultural labor movement in Colorado second only to that in southern California as the most active of the decade.[42]

Chicanas joined Chicanos in the unions and protests of the 1930s. Though they did not achieve the prominence of Chicanas in cities such as Los Angeles and San Antonio, with a large female semi-industrial sector, they joined the attempt to redefine the terms of their northern existence. Hispanic women in New Mexico and Colorado addressed union rallies of miners and beetworkers, joined picket lines, and went to jail. Some politically active Hispanic women lobbied for better wages; Mrs. Mauricio Trujillo of Gardner and Mrs. Aurelia Sanchez of Frederick agitated in W.P.A. unions, and Helen Lucero organized against police brutality in Denver.[43] For these women, mutuality of interests between the sexes and in occupational patterns overcame a tradition which placed interethnic contact in the male sphere, and their actions returned these women, even in northern Colorado, from the margin to the center of community life.

Myriad difficulties beset any attempt to organize Chicano beetworkers. Though at least one Hispanic beet local moved with its constituents from Walsenburg, Colorado, in the winter to Vale, South Dakota, in the summer, few were so successful in maintaining contact with workers. Even when they wintered in the north, beetworkers usually changed residence during the beet season. In addition, in most areas in the 1930s, Anglos as well as Hispanics performed beet labor, and ethnic tensions arose within mixed and between rival ethnically-based locals. Moreover, members often lacked the money for dues; hostile city and county officials canceled scheduled meeting places and jailed union leaders, whom they designated as outside agitators, on charges of vagrancy; and neither the sugar companies nor the growers admitted responsibility for bargaining with labor.[44]

Despite all these difficulties and several particularly low points, at least some locals, many of which remained independent throughout the decade, agitated each year. Conferences attempting to build ever larger and more effective coalitions at the state and national level convened in Colorado with great persistence. In 1930 a beet-union conference hosted 200 delegates with a Colorado constituency placed at 7500 workers. Six years later, a conference of 120 delegates appointed committees to meet with the growers, the company, and W.P.A. officials. In 1937, the movement culminated in a broadly based national convention in Denver from which emerged the United Cannery, Agricultural and Packing and Allied Workers of America (UCAPAWA) under a C.I.O. (Congress of Industrial Organizations) charter. At least ten of the one hundred delegates represented the purported 8000 Colorado beetworker members.[45]

The persistence of these organizational efforts, like the political organizations and mutualistas, measured the declining effectiveness of the regional community as a viable strategy. As avenues of retreat and aid were cut off and Chicano beetworkers formed increasingly permanent communities in the north, they sought newer, more confrontational organized means, such as these unions, to gain some control over their conditions and interaction with the Anglo economy and society.

Beet unions demanded wage increases, an end to growers withholding pay, and that the sugar company guarantee payment of wages by the growers. Beyond these monetary items, the unions sought adequate housing, drinking water, and garden plots large enough for a family food supply. They also demanded the right to conduct all negotiations where the majority of the laborers belonged to a union, and non-discriminatory work relief and hiring policies.[46] Together these demands would have increased the economic base for Chicanos in the north until it more nearly approximated that of the Hispanic villages in the south, and increased their control over their environment.

They seldom won any of these demands from the growers. Yet although they threatened almost every year, only in 1932 did they actually strike.[47] It was perhaps the legacy of this strike that prevented them from repeating it.

In response to massive wage reductions in early 1932, a new beetworkers' committee called a strike for May 16. The United Front

Committee represented a coalition under radical leadership of the sur-
viving politically and ethnically varied grass-roots beet locals in Colorado, and it attempted an unprecedented scale of organizing to culmi-
nate in the first state-wide beetworkers' strike. Mass meetings were held
the Sunday before the strike, and the following Monday carloads of Chicano organizers toured the beetfields. They persuaded quite a few of the
workers to declare themselves on strike and to walk off the field. Some
accusations of intimidation were made but none were confirmed. As in
the 1920s, the areas near the coal mines in Weld County, the Chicano
clusters on the edges of rural towns, and the beet colonies contained the
most enthusiasts. Coal-mining areas had the most exposure to union
organizing in the mines. Clusters and colonies—more permanent Chicano settlements—shared the most homogeneity in ethnicity and class,
and there a sense of neighborhood, of common interest, had grown
deepest.

Many Anglos claimed the strike leaders were outsiders. Weld County
and Greeley officials and the press labeled them "oily tongued" communists and agitators from Denver. But four of those jailed on May 17
for investigation of such charges turned out to live in Greeley's own
Hispanic colony. The twenty-four Chicanos arrested three days later not
only were local, but represented, with six women and ages ranging from
22 to 73, a wide sector of the Chicano community.

As the strike continued, tensions rose. Deputies began to patrol beetfields in the coal-mine section of the county. When they arrested seventeen more Chicanos and one Anglo on the twenty-first, strike leaders
protested at open-air meetings. The Greeley Hispanic colony, a union
stronghold, hosted a Communist party meeting. These colonists felt
themselves pushed further and further outside the Anglo community.
Farmers armed themselves, and "squads of deputy sheriffs and volunteers" arrested unarmed "rioters." Repatriations also continued, and
strike leaders were jailed for twenty to thirty days. A Communist journal claimed that 18,000 beetworkers had gone on strike in Colorado.
But by May 30, the fields were quiet, the beet tenders were back at work,
and none of their aims had been achieved.[48]

The strike was plagued from the beginning with more than arrests or
red-baiting. Even before the strike began, the *Greeley Daily Tribune*
reported that "local men were free with the prediction that for every
man that joins the strike there would be two to take his place," and at
least one farmer replaced his troublesome "Mexican" beet labor with
"Anglo-Saxons." And beyond that, the area the strikers attempted to

cover was too wide, too difficult to police, and their resources too small, the Hispanic settlements too vulnerable. The union had promised food during the strike, but failed to provide it, and in the northern enclaves there was no alternate source of wages or subsistence.[49]

Of course the failure of the strike did not mean that Chicanos found labor organizing a useless strategy, a useless alternative or addition to the retreat to the villages. At least eight Hispanic beet-labor locals survived in Colorado into the 1940s. And the leftist Liga Obrera de Habla Española, or Spanish Speaking Workers Union, established with the aid of the I.W.W. in the Colorado beetfields in 1928, also survived. It retained branches in Denver and other parts of northern Colorado. And it even reached the remote Hispanic villages of the Upper Rio Grande, traveling with its members along the now fragile routes of the regional community to become the largest lay organization there.

Although its members undertook no regional action, the Liga exemplified the way in which the region's Chicanos used their labor organizations most effectively in the 1930s: as pressure groups. It had branches also in Gallup, Las Vegas, and Santa Fe, New Mexico, and became increasingly demonstrative and political. In 1935 the Liga's eight thousand New Mexico members succeeded in defeating a New Mexico criminal syndicalism bill. And two years later members occupied the New Mexico governor's office.[50] In the villages, Hispanics saw the Liga as powerful enough to force its demands on political authorities, to gain for the villagers more relief and work projects, and so they flocked to its standard.

In Colorado the beet-labor unions lobbied with some success for their constituents. In 1933, beet-labor leader Leo Rodriguez of Fort Lupton hitch-hiked to Washington to testify on low wages and child labor. After the 1934 Jones-Costigan Act extended the Agricultural Administration Act to cover sugar beets, Rodriguez and other union leaders petitioned for on-site hearings and represented beet labor at those hearings. They also kept pressure on the federal government and relief officials between the invalidation of that act and the passage of the Sugar Act in 1937. They policed the enforcement of wage determinations and policies, and kept beet-labor conditions before the public eye.[51]

Despite their inability to force a settlement on the beetgrowers or the sugar company, Chicanos had achieved at least a limited measure of success in creating a strategy for confronting the Anglo economy that did not depend on the survival of the regional community. As the efficacy of the ethnically based regional community declined, Chicanos in both Colorado and New Mexico turned to a more class-based solidarity.

The unions, the growth in school enrollment, and the burgeoning organization of Chicano settlements in northern Colorado all pointed to a Chicano effort to replace the fragmented regional community with other means to achieve some control over their fate. But federal intervention as well as interference on the local level limited this new effort. In a context of general economic disaster, overstretched budgets and unrest, when faced with the enhanced militance of the non-disappearing "Mexicans" and the potential threat to order from the increasingly radical nature and pervasiveness of their unions, local, state, and federal governments, too, adopted new strategies. Repatriations, state border closings, and Immigration and Naturalization Service investigations of Liga members were only the most obvious.[52]

A contributing factor in the formation of government policies was the ongoing tension between Anglos and Hispanics, a tension exacerbated by the economic crisis as the two groups became rivals for scarce resources.[53] While increased enmity and growing urban concentrations did lead to some new efforts to reduce these tensions—for example the Denver Interracial Commission's adoption of the issue in 1935—many Anglos throughout Colorado and New Mexico, in company with many Spanish Americans, blamed the nation's ills on the Mexicans. Unlike the Spanish Americans, however, the Anglos continued to confound Chicano citizens with Mexican aliens.[54] After all, had not "Mexican" officially been designated a race in the 1930 census? It was not a matter of citizenship. Mexican and Spanish American alike were now "Mexican." The "White Trade Only" signs which still graced shop windows in Greeley, Fort Collins, and other cities excluded all Chicanos—both Spanish American and Mexicans. Public recreation facilities were occasionally segregated, clubs almost always so, and some towns did not allow Chicanos to build or live within their borders. The Ku Klux Klan again demonstrated in sugar-beet towns; handbills that warned "ALL MEXICANS AND ALL OTHER ALIENS TO LEAVE THE STATE OF COLORADO AT ONCE BY ORDERS OF COLORADO STATE VIGILANTES" floated over not just Mexican neighborhoods but the Spanish American colony in Greeley in 1936.[55] The pervasiveness of Anglo hostility toward Mexicans and, by association, Spanish Americans, emerged fully when a 1940 questionnaire distributed to 915 junior and senior high school students in a "representative" Colorado county elicited the information that 31 percent of the students would not grant Mexicans United States citizenship, 35 percent would not allow them in the same school room, and 42 percent not in the same church. Forty-eight percent would not accept a Mexican as a friend, 69 percent would not accompany one to a social function, and 94 percent would not marry one.[56] These tensions were not, however, geographically limited. Even in the heavily Hispanic areas of New Mexico and the San Luis Valley, Chicanos faced similar problems.[57] Hardship had clearly not made the Chicano and Anglo communities as one.

The universality of the hostility portended a more or less uniform attitude across the region regarding Chicano employment and relief. Employment agencies, public and private, encountered difficulty placing their Chicano clients because, as they reported, "an employer will often refuse to take a Spanish-speaking person unless a special effort is made by the placement officer." The jobs Chicanos found tended to be on public relief projects or in poorly paid domestic work.[58]

Hispanic dependence on public works projects, in turn, led Anglos to label W.P.A. projects in the Arkansas Valley "Mexican Projects," and the state sales tax, the "Mexican bonus."[59] It seemed to some that Chicanos actually received preference over Anglos for work relief. This possibility appalled Anglos who saw Chicanos as un-American. "Keep our Americanism," pleaded one irate Fort Collins citizen who reported that the "Mexicans" would not or could not "speak American."[60] Colorado's Spanish American heritage had made no impression on these Anglos. An outraged Rocky Ford resident posited that the relief load in the Arkansas Valley town was half Chicano; "[T]he skunks," he warned, "are claiming now that they were born in the United States."[61] If Chicanos, wherever they were born, however persistent, were not to be part of the United States polity in the prosperity of the 1920s, they certainly would not be admitted during the Depression.

Many Anglos, including relief officials, took the less overtly resentful line that relief was actually damaging to Chicano recipients. Freddy Falogrady, secretary of the National Reemployment Service in Las Animas County, a county one-third to one-half Spanish American, revealed that "the greater number of those receiving relief are Spanish Americans, and the Chairman of our relief committee feels, and we believe justly so, if these people are not held down to the minimum of help from Federal Relief, they will settle down to live on the country for the rest of their lives and it will be impossible to persuade them to work even when conditions are better."[62] Continuing to label local Spanish Americans in the same way they had for at least thirty years, as "childish" in their attitude toward money, passive, complacent, resistant to progress, and incapable of any but common or manual labor, Anglos in Colorado and New Mexico saw government relief as reinforcing these tendencies which, many believed, lay at the root of Hispanic need even more fundamentally than did the Depression. "Before the advent of the WPA," claimed a naïve Anglo graduate student at the University of New Mexico, "the people of Rio Arriba County were on the whole self supporting. . . . Since the inauguration of the WPA there has been a noticeable decrease of small farms and an increased dependency on the relief agencies." Other Anglos were dismayed to find that once Hispanics discovered the possibilities of relief, they demanded food, medical care, and clothes for the children. "I believe they could easily become quite inclined to beg," concluded one teacher.[63]

Along with this sense of the peculiar moral vulnerability of Chicanos went a greater fear on the part of some Anglos that the existence of relief work endangered the survival of that facet of the regional community which served Anglo employers. It threatened the reliance of Hispanics on beet, railroad, and sheepherding labor and to destroy the region's system of low-wage labor. "All Mexicans who refuse to work in the beet fields," demanded a Denver Anglo, "should be cut off from *all* relief. We have coddled them entirely too long and they think they have us bluffed."[64]

Indeed, beetworkers did try to exploit this new opportunity to better their condition. Year-round government work relief allowed increased stability, a highly desirable condition since the decline of the regional community. Beginning in 1934, however, federal policy was to remove potential beetworkers from relief rolls in the early spring, several weeks before beetwork began. Harry Hopkins, in charge of the Federal Emergency Relief Administration, explained that after "very careful consideration" the administration had concluded the policy was "necessary in order to overcome the reluctance on the part of these people to move off relief rolls when employment does become available."[65] Yet Chicanos knew that the end of the beet season would find them again in need and with no certainty of regaining work relief or any other employment. Forcing these workers to migrate for seasonal labor threatened their local relief status as residents; it also meant either a return to abbreviated school years for their children or leaving their families behind for work at wages lower than those the work relief paid, wages too low for year-round survival. Nor could these workers rely, as they had earlier, on village kin to make up the difference. Contrary to popular Anglo opinion, observers found among villagers and ex-villagers "general dissatisfaction with remaining dependent upon the generosity of the Governmental agencies," but in a situation where it required the work of four family members for an entire season—from May to early November—to equal the annual wage of a single worker on relief work wages, Chicanos, particularly those with small families, resisted being forced to accept jobs in the private sector at less than subsistence wages. The increasingly organized Chicano workers attempted to use their work relief jobs to allow them to survive while pressuring growers and other employers for higher wages.[66] They resisted being forced to participate in an Anglo version of the regional community's migratory labor which held few benefits for Hispanics.

In the interests of stability and of maintaining the status quo ante, however, government relief agencies could not allow themselves to be governed by sympathy for the beetworkers' new strategies. Hopkins added to his explanation a warning: "The Relief Administration cannot take part in any efforts to influence the wages in such fields which are outside its own Work Division activities." In the years following, as federal work relief directors continued to drop beetworkers long before beetwork became available, they reiterated that they were "not interested in the terms of the beet labor contract offered by farmers."[67] Administrators publicly ignored the effect their timely removal of workers had on the bargaining power of those workers, and argued that springtime reductions in W.P.A. rolls affected all states and all ethnic and racial groupings. But in Colorado, at least, the greatest impact of those reductions fell on the Chicano workers, and covert discrimination in this area was recognized by all parties, however often they publicly denied it. Terry Owens, District W.P.A. Director for Pueblo, Colorado, confided to his regional administrator, "I cannot help but feel that our procedures in this matter have been eminently fair and intelligent," but, he admitted, "the fact that other nationalities are not acceptable to the sugar beet farmers may be interpreted as racial discrimination." Paul Shriver, on the other hand, as state W.P.A. director, was "not particularly proud of the way in which it was handled." "Men were laid off on the assumption that they were beet laborers," he explained, "because of their names—Spanish and Mexican."[68]

The federal government adopted as the official view the myth that only Chicano labor would or could perform beet and other underpaid work. What had been a convenient rationale in the private sector for the continued importation at low wages of Chicano workers in the 1920s now became a government rationale for reducing the work relief load. Equally important, the government's adoption of this rationale perpetuated and legitimized discrimination on ethnic lines already prevalent in northern Colorado's labor market. By April 1937, when the beetworkers were at the height of their organizing, the W.P.A. of both New Mexico and Colorado had already agreed, in conference with the sugar companies who threatened to return to active recruitment of out-of-state labor, to "make available" qualified beet labor.[69] With federal manipulation of relief jobs governing the ebb and flow of migration and the wages received, the government was perpetuating the migratory and economic aspects of the regional community at the same time that Hispanics were rejecting them.

Chicano individuals and organizations protested these relief policies. Spanish Americans demanded, "Why should only the Spanish Americans be sent when they like the rest have been born and raised right here in the United States?" And one World War I veteran bitterly complained that "only in times of war and during elections are we noticed . . . after that we have no country or no flag." A sympathetic but powerless Paul Shriver explained, "We have to work this thing out realistically. We are working under a capitalist system in this country." The W.P.A.'s Director of Labor Relations in Washington added, "The law is on the side of the sugar companies and there is nothing we can do about it."[70]

The Jones-Costigan Act of 1934 could be seen as a compromise between the government's rigid relief policies and the laborers' demands. It stipulated that in order to receive full benefits, a grower had to pay beet labor in full; the Secretary of Agriculture could set minimum wages in the event of a dispute; and the growers had to accept the Secretary of Agriculture's decisions as adjudicator. In 1935 an amendment was passed that restricted the use of child labor. After an initial year of confusion and indecision, rates for 1935 were set at $19.50 per twelve-ton acre, a great increase over the $14 of the previous year, though less than beetworker's demands. But the Sugar Act passed in 1937 to replace that which the Supreme Court invalidated the previous year lacked the provision empowering the Secretary of Agriculture to enforce a minimum wage or to adjudicate disputes between growers and labor.[71]

In the absence of wage-enforcement power, the act had less to offer the beetworkers. Even the child-labor provisions proved a mixed blessing. In 1939 child labor in northern Colorado declined to 12 percent of beetworkers' children aged six to fourteen, as compared to 73 percent in 1920, and, as a result, children stayed in school for more of the school year. But a social worker at the Greeley Hispanic colony explained the drawbacks: "By the time the fathers employ men to do the labor which the children used to do, the money is out of the family and the children do not have the food, clothing, and warmth that they used to have."[72] Wages rose slightly after 1937, but each spring, 78 percent of beet families found themselves living on store credit, 11 percent on relief, and 4 percent on advances from the grower. Thirty-eight percent still ended the season with no cash on hand after settling bills.[73] Federal action taken via the Sugar Acts may have restored conditions to the status they had before the Depression, but it had not improved on them. Through both its relief policies and the Sugar Acts the federal government had sustained the economic structure of the regional community and had hindered any attempts, whether Chicano or Anglo, to alter the relations it imposed.

In the same vein, New Deal jobs programs reflected less the aspirations of Hispanics than the old order Hispanics were trying to escape. While alterations in power dynamics and resources on the Anglo-Hispanic frontier encouraged Hispanics to depend less on their enclaves and more on winning a better and more permanent place in the larger society through such avenues as unions and education, New Deal jobs programs had their own definition of Hispanic improvement. The New Deal's focus on improvement within the confines of the old order, in the name of stability and neutrality, like their relief policies regarding beetworkers, frustrated new Hispanic strategies and aspirations. The conundrum appeared with particular clarity with regard to gender.

As it did elsewhere and for other women, the New Deal's jobs programs tended to reinforce older labor patterns rather than to create new patterns for Hispanic women. Trends that had begun in the 1920s as a result of greater school attendance and political opportunities continued. By 1937 Hispanic women teachers in Rio Arriba County outnumbered the Hispanic men at last. And the ranks of Hispanic clerical and health workers increased.[74] Hispanic women in Hispanic culture areas also continued to be politically active. (At least five Hispanic women were in the New Mexico state legislature in the 1930s.)[75] A substantial village could still support a few teachers, a seamstress, a laundress, a postmistress, and a midwife, and women still maintained their own bartering economy; they worked in each other's fields, plastered, and traded fruit and vegetables. Packing, sorting, and stringing chili brought a cash income to many women, and a few others ran family stores.[76]

In the 1930s, as they had before, however, particularly landless and urban Hispanic women faced limited cash-earning opportunities. Plagued by discriminatory hiring practices of stores and offices, lack of education and English, poverty, and increased Anglo competition, they could make little headway in improving their labor-market choices. In the cities a few worked in canneries or as waitresses. But for the rest, earning cash still meant taking in laundry or doing domestic service, and many women did both.[77]

Across the nation, women beset by declining alternatives and dis-appearing incomes sought housework, and the proportion of employed women in domestic service went up during the 1930s for the first time in this century. Chicanas were part of the trend and suffered from it. Sixty-five percent of unmarried Chicanas between the ages of fifteen and nineteen worked outside the home both in suburban Albuquerque and in Denver, almost two-thirds of them in low-paying housework or cleaning. Even in the villages it became increasingly common for a daughter or a mother to do housework for wages. Prospective employ-ers continued to greet them with both distrust and the expectation that they would work for a lower wage than other domestic servants. And the relative difficulty with which employment services placed Chicanas bore out that Chicanas in Denver, at least, seeking wage-work in increasing numbers, continued to find the market for their labor even more constricted than for Hispanic men or for Anglo women.[78]

Into this fairly static picture came the New Deal's work programs. As in other states, the work programs became embroiled in state and local politics, triggering a constant barrage of angry and contradictory letters from Hispanics and Anglos, males and females alike. But although Hispanic politicians did exploit these new opportunities for patronage, Hispanic men and women, even in areas of Hispanic major-ities, remained underrepresented in these programs at all levels. A work project in Rio Arriba County, for example, a county 90 percent His-panic, had no Hispanic supervisors. Although Hispanics numbered an unusually high 35 percent of the project's 45 skilled workers, they com-prised 87 percent of the 139 unskilled laborers.[79]

Hispanic women, too, found that New Deal jobs programs offered them less than it offered their neighbors. A few Hispanic women partic-ipated in sexually mixed work projects, and at least two rural school projects employed women plasterers, but the director of women's work in New Mexico, Helen Dail Thomas, felt obliged to apologize "that we have so few purely women's work projects to report." The paucity was not, in her view, her fault, or that of the program. "During the summer, practically all of the women are busy working in the gardens," she explained, and, in any case, "our native women are not good sewers."[80]

The most fundamental reason New Mexico lacked work projects for Hispanic women, however, lay beyond either gardens, often suffering from drought in any case, or ignorance of needlecraft. It lay in the same perspective which differentiated relief needs of Anglo and Hispanic beetworkers. Margaret Reeves, New Mexico State Relief Administrator in 1933 and 1934, baldly replied to a query sent by Ellen Woodward, Director of Women's Work in Washington, "I do not believe that there should be many more women working in New Mexico, nor many more projects for women than we have at present. You may know that seventy per cent of the population of this state is Spanish-speaking. . . . I feel that women projects are better adapted to Anglo-American communities and to industrial areas." While Reeves claimed to have made a "special effort to help the man of the family to employment," she insisted that Spanish American mothers, because of the large families, (somewhat exaggerated by Reeves) were "badly needed in the home." Apparently Anglo mothers, in her view, were not. Sympathetic observers, while recognizing the declining resources of the villagers, also believed that Hispanics were habituated to a less expensive diet and standard of living than most Anglos and so, in their view, "needed" fewer of the scarce dollars relief directors had to spend.[81]

Although Reeves and Thomas both soon disappeared from the scene, Woodward continued to find New Mexico's Hispanic women's projects inadequate. In late 1936, for example, spurred by complaints received from women on sewing projects, she questioned "most emphatically whether we should sanction part-time employment, even in New Mexico where the situation in connection with the Mexican women is quite unique." Woodward was not blind to the racial issue. "It seems to me," she explained to the regional director at Salt Lake City, "that when we did not lower the standard in the southern states where the problem of the negro women is so acute it was a great pity to discriminate against the Mexican women in New Mexico." But Woodward bowed, in this instance, to the greater authority of the woman on the spot, Mrs. Andrews, who contended that the W.P.A. program's wage, which could reach fifty-five dollars per month in urban centers, lured women from their private employment at three to five dollars per week or fifteen cents per hour. It led to "far more women certified than it would be possible for us to work if we worked them full time." Part-time employment, with its reduced wages, she argued, would not only lessen the incentive to leave other low-paying jobs, but would increase the number of women the project could reach. Andrews insisted that though a few had complained, the majority of women preferred the new arrangement as it gave them more time at home. As with the relief policies of Colorado in regard to beetworkers, the aim was not to change the economic structure, but to sustain it.[82] And by giving more cash-earning jobs to men, the New Deal sustained a pattern where village men, preferring work to relief and desperate for cash, left the gardens and irrigated lands in the hands of women. For landless, unmarried, and urban women, however, the Anglo and male bias brought few rewards.

This is not to deny that New Deal jobs programs offered desperately needed employment and some lasting benefits to Hispanics. New Deal agencies provided modern technical and professional training for some Hispanic men and women, and hired a few Hispanic men and women to administer extension programs among Spanish Americans. In general, however, New Deal programs, when they placed Hispanic women at all, tended to channel them, as they did minority women elsewhere, into traditional or marginal occupations. In rural areas, crafts projects that employed both men and women were often seen particularly as a way to produce added income for the difficult-to-place women.[83] In urban centers, besides the ubiquitous sewing projects and despite the fact that some young Hispanic women earned as little as fifty cents a week doing housework, W.P.A. officials argued for and won household-training projects. Mary Isham, State Director of Women's Activities for Colorado in 1935, contended, "[W]e have many girls from Spanish speaking and negro families whom we greatly desire to do something worthwhile for in the way of permanent training." The most suitable permanent training for Chicanas seemed to Isham, as to others in previous decades, training for domestic service, though Chicanas disliked the work so much that the programs went begging for candidates.[84] Even the National Youth Administration, which sometimes offered training in office skills, had most of its Hispanic female participants in Colorado and New Mexico making quilts and mattresses, cleaning, and in domestic training. George Bickel, Assistant State Director of the W.P.A. for Colorado, justified this use of N.Y.A. funds as appropriate to the future he foresaw for San Luis Valley's Hispanics. "Many of the valley's youth," he claimed, "have little to anticipate in life save an existence of peonage. The average Spanish-American girl on the NYA program looks forward to little save a life devoted to motherhood often under the most miserable circumstances." Heading neither for higher education nor industry, such a Hispanic girl, Bickel argued, "must have opportunity to learn and work in a program of sewing, budget management, commodity usage, and personal hygiene." For the boys, too, Bickel envisioned the future as static in terms of occupational mobility: "these boys will be sheepmen, tenant farmers, laborers and craftsmen. Our challenge is to help them from relief to self sufficiency in these fields." What Bickel and his New Deal cohorts seemed to want for Chicanos and Chicanas, as one Nambé Community School teacher expressed it, was "to improve but not to change" conditions. But the stipulation of stasis frustrated evolving Hispanic strategies and limited the improvement that such New Deal programs could achieve.[85]

Federal relief and employment policies principally affected the economic structure and migratory patterns of the larger regional community. They rarely entered directly into the internal cultural dimension of specific Hispanic communities. But as during World War I, the government and the public were no longer indifferent to what happened in the village. Other government and private services brought the New Deal home to village and enclave. With it they brought the potential for enormous benefits in education and living standards, but they also brought a cultural contest. The Depression had undermined villagers' control over the dynamics of the regional community; it now directly threatened their control over their cultural development.

New services assailed Hispanics on every side. For the first time since World War I, many remote Hispanic villages in New Mexico and southern Colorado and many Hispanic colonies in northern Colorado received visits and technological advice from agricultural and home demonstration agents, from county, state, or Children's Bureau healthcare personnel, from W.P.A. recreation advisers, and from literacy-program teachers whose sympathies became apparent when they included in beetworkers' English lessons, sentences such as "we came here as persons of equal rights" and "the unemployed workers have no money to buy what the machines produce." Programs increasingly hired Hispanics to teach Hispanics, and the Denver Junior Consultation Center, funded by the N.Y.A., W.P.A., Adult Education, and Y.W.C.A. in 1936, appointed a Mr. Gilbert Martinez "to act as counselor (under supervision) for Spanish and Mexican youth." In addition, Catholics founded new mission stations in Fort Collins and other beetgrowing towns; Presbyterians turned increasingly to their Houses of Neighborly Service in the Hispanic areas of northern Colorado cities; and evangelical Protestants began to make headway in the villages. New Mexico also witnessed the inauguration of several public educational experiments supported by private foundations. They ranged from those placing renewed emphasis on the learning of English before the first grade and designed to answer the question "can the intelligence quotient of these children be raised?" to the introduction of the bilingual method in Taos County and the involvement of the entire village in school management and curriculum planning at Nambé. By 1938, sociologist Daniel Valdes could report, "[N]early every person who has even the faintest glimmering of social conscience wants to do something for or about 'the poor Mexicans.'"[86]

Amidst all the excitement and missionary fervor of the agents, both public and private, the impoverished Hispanics did their best to maintain control, to resist pressure, and to select from among the varied messages and services. The New Deal was no monolith. Its agents and those of the other experiments differed among themselves in viewpoint and method. And yet most found the Hispanics anxious for advice and aid on some matters, but, particularly in the villages, skeptical of almost everything the Anglos had to offer.

Hispanics found Anglo notions of agricultural development particularly troublesome. Federal Rural Rehabilitation and Farm Security Administration officers, for example, met with great suspicion. They railed against the villagers' reactionary nature as they unsuccessfully urged them to use their land to secure farm improvement loans. But having lost land put up for collateral on government loans in the early days of the Depression, villagers trusted neither the banks nor the advice. And their experience with Anglo-style agricultural development had been almost entirely negative. Since the commencement of the Santa Cruz Valley irrigation project in the upper Rio Grande Valley, reported one federal survey, "the only land that has been profitably cultivated has been the land that did not come into the irrigation district." And in 1937, two thousand Spanish American landholders, unable to meet bond payments on the middle Rio Grande Valley irrigation project, were spared eviction only by a court injunction. Federal development seemed linked to debt and dispossession. "One old woman," reported rural rehabilitation worker Charles Loomis, "who since the death of her husband has operated her own enterprise with her sons . . . told others that the supervisors were 'out to get the land for the Texans.'"[87] As a substitute for the regional community strategy of temporary entry into the Anglo economy to sustain Hispanic village autonomy and communalism, such development held little appeal. Villagers preferred to take W.P.A. work, even when it meant neglecting their land, as it brought cash with no strings attached.

Designed with the hope of effecting a permanent solution, of making villagers independent of relief and wage labor, development projects were often received by villagers as stop-gap measures of last resort. At the end of the decade, even when federal rural rehabilitation planners approached the village as a unity, villagers were inclined to doubt the permanent efficacy of these efforts. The planners had the cooperation of village leaders, used natural kinship groupings to form cooperatives, and arranged the use of range for the villagers, but it was still not clear to the villagers how their small cooperative ventures would be able to compete with the big livestock enterprises.The village skeptics had a point, as even the Anglo rural supervisors admitted. Village survival without migratory wage labor, one supervisor acknowledged, would require a far more drastic redistribution of land and range rights than could be effected by either the village rehabilitation experiment or the Taylor Grazing Act of 1934, which essentially maintained the status quo.[88]

Private and public welfare workers who reached out particularly to women also found a good deal of skepticism about and resistance to this new Anglo intrusion. Anglo women came into the Greeley beetworker colony to teach cooking and sewing. "I already knew how to cook," a resident recalled, and commented with bitter irony on the recent proliferation of "Taco Bell" fast food restaurants, now serving Anglos the once despised tortillas and beans. Home demonstration agents in New Mexico, both Anglo and educated Hispanic, seemed surprised that suggestions about child care and home decorating elicited resentment and required great tact among women who insisted that they did their best with their meager resources.

These Anglo and Hispanic social service workers in both north and south belonged to the tradition of the women who had gone to the villages decades before. They were missionaries by other names. They saw themselves as organizers and advocates of the women they taught and as inculcators of proper gender roles and values. Home demonstration agent Vernita Conley complained in 1937 that "it is found quite difficult to break down their 'old Spanish customs,'" and her predecessor, Mrs. Ivie Jones, confessed, "[T]he Agent has not yet succeeded in getting the men to plaster the outside of the houses, although she has often tried to persuade them that the plastering is their job"—and not, as the villagers would have it, that of their wives. One such agent even encouraged a promising female Hispanic college student "to major in home economics instead of in business and commerce."[89]

These agents, however, also urged women to come to mixed meetings, encouraged handicraft work as a means of income earning among women, found markets for women's crafts and produce, and fostered the development of women's clubs and women's club leaders. And like the remaining missionaries, nuns, and priests, they became intermediaries. They channeled new services, technology, and knowledge of relief and work programs to Hispanics. New services fit into older patterns of interaction among women of different cultures; the missionaries, old and new, saw themselves not as restricting Hispanic women but as guiding them to areas of proper fulfillment.[90]

The inauguration of several midwife training programs in the late 1930s, made possible in part through federal funds provided under Title V of the Social Security Act of 1935, created the greatest direct intrusion into the women's sphere of the villages. Both the Hispanic birth rate and the infant mortality rate, though falling, remained higher than the national or even local Anglo rates throughout the region. Malnutrition and primitive sanitation received some of the blame for the high infant mortality rates, but many observers blamed "the practice of untrained and incompetent midwives." The new programs cost less than importing doctors, and, though small, deserve some of the credit for the declining infant mortality rate. They also, however, attempted to alter almost every aspect of what had been the village women's system of midwifery.[91]

Despite midwife Susana Archuleta's assertion that "you can't look at midwifery in terms of dollar signs," one investigator reported that "under the Supervision Plan midwives are encouraged to charge their patients from a minimum of $10.00 to a maximum of $25.00." This rate represented two to five times more in cash than they previously had received in kind at the patient's discretion, though still less than a doctor's fee. In addition, whereas the local village women had selected midwives on the basis of their altruism as well as their skill, midwifery training program directors and teachers had their own, more academic, criteria for midwives, and selected them for further training on that basis. They also standardized procedures, gave examinations, and issued certificates over which local village women had no control.

Not all midwives followed this route to the professionalization and monetarization of their craft, nor did they immediately replace their healing lore with the new medical teaching, which they perceived "as different from but no more reliable than theirs." One woman from Ranchos de Taos, New Mexico, did become a full-time midwife, in itself a break with tradition, and added a two-bed ward to her home, along with a phone. But in this example of selective acculturation, unlike the Anglo hospitals and doctors, she provided transportation for her patients and allowed relatives of the mothers to help with nursing, a feature her customers found particularly attractive.

As with other new services and policies of the 1930s, the midwifery supervision plan threatened the cultural autonomy of the villages, in this case of village women in particular. But like most of the other new services, limited funds that in this case allowed the assignment of only a single county health nurse to the program, mitigated the threat as well as the benefits and allowed many of the villagers to continue selecting those aspects of the services that best suited their own view of their cultural development.[92]

Perhaps the most direct intervention in Hispanic cultural development came in the form of the federal adoption of the Spanish colonial arts revival. In this program came together almost all the aspects of the villagers' confrontation with the Depression and the New Deal. It involved federal job and relief policies and Hispanic strategies, and it encompassed the competing views of Hispanics and Anglos regarding the future place of Hispanics in the United States.

In pondering the condition of the migrant Chicano sugar-beet workers, a conference of sugar company, relief, labor, and government officials focused briefly on the Hispanics' reversion, whether in New Mexico or Colorado, to the status of relief recipients after each season. The conference concluded that "some effort is needed to establish this group on the land."[93] The policy of stabilizing agricultural groups on the land had roots in the 1920s and even earlier as the government sought through federally funded agricultural and home extension work to stem the flow of migrants from the farms to the crowded cities. "During recent years it has been realized," reported Juan Ramirez, agricultural extension agent for Santa Fe County in 1929, that despite the lack of urban services, such as electricity and plumbing, "a little increase in the attractiveness of the farm home for its comfort through shade and added beauty aids materially in keeping the family contented on the farm." Increased productivity, food preservation, and home management, it was hoped, would also make the farm family more self-sufficient and compensate for declining commodity prices and rising prices of consumer durables.[94]

During the 1930s, new home demonstration agents in Hispanic counties brought this message and new techniques to the villagers. But in New Mexico and Colorado, a major avenue through which the state and federal governments hoped to render the philosophy of "live at home" a reality was the revival of Spanish colonial arts. In adopting this approach, the government, as it had in regard to labor and migration patterns, again took a largely private and piecemeal program and a popular public opinion—in this case a movement to preserve Hispanic arts and the notion that Chicanos were specially suited to handicrafts—and made them official policy.[95] This particular policy required a federal intrusion into the villages not merely in the interests of bringing Anglo culture and technology, but to supervise Hispanic culture itself.

Hispanic culture, even in the villages, had not remained static. Hispanics in New Mexico and Colorado had instead continued eagerly to adopt those facets of Anglo culture they found most useful. In 1937, a Denver Public Schools investigator who otherwise found little evidence of assimilation noted, "[T]he American point of view that an automobile is an essential item of family equipment seemed to have been accepted by the Spanish-speaking American people." Approximately one-third each of Spanish American and Mexican beetworkers owned cars, while each village in northern New Mexico boasted at least one and many had more than twenty. Anglo employers who preferred less mobile workers may have inveighed against such cars as "unwise and unthrifty investments in a luxury," but the Chicanos used the cars to search for beet and mine work, to buy food in bulk at lower cost, to get hauling jobs in the winter, and to transport themselves to and from the fields, as well as for family recreation and social life in isolated farm areas.[96]

Sewing machines and stoves also continued their popularity of previous decades. In Santa Fe County, the home demonstration agent, Fabiola Cabeza de Baca Gilbert, claimed in 1930 that 90 percent of the women had sewing machines.[97] And the villages had changed in other ways. Many houses now had slanted metal, not flat adobe, roofs; many women wore high-heeled shoes and elaborate hats instead of shawls, danced modern dance steps, got permanents, and occasionally, in urban areas or villages with cars, went on dates while a mildly scandalized older generation looked on.[98]

Even the habits of food preservation changed rapidly as home demonstration agents introduced pressure cookers to the village women. Within the decade, the number of pressure cookers soared from two or three in each northern New Mexico Hispanic county to hundreds. As supplemental sources of income diminished, the garden and its preserved produce became ever more important. Where they could, women sold and traded not only dried chili, cornmeal, pumpkins and other produce, but canned green chili. In Nambé, in 1938, Anglo school teachers noted that while not every home had the coveted "nice linoleums . . . for their kitchens," every home had a pressure cooker.[99]

Commenting on the furnishings of a typical Spanish American home in 1940, Erna Fergusson admitted, "[N]one of this conforms to the taste of precisely today, but," she added, "it has the consummate taste of expressing perfectly the family whom it serves." As they had been at the onset of the regional community, Hispanics remained wary of Anglos and feared losing their remaining lands, but they were eager for knowledge of new technology and language. Almost alone among Anglo observers of the time, sociologist Paul Walter realized that "the effect of increasing resistance to assimilation is not so much to retard the rate of social change as to give rise and support to selective processes by which the group readily acquires some innovations but rejects others." Through their selective cultural borrowing in the 1930s, Hispanics continued to try to control both the acculturation process and the direction their own evolving culture would take.[100]

To most Anglos, in particular to those very Anglos most convinced of the benefits of cultural pluralism, Hispanic-controlled acculturation proved less than satisfactory. They labeled Hispanic choices "naive." They lamented the disappearance of the picturesque black shawls and the appearance of cars. They complained that Spanish Americans "too often choose their styles from the mail order catalogues," and that all that was "genuinely cultural in the social life of the native New Mexican village, has dwindled almost to the vanishing point." And they, as author Mary Austin did, feared that if left to themselves, villagers would become "average installment plan sub-Rotarian middle-class Americans."[101] These Anglos had different aims for Hispanic culture than either the overtly assimilationist Americanizers or the Hispanic villagers, and it did not seem to occur to them that in imposing their own cultural choices on Hispanic villagers they rendered their pluralism, their respect for other cultures and in particular the right of those cultures to autonomous development, at least on this one level, only empty rhetoric.

Anglo sponsors of Hispanic cultural "revival" tended to view New Mexico as artists and authors did since before the turn of the century, as an antidote to modern mechanization, a land of exotic primitivism, pure emotions, and simple truths. In much the same way New York's avant-garde turned to Harlem in the 1920s, New Mexico's literati, clustered in their bohemian colonies in Santa Fe and Taos, turned to Spanish American and Indian arts. The educated elite of both Anglo and Hispanic society lauded "the land of Mañana," where "the Machine Age with its confusion has not deeply impressed us" and where "the luckiest poor people in America" could be seen in "the contented native tilling the soil and idling his leisure time unconcerned and happy."[102] These patrons of the Hispanic arts, themselves artists, educators, and disenchanted millionaires, in their various Anglo art societies from 1915 through the 1930s sought not only to revive native arts, but to revive their own American culture through them. Alice Corbin Henderson, in her poem, "Litany of the Desert," called on northern New Mexico as her contemporaries called on other folk cultures, to "recreate us" after the carnage of the First World War.[103]

The participants in these arts revival movements appointed themselves sole guardians. They saw themselves as rescuing a beleaguered Hispanic culture both for themselves and for the villagers. "We are keeping alive all the beauty and the grace of the Spanish culture," claimed one Anglo artist; "I set the revival of the Spanish colonial arts in motion," asserted Mary Austin.[104] They tended to interpret their discovery of native arts as creation or revival, despite continuous activity and even spread of the arts, such as wood carving and weaving, by Hispanic villagers. José Dolores Lopez began embellishing his carving in 1917, well before the Santa Fe artists "discovered" him. Similarly, Elena Vigil from Chimayo had long before this Anglo-sponsored revival taught men and women in her husband's village of Cundiyo to weave for the market. And Hispanic weavers displayed a canny market awareness throughout the 1920s and 1930s, with or without Anglo aid. Indeed, the Chimayo weavers, long famous, remained outside the "revival" almost entirely, due to their use of commercial dyes and yarns and their access to other markets. Much as women missionaries had exaggerated the darkness of village life to legitimize their mission, these Anglos, to legitimize their role as cultural directors, tended to exaggerate the demise of Hispanic culture.[105]

Because these Anglos believed that, as arts store manager Helen McCrossen put it in 1931, "to some extent native taste has been corrupted by contact with an alien civilization and cheap, machine-made articles," they took it upon themselves to provide "good examples" of "authentic" Spanish colonial art for the purpose of "restoring to the Spanish Americans something of their former expressiveness." And despite their avowed rejection of competition, they sponsored contests which pitted the Hispanic artists against each other to create the most authentically colonial Hispanic art for cash prizes. On similar lines, Hispanic arts benefactor and wealthy Chicago publisher Cyrus McCormick, who claimed that "a nation which neglects home industries loses a large opportunity for self-expression," found that untutored Spanish Americans in Colorado and New Mexico used "atrocious colors, with a design that lacks a great deal of being artistic." In regard to one furniture maker in Nambé, where the McCormicks had a second home, McCormick was "very much afraid that [the artist] was applying too many of his own ideas." McCormick, who disparaged even the most lauded of the revived artists, wanted these artists "to follow accepted models," and warned Mary Austin that "they are not fundamentally assisted by a shop through which their work, which seems to me to be poor, is brought before the notice of an uncritical, jitney public." He, at least, seemed less interested in developing Spanish American culture and self-expression than in pushing it back and holding it, for the benefit of the spirit of the nation, in the Spanish colonial era.[106]

There was a scattering of educated Hispanics involved in the sponsorship of the arts movement. They included such wealthy and prominent figures as Concha Ortiz y Pino, a member of the state legislature from 1936 to 1942 and a proponent of bilingual education. She borrowed a house from her father in the family village of Galisteo and erected a vocational crafts school there in the early 1930s. Carmen Espinosa, the sister-in-law of the politically powerful Dennis Chavez, helped organize the Folklorida de Santa Fe. Fabiola Cabeza de Baca Gilbert, niece of a former governor, fostered Hispanic crafts and legitimized Hispanic recipes in her work as a home demonstration agent. And Adelina Otero-Warren, who referred to her heritage as "Spanish" and "patron," as superintendent of schools in Santa Fe County encouraged schools to incorporate Hispanic crafts in their curricula.

None of these women personally identified with the class of Spanish Americans she now patronized. Several referred to "matriarchs" in their family, and a tradition of noblesse oblige. Villagers did not treat them as peers, and the attitude of these women toward Spanish Americans not of the elite was virtually indistinguishable from that of their Anglo counterparts.[107] The participation of these women did not make the arts patrons' revival of "dormant" arts and guidance of living ones indigenous or authentic.[108] Both the Anglo and the Hispanic patrons stood, in large measure, outside the villages and their culture, and both used the arts to render the villages closer to the romantic vision they wanted Hispanic culture to fulfill.

With the government's adoption of the Spanish colonial arts revival as a solution to village relief and poverty, what had been a limited private endeavor became considerably broader, though it altered few of its attributes. The older tradition regarding Hispanic arts blended with a newer brand of cultural regionalism promoted by eastern sociologists who sought cultures that could withstand the onslaught of industrialism's mass-production cultural leveling and could help provide a healthy balance for city dwellers between the rural and the urban, the natural and the man-made. With this motive, government programs continued the practices of the private patrons, some of whom assisted the new efforts. They occasionally hired Anglos to teach villagers to make "authentic examples of old Spanish Colonial home furnishings." They insisted "there should be a development of better designs and the use of homespun yarn in the making of their textiles." And they imposed their own aesthetics. These patrons, too, through their supervision of "traditional" handicrafts, aimed to direct Hispanic artists "in the right path."[109]

The significance of the government's program, however, lay beyond taste and style. It was through the use of National Youth Administration, Works Progress Administration, Agricultural Extension, and Smith-Hughes Vocational Training funds and personnel for crafts education, training, and marketing in the villages of southern Colorado and New Mexico that the program most affected Hispanic options.[110]

When searching for "a project that would be of value to the Spanish-American population," federal officials took into account the lack of an industrial infrastructure in northern New Mexico. They also shared popular assumptions that many of the Hispanic young people "through lack of previous educational advantages, cannot profit by a high school education," and that Spanish Americans lacked "mechanical mindedness." In search of "practical" instruction for unemployed village youth, these men and women looked to "the hand trades which can be carried on in the village," such as spinning, weaving, pottery, carpentry, and tanning, and called the cultural values inherent in such a choice "a by-product" of a program that had as its main concern the economic returns to the worker.[111] As a result, twenty-four communities in New Mexico, including many in the Hispanic northern counties, had government-sponsored craft schools by the end of the decade, and Las Animas, Costilla, and Archuleta counties in southern Colorado had "Spanish Colonial" or "Native Arts and Crafts/Vocational Training" projects. The crafts were seen as offering life-long careers to Spanish Americans, although by the end of 1941 the crafts industries had yet to be self-supporting.[112]

By channeling vocational education funds almost exclusively into crafts training at a time when Anglo youths even in rural ranching communities received industrial or commercial training, the federal interest in Spanish colonial arts affected future opportunities for Spanish Americans.[113] This brand of cultural pluralism had troubling implications. The crafts programs brought some income and sustenance to impoverished villages, and they signaled at last an official recognition of diversity as legitimate and even beneficial. But, intentionally or not, by their methods they perpetuated not only a distinct and not entirely self-sufficient or autonomous group but also a marginalized, cheap labor force. Such pluralism relieved the tension created by what sociology professor R. W. Roskelley of Colorado noted as "the impossibility of scoffing at the Mexican culture patterns, of indoctrinating them with those of the Nordics and still expecting them to perform a type of labor and live under conditions which Nordic standards taboo."[114] Successful cultural assimilation, in the eyes of Anglos who continued to look to culture as a comforting explanation for persistent inequities, would create a dissatisfied Chicano work force, one barred nakedly by race and structural discrimination from occupational mobility. Colorado and New Mexico had witnessed Chicano labor upheaval and increasing radicalism, which some onlookers attributed to the beginnings of such assimilation. Whether or not any of the more pluralistic Anglo revivers of Spanish colonial arts had this particular conundrum in mind, some of the crafts programs' most earnest practitioners were assailed by doubts. Among the most articulate of these was an Anglo male teacher in Nambé in early 1938, who insisted, "[W]e do live in an American society and its influences reach into the community." As he wrestled with the implications of the cultural program, he demanded, "[I]s it safe to say that Spanish culture which we encourage will enhance and enrich their living instead of helping to emphasize racial differences?"[115]

Great claims were made for the success of Spanish colonial arts in restoring pride, community, and economic viability to the villages. Of one pilot project in Chupadero, outside Santa Fe, the New Mexico Emergency Relief Administration *Bulletin* glowed:

> From a reconstruction problem, this community has raised itself to a more self-sustaining rural community demonstrating the extent to which the Arts and Crafts of the native Spanish American Population may develop themselves. Meanwhile the community is happy and contented in the strength of its own independent and harmonious enjoyment of life.[116]

In other areas of Colorado and New Mexico Hispanics also became more "self-sufficient" through their crafts, and some of the unemployed beetworkers and miners who returned to the villages took up this work. In 1935/36, the reported value of handcrafted products sold by over fifteen participating communities in Rio Arriba County reached $21,210. At least one village, Cundiyo, owed its survival during the Depression to its weaving.[117]

Claims for the crafts program, however, had gone beyond temporary supplemental income. And in linking these Spanish colonial crafts to the totality of ongoing Hispanic village culture, private and government arts proponents defined and limited the development of that culture in ways the villagers and other Hispanics themselves often rejected. A conference that included many Hispanic educators and focused on educational problems in Spanish-speaking communities reported on the matter in 1943:

> in certain regions many of the customs and practices among the Spanish speaking groups that are in fact survivals of specific phases in the historic development of all mankind are frequently mistaken for basic elements of the Hispanic character. This popular misconception has resulted in the indiscriminating exploitation of the picturesque aspect of Hispanic American life by groups and persons who are genuinely concerned with the welfare of the group, and who believe that these have basic cultural values.

This critique of colonial arts programs as well-meant but imposed, misdirected, and retrogressive was followed by a warning that Hispanic participation in the programs often hinged more on lack of alternatives than on genuine interest. Rather than mire reluctant villagers in amber for the benefit of alien onlookers, the conference committee recommended that crafts fostered in the villages should be limited to those which provided articles villagers could not otherwise afford "or that bring economic returns equal to those offered by other available occupations demanding equal skill." What many conference participants feared, in sum, was the result of a policy which seemed too little to take into account the aspirations, future needs, tastes, and interests of the villagers as participants in a heavily industrial economy. This cultural intersection that seemed to benefit both groups, could too easily, by training Hispanics only in manual industries, simply perpetuate the low-income status of the Hispanics.[118]

The fears expressed seemed borne out by experience. The economic returns afforded by the colonial arts never did, in this era, match those of other occupations. Nor did they even begin to replace the two million dollars earned outside the villages yearly in the 1920s. The investigators who in 1935 conducted the federal Tewa Basin study of northern New Mexico villages found that few Spanish Americans attempted or planned to attempt to make a living from the crafts as "the wages per hour on handicraft work remain extremely low, 15 cents at best." That these wages were considerably lower, for example, than government road project wages, but not lower than many of the domestic service jobs open to women, may help to explain the relatively high participation among women in these projects. Only a truly exceptional craftsperson might make as much as twenty-five cents per hour. By the late 1930s some Hispanics complained not only that "too often a feeling of condescension or sentimentality was involved in movements to sponsor the arts," but that "the artisans themselves were given a false idea of the value of their work."[119]

Anglo marketers had placed great faith in the validity of their vision of Hispanic crafts. They often found, however, their Hispanic craftsmen and women resistant to interference in their designs, unable or unwilling to make required items from suggested materials, unable to complete orders within the allotted time for want of materials or because they were busy with other tasks or school, or reluctant to learn the trade at all.[120] In addition, the artisans resisted a downward pressure on prices and occasionally had difficulty extracting funds from the movement's shops, which were never self-sustaining but relied on contributions from such patrons as Cyrus McCormick.

Anti-modern Anglos' hopes for a viable arts revival had also relied in part on a misplaced faith in two other seemingly antagonistic phenomena: tourism and advertising. In actuality, neither could sustain the movement or its artisans. Although by 1937 tourism had become the main source of income in Santa Fe and the chamber of commerce did recognize the connection with the arts revival in maintaining a local atmosphere of exoticism, it proved too seasonal. Advertising, despite the fashionableness of simplicity and Spanish architecture, proved incapable of overcoming the realities of handcraft production in a machine age.[121] Relative irregularity of design, slowness of production, and cost of manufacture and shipment had become distinct handicaps.

However noble their intentions, success on the part of government or private Spanish colonial arts revivers would have meant not only the permanent marginalization of Hispanics through teaching them only skills of limited application and economic value in an industrial age, but would also have cast the villages in an amber of largely Anglo design, rendering theirs a captive culture. Perhaps the best indication of the rejection of this scenario by most Hispanics lies in the occupational choices they themselves made when given the opportunity. In 1930, a teacher at the Presbyterian high school in Santa Fe described the "commercial department" as among the most popular and reported "few of the girls return to the plazas to live unless they go as teachers. There is little opportunity for employment there." In 1937, after the introduction of the arts programs, a teacher from the northern New Mexico village of Embudo still found "a tendency for young folks to feel that only those who go away to school and enter one of the so-called professions really make something of themselves." And even for those who had no such professional aims, when the Second World War brought a revived economy, villagers left their crafts and returned to their seasonal migrations.[122]

Villagers had turned to crafts largely as a temporary measure, rarely as a permanent career. Crafts were a means to retain their way of life at a time when they had, and the government provided, few alternatives. During an era when the collapse of other ethnic communities heralded their increasing integration into the United States mainstream culture, the federal adoption of the private Spanish colonial arts programs both threatened the autonomy of Hispanic culture by seeking to direct it and simultaneously allowed the survival of the villages without assimilation despite the breakdown of their own economic strategies. In the eyes of its creators, the vocational program may have had no lasting success. It did not develop a self-sufficient Anglo-guided handicraft industry. But by sustaining the villages as a place apart, it enabled Hispanic villagers in the 1940s to recapture their still distinct cultural dynamic.

The 1930s had brought new Anglo and Hispanic strategies. Like the arts program, most faded with the decade. By 1939, for example, only six UCAPAWA locals still organized beetworkers in northern Colorado. In 1941, UCAPAWA abandoned the field. Yet grievances remained. The Farm Security Administration revealed that most beet-labor houses in northern Colorado still lacked "adequate waste disposal facilities, refrigeration, or indoor toilets, while two thirds had leaky roofs and were without proper drainage," and in Denver 89 percent of Spanish Americans resided in substandard housing. Fewer than 11 percent of Denver Hispanics owned their homes, as compared to 34 percent of black and 41 percent of Anglo residents, and half the Chicanos still depended on WPA work, a proportion five times that of any other racial or ethnic group. In rural areas, investigators reported in 1943 that "practically none have acquired self-subsisting farms." Infant mortality among Denver's Chicanos remained at almost three times that among Anglos. And a 1945 Department of Labor report concluded that conditions in the beetfields showed no improvement notwithstanding federal government regulations.[123] Despite federal programs and new Anglo services, the Depression had witnessed little progress in the northern Colorado Chicano community.

Continuing isolation in northern Colorado, poverty, substandard housing, and lack of non-seasonal employment opportunities there help to explain why sociologist Kalervo Oberg found Hispanics in 1940 still looking to their New Mexican villages rather than outside them for their life's center. "As poor and insecure economically as the Spanish-American undoubtedly is, he still holds tenaciously to a community life that offers him more than he can find elsewhere."[124] Yet these northern New Mexico communities had weathered the Depression little better. In 1941 an El Cerrito resident told investigators, "[T]he people here are worse off than they have ever been in their lives." Despite federal rehabilitation, crafts, and other programs, their farms were still too small or too dry to provide a living; they continued to lack adequate grazing land; and steady wage work remained elusive. After seven years of federal subsidies through work projects and relief, the investigators reported, basic conditions remained unchanged.[125]

Both in the villages and in northern Colorado, some Chicanos had benefited from the increased schooling that greater stability coupled with child-labor laws had made possible. In addition, literacy programs, workers' education, and other federal outreach programs that hired Hispanics to serve Hispanics, although established only late in the 1930s,

did help foster leaders and organized community groups in some localities. These government-sponsored community organizations could
supplement the dwindling, more radical grass-roots unions that, in contrast, the government (local, state, and federal) as well as employers had
discouraged. But the new organizations were limited in scope and aims,
and most of the Hispanics would have to await the greater prosperity
and opportunities of the 1940s to garner any reward for their increased
education.

The federal government had intervened at almost every level of the
regional community during the Depression, from work-relief policies in
northern Colorado to crafts programs in the villages, from rural rehabilitation to midwifery, in the name of welfare, stability, and order.
Health and nutrition officials, home economic and agricultural agents,
literacy and cooperative teachers had entered Hispanic communities,
each "missionary" bringing with him or her a cultural message. Yet the
pattern that remained after 1940 was not that of stabilized and self-sufficient Anglo-style communities. And even the alternate patterns Chicanos themselves had been building, based on unions and other community organizations, lay diminished or in disarray. The Chicano
organizations that had not suffered at the hands of federal and local
investigators by having leaders arrested or deported called off their
struggles for Chicano rights for the duration of the Second World War.
The "rehabilitated" villagers returned to seasonal labor, while the
youths, "interested," as New Mexico's director of vocational education
found, "in learning more lucrative trades than traditional craftsman-
ship," turned eagerly to the war industries. What remained, after all,
was the migratory and interdependent pattern of the regional community. As late as 1979 anthropologist Paul Kutsche observed the regional
community still operating in the New Mexican villages: "a network promoting the survival of its members in a variety of subsistence situations. . . . Those more established on the periphery provide bases for
migrating kinsmen seeking work or education." Had the regional community survived the Depression despite federal intervention or because
of it?[126]

World War I had given a brief glimpse of what the federal government could accomplish in the way of Americanization given enough
money, attention, and time. But in the 1930s the aims were different.
Just as Chicanos were forming new strategies less dependent on the
regional community with its migratory patterns and ethnic isolation,
the federal government began working instead to maintain it. Under-

mining stability in the north by manipulation of migration patterns through relief timing, the federal government also fostered ethnic distinction through crafts and village rehabilitation programs. A homogenized America no longer seemed the government's ultimate goal. This new federal policy was a major reason not only for the survival of the villages and Hispanics as a group apart but for the limited success of the new Chicano strategies.

By the end of the 1930s, the villagers, men and women alike, had lost, at least temporarily, much of their remaining autonomy, their ability to choose for themselves among income opportunities and cultural adaptations. This loss of autonomy had not come, as might have been expected, through assimilation. It had come through government "preservation" of Hispanic village culture. When the kinship and regional strategies proved inadequate to the task, the federal government helped sustain both the villages and the migratory patterns. It adopted private methods of labor discrimination and cultural patronage to do so, though it also returned wages closer to the admittedly inadequate level of the mid-1920s. Tempered by Hispanic resistance, bureaucratic inefficiency, and limited funds, the government thus suspended the dynamic of Hispanic culture, including the growth of alternatives to the regional community strategy. In effect in the 1930s the government succeeded in taking over the regional community erected on the Anglo-Hispanic frontier and used it to restore order, despite economic dislocation. What had begun as a Hispanic strategy to retain autonomy and cultural control became, in other hands, an instrument against both. But, ironically, the government also thus suspended the destruction of the villages as a separate culture. And it was largely due to this federal intervention that the regional community survived the 1930s at all.

Conclusion

The United States conquest of Hispanic New Mexico and Colorado was not, after all, an instant one. Long after the United States had established political hegemony over the region as a whole, Hispanic villagers continued to enjoy a life relatively untrammeled by the immediate presence of government officials, much as they had under the distant and somewhat relaxed Spanish colonial and Mexican governments. This neglect afforded the villages its own protection, left them free from interference in developing their own cultural and economic strategies. But though government authority kept its distance for some time, other elements of Anglo society pursued the conquest by other means. Indeed, the history of Anglo-Hispanic relations in the Southwest from 1880 to 1940, in one sense, took the form of continuous Anglo efforts to perfect the incomplete conquest and of continually evolving Hispanic strategies to prevent it. This struggle embroiled issues of both gender and class, and it is only in the nexus of these three elements, culture, class, and gender, that the ramifications of this Anglo-Hispanic frontier become clear.

Culture exists as a fluid rather than a static phenomenon, as something people develop rather than something that existed in its true form only at some golden age in the past. The focus in examining intercultural relations thus lies, as anthropologist David Snow has pointed out, on "processes of reorganization (rather than disorganization) of local groups and the re-establishment of viable economic patterns following stress."[1] The focus lies, in other words, on the strategies whereby people

200

who are fundamentally threatened retain or gain control of cultural development and change, as well as on the cultural changes themselves.

By the 1880s, Hispanics in northern New Mexico and southern Colorado faced numerous threats to their livelihood from Anglo enterprises and found few successful avenues of defense. Railroads made Hispanic freighting unprofitable. Railroads and commercial stockgrowers, as well as timber and mining companies and the government, legally and illegally absorbed more and more of vital Hispanic grazing lands. And the neglect of the villages by the federal government was mirrored by the failure of politics as a strategy of protection for Hispanic villagers as a group. Despite the entreaties of the Spanish language press, politics and the spoils they promised proved more divisive than unifying. Other strategies, such as homesteading, economic collaboration, and violent resistance also proved unsatisfactory in preserving general Hispanic control over their own cultural and economic dynamic.

Like similarly placed people in Europe, Africa, South America, and even elsewhere in the United States, who found their culture relying on an inadequate economic base and challenged by an economic system not only different but controlled by an often antagonistic culture, Hispanic villagers turned to seasonal migration.[2] This was a strategy that, with the labor of women in the villages, could preserve the small farms and communal villages by welding them to a new regional economic system. The villages preserved migrant workers, sons, brothers, husbands, and whole families of villagers against the exigencies of seasonal flux and national depressions. And the migrant workers, by their earnings, preserved the villages. Migration diversified the village economy and stretched the village into a regional community consisting of migrants and villagers with bonds crossing hundreds of miles. It allowed households to bridge safely the gap across cultural and production systems, to remain culturally aloof from the Anglos by supplementing the village economy with migrants' earnings instead of supplanting it by fully entering the Anglo economy.

This regional community and its migrant system could survive as an effective strategy only so long as Anglos continued to neglect the villages and so long as the Hispanic strategy met the needs of both parties on this frontier. As the decades progressed, however, Anglo aims for Hispanics and Hispanic aims for themselves increasingly diverged. Even in the early years, the intersection had not been perfect. While the regional community supplied Anglo developers with a large source of labor made cheap by providing much of its own subsistence, it also permitted the Hispanics to remain outside overwhelming Anglo control, only partly dependent on wage labor, and with a mobility that allowed protest of unpalatable working conditions. This independence was further symbolized by the Hispanic villagers' refusal to conform to Anglo individualist competitive behavior, sexual structure, and language. The regional community permitted Hispanics to select and incorporate into village life only those aspects of Anglo culture, such as sewing machines, cars, and clothing, which most suited their own concept of their needs. Women continued to work outside as well as within the house; men sought and left work based as much on their own limited cash needs as on labor-market demands; villagers continued to share resources; and school children learned Spanish. Anglos themselves developed strategies to combat this independence, to complete the conquest and effect control over the culture, as they did elsewhere when confronting other newcomers to the industrial work ethic. Their strategies and the Hispanic ones evolved in response to one another as well as to changing economic conditions.

Women in particular, as missionaries, teachers, and social service workers, were enlisted on this Anglo frontier as elsewhere to transmit Anglo culture and effect social control. But isolated missionaries in the villages had extremely limited funds and were often ambivalent about the Anglo industrial culture they supposedly represented. Though many became respected and authoritative members of the village, they proved incapable of imposing a transformation of village culture on the Hispanic inhabitants. They could not create a homogeneous "Americanized" population endowed with an industrial work ethic and separate sexual spheres. As long as the village strategy of a regional community and the demand for Hispanic labor on which it relied continued to meet village needs, villagers could fend off such cultural threats, including interference with the essential flexible sexual structure and communal mores.

In the southern Colorado coal fields, however, Hispanics witnessed a better financed and more complete Anglo invasion than that of the women missionaries. The Colorado Fuel and Iron Company in particular had great success in replacing Hispanic plazas with company towns. In the camps, the Hispanic miners whose plazas had been so replaced, were more committed to their jobs than were the village migrants who joined them, and less able to take refuge in the networks of the regional community or to protect their autonomy through migration. With the erosion of property ownership and village exchange, the varied income base of their family economy had suffered. The women's economy that had sustained the village was not completely restored by taking in boarders and laundry. Women in the camps could not to the same degree as in the villages make up for the deficiencies of an industrial employer.

Along with their coworkers of other ethnic groups, these Hispanics nonetheless had the same tendency, so distressing to their Anglo instructors, to interpret Anglo messages through the prism of their own culture and needs, as the Hispanic villagers had. While C.F.I.'s Sociology Department strove to create a unified, Americanized, and docile labor force, Hispanic participation in mining strikes showed that the message of common interest between employer and employee had made less headway than that of common interests across ethnic lines. The greater dependence of these Hispanic miners on wage labor had not necessarily made them more quiescent and dependable workers than the migrant villagers whose independence so irked some observers. It resulted instead in these early Hispanic attempts to shift their strategy and to join in a redefined community, which embraced non-Hispanics. Such activity convinced at least some Anglo mining companies of the limits of Americanization and the benefits to themselves of ethnic differences.

Sugar companies and growers also depended on cheap Hispanic labor, and they, too, discovered the uses of ethnic diversity. In the 1930s, investigators found that many Hispanic school children in Colorado answered the question, "Why did the English colonize America?" with the reply, "To get beet contracts."[3] In the 1910s and 1920s, sugar companies built adobe colonies for Hispanic beetworkers to decrease recruiting costs by creating a permanent labor force on the site. Unlike the company mining towns, however, these colonies formed almost a mock miniature of the regional community. The houses were distinctly different—adobe—not the frame and brick of the Anglo homes in the area, and the colonies were isolated, always some distance from the nearest Anglo community, usually out of sight.

The colonies mimicked those aspects of the regional community that made Hispanics an acceptable, cheap, and perpetual labor force. The colonies removed them from the Anglo community when they were not wanted as labor, and allowed them to furnish part—but only part—of their own subsistence. The colony gardens were inadequate for full subsistence. Colony residents, like many villagers, had to seek wage labor. But the colonies did not fully duplicate the villages. The colony infrastructure, lacking a unified church, ultimate control over even residential land, and a permanent population, could not replicate the stable refuge, the female core and authority of the village. The company colonies thus kept some Hispanics in the north free of recruiting costs, isolated from Anglo society and economic mobility, and culturally and economically distinct.

Nonetheless, this experiment in ethnic separation, like coal-company Americanization, failed to adhere strictly to Anglo design. The company coal camps had the advantage of closely monitored polyglot populations, but the beet colonies contained only loosely supervised Chicanos who already had much in common. Though most Hispanic migrants came from landowning families in the village, they performed only wage labor outside it; in the Anglo world, these migrants shared not only a culture but a class. As the number of Chicanos settling permanently in the north increased, and as they formed more stable communities there, they, like the miners, shifted to a strategy more confrontational than migration was. This strategy depended on both ethnic and class ties, and at least some beet colonies became not only self-governing communities, but foci of Chicano unrest. Isolation as well as integration could foster autonomous organization.

As more Hispanics settled permanently in the north, inside and outside the colonies, and as economic disasters and continued deprivation of land further diminished the efficiency of the regional community as a strategy of autonomous survival, Hispanics at all points of the regional community moved from their strategy of resistance to a more assertive one. They began to redefine their communities on the frontier of their region and to develop strategies less dependent on ties between these communities and the villages. They looked instead toward winning a broader place for themselves within the Anglo community. Their aims were not necessarily Anglicization, but involved permanent residence, greater economic opportunities, and full social incorporation into the Anglo world.

Anglos, however, in part in response to this new Chicano assertion, simultaneously moved from an ideology of homogeneity and integration through Americanization, as at the coal camps, to one more pluralistic and exclusive, at least with regard to Hispanics, as in the beet colonies. Determined to keep the Mexican border open, employers after World War I had exploited the patterns of the Hispanic regional community to promise that the conflated Mexicans and Spanish Americans would disappear when not wanted, would remain a dispensable marginal presence, a reserve, in the Anglo polity. In the 1920s, the private and informal determination to keep Chicanos, citizens and non-citizens alike, in the status of a distinct, permanent manual-labor class, became more and more imbedded in the area's institutions. It appeared in schools as separate classrooms, attendance policies, and vocational training, and it affected relief policies. Though inhibiting the growth of an integrated Chicano community in the north, this strategy of exclusion was not incompatible with the semi-autonomous survival of the villages as long as it was accompanied by a large seasonal demand for Hispanic labor. When the Depression ended that demand, such Anglo responses as the repatriations of 1932 and the border closing with New Mexico in 1936 revealed both the effectiveness of the exclusion in keeping the Chicano community in the north vulnerable, and the entrenched legitimacy of the exclusion in the minds of many Anglo Coloradans.

The early 1930s witnessed the collapse of the regional community, a collapse brought about not only by the disappearance of demand for Hispanic labor and the almost total agricultural ruin of the never fully sufficient villages, but by the failure of Hispanic communities in the north to become new bases for Hispanic expansion and power. Structural discrimination had fostered unfair employment and realty practices, and limited opportunities for Chicanos and Chicanas in northern Colorado. In addition, the sexual structure of northern Colorado bore little resemblance to that of the villages. Chicanas found their opportunities narrowed even further than those of the men, and could not recreate the village core.

For Hispanic villagers, the autonomy of women and the autonomy of the community depended on each other. The regional community had sustained, in the villages, a place where Chicanas could continue to fill a large variety of positions, and experience centrality and authority. They led church services, ran businesses and post offices, tended gardens, fields, and domestic livestock, ran for political office, built ovens, and plastered walls. Increasingly the distinction between male and female relation to the cash economy diminished, and more and more women not only worked outside the home, but left the village for wage work.

This sexual division of labor that sustained the village and the regional community had no northern counterpart. Chicanas in the north lacked not only sufficient land to produce a subsistence living or marketable produce, but the wage-earning power of the men. As varied sources of income diminished, so, too, did the autonomy of the community, whether the regional community, the villages, or the nascent communities in northern Colorado.

The work of the village women had largely made possible the Chicano exploitation of the symbiosis of Anglo and Chicano economies through the regional community. The permanent Chicano settlements in the north could not recreate this system, could not achieve a secure economic base apart from the villages. Their attempts at community-building based on other labor patterns—their attempts to unionize, for example—tended to fall victim to their heavy dependence on a single income source. When the regional community collapsed, these Chicanos had no separate refuge.

As Hispanic women moved away from the villages, they, like the men, moved away from their center of power. But while the men lost power in the wider multiethnic arena, the women lost it within the Hispanic community as well. Both in the mining towns of southern Colorado and the beet towns of northern Colorado, Chicanas found that without their property and their garden to give them a right to an independent place in the community as land owner and producer, their roles were increasingly limited to consumer and reproducer. In addition, as families came to rely increasingly on money and on labor, women, as inferior wage-earners, lost authority, and widows became merely titular heads of households. Hispanic women's institutions that had provided positions of authority for women in the village, such as the church, lacked a unified community-wide constituency in the Anglo north. And itinerant midwives, here today and gone tomorrow, could not create bonds of trust and support. As non-migrants, women had been the principal creators as well as sustainers of community and neighborhood in the villages, a stable central force of village society. Outside the villages they were, instead, mobile and marginal.

Both in the villages and in the northern communities, Anglo female social-service workers reached out to women in particular. But even when they successfully established contact, and their community was willing to incorporate Chicanas into it, the position these Anglo women offered did not match the authority, variety, and centrality of Hispanic women's village roles. Hispanic women in the villages, in keeping with their own cultural roles, had strived to integrate the women missionaries into village life on several levels and to temper their threat to village harmony. Anglo women "missionaries" on all sites, however, concentrated for the most part on a narrower round of experience in their contact with Hispanics. They reached into the heart of the family and the home. They concentrated on childrearing, on cooking and preserving food, and on the aesthetics of home furnishings. In the 1930s, they tended less overtly to identify Americanism with Anglo culture or with Protestant Christianity, but they still emphasized, in this era of pluralism, their own aesthetics and tastes, and their own concept of women's proper role.

Anglo women, like the men, sought to fit Hispanic women into roles Anglos had designed for them. They did not envision them as semi-autonomous property-owners who worked outside the house as well as within it and who had little compunction in performing, in case of need, tasks usually in the men's realm. Instead, they saw Chicanas either as women thrust outside their true role by circumstance and improvident men, or as martyrs to domestic ignorance and its result: bad housekeeping. From the missionaries in the villages to the agricultural extension agents and Works Progress Administration directors, these middle-class Anglo women sought to transform Hispanic women into ideal domestic servants and housewives.

Minority status clearly played a role in keeping Chicanas in a secondary position in Anglo areas, but neither it nor the cultural heritage so many have mistakenly blamed is a sufficient explanation.[4] Anglo women, too, experienced marginality in the Anglo society of the time. Indeed, like the Hispanic women, Anglo women missionaries found that they enjoyed a central position in the Hispanic villages that they did not have in the Anglo world. In Anglo areas, as cross-cultural bridges Anglo women fell short; they could not lead Hispanic women to a centrality in the new society that would match the power of their village roles. Hispanic men and women alike suffered a loss of status at the northern edges of the regional community, but for the women, full integration and assimilation into the Anglo community would not remedy that loss.

By the 1930s, among Anglos assimilation was in any case increasingly unfashionable. Pluralism had so displaced homogeneity in government thinking, that even when Hispanics showed signs of abandoning the regional community for other strategies, the government and other Anglos, abandoning the agenda of conquest, took it up. When the regional community's collapsing support lines had rendered retreat difficult and fostered the growth of new, more assertive Chicano organizations, government policies restored the lines of retreat and saw to it that they were taken, defusing the confrontations of the mid-1930s. As Chicanos tried to build unions and other advocacy organizations dependent on a stable community, these policies encouraged migration by removing Chicanos from relief work and relief rolls weeks before beetwork began.

Just as the New Deal's pluralism fostered a static economic role for Chicano labor as migrants, it propagated a view of Hispanic culture as static, unchanged since the United States conquest, and furthered this view's transformation to a reality. By channeling relief funds for Hispanic areas into such projects as Spanish colonial crafts training, government programs encouraged cultural isolation, whether or not they intended it. Anti-modernist Anglos, grappling with real problems of geographic isolation and poverty in the villages, saw in colonial cultural revival the economic salvation of the Hispanic villages, and the spiritual salvation of modern America. But however beneficent their impulse, they often did not understand Hispanic villagers' mores and desires, and their movement had other implications. Spanish Americans could not, because of their citizenship, be forever denied a place in the United States polity, but the place tendered them could remain on the margins. They could provide the useful "other" that anti-modernists wanted to preserve for balance and as part of the human heritage.

At its most sanguine, the New Deal hoped to restore the regional community to its healthiest state, that which served both Hispanics' desire for autonomy and Anglos' need for semi-self-sufficient labor. Government agencies did not only teach villagers woodcarving instead of auto mechanics and force reluctant Chicanos to take beetwork, they also, at various points, attempted to raise beetwork wages, increase the productivity of remaining village lands, and provide more pasturage than depleted communal holdings offered. That these latter policies proved, in their implementation, sporadic, underfunded, and spotty frustrated many New Dealers as well as Chicano laborers and villagers. But in the end, the more persistent government policies dominated Anglo-Hispanic interaction in the 1930s. These policies that fostered migrant labor and cultural "revival" under Anglo direction limited the freedom with which Hispanics could recreate their own strategies, limited the expansion of the Hispanic community on its own terms beyond the margins of either the Hispanic regional community or the Anglo society of the north. And it made the culturally autonomous Hispanic homeland an increasingly besieged enclave, an internal colony. By the late 1930s, Hispanic control over both their cultural development and their strategies of resistance and confrontation had been severely if not completely eroded, in part at least, by federal government intrusion at virtually every level of their community. This was, perhaps, the ultimate Anglo conquest.

The conflict between Anglo and Hispanic on this frontier involved more than the conflict between an agricultural and an industrial society, although that was one aspect. The regional community created by the villagers within the Anglo Southwest, bound by kinship ties across hundreds of miles and disparate economic and cultural conditions, became an arena for a struggle that involved culture, class, and gender. In a confrontation where one culture dominated the economy and the state, cultural differences evolved into class lines, and sexual structures played a crucial role in the increasing dependence of the subordinate group. The regional community, ultimately limited to a Hispanic strategy of retreat, did not succeed as a strategy of integration. The margins of the regional community could not be converted, even with the aid of unions, into centers of intercultural communities. By the 1930s, structural discrimination was too strong a barrier.

In this struggle, Anglo definitions of gender behavior and race, and the economic realities of Anglo areas, acted at least as strongly as Hispanic traditions of village women and migratory men to move women, the community builders, to the margins of Chicano society and economy when they settled outside the villages. And Anglo economic control, in tandem with a government that was no longer neglectful, enclosed and perpetuated a distinct Hispanic culture in its village heartland and kept Hispanic workers in a seasonal laboring class. Hispanics found the perversion of their strategy had made them collaborators in their own permanent marginality even when such marginality no longer served their purposes. The two cultures had not melded into one; the frontier still existed, but it was unclear whether this survival was, in fact, anyone's victory.

Abbreviations Used in Notes and Bibliography

AAA	Agricultural Adjustment Administration
AFL	American Federation of Labor
Alb. Trib.	*Albuquerque Tribune*
C&P	*Camp and Plant* (Colorado Fuel and Iron's magazine)
CB	Children's Bureau
CFI	Colorado Fuel and Iron
CHS	Colorado Historical Society, Denver
CLA	*Colorado Labor Advocate*
CSA	Colorado State Archives, Denver
CSFL	Colorado State Federation of Labor
DPL	Western History Department, Denver Public Library
DPS	Denver Public Schools
GDT	*Greeley Daily Tribune*
Gov. Rec.	Governor's Records
GWSCo	Great Western Sugar Company
HMM	*Home Mission Monthly*
JCCC	Joint Convention Contest Committee
MHL	Menaul Historical Library of the Southwest, Albuquerque
Ms. Census	Manuscript Census of the United States
NA	National Archives
NMAES	New Mexico Agricultural Extension Service, Annual Reports of County Agents, National Archives microfilm

NM ERA	New Mexico Emergency Relief Administration
NMHL	New Mexico Historical Library, Santa Fe
NMHR	*New Mexico Historical Review*
NMJE	*New Mexico Journal of Education*
NMSR	*New Mexico School Review*
NMSRCA	New Mexico State Records Center and Archives, Santa Fe
NMWN	*New Mexico War News*
NYA	Records of the National Youth Administration
PHR	*Pacific Historical Review*
PHS	Presbyterian Historical Society, Philadelphia
RACo	Rio Arriba County, New Mexico
RB	Regional Bulletin
RG	Record Group
RMFCo	Rocky Mountain Fuel Company
RMN	*Rocky Mountain News*
SANS	Spanish American Normal School
SCS	Soil Conservation Service
SLVH	*San Luis Valley Historian*
TCN	*Trinidad Chronicle-News*
TTL	*Through the Leaves* (Great Western Sugar Company's magazine)
UNM	Special Collections, University of New Mexico, Albuquerque
U.S.C.W.A., *Interviews*	United States Civil Works Administration, *Interviews Collected During 1933–1934 for State Historical Society of Colorado*
USDL	United States Department of Labor
W&M	*Women and Missions*
WCTU	Women's Christian Temperance Union
WHC	Western Historical Collections, University of Colorado, Boulder
WHQ	*Western Historical Quarterly*
WPA	Records of the Works Progress Administration, State Series

Notes

Introduction

1. See, for example, David H. Dinwoodie, "Indians, Hispanos, and Land Reform: A New Deal Struggle in New Mexico," *WHQ* 17 (July 1986), 291–323; Frances Leon Swadesh, *Los Primeros Pobladores: Hispanic Americans of the Ute Frontier* (Notre Dame, 1974); Alvar Carlson, "El Rancho and Vadito: Spanish Settlements on Indian Lands," *El Palacio* 85 (Spring 1979), 29–39; William deBuys, *Enchantment and Exploitation: The Life and Hard Times of a New Mexico Mountain Range* (Albuquerque, 1985).

2. See John Bodnar, *The Transplanted: A History of Immigrants in Urban America* (Bloomington, Indiana, 1985), xv, xvii, xx; Mario T. García, *Desert Immigrants: The Mexicans of El Paso, 1880–1920* (New Haven, 1981), 1. This is not to deny the validity of the colonization theory recently propounded by some Chicano historians, for example, Mario Barrera, *Race and Class in the Southwest* (Notre Dame, 1979); Mario Barrera et al., "The Barrio as an Internal Colony," pp. 281–301, in *La Causa Política: A Chicano Politics Reader,* F. Chris Garcia, ed. (Notre Dame, 1974); and Rodolfo Acuña, *Occupied America: The Chicano's Struggle Toward Liberation* (San Francisco, 1972). (N.B.: Acuña in his second edition, *Occupied America: A History of Chicanos* (New York, 1981), vii, dropped the internal colonial model as irrelevant to the twentieth-century Chicano experience.) It is rather to argue that despite their colonized status, the actual experience of Chicanos in the Anglo-dominated enclaves of the Southwest had great similarities to the European experience, and that theories derived from the one case may illuminate the other.

3. Anthropologists are apparently a decade or so ahead of most historians in this regard. Cf. Renato Rosaldo, "Chicano Studies, 1970–1984," *Annual Review of Anthropology* 14 (1985), 406–407.

4. Jack Holmes, "Success and Failure: The Limits of New Mexico's His-

213

panic Politics," in Renato Rosaldo et al., eds., *Chicano: The Evolution of a People* (Minneapolis, 1973), 239.

5. Clark S. Knowlton, "Patron-Peon Pattern Among the Spanish Americans of New Mexico," in Rosaldo et al., 235. See also Florence Kluckhohn and Fred Strodtbeck, *Variations in Value Orientations* (Evanston, Ill., 1961); Paul Kutsche, "Introduction: Atomism, Factionalism and Flexibility," in Kutsche, ed., *The Survival of Spanish American Villages* (Colorado Springs, 1979); Paul Kutsche and John R. Van Ness, *Cañones: Values, Crisis and Survival in a Northern New Mexico Village* (Albuquerque, 1981); Margaret Mead, ed., *Cultural Patterns and Technical Change* (Paris, 1953).

6. See Reyes Ramos, "Discovering the Production of Mexican American Family Structure," *De Colores* 6 (1982), 5–6, 8.

7. Milton Callon in interview of Carlos Jimenez, Denver Public Library, Oral History 72. In discussing the condition of Chicanos in Denver, Jimenez blamed poverty and economics; Callon blamed folk culture.

8. For example, *C&P* 3 (23 May 1903), 461, and 4 (19 Sept. 1903), 222–223; *HMM* vols. 1–4 (Nov. 1899–1904); and Rev. Robert M. Craig, *Our Mexicans* (New York, 1904), 27.

9. George I. Sanchez, *Forgotten People: A Study of New Mexicans* (Albuquerque, 1940), 10–11.

10. Carolyn Zeleny, *Relations Between the Spanish-Americans and Anglo-Americans in New Mexico* (1944, reprint ed. New York, 1974), 43.

11. Andrew Schlesinger, "Las Gorras Blancas, 1889–1891," *Journal of Mexican American History* 1 (Spring 1971), 90.

12. Jose de Onís, ed., *The Hispanic Contribution to the State of Colorado* (Boulder, 1976), xviii. And see Arthur Campa, *Hispanic Culture in the Southwest* (Norman, 1979), 211–216, 282–290.

13. For an example of a traditional view see William May, Jr., "The Great Western Sugarlands: History of the Great Western Sugar Company" (Ph.D. dissertation, Univ. of Colorado, 1982), 403. See Barrera, *Race and Class,* 53–54, on isolation and self-sufficiency. See also Octavio Romano-V., cited in Salvador Alvarez, "Mexican American Community Organizations, " *El Grito* 4 (Spring 1971), 69. For depictions of Hispanics as shapers of their history, see Jack Holmes; Reyes Ramos; and, in part, Frances Swadesh, and Alvar Carlson. Kutsche, "Introduction," 7, 9, 11, describes the other side of the passivity coin: researchers owing allegiance to conflict theory depict villages paralyzed by intense factionalism. Kutsche himself finds in village communalism flexibility and cohesive strength. See David J. Weber, "Turner, the Boltonians, and the Borderlands," *American Historical Review* 91 (Feb. 1986), 69–75, on the Anglo tradition of a stultified Spanish frontier. And of the newer school see works by John R. Chávez, Arnoldo De León, Mario García, Richard Griswold del Castillo, and Ricardo Romo, among others cited below.

14. See, for example, Albert Camarillo, *Chicanos in a Changing Society:*

From Mexican Pueblos to American Barrios in Santa Barbara and Southern California, 1848–1940 (Cambridge, Mass., 1979).

15. Frank Thistlethwaite, "Migration from Europe Overseas in the Nineteenth and Twentieth Centuries," in H. Moller, ed., *Population Movements in Modern European History* (New York, 1964), 73–91.

16. Ricardo Romo, "Work and Restlessness: Occupational and Spatial Mobility among Mexicanos in Los Angeles, 1918–1928," *PHR* 46 (May 1977), 180.

17. Ricardo Romo, *East Los Angeles: History of a Barrio* (Austin, 1983), 8–10, 12; Arnoldo De León, *The Tejano Community, 1836–1900* (Albuquerque, 1982), xii–xiv, 111, 153; Richard Griswold del Castillo, *The Los Angeles Barrio, 1850–1890: A Social History* (Berkeley, 1979), xi, 150. Cf. Virginia Yans-McLaughlin, *Family and Community: Italian Immigrants in Buffalo, 1880–1930* (Ithaca, 1977); Rudolph J. Vecoli, "Contadini in Chicago: A Critique of *The Uprooted*," *Journal of American History,* 51 (Dec. 1964), 404–417. Many observers of Chicanos, e.g. Carey McWilliams, Paul Taylor, and Nancie González, address the most recurrent and classic manifestation of social disorganization: high crime rates. All conclude that where these rates were disproportionately high, the primary cause was impoverishment, not cultural collapse.

18. Josef J. Barton, *Peasants and Strangers: Italians, Rumanians and Slovaks in an American City, 1890–1950* (Cambridge, Mass., 1975), 64; Griswold del Castillo, 138; Jose Amaro Hernandez, *Mutual Aid for Survival: The Case of the Mexican American* (Malabar, Fla., 1983), 4, 6, 9, 97–98, 128.

19. De León, xiii, 111.

20. Camarillo, 4; and see García, 5, 223.

21. Barrera et al., 282, 286.

22. David Snow, "Rural Hispanic Community Organization in Northern New Mexico: An Historical Perspective," in Kutsche, 51–52, on the fluidity of population and community in the face of cultural and natural stress, a fluidity which allows the community to reorganize instead of disintegrate, and to reestablish viable economic patterns. And see Romo, "Work and Restlessness."

23. See, for example, Donald W. Meinig's otherwise wonderful *Southwest: Three Peoples in Geographic Change, 1600–1970* (New York, 1971).

24. See works cited above by Griswold del Castillo, Camarillo, and García; and Julia Kirk Blackwelder, *Women of the Depression: Caste and Culture in San Antonio, 1929–1939* (College Station, Tex., 1984); Charles Briggs, "'Our Strength Is in the Land': The Structure of Hierarchy and Equality and the Pragmatics of Discourse in Hispano ('Spanish-American') 'Talk About the Past'" (Ph.D. dissertation, Univ. of Chicago, 1981), and Briggs, *The Woodcarvers of Córdova, New Mexico: Social Dimensions of an Artistic 'Revival'* (Knoxville, 1980).

25. Stephen Olsen aptly defined regional analysis as "an attempt to understand social and cultural organization in terms of spatial differentiation and

organization," in "Regional Social Systems: Linking Quantitative Analysis and Fieldwork," in Carol A. Smith, ed., *Regional Analysis,* vol. 2, *Social Systems* (New York, 1976), 21. Smith herself claimed "the adaptation of a part (local community) can no more be explained without reference to the system than can the adaptation of an organism be explained without reference to the web of relationships involved in defining its niche." Carol A. Smith, "Analyzing Regional Social Systems, " in *ibid.,* 13. See also Claude Meillassoux, "'The Economy' in Agricultural Self-Sustaining Societies: A Preliminary Analysis," in David Seddon, ed., *Relations of Production: Marxist Approaches to Anthropology* (London, 1978), 154. On people's ability to participate in different economic systems and hierarchies simultaneously, see Clifford Geertz on the Javanese, cited in Carol A. Smith, "Exchange Systems and the Spatial Distribution of Elites: The Organization of Stratification in Agrarian Societies," in her *Regional Analysis,* vol. 1(New York, 1976), 350.

26. Eugen A. Archuleta, "Hispanic Villagers, the CCC and the Beginning of Social Mobility in the San Luis Valley," 6, in Mexican Americans in Colorado Collection, WHC.

27. Extremely interesting in this regard is G. William Skinner, "Chinese Peasants and the Closed Community: An Open and Shut Case," *Comparative Studies in Society and History,* 13 (July 1971), 271–281, and "Mobility Strategies in Late Imperial China: A Regional Systems Analysis" in Smith, *Regional Analysis,* vol. 1, 327–364.

28. Weber, 71–72, 81.

29. Edward H. Spicer, "Ethnic Boundaries as Situations," in Edward Spicer and Raymond H. Thomas, eds., *Plural Society in the Southwest* (New York, 1972), 54–55.

30. See works by Sandra Myres, Joanna Stratton, Glenda Riley, Lillian Schlissel. Many of these authors do address some issues of ethnic and racial differences, but their main focus lies elsewhere. There is an increasing literature on native American women; see works by, for example, Sylvia van Kirk, Gretchen Bataille, and Kathleen Sands. For important exceptions covering 19th-century Mexican women, see Janet Lecompte, "The Independent Women of Hispanic New Mexico, 1821–1846," *WHQ* 12 (Jan. 1981), 17–35; Joan Jensen has published several articles which are sensitive to the importance of ethnic differences. On Chicanas see the urban studies cited earlier; Mario T. García, "The Chicana in American History: The Mexican Women of El Paso, 1880–1920—A Case Study," *PHR* 49 (May 1980), 315–337; and Richard Griswold Del Castillo, *La Familia: Chicano Families in the Urban Southwest, 1848 to the Present* (Notre Dame, 1984).

31. Cf. Elinor Lerner, "Into the Melting-Pot," *The Women's Review of Books* 3 (June 1986), 12; Rosalinda M. Gonzalez, "Chicanas and Mexican Immigrant Families 1920–1940: Women's Subordination and Family Exploitation," in Joan Jensen and Lois Scharf, eds., *Decades of Discontent: The Wom-*

en's Movement 1920–1940 (Westport, Conn., 1983), 59–84; and Blackwelder, e.g. 102, 162. Alfredo Mirandé and Evangelina Enríquez, *La Chicana: The Mexican American Woman* (Chicago, 1979), and Maxine Baca Zinn, "Gender and Ethnic Identity among Chicanos," *Frontiers* 5 (Summer 1980), 18–24, also complain about these assumptions, but while work on contemporary Chicano gender roles is mushrooming, there have still been few examinations of actual patterns of behavior in the period and for the locations covered in this book.

32. See, for example, Yans-McLaughlin; Maxine Seller, "The Education of the Immigrant Woman 1900–1935," *Journal of Urban History* 4 (May 1978): 307–330; Betty Boyd Caroli et al., eds., *The Italian Immigrant Woman in North America* (Toronto, 1978); Paul Taylor, *Mexican Labor in the United States Valley of the South Platte, Colorado,* Univ. of California Publications in Economics, vol. 6 (1929), 234.

33. Cf. Tamara Hareven, "Family Time and Industrial Time: Family Work in a Planned Corporation Town, 1900–1924," *Journal of Urban History* 1 (May 1975): 365–389; Hareven, "The Laborers of Manchester, New Hampshire 1912–1922: The Role of Family and Ethnicity in Adjustments to Industrial Life," *Labor History* 16 (Spring 1975): 249–265; Judith Smith, "Our Own Kind: Family and Community Networks in Providence," in Nancy Cott and Elizabeth Pleck, eds., *A Heritage of Her Own: Toward a New Social History of American Women* (New York, 1979), 393–411; and Pleck, "A Mother's Wages: Income Earning Among Married Italian and Black Women, 1896–1911," in *ibid.,* 367–392; Julia Kirk Blackwelder, "Women in the Work Force: Atlanta, New Orleans, and San Antonio, 1930–1940," *Journal of Urban History* 4 (May 1978), 331–358.

Chapter 1. The Expanding Chicano Frontier

1. Elsewhere, in southern New Mexico, for example, the government gave large grants instead to individuals or empresarios. Antonio Goubaud-Carrera, "Food Patterns and Nutrition in Two Spanish-American Communities" (Master's thesis, Univ. of Chicago, 1943), 6–7; and, for example, Jerold Widdison, "Historical Geography of the Middle Rio Puerco Valley, New Mexico," *NMHR* 34 (Oct. 1959), 264. Renato Rosaldo, "Chicano Studies, 1970–1984," *Annual Review of Anthropology* 14 (1985), 413.

2. On variations, see, for example, John Van Ness, "Hispanic Village Organization in Northern New Mexico: Corporate Community Structure in Historical and Comparative Perspective," in Paul Kutsche, ed., *The Survival of Spanish American Villages* (Colorado Springs, 1979), 38; Goubaud-Carrera, 6–7; Allan Harper et al., *Man and Resources in the Middle Rio Grande Valley* (Albuquerque, 1943), 18–19; George I. Sanchez, *Forgotten People: A Study of New Mexicans* (Albuquerque, 1940), 58; Alvar Carlson, "El Rancho and Vadito:

Spanish Settlements on Indian Lands," *El Palacio* 85 (Spring 1979), 32; Mario Barrera, *Race and Class in the Southwest* (Notre Dame, 1979), 23.

3. Emilio Lobato, Sr., interview by Elinor Kingery and Nancy Demious, 19 Nov. 1962, 0–104, CHS; Hayden Manuscript, 59, 61–62, Charles Hayden Papers, WHC; Daniel Valdes, *The Spanish-Speaking People of the Southwest* (Denver, 1938).

4. Valdes; Lobato; and John Philip Andrews, "History of Rural Spanish Settlement and Land Use in the Upper Culebra Basin of the San Luis Valley, Costilla County, Colorado" (Master's thesis, Univ. of Colorado, 1972), 52–53.

5. Goubaud-Carrera, 28.

6. *Ibid.*, 31; Nancie González, *The Spanish Americans of New Mexico: A Distinctive Heritage* (Los Angeles, 1967), 29.

7. Ms. Census, RACo, 1880; and Vigil Family Collection, Box 1. See also Janet Lecompte, "The Independent Women of Hispanic New Mexico, 1821–1846," *WHQ* 12 (Jan. 1981), 17–35; and Ricardo Romo, *East Los Angeles: History of a Barrio* (Austin, 1983), 19. On women and property, see, for example, John Lawrence Diary; Vigil Family Collection, Box 1; and Rio Arriba County Reception Book, 1887–1912 (at NMSRCA). And see Chapter 2 of this work.

8. Frances Leon Swadesh, *Los Primeros Pobladores: Hispanic Americans of the Ute Frontier* (Notre Dame, 1974), 152–153; Anselmo F. Arellano, ed., *La Tierra Amarilla: The People of the Chama Valley* (Tierra Amarilla, 1978), 106. Teodora Abeyta in the U.S.C.W.A., *Interviews,* UN3CWA M216, reel 5, p. 76. See Maurice Godelier, *Perspectives in Marxist Anthropology* (Cambridge, 1977), 20, 32 on the naïveté of assuming social inequality and rivalry do not exist in non-capitalist societies, and Georges Dupré and Pierre Philippe Rey, "Reflections on the Relevance of a Theory of the History of Exchange," in David Seddon, ed., *Relations of Production: Marxist Approaches to Anthropology* (London, 1978), 195 on the exploitation of juniors by seniors.

9. Kutsche, "Introduction," 15–17. Many villagers of various wealth had one or two Navaho slaves before the Civil War, acquired on trading or raiding forays. These slaves were treated as subordinate family members. By the 1880s, their descendants had often married into Hispanic village families, though some villagers attached a stigma to that connection. See D. Gene Combs, "Enslavement of Indians in the San Luis Valley of Colorado," *SLVH* 5 (1973), 1–29, and Ms. Census, RACo, 1880 for examples.

10. Olen E. Leonard, *The Role of the Land Grant* (1943; reprint ed. Albuquerque, 1970), 134–135.

11. Cleofas Jaramillo, *Romance of a Little Village Girl* (San Antonio, 1955), 9–15, 31, 71, 93–99, 111, 114; Donovan Senter and Florence Hawley, "The Grammar School as the Basic Acculturating Influence for Native New Mexicans," *Social Forces* 21 (May 1946), 399–400; Charles Briggs, "'Our Strength Is in the Land'" (Ph.D. dissertation, Univ. of Chicago, 1981).

12. Carlson, "El Rancho and Vadito," 32; Harper et al., 59.

13. Swadesh, 4; Mrs. A. I. Moloney Collection, Belinda Salazar, "The Story of the First Mercantile Business in Colorado," 4; Carolyn Zeleny, *Relations Between the Spanish-Americans and Anglo-Americans in New Mexico* (1944, reprint ed., New York, 1974), 82; Betty Naster, "Casimiro Barela, Colorado's 'Perpetual Senator' 1847–1920" (Master's thesis, Univ. of Denver, 1974), 5.

14. Alvar Carlson, "New Mexico's Sheep Industry, 1850–1900: Its Role in the History of the Territory," *NMHR* 44 (Jan. 1969), 27, two hundred thousand a year had gone to Mexico; and see Agapito Duran in U.S.C.W.A., *Interviews,* reel 5.

15. Arthur Campa, "Hispanic Folklore in Colorado," in José de Onís, ed., *The Hispanic Contribution to the State of Colorado* (Boulder, 1976), 91; Swadesh, 82; Marshall Sprague, *Colorado: A Bicentennial History* (New York, 1976), 58; Andrews, 65–66.

16. González, 24; *SLVH* 14 (1969), 1–7; Chris Romero, interview by Bette D. Peters, Feb. 1983, DPL, uncatalogued; William Shellabarger in Shellabarger Papers; Andrews, 34.

17. Swadesh, 64, 72; Donald Meinig, *Southwest: Three Peoples in Geographical Change, 1600–1970* (New York, 1971), chpt. 4; Carlson, "El Rancho and Vadito," 34; Eugen Archuleta, "Hispanic Villagers, the Civilian Conservation Corps and the Beginning of Social Mobility in the San Luis Valley" (unpublished ms., n.d. [1973]) in Mexican-Americans in Colorado Collection, WHC. See Bishop Lamy's attempt to resuscitate, in more standard form, the Catholic Church in New Mexico. Howard Roberts Lamar, *The Far Southwest 1846–1912: A Territorial History* (New York, 1970), 102–103.

18. Carlson, "New Mexico's Sheep Industry," 27; and see, for example, Andrews, 60.

19. Elfido Lopez, Sr., Collection 813, CHS; also doing wage work to rent land was Lucas Martinez, 0–200, CHS.

20. Meinig, chpt. 4; Andrews, 67; Swadesh, 101; U.S.C.W.A. *Interviews:* Nicholas Vigil, reel 5, 161, Agapito Duran, 327, Senator Madrid, 80, and C. T. E. Bigson, Jr., re: Lucian Lucero, reel 2, 81; Lobato; Romero.

21. R. W. Roskelley, "Population Trends in Colorado," Cooperative Plan of Rural Research, Colorado Agricultural Experiment Station, Fort Collins, and Rural Section, Division of Research, Federal WPA, Bulletin 462 (Sept. 1940), 12–13.

22. Edith Agnew and Ruth Barber, "The Unique Presbyterian School System of New Mexico," *Journal of Presbyterian History* 49 (Fall 1971), 207; Joan Moore with Alfredo Cuéllar, *Mexican Americans* (Englewood Cliffs, 1970), 15; Barrera, 7–16; Arellano, 13, 108; Swadesh, 83.

23. Stephan Abbott, 1913, cited in Swadesh, 109.

24. John W. Reps, *Cities of the American West: A History of Urban Planning* (Princeton, 1979); Owen Meredith Wilson, "A History of the Denver and Rio Grande Project, 1870–1901" (Ph.D. dissertation, Univ. of California,

Berkeley, 1942), 22: lack of federal subsidies for the Denver and Rio Grande made land speculation vital to its building. And see David Lavender, *The Southwest* (New York, 1980), 268.

25. Carlson, "New Mexico's Sheep Industry," 37. On the necessity of access to outside capital see Peter Decker, *Fortunes and Failures: White Collar Mobility in Nineteenth-Century San Francisco* (Cambridge, Mass., 1978).

26. Rio Arriba County, New Mexico, Applications for licenses, 1884–1923, NMSRCA. Even on this level, Anglo stores in Hispanic villages uniformly involved more capital than did Hispanic ones. By the 1880s, in the cities few Hispanics appeared in commercial directories or organizations. Harper et al., 64; and see, for example, U.S.C.W.A., *Interviews,* reel 5, 165–166.

27. See, for example, Andrew Schlesinger, "Las Gorras Blancas, 1889–1891," *Journal of Mexican American History* 1 (Spring 1971), 92; Carlos Jimenez, interview by Milton Callon and James Davis, 31 March 1969, DPL, OH-72: Jimenez's great uncle's land was opened to homesteaders.

28. Warren Beck and Ynez Haase, *Historical Atlas of New Mexico* (Norman, Okla., 1969), 21; Robert Rosenbaum, *Mexicano Resistance in the Southwest: "The Sacred Right of Self Preservation"* (Austin, 1981), 138.

29. Beck and Haase, 21. The court sat until 1904, but the loss of land continued afterward.

30. Zeleny, 154.

31. William Keleher, "Law of the New Mexico Land Grant," *NMHR* 4 (Oct. 1929), 358–359.

32. Zeleny, 159; Jimenez; Swadesh, 70; Court Records, Rio Arriba County; Lamar, 137–139, 145–147, 150. Robert Torrez, "'El Bornes': La Tierra Amarilla and T. D. Burns," *NMHR* 56 (April 1981), 171. Burns started buying portions from heirs up to 42,000 acres in a single month, and acquired others from debts and possibly even by destruction of deeds given him for safekeeping. Local bitterness still lingers. See also Olen Leonard and Charles Loomis, *Culture of a Contemporary Rural Community: El Cerrito, New Mexico* (Washington, D.C., 1941), 111–112. Land grant literature and cases are extensive. See, for example, U.S.D.A., Soil Conservation Service, "Notes on Community Owned Land Grants," Aug. 1937, in the Eastburn Smith Collection, NMSRCA; William deBuys, "Fractions of Justice: A Legal and Social History of the Las Trampas Land Grant, New Mexico," *NMHR* 56 (Jan. 1981), 71–97; Clark S. Knowlton, "Causes of Land Loss Among the Spanish Americans in Northern New Mexico," *Rocky Mountain Social Science Journal* 1 (April 1964), 201–211.

33. deBuys, 77, 79, 80, 81–82. Keleher, 364. When the Rocky Mountain Timber Company, a sister company of the Colorado Fuel and Iron Company, bought a large section of the (confirmed) Maxwell Land Grant along the southern Colorado border, some residents had to renegotiate leases while others were forced off land reserved for CFI use. See Gary Beardsworth, "The Effects of the Denver and Rio Grande Railway on the Resident Population of Southern Col-

orado Between 1860 and 1885," May 1973, in Mexican-Americans in Colorado Collection; and William Taylor and Elliott West, "Patron Leadership at the Crossroads: Southern Colorado in the Late Nineteenth Century," *PHR* 42 (Aug. 1973), 341. Not until 1913 did a New Mexico statute prohibit alienation of common lands without approval of a grant board of trustees.

34. Taylor and West, 342. See also the impact on surrounding lands of wool-washing concerns and tie pickling plants in Las Vegas, New Mexico.

35. Lela Weatherby, "A Study of the Early Years of the Presbyterian Work with the Spanish Speaking People of New Mexico and Colorado and Its Development from 1850–1920" (Master's thesis, Presbyterian College of Christian Education, 1942), 31; Beck and Haase, 59; Barrera, 23ff; Gov. Miguel Otero in Wayne Moquin with Charles van Doren, eds., *A Documentary History of the Mexican Americans* (New York, 1971). Gov. Otero's plea for statehood rested partially on the grounds that the federal government was stripping New Mexico of its public domain. See also Carlson, "New Mexico's Sheep Industry," 37.

36. For example, Andrews, 68; John Lawrence Collection, diary, 13 March 1906, WHC; and Wesley Robert Hurt, Jr., "Manzano: A Study of Community Disorganization" (Master's thesis, Univ. of New Mexico, 1941), 100.

37. Andrews, 66; Harper et al., 60.

38. Paul Walter, Jr., "A Study of Isolation and Social Change in Three Spanish Speaking Villages of New Mexico" (Ph.D. dissertation, Stanford Univ., 1938), 40; Harper et al., 60, 62; Barrera, 23ff; Leo Grebler et al., *The Mexican-American People: The Nation's Second Largest Minority* (New York, 1970), 49; Taylor and West, 356.

39. Frank H. Grubbs, "Frank Bond: Gentleman Sheepherder of Northern New Mexico 1883–1915," *NMHR* 35 (July 1960), 172; statistics on sheep from Carlson, "New Mexico's Sheep Industry," 36.

40. Grubbs, 181.

41. Carlson, "New Mexico's Sheep Industry," 36.

42. Harper et al., 79; Carlson, "New Mexico's Sheep Industry"; Grubbs, "Frank Bond," *NMHR* 35 (July 1960), 182–187, and 36 (Oct. 1961), 299. By 1900 the Bonds had 18,000 sheep on shares at Española and 30,000 at Wagonmound by 1904, and 24,000 at Trinidad. In 1911 they had over 37,000 on 90 separate contracts.

43. Grubbs, "Frank Bond," *NMHR* 35 (July 1960), 17.

44. Carlson, "New Mexico's Sheep Industry," 37.

45. Arellano, 16; Torrez, 168.

46. Ms. Census, RACo, 1880, 1900; Carlos Jimenez; Elfido Lopez; William Parish, ed., "Sheep Husbandry in New Mexico, 1902–1903," *NMHR* 37 (July 1962), 209.

47. Harper et al., 64; Carlson, "El Rancho and Vadito," 38.

48. John Lawrence, Diary, 27–31 Oct. 1902 and 3 Jan. 1904; on intermarriage see Darlis Miller, "Cross-Cultural Marriages in the Southwest: The New

Mexico Experience, 1846–1900." *NMHR* 57 (Oct. 1982), 335–360. Marriage registers from Rio Arriba County indicate a static rate as do census records from 1880 and 1900. In Las Animas County, Colorado, the intermarriages, according to the marriage registers, increased from 2.5% in 1900 to 6.6% in 1906 and 8.4% in 1916, concentrated in the mining camps.

49. Robert Larson, *New Mexico Populism: A Study of Radical Protest in a Western Territory* (Boulder, 1974), 50; see Schlesinger, and Rosenbaum, on which this account heavily relies as well as Carlos Jimenez. And see also Robert Rosenbaum, "Las Gorras Blancas of San Miguel County, 1889–1890," in Renato Rosaldo et al., eds., *Chicano: The Evolution of a People* (Minneapolis, 1973), 132, 136n.

50. Schlesinger, throughout, quoting the Las Vegas Optic's editor. The Knights of Labor district organizer may have used his organizing talents for both groups.

51. Quoted in *ibid.,* 115.

52. Lavender, 248; Swadesh, xix, 231 n 42. In the Estancia Valley in 1911, a large arsenal was found in a barn at Abo, purportedly collected with the intention of driving the Anglos from the valley. Hurt, 99.

53. Schlesinger, 113; Parish, *NMHR* 37 (Oct. 1962), 289; Keleher, 364; Callon Papers, Box 5, File 9.

54. See the 1915 libel law passed with Penitente influence. Jose Amaro Hernandez, *Mutual Aid for Survival: The Case of the Mexican American* (Malabar, Fla., 1983), 17–28. The degree of Penitente political solidarity from 1880 to 1940 is hotly disputed. See Jack E. Holmes, "Success and Failure: The Limits of New Mexico's Hispanic Politics," in Rosaldo et al., 238–248.

55. New Mexico State Corporation Commission, *Annual Reports;* José Timoteo López, *La Historia de la Sociedad Protección Mutua de Trabajadores Unidos* (New York, 1958), 8–20; Frederick Sanchez, "A History of the S.P.M.D.T.U." *SLVH* 3 (Winter 1971), 3–4; Rosenbaum, *Mexicano Resistance,* 131, 146; Paul Walter, Jr., "The Press as a Source in the Study of Social Problems" (Master's thesis, Univ. of New Mexico, 1933). Representatives of seven newspapers in 1892 formed an association.

56. In Antonito. In their determination to retain control of the new organization, S.P.M.D.T.U. banned holders of political or religious office from becoming members. José López, 9, 12.

57. For example, "Constitution and Bye-laws of the Association of the Brotherhood for the Protection of the Rights and Privileges of the People of New Mexico," in L. Bradford Prince Collection.

58. Callon Papers, Box 4, File 6; Schlesinger, 122–124; Rosenbaum, *Mexicano Resistance,* 135.

59. Schlesinger, 123; *NMJE* 7 (Oct. 1910), 4, listing New Mexico delegates to the constitutional convention. For Rio Arriba, Taos, and Mora Counties, where the population was approximately 90% Hispanic, about half the delegates were Hispanic.

60. Grubbs, *NMHR* 36 (Oct. 1961), 316.

61. New Mexico Superintendent of Public Instruction, *Report,* 1910–1912, 44.

62. See various issues of *HMM* on the shortness of the term; Lois Huebert, "A History of Presbyterian Church Schools in New Mexico" (Master's thesis, Univ. of New Mexico, 1964), 28 states that in 1891 the average length of the rural public school term in the state was two months; Louisa Vigil in Nan Elsasser et al., *Las Mujeres: Conversations from a Hispanic Community* (Old Westbury, N.Y., 1980), 13–14; Weatherby, 46–47; Zeleny, 273.

63. On the Penitentes as resisting the new Anglo-Catholic hierarchy, eager for literacy, prone to conversion by Protestant missionaries who simultaneously saw in them the most horrific symbol of idolatry and Romanism, see Schlesinger, 105; Zeleny, 140, 145, 149–150; Swadesh, 77; Sherman Doyle, *Presbyterian Home Missions* (New York, 1905), 216.

64. Minutes of the Synod of Colorado, 18 May 1880, cited in R. Douglas Brackenridge and Francisco O. García-Treto, *Iglesia Presbiteriana: A History of Presbyterians and Mexican Americans in the Southwest* (San Antonio, 1974), 69.

65. Doyle, 214; *HMM* 14 (Nov. 1900); "History of the Presbytery of Pueblo," 1907, in Darley Family Collection, Box 3, WHC. The College at Del Norte lasted from 1884–1901.

66. Brackenridge and García-Treto, 61; Weatherby, 42. Double villages include, for example, Garcia-Costilla, San Pablo-San Pedro, San Rafael-Mogote. Compare impact of missionaries on native Americans, see Robert F. Berkhofer, Jr., *Salvation and the Savage: An Analysis of Protestant Missions and the American Indian Response, 1787–1862* (New York, 1972).

67. Brackenridge and García-Treto, 54, 55, 73.

68. *Ibid.,* 52. Similarly, the territorial government found it necessary to establish a separate Spanish American Normal School in 1909 to train Spanish American teachers, something the New Mexico Normal University at Las Vegas had signally failed to do. The school provided the first opportunity many Hispanics in Rio Arriba and Taos counties had for education beyond the fourth grade, but few positions opened for Hispanic teachers outside their own culture area. Spanish American Normal School, reports to the governor, in Governor McDonald Papers, NMSRCA.

69. Maria Girard Vincent, "Ritual Kinship in an Urban Setting: Martineztown, New Mexico" (Master's thesis, Univ. of New Mexico, 1966), 147; Emilio Lobato, Sr.; Catron Papers, Archive 29, Box 502:1, folders 15, 16; Las Animas County School records, Box 13100, District 4 (Madrid) cashbook; Roy Banner and Arthur Maes, "The Justice of Peace Courts of New Mexico with Particular Emphasis on Those of Bernalillo County," *Research* (Univ. of New Mexico) 1 (April 1937), 100, 105–106; Dena Markoff, "Beet Hand Laborers of Sugar City, Colorado, 1900–1920," in Sidney Heitman, ed., *Germans from Russia in Colorado* (Ann Arbor, 1978), 180; Florence Kluckhohn and Fred Strodtbeck, *Variations in Value Orientations* (Evanston, Ill., 1961), 184; Walter, "A Study of

Isolation," throughout; Taylor and West, 340; Hurt, 170; Clark S. Knowlton, "Patron-Peon Pattern Among the Spanish Americans of New Mexico" in Rosaldo et al., 233–234.

70. Swadesh, 59; Taylor and West, 337; Zeleny, 166–167; Barrera, 27–33; Fabiola Cabeza de Baca Gilbert, *We Fed Them Cactus* (Albuquerque, 1954), ix–x, 6; Maurilio Vigil, *Los Patrones: Profiles of Hispanic Political Leaders* (Washington, D.C., 1980), 63–65 etc.

71. Zeleny, 170; Moore, 15. And see Naster, 12–13, 87, 89, on Casimiro Barela, Colorado State senator from 1876 to 1916.

72. Zeleny, 166–167; Parish, *NMHR* 37 (Oct. 1962), 284.

73. A. C. Campbell to Otero, 17 June 1901, Otero Collection, Archive 21, Box 1.

74. Swadesh, 136, 176; Paul Kutsche and John Van Ness, *Cañones: Values, Crisis and Survival in a Northern New Mexico Village* (Albuquerque, 1981), 96–97. Kutsche, "Introduction," 15–17.

75. Holmes, 240, 242, 244–245.

76. Rosenbaum, "Las Gorras Blancas," 131, 138, 143; Rosenbaum, *Mexicano Resistance,* 144.

77. Petitions 1912: Colfax County, Governor McDonald's Papers; see also Taylor and West, 341, 356–357; Barrera, 454; Knowlton, 235–236.

78. Lena Granger, San Pablo, *HMM* 17 (Nov. 1902), 16.

79. John LaFont, *The Homesteaders of the Upper Rio Grande* (Birmingham, 1971), 25; John Lawrence Diary, 5 June 1901 and 4 June 1902; Lucas Martinez.

80. Kalervo Oberg, "Cultural Factors and Land-Use Planning in Cuba Valley, New Mexico," *Rural Sociology* 5 (Dec. 1940), 441; Harper et al., 21; Lucas Martinez supported his 1908 homestead in northern Colorado with beetwork and partido contracts even after he proved up, concluding, "El que es pobre es pobre" and the rich stay rich.

81. James Atkins, *Human Relations in Colorado—A Historical Record* (Denver, 1968), 99.

82. Jonathan Van Arsdale, "Railroads in New Mexico," *Research* 2 (Dec. 1939), 5–7; Beck and Haase, 58.

83. In Mexico the range of railroad work open to Chicanos was broader. Victor Clark, *Mexican Labor in the United States,* U.S. Labor Bureau Bulletin no. 78 (Sept. 1908), 477.

84. *Ibid.,* 478–481; Zeleny, 179; Goubaud-Carrera, 78. Steve Martinez, "Frank Romero," *SLVH* 8 (1976), 20. Ms. Census, RACo, 1900.

85. The Hispanic miners could earn up to $55 per month. Clark, 487–488; *C&P* 1 (14 Dec. 1901), 6, and 3 (25 April 1903), 364; U.S. Congress, Senate, Commission on Industrial Relations, *Rockefeller Interests in Colorado,* 64th Cong., 1st sess., S.doc. 415, 1916, 8905–8906. Colorado Coal Mine Inspector, *Annual Reports,* 1901–1910.

86. Clark, 488.

87. Thomas W. Shomburg, March 3, n.d., oral history at CHS, re: Rocky Mountain Timber Company 1902; Clark, 494; Swadesh, 87–88; *C&P* 4 (26 Sept. 1903), 245–247.

88. Ms. Census, RACo, 1880.

89. *Ibid.,* 1880, 1900, and Las Animas County, 1900; and Catron Papers, Box 502:1, folders 15 and 16; Delphino Salazar in U.S.C.W.A., *Interviews* reel 2, p. 106; Shomburg; Miller, 340, 342–343, 346.

90. Ms. Census—in addition, eight women and sixty-six men were listed as farmers in Embudo; U.S.C.W.A., *Interviews* reel 2, p. 105.

91. Bound histories of factory districts, and statistical data 1901–1924, Box 16A, Great Western Sugar Company Papers, Univ. of Colorado; William May, Jr., "The Great Western Sugarlands: History of the Great Western Sugar Company" (Ph.D. dissertation, Univ. of Colorado, 1982), 4–21, 40–53.

92. For example, Clark, 472, 484.

93. The companies had originally imported the German-Russians from Russia for their knowledge of beet cultivation. Markoff, 85, 95; Clark, 484; J. C. Ross, *HMM* 16 (Nov. 1902), 12; U.S. Congress, Senate, Committee on Immigration, *Report of the Immigration Commission,* 61st Cong., doc. 85, part 25, vol. 2, 1911.

94. Notes, 7 May 1904, p. 4, Callon Papers, Box 4, file 2; Lucas Martinez. Some of the families who came north homesteaded there while working in beets to earn cash, for example, see Ft. Collins *Coloradan,* May 18, 1975, "Mexican Americans Have Deep Roots Here," in DPL clipping file under "Spanish-Americans," and see Chris Romero.

95. Clark, 484; Harry Schwartz, *Seasonal Farm Labor in the United States with Special Reference to Hired Workers in Fruit and Vegetable and Sugar-Beet Production* (New York, 1945), 108.

96. May, 412; Weld County School Records, Box 13376, CSA; Clark, 496.

97. Edward Clopper and Lewis Hine, *Child Labor in the Sugar Beet Fields of Colorado* (New York, 1916), 22–24; Deaconess Mission, June 10, 1913, Board of Charities and Corrections, Box 66924, CSA.

98. By 1909, Denver and Pueblo each had licensed employment agencies run and owned by Spanish Americans. Colorado Bureau of Labor Statistics, *Biennial Report* (1909–1910), 213, 215.

99. Rio Arriba County school census Aug. 1915, and Rio Arriba County marriage records, Jan. 1907–Feb. 1911, NMSRCA; *HMM* 27 (Nov. 1912), 4; Clark, 502.

100. In 1906, 27.2% of the Hispanic marriages involved people of different towns, and there were nine mixed marriages (or 6.6% of Hispanic marriages). Clark, 519; Las Animas County, Colorado, marriage registers.

101. Clark, 502.

102. *Ibid.,* 485.

103. *Ibid.*, 481, 485.

104. *Ibid.*, 488, 496, 498. Barrera (on structural discrimination), 50.

105. *C&P* 4 (26 Sept. 1903), 246.

106. Alice Blake, "Presbyterian Work in New Mexico" (unpublished manuscript, 1935), 100; Clark, 502–503.

107. Joan Jensen, "Women Teachers, Class, and Ethnicity: New Mexico, 1900–1950," *Southwest Economy and Society* 4 (Late Winter 1978–1979), 3; Herbert Gutman, *Work, Culture and Society in Industrializing America* (1966, reprint ed., New York, 1977), on Americanizing industrial work habits. Ruth Laughlin Barker, *Caballeros* (New York, 1931), 268; Clark, 501, 503, 522; Arnold Anderson, 1909, cited in Nancie González, *The Spanish-Americans of New Mexico: A Heritage of Pride* (Albuquerque, 1969), 54.

108. Morton Fried quoted in Zeleny, 238 n 19.

109. Archuleta, 4; and see Swadesh, 200.

110. Clark, 498, 501, 504; Luisa Torres, "Palabras de Una Viejita/The Words of an Old One," *El Palacio* 84 (Fall 1978), 10; Goubaud-Carrera, 19–20, 57.

111. Clark, 504; Torres, 10.

112. Clark, 502.

113. Zeleny, 300. See Alan Dawley, *Class and Community: The Industrial Revolution in Lynn* (Cambridge, Mass., 1976), for a discussion of the disparity in views held by different groups on technology, culture, and economy. Cf. Manuel Gamio, *Mexican Immigration to the United States* (Chicago, 1930), 67–75, 138.

114. Zeleny, xi.

115. Charles Loomis, "Systematic Linkage of El Cerrito," *Rural Sociology* 24 (March 1959), 55–56.

116. Swadesh, 154–155, 187; Kluckhohn quoted in González, *A Distinctive Heritage*, 45; Kutsche, "Introduction," 12.

Chapter 2. Hispanic Village Women

1. Luisa Torres, "Palabras de Una Viejita/The Words of an Old One," *El Palacio* 84 (Fall 1978), 12. And see also Annette Thorp, "Vicenta," WPA 5.5.53, no. 1, NMHL.

2. Some of the material presented in this and the following chapters has appeared in Sarah Deutsch, "Women and Intercultural Relations, the Case of Hispanic New Mexico and Colorado," *Signs* 12 (Summer 1987). See Maxine Baca Zinn, "Gender and Ethnic Identity among Chicanos," *Frontiers* 5 (Summer 1980), 18–24, and her "Mexican-American Women in the Social Sciences," *Signs* 8 (Winter 1982), 259–272; Alfredo Mirandé and Evangelina Enríquez, *La Chicana: The Mexican American Woman* (Chicago, 1979), 108–117; and Richard Griswold del Castillo, *La Familia: Chicano Families in the Urban South-*

west, 1848 to the Present (Notre Dame, 1984) for protests and summaries of relevant literature. The connection between concrete life and ideology is tricky. Ramon Gutierrez, "Marriage, Sex, and the Family: Social Change in Colonial New Mexico, 1660–1846" (Ph.D. dissertation, Univ. of Wisconsin, Madison, 1980), and Griswold del Castillo argue that despite differences between ideology and practice, a patriarchal ideal of unlimited male authority persisted in the upper and middle classes, and was probably aped by the lower classes. Some recent works which do depict village women as more autonomous include Facundo Valdez, "Vergüenza," in Paul Kutsche, ed., *The Survival of Spanish American Villages,* Colorado College Studies no. 15 (Spring 1979), 102; Joan Jensen, "Canning Comes to New Mexico: Women and the Agricultural Extension Service, 1914–1919," *NMHR* 57 (Oct. 1982), 361–386; Janet Lecompte on an earlier period, "The Independent Women of Hispanic New Mexico, 1821–1846," *WHQ* 12 (Jan. 1981), 17–35; and Frances Swadesh, *Los Primeros Pobladores* (Notre Dame, 1974). Recent works on Chicano urban history cover urban but not village women, see the introduction to this work.

3. Valdez, 102.

4. Antonio Goubaud-Carrera, "Food Patterns and Nutrition in Two Spanish-American Communities" (Master's thesis, Univ. of Chicago, 1943), 59.

5. Olen Leonard, *The Role of the Land Grant in the Social Organization and Social Processes of a Spanish American Village in New Mexico* (1943, reprint ed. Albuquerque, 1970), 70.

6. Thorp, "Chana," WPA 5.5.52, no. 71, NMHL; Grace Farrell, "Homemaking with the 'Other Half' Along Our International Border," *Journal of Home Economics* 21 (June 1929), 416; Fabiola Cabeza de Baca Gilbert, *We Fed Them Cactus* (Albuquerque, 1954), 83.

7. Occasionally a group of women would sponsor one. John Lawrence Diary, 23–24 Oct. 1904, WHC.

8. Nan Elsasser et al., *Las Mujeres: Conversations from a Hispanic Community* (Old Westbury, N.Y., 1979), 9; Thorp, "Weddings," WPA 5.5.52, no. 67, NMHL, and "Chana." According to Mary Wilson in Santa Fe in 1919, "The house is always open to receive callers, and no young man stopping on an errand is ever in too great haste to chat for a brief time with any member of the family he may meet." "The Place and Influence of Mexican Women," *HMM* 33 (Aug. 1919), 222.

9. Thorp, "Satan and the Girl," WPA 5.5.53, no. 4, NMHL.

10. Fran Leeper Buss, *La Partera: Story of a Midwife* (Ann Arbor, 1980).

11. Farrell, 416; Lawrence Diary, 16 Aug. 1903 and 29 July 1904.

12. Described many places, for example, Thorp, "Weddings," and Clark, *HMM* 16 (Nov. 1901), 11; Leonard, 78, is the only reference I have seen describe the mother's participation in this phase of the process. Illiterate parents often left a squash; the way in which it was returned signified a positive or negative response.

13. Thorp, "Weddings."

14. *Ibid.* Re: property, see, for example, Cleofas Jaramillo, *Romance of a Little Village Girl* (San Antonio, 1955), 131. She had a herd of sheep in her own right, which she continued to hold as such, given her by her father. Grace Russell, "Wedding Customs," *HMM* 35 (May 1921), 153.

15. See Ms. Census, RACo, Chimayo, El Rito, Embudo, 1910; only in the 1880s did an unusually large number of women, up to 25%, marry under the age of fifteen, while from 1900 to 1910 less than 8% did so, in the 1890s less than 6%; in the 1860s and 1870s the figure is 19%, but it must be recalled that a disproportionate number of youthful marriages is likely to have survived the intervening fifty years.

16. See RACo Records, Criminal and Civil Docket, vols. D, E; Reception Book 1887–1912; and Juez de Paz Record Book, Abiquiu, NMSRCA; Dorothy Woodward, "The Penitentes of New Mexico" (Ph.D. dissertation, Yale Univ., 1935), 281; WPA files; and Lawrence Diary, 16 April 1903. On fathers refusing daughter's choice in marriage, see, for example, "Manuela," WPA files, 11, pp. 275ff, NMSRCA. See also Mirandé and Enríquez, 116.

17. As can be seen in marriage procedures above, in Elsasser et al., in my interviews, and in Donovan Senter and Florence Hawley, "The Grammar School as the Basic Acculturating Influence for Native New Mexicans," *Social Forces* 24 (May 1946), 402.

18. Elsasser et al., 87–88; Buss, throughout; Granger, *HMM* 16 (Nov. 1901), 16; *HMM* 23 (Nov. 1908), 16. It seems to have been Hispanic men who reached adolescence in such urban environments as Albuquerque and San Francisco after 1940 who insisted that wives stay at home, that men control household funds, and that children and household chores were not in the man's sphere. See Elsasser et al. and Chapter 6.

19. Wayne Moquin, with Charles Van Doren, eds., *A Documentary History of the Mexican Americans* (New York, 1971), 268: William Shepherd. Leonard, 119. On Hispanic vs. Anglo marital property law, see Richard Griswold del Castillo, *The Los Angeles Barrio, 1850–1890: A Social History* (Berkeley, 1979), 69–70, 154; and Joan Jensen, who warns against romanticizing this community property practice in "'I've Worked, I'm Not Afraid of Work': Farm Women in New Mexico, 1920–1940," *NMHR* 61 (Jan. 1986), 30.

20. Leonard, 53. Ms. Census, RACo, for example Ojo Caliente, Chimayo, and Embudo, 1900, 1910. Case 680, RACo. Records, District Court, vol. E, 1905–1911. This case involved both a woman who cultivated the land with the help of her son and tenants to about 1900, and a woman who planted seed and defended her land (successfully) against other claimants after that.

21. Mrs. J. B. Martinez to Vigil, 24 Jan. 1900, Vigil Family Collection, Box 1, WHC (my translation). On women and property, see also John Lawrence Diary; Vigil Family Collection, Box 1; and Rio Arriba County Reception Book, 1887–1912 (at NMSRCA). The latter actually shows a decline in women's participation in property transfers, from 25% of transfers in the 1880s to 2.5% for

1909–10, but increasing to 12.3% for 1911–12. The percent of property transactions involving Hispanic women acting on their own, as opposed to acting jointly with a husband or other male, followed the same pattern, at all times forming approximately half the number of women's property transactions.

22. John Lawrence Diary, 5 Nov. 1901 and 27 Oct. 1901; Jaramillo, 131.

23. Re: partido contracts, this was sometimes insisted on by Anglo contractors to avoid a bankruptcy dodge. Case 337, Lujan v. Lujan, Catron Papers, Archive 29, Box 201:10, folder 1, UNM. 1896 Juez de Paz Record Book, Abiquiu, 15 June 1909, NMSRCA. RACo Records, District Court, vol. E, 1905–1911, Docket Book, 1895–1905, and Reception Book, 1887–1912, NMSRCA. Dona Josefita Atencio, wife of Don Agapito Atencio, Las Animas County, "possessed strong opinions of her own. . . . To the last of her days she continued to sell her grain by the 'fenega' and in 'Reales' she counted the cash received for her grain"; Louis Sporleder, *The Romance of the Spanish Peaks* (n.p., 1960), 16.

24. Elsasser et al.: Vigil, 13.

25. For example, of El Rito's 117 households in 1880, only 9 were headed by women; in 1900, 16 of 120; and in 1910, 18 of 164. Respectively, 6, 16 and 17 of these were widows; 2, 1, and 3 were single women, and 1, 1, 0 were divorcées. Ms. Census, RACo, 1880, 1900, 1910; and see Thorp, "Chana."

26. As few single males as single females headed households. Ms. Census, RACo, 1880, 1900, 1910.

27. Ruth Laughlin Barker, *Caballeros* (New York, 1931), 277. Case 253, Maria Rita M. De Montoya vs. Juan Sanchez and Mrs. Remedio de Sanchez, 1915, Santa Fe County, Catron Papers, Box 201:8, folder 15. Anaria Margarita Vasquez to Vigil, 24 Nov. 1912, Vigil Family Collection, Box 1. As did men, widows without access to cash earnings had trouble meeting their property taxes. Jaramillo, 125–137. Mrs. Eva Montoya to Vigil, 19 March 1913, Vigil Family Collection, Box 1. She had an adult son, but conducted her own business. See also Mrs. J. B. Martinez to Vigil, 11 April 1913, Notary's Record 1906, and file 19, *ibid.* RACo Civil Docket, District Court, vol. D, 1895–1915, shows women involved in five cases regarding taxes and other land disputes, and one ejectment.

28. For example, Laurel Ulrich, *Goodwives: Image and Reality in the Lives of Women in Northern New England 1650–1750* (New York, 1982), 50. Similar to the environment Ulrich describes is the personal nature of business transactions within the community.

29. Buss, 51; Sister M. Lucia Van der Eerden, *Maternity Care in a Spanish-American Community of New Mexico* (Washington, D.C., 1948), 34; and Thorp, "Curandera," WPA 5.5.52, no. 70, NMHL. Curanderas were also exempt from this sexual taboo and could treat men alone and go to widowers homes and give, for example, massages, see John Lawrence Diary, 2 Dec. 1907.

30. "Parteras," WPA 5.5.53, no. 8, NMHL.

31. Buss, 34–35; Van der Eerden, 13–15.

32. Van der Eerden, 33; Elsasser et al.: Sedillo, 19.

33. Van der Eerden, 15, 21, 26, 34.

34. Buss, 50; and see "Parteras."

35. Lou Sage Batchen, "La Curandera," *El Palacio* 18 (Spring 1975), 22.

36. Thorp, "Curandera."

37. *Ibid.,* and Van der Eerden, 37.

38. Van der Eerden, 10; John Lawrence Diary, 16 April 1903; and various issues of *HMM*. Doctors charged, in addition to their set fees, one dollar each mile traveled, which added up rapidly as there were only four doctors in New Mexico north of Santa Fe in this period.

39. Elsasser et al., 41.

40. Buss, App. I: Rackley, 116.

41. Buss, 6–7.

42. Thorp, "Partera. 'Midwife,'" WPA 5.5.53, no. 8. See also Buss, App. I: Rackley, 116. Cf. Eleanor Leacock, *Myths of Male Dominance* (New York, 1981), 146, that women gained public recognition as herbal doctors.

43. Goubaud-Carrera, 59. Buss, 27. Thorp, "Vicenta." "Co-parent" is a more accurate translation of the duties of the comadre or madrina than "god-parent"; see, for example, Hayden manuscript, Hayden Papers, WHC.

44. See, for example, Thorp, "Lina," 5.5.52, no. 74 and Thorp, "Weddings." Co-parents were usually close relatives, partly because one could not marry co-parents, so they were taken from among already ineligible mates of the small villages. See Swadesh, 189. Widowhood, remarriage, and large families were all common. To contrast Los Angeles practice in naming co-parents, see Griswold del Castillo, *Los Angeles,* 97.

45. *HMM* 14 (Nov. 1899), 10; and see Elsasser et al.: Luisa Vigil, 11; "Alita," *HMM* 14 (Nov. 1899), 8.

46. Cf. Nancy Grey Osterud, "Strategies of Mutuality: Relations Among Women and Men in an Agricultural Community" (Ph.D. dissertation, Brown Univ., 1984).

47. Leonard, 75–76, 113; Prudence Clark, *HMM* 24 (Nov. 1909), 5.

48. Benham, *HMM* 16 (Nov. 1901), 8; Elsasser et al.: Vigil, 14; John Lawrence Diary, WHC. And see Griswold del Castillo, *La Familia,* 42–43.

49. Thorp, "Chana"; Hayden manuscript, 66; *HMM* 19 (Nov. 1904), 13; C. Jimenez, Oral History 72, DPL; "Alita," *HMM* 14 (Nov. 1899), 8; Carolyn Atkins, ed., *Los Tres Campos—The Three Fields* (Albuquerque, 1978): Romero, Lopez, 18, and Ortega, 48.

50. Lorin Brown (Lorenzo de Cordova), *Echoes of the Flute* (Santa Fe, 1972), 22.

51. *Ibid.,* 41–42; *HMM* 19 (Nov. 1904), 7; Alice Corbin Henderson, *Brothers of Light* (Santa Fe, 1937), 76–77; Marta Weigle, *Brothers of Light, Brothers of Blood* (Albuquerque, 1976), 144. Paul Kutsche and Dennis Gallegos, "Community Functions of the *Cofradía de Nuestro Padre de Jesús Nazareno*," in

Kutsche, 94; William Wallrich, "Auxiliadoras de la Morada," *Southwestern Lore* 16 (June 1950), 4–10.

52. Kutsche and Gallegos, 97; *HMM* 15 (Nov. 1900), 10, and 21 (April 1906), 5. Thorp, "Lina."

53. F. Maes, *HMM* 16 (Nov. 1902), 8; Rev. Robert Craig, *Our Mexicans* (New York, 1904), 32. Clark, *HMM* 16 (Nov. 1901), 10; and Hyson, *ibid.,* 16. Jaramillo, 42, 44; Elsasser et al., 9. Alice Blake, "Presbyterian Mission Work in New Mexico" (unpublished manuscript, 1935), 61.

54. John Burma, *Spanish Speaking Groups in the United States* (Durham, 1954), 24. Florence Kluckhohn and Fred Strodtbeck, *Variations in Value Orientations* (Evanston, 1961), 230. Estelle Warner, "Mountain Villages of New Mexico," *HMM* 34 (May 1920), 147: "The visiting priest and the reader who takes his place when he is not there, generally a woman . . . " Farrell, 415. Jaramillo, 33. Leonard, 71. Wallrich, 4–10.

55. Men and women also sat separately at religious services, and fiestas had both a mayordomo and a mayordama. Henderson, 50; Thorp, "Lina." Farrell, 415. When faced with a Protestant missionary threat, neither sex monopolized the role of guardian of the faith. Alphonso Esquibel, *Vaquero to Dominic* (Santa Fe, 1978), 9. *The Church at Home and Abroad* 18 (April 1895), 289. Blake, "Presbyterian Mission Work," 99. Jane Atkins Grainger, *El Centenario de la Palabre* (Albuquerque, 1980), 96–97. Lydia Zellers, OH, TC93, MHL. Blake, *HMM* 14 (March 1900), 99; Allison, *HMM* 17 (Jan. 1903), 58; *HMM* 19 (Nov. 1904), 6, 11; Clark, *HMM* 20 (June 1906), 178; Hyson, *HMM* 22 (Aug. 1908), 243; *HMM* 26 (Nov. 1911), 28; and Lela Weatherby, "A Study of the Early Years of the Presbyterian Work with the Spanish Speaking People of New Mexico and Colorado and Its Development from 1850–1920" (Master's thesis, Presbyterian College of Christian Education, 1942), 62. These are instances of parents refusing to let spouses or children convert to Presbyterianism; despite the impressions of some missionaries, there is no indication that either mothers or fathers predominated among resisters or converts.

56. Thorp, "Lina." Ester Gallegos y Chavez, "The Northern New Mexico Woman: A Changing Silhouette," in Arnulfo D. Trejo, ed., *The Chicanos as We See Ourselves* (Tucson, 1979), 70.

57. Charles Briggs, "'Our Strength Is in the Land': The Structure of Hierarchy and Equality and the Pragmatics of Discourse in Hispano ('Spanish American') 'Talk About the Past'" (Ph.D. dissertation, Univ. of Chicago, 1981), 264ff.

58. Thorp, "Chana." Flora Lucero Garcia, "Margarita Ruyball Lucero," *SLVH* 8 (1976), 3–5; Allison, *HMM* 23 (Nov. 1908), 9.

59. Ms. Census, RACo, Chimayo, 1880, 1900, 1910.

60. For example, Hayden manuscript, 68–69.

61. On processing (butchering, rendering lard, drying meat, shelling, toasting, sifting, and sometimes harvesting grains) see Clark, *HMM* 15 (March 1901),

104–105; MacArthur, *HMM* 24 (Nov. 1909), 16. Jensen, "Canning," 365; Thorp, "Chana"; Hayden manuscript, 69.

62. Paul Kutsche and John Van Ness, *Cañones: Values, Crisis and Survival in a Northern New Mexico Community* (Albuquerque, 1981), 22.

63. Blake, *HMM* 27 (Nov. 1912), 18; Goubaud-Carrera, 59. Hayden manuscript, 64.

64. Thorp, "Vicenta."

65. Leonard, 74.

66. Goubaud-Carrera, 64. Cf. George Foster, "The Dyadic Contract: A Model for the Social Structure of a Mexican Peasant Village," in Jack M. Potter et al., *Peasant Society: A Reader* (Boston, 1967), 218–220.

67. "Parteras," WPA 5.5.53, no. 8, NMHL.

68. For example, Buss, 21; Leonard, 80; and Olen Leonard and Charles Loomis, *Culture of a Contemporary Rural Community* (Washington, D.C., 1941), 19 on definitions of male virtue.

69. Thorp, "Vicenta." See also Ann Lucero, "Memories of Mr. Abel Chavez," *SLVH* 8 (1976), 23–24.

70. For example, Ruth Barber, Oral History TC 35C, MHL, and various issues of *HMM*.

71. Thorp, "Vicenta"; and Catarina Padilla, WPA B.C. no. 538:5, NMSRCA; and Barker, 306–308.

72. Quoted in Robert Coles, *The Old Ones of New Mexico* (Albuquerque, 1973), 25.

73. For example, Blake, *HMM* 27 (Nov. 1912), 18; Granger, *HMM* 16 (Nov. 1901), 16; *HMM* 26 (Nov. 1911), 14, and 19 (Nov. 1904), 4; and Thorp, "Chana." For communal plastering of homes see interviews and Van der Eerden, 5–6 on exchange of labor.

74. Ms. Census, RACo, 1910.

75. Kutsche and Van Ness, 35.

76. Men: *HMM* 19 (Nov. 1904), 11; William Parish, ed., "Sheep Husbandry in New Mexico, 1902–1903," *NMHR* 37 (Oct. 1962), 263. Women: "Manuela," pp. 275–276, WPA files, 11, NMSRCA; Parish, 285; Thorp, "Chana" and "Vicenta"; M. K. Marquez, "Juanita Ortega de Gomez," *SLVH* 8 (1976), 19–23, Juanita sheared and butchered her own sheep on her homestead after her husband died in 1908 and was also a curandera; Buss, 23–25, Jesusita herded and sheared sheep as her father had no sons, and found no stigma attached to attending village dances in jeans: "Not like a girl, like a boy. And nobody bothers me, no. Everybody likes me." See also Gilbert, 131–132.

77. *HMM* 18 (Nov. 1903), 10.

78. Sue Zuver quoted in Blake, "Presbyterian Mission Work," 122. Brengle, *HMM* 25 (Nov. 1910), 15.

79. Case 598, RACo Court Records, District Court, 1895–1905, Docket Book D.

80. "Deep Village," WPA files, 220, RACo History, NMSRCA; Leonard, 27, 29; Juan B. Rael et al., "Arroyo Hondo . . . ," *El Palacio* 81 (Spring 1975), 8, 10.

81. Ms. Census, RACo, 1910. In Chama, nine women did washing, three did odd job labor, three took in lodgers, and six did housework. See also "Alita," *HMM* 14 (Nov. 1899), 8; Leadingham, *HMM* 18 (Nov. 1903), 14.

82. See Laila Shukry Hamamsy, "The Role of Women in a Changing Navaho Society," *American Anthropologist* 59 (1957), 105 on Navaho women giving up the land because of husbands' absences for wage work; and Ulrich, 8, 36 on the ability to tolerate deviations from the norm without destroying the norm.

83. Ms. Census, RACo, New Mexico and Las Animas County, Colorado, 1880, 1900, 1910; for sewing, see Thorp, "Vicenta," and for mattresses see Hayden manuscript, 70.

84. Divorce thus seems more common than legend would have it. For example, see Darlis Miller, "Cross-Cultural Marriages in the Southwest: The New Mexico Experience, 1846–1900," *NMHR* 57 (Oct. 1982), 350, and Hayden manuscript, 66, as opposed to RACo Court Records, District Court Docket Book, vols. D and E, NMSRCA.

85. RACo Criminal and Civil Docket, District Court, June 1913, Catron Papers, Box 901:1. RACo, *ibid.,* June 1914, NMSRCA.

86. Case 337, Lujan v. Lujan, Catron Papers, Box 201:10, folder 1; Case 4958, Renehan Gilbert Papers, file 3, NMSRCA; Case 662, RACo District Court Records, NMSRCA; Case 1480, Padilla v. Padilla, Truchas, June 1914, Catron Papers, Box 201:4, folder 24.

87. Case 4958, Renehan Gilbert Papers. Case 262, Lopez v. Lopez, 1914–1915, Catron Papers, Box 201: 8, folder 25; the Lopezes remarried each other and sought a second divorce.

88. Ms. Census, RACo, 1910, see, for example, a Vallecitos divorcée whose father was a farmer. She was twenty-four with two children. And see also Ojo Caliente and Espanola.

89. *Ibid.:* divorced woman farmer in Vallecitos; washerwomen in Petaca and Chimayo, houseworker in Chama.

90. Case 337, Lujan v. Lujan.

91. "Tia Lupe," pp. 96–102, WPA files, 20, NMSRCA; Lorin Brown, with Charles Briggs and Marta Weigle, *Hispanic Folklife of New Mexico* (Albuquerque, 1978), 136–137. And see also Isidoro Montano, "La Vida de Anita Romero," in Anselmo Arellano, ed., *La Tierra Amarilla: The People of the Chama Valley* (Tierra Amarilla, 1978), 73–74. Anita left drudgery and a lazy husband for a man who treated her with more respect. In "Amelia Lucero," WPA 5.5.53, no. 7, NMHL, a young wife returns to her parents because of the parsimony of her spouse, and eventually receives child support payments from him.

92. Ms. Census, RACo, 1910, Chama, Cebolla, and Canjilon. There were

also women living apart from their husbands. *Ibid.,* for example, Chimayo, Tierra Amarilla, and Cebolla.

93. Daniel Valdez, *A History of the San Luis Valley* (Alamosa, 1930).

94. Barker, 277; Case 130, Catron Papers, Box 201:5, folder 24; Thorp, "Tita," WPA 5.5.52, no. 75, NMHL.

95. St. Vincent Orphans' Home and Industrial School, list of orphans, 1909, 1912, 1913, 1915, 1916, Gov. MacDonald Papers, NMSRCA.

96. *New Mexico Penitentiary Records,* reel 1, NMSRCA.

97. Cf. Leacock, 42.

98. Thorp, "Stories," WPA 5.5.53, no. 5, NMHL.

99. Briggs, 178, 401. In the 1930s, a Spanish Colonial Arts store manager who employed Hispanic spinners on the premises found that a new, relatively young Hispanic woman became the target of such accusations because she spun so much faster than her older coworkers. See Sarah Nestor, *The Native Market of the Spanish New Mexican Craftsmen, Santa Fe 1933–1940* (Santa Fe, 1978), 23.

100. Marc Simmons, *Witchcraft in the Southwest* (Flagstaff, 1974), 36, 41–42, 56 for examples of male witches or sorcerors, and 2, 40 for the rest.

101. *New Mexican Review,* 8 Sept. 1884 and *Santa Fe Daily New Mexican,* 2 Oct. 1882, cited in *ibid.,* 36–38.

102. Simmons, 48–49, 154; Cleofas Jaramillo, *Shadows of the Past* (Santa Fe, 1941), 99, 102; Marta Weigle, *Spiders and Spinsters: Women and Mythology* (Albuquerque, 1982), 41–42 on the particular vulnerability of spinsters; WPA files, B.C. no. 329:99, NMSRCA; Nina Otero-Warren, *Old Spain in Our Southwest* (New York, 1936), 124; Gallegos y Chavez, 71.

103. On going to great lengths to foster a child, see "Parteras."

104. Cf. Alice Schlegel, "An Overview," in Schlegel, ed., *Sexual Stratification: A Cross-Cultural View* (New York, 1977), 356.

105. *Ibid.,* 355; Leacock, 144.

106. Cf. Hamamsy, 102.

107. Leonard, 80; Goubaud-Carrera, 60; Margaret Mead, ed., *Cultural Patterns and Technical Change* (Paris, 1953), 182. Anthropologist Beverly Brown tells the story of a man filming an African village while questioning a man on what women did. As women erected a house in the background, the man, after a long pause, responded, "Well, they take care of the children, yes, that's what they do; they take care of the children." Conversation at 6th Berkshire Conference on the History of Women, 1984.

Chapter 3. Women Missionaries and Women Villagers

1. Benham, *HMM* 15 (Nov. 1900), 4.

2. Valentin Rabe, "Evangelical Logistics: Mission Support and Resources

to 1920," in John Fairbank, ed., *The Missionary Enterprise in China and America* (Cambridge, Mass., 1974), 80–81.

3. Quoted in Katharine Crowell, *Our Mexican Mission Schools* (New York, n.d. [c. 1913]), 82.

4. Ruth Barber and Edith Agnew, *Sowers Went Forth* (Albuquerque, 1981), 70.

5. Rev. Robert Craig, *Our Mexicans* (New York, 1904), 69–70.

6. Honora deBusk, "Evening in a New Mexico Mission" (n.d.), DeBusk Papers, Box 1, WHC.

7. *HMM* 27 (Aug. 1913), 235.

8. Blake, *HMM* 24 (July 1910), 204–205.

9. Hoff, "The Life . . . ," *HMM* 29 (Nov. 1914), 12–13; Kennedy, *HMM* 15 (Nov. 1900), 15; Anon., *HMM* 21 (April 1906), 6.

10. Allaben, at interdenominational conference, *HMM* 28 (Nov. 1913), 14. On doubters, see S. H. Pingrey to "My dear," 14 Nov. 1900, Record Group 51, Women's Board of Home Missions, Box 2, folder 8, PHS.

11. *NMJE* 12 (June 1916), 14, and 3 (Dec. 1906), 13–14.

12. New Mexico Superintendent of Public Instruction, *Biennial Report,* 1910–1912.

13. State Superintendent Alvan N. White, Report of the Dept. of Education, Gov. McDonald Papers, Exp. 2, NMSRCA.

14. W. B. Wilson, *NMJE* 11 (March 1915), 17–18; *NMJE* 3 (Dec. 1906), 13–14.

15. Mrs. O'Connor Roberts, "Difficulties Met . . . ," *NMJE* 3 (April 1907), 10–11.

16. Supt. Charles George, Alamagordo, *NMJE* 8 (March 1912), 27.

17. Nan Elsasser et al., *Las Mujeres: Conversations from a Hispanic Community* (Old Westbury, N.Y., 1979): Andreita Padilla, 24. Blake, *HMM* 26 (Nov. 1911), 17.

18. Galbraith, *HMM* 24 (Nov. 1909), 5. She excused the stymied public school teachers. And see Zellers, Oral History TC93, p. 1, MHL.

19. Agnes Smedley, *Daughter of Earth* (1929, reprint ed., Old Westbury, N.Y., 1973), 120–123. Approximately one-third of Rio Arriba County's teaching force had not qualified in the state's exams. The next closest counties were Torrance and Socorro, with nine each. *NMJE* 10 (March 1911), 3.

20. Alice Blake, "Presbyterian Mission Work in New Mexico" (unpublished manuscript, 1935, at MHL), 266. On Sisters of Loretto schools as limited to the wealthy, see Cleofas Jaramillo, *Romance of a Little Village Girl* (San Antonio, 1955), 28–30, 48–52; Ruth Barber, Oral History TC139C, MHL. On lack of Hispanics in higher education, see reports from New Mexico College of Agriculture and Mechanical Arts and New Mexico Normal University in Governors' Papers, NMSRCA; and *NMJE* 1 (July 1905), 18 on the Univ. of New Mexico.

21. *NMJE* 11 (Oct. 1914), 16–17; SANS, Gov. McDonald Papers, Exp. 2.

22. *NMJE* 9 (Feb. 1913), 3.

23. The school's sex ratio was, however, far nearer to equal than the ratio among extant teachers in Rio Arriba County, where most of the students lived. In 1913, 87% of the teachers in the county were male. In contrast, at the state-wide level, only 30% of New Mexico's teachers were male. New Mexico Dept. of Education, *Educational Directory* (1913), 38.

24. Reports of the Trustees, 1909–1910, and of the Board of Regents, 1914–1916, transcript of students, 1913, 1916–1917, registration and withdrawals, 1917–1918, Gov. McDonald Papers, Exp. 2, SANS.

25. Board of Regents meeting, 23 July 1918, Gov. McDonald Papers, SANS.

26. Lela Weatherby, "A Study of the Early Years of the Presbyterian Work with the Spanish Speaking People of New Mexico and Colorado" (Master's thesis, Presbyterian College of Christian Education, 1942), 72. Besides the sixty Presbyterian schools were three United Brethren day schools in these years in northern New Mexico, at Alcalde (1917), Velarde (1912) (previously a Baptist school, 1897–1909), and Vallecitos (1930), as well as the McCurdy School (boarding and day high school) in Santa Cruz (1915), a spot previously abandoned by the Presbyterians to the resident Catholic orders. See Leland Corbin, "The Educational Activities of the Evangelical United Brethren Church in New Mexico" (Master's thesis, Univ. of New Mexico, 1949), 1, 24–31. *HMM* 16 (Nov. 1902), 2.

27. "Our Stations," *HMM* 18 (Nov. 1903), 9; Craig, 98.

28. Allison School Scholarship List, 1902, MHL.

29. Catherine Wallace, "Santa Fe," *HMM* 15 (Sept. 1901), 107.

30. *HMM* 24 (Nov. 1909), 12, 16. *HMM* 22 (Nov. 1907), 16. From 1888 to 1907 about 560 pupils had passed through her school.

31. A brief summer training session was held by each county; all teachers were to attend. *HMM* 24 (Nov. 1909), 15, and 27 (Nov. 1912), 7.

32. Joan Jensen, "Women Teachers, Class, and Ethnicity: New Mexico, 1900–1950," *Southwest Economy and Society* 4 (Late Winter 1978–1979), 5. Ms. Census, RACo, 1910, e.g. Velarde's teacher, Cirila Martinez, age 20, lived with her father, a farmer; in Ojo Sarco, teacher Librada Sanchez, age 22, was a farmer's wife of six years with three children.

33. Nearly half of these women were Anglos, and only 3% of the men were. But half the Hispanic women were married or widowed. New Mexico, Dept. of Education, *Educational Directory* (1913), 38, and (1915–1916), 49–51.

34. Collective biography compiled from information on over 88 women, mainly derived from *HMM, W&M,* Blake, "Presbyterian Mission Work," and personnel files (H5) at PHS.

35. Jensen, 5–6, covers this trend for southern New Mexico, and patterns of Anglo women missionaries replacing Hispanic men or women are illustrated in Barber and Agnew, 57, 72.

36. *HMM* 19 (Nov. 1905), 6. And see D. F. McFarland to Mrs. Cornelia Martin, 1867, quoted in Barber and Agnew, 12.

37. Catharine Beecher, *The Duty of American Women to Their Country* (New York, 1845), 3, 65, and *Educational Reminiscences* (New York, 1874), dedication, 101, 106, 107; and see Redding Sugg, "The Pedagogy of Love," *Virginia Quarterly* 54 (Summer 1978), 411–412.

38. *HMM* 19 (Nov. 1905), 6 (emphasis mine).

39. "The Social and Economic Background of State Teachers College Students," *Colorado State Teachers College Bulletin* 6 (Sept. 1925), v; John Higham, "The Reorientation of American Culture in the 1890s," in Higham, *Writing American History: Essays on Modern Scholarship* (Bloomington, 1970), 94; Jane Hunter, *Gospel of Gentility: American Women Missionaries in Turn-of-the-Century China* (New Haven, 1984), 30–31. Cf. Hunter's sensitive treatment throughout for fascinating similarities and contrasts.

40. Mrs. Mary Goodall to Pierson, 28 May 1900, Record Group 51, Women's Board of Home Missions, Box 2, folder 6, PHS; and see, for example, H5 (personnel) files of Hunt, Riley, and Sutherland, PHS. For example, Craig, *HMM* 28 (Nov. 1913), 10, and Blake in Barber and Agnew, 65.

41. Hyson, "Reminiscences," *HMM* 29 (Nov. 1914), 8; and see Leadingham, *HMM* 18 (Nov. 1903), 267; Fish, *HMM* 26 (Nov. 1911), 13–14 and English, *ibid.,* 21 on their new teachers' homes with rainproof roofs; Barber and Agnew, 91; Romero in Carolyn Atkins, ed., *Los Tres Campos—Three Fields: A History of Protestant Evangelists and Presbyterians in Chimayó, Córdova and Truchas, New Mexico* (Albuquerque, 1978), 25; various issues of *HMM*.

42. Atkins, 22; Barber and Agnew, 115.

43. Meeker to Craig, 26 Jan. 1906, H5 Olinda Meeker, PHS.

44. Meeker to Craig, 4 June 1906, H5 Olinda Meeker, PHS; and see Blake, *HMM* 17 (March 1903), 114; and, for example, Hyson, *HMM* 29 (Nov. 1914), 9.

45. Clements to Allaben, 4 May 1918, H5 Clements, PHS. These qualities of strength could also lead to friction among headstrong coworkers where plazas had more than one teacher and at the boarding schools. See the Women's Board of Home Missions files (Record Group 51) at PHS for several incidents at the Allison School in Santa Fe, and at least one in Chimayo, and see, for example, Frances Robe's sister-in-law's complaints about Robe's perfectionism.

46. Brown to Boyd, 9 May 1911, H5 Emma Brown, PHS. See also Murray to Allaben, 3 Feb. 1913 and 19 May 1913, H5 Louise Murray; Sutherland to Mrs. Miller, 1 Nov. 1894 and 21 Dec. 1893, H5 Sutherland; and Sterret to Boole, 19 June 1906, Record Group 51, Box 2, folder 8, PHS.

47. Hyson, "Reminiscences," 8; Orton, "A New . . . ," *HMM* 24 (Nov. 1909), 16. See also, for example, Randi Walker, "Protestantism in the Sangre de Cristos: Factors in the Growth and Decline of the Hispanic Protestant Churches in Northern New Mexico and Southern Colorado, 1850–1920" (Ph.D. dissertation, Claremont Graduate School, 1983), 168, and *HMM* 22 (Nov. 1907), 16.

48. For example, Blake, "Presbyterian Mission Work," 162, 200; Jane Atkins Grainger, *El Centenario de la Palabre: El Rito Presbyterian Church, 1879–1979* (Albuquerque, 1980), 99.

49. *HMM* 29 (May 1916), 6–7.

50. *HMM* 14 (Aug. 1900), 227.

51. Interviews with Edith Agnew, Santa Fe, 8 Nov. 1983, Arthur Maes, Denver, 12 Sept. 1983, and Alfonso Esquibel, Santa Fe, 9 Nov. 1983.

52. See Higham, 86–88 on strenuosity and rebellion against "excessive" refinement.

53. *HMM* 19 (Nov. 1904), 9; Sawhill, *HMM* 29 (Nov. 1914), 6; see also Clark, *HMM* 23 (Nov. 1908), 18; Mabel Parker, *HMM* 29 (Nov. 1914), 3.

54. Allison, *HMM* 22 (Nov. 1907), 17; McNair, *HMM* 18 (Nov. 1903), 13.

55. Clark, *HMM* 16 (Nov. 1901), 9; "Sojourn in Santa Fe," *ibid.,* 4; Hoff, "The Life of a Recent Graduate . . . ," *HMM* 29 (Nov. 1914), 12–13; Marion LeDuc, *HMM* 23 (Nov. 1908), 15.

56. Orton, *HMM* 23 (Nov. 1908), 6; Elliot quoted in Blake, "Presbyterian Mission Work," 169.

57. See H5 files, PHS; because most of these women applied for home mission service only, only a few instances of preference for foreign service appear, but many women preferred work among blacks, Appalachians, and Mormons, and indications are that over one-quarter of the women served in other fields in addition to their Hispanic service. In her introduction to Harriet Kellogg's *Life of Mrs. Emily J. Harwood* (Albuquerque, 1903), Mary Teats wrote, "I partook somewhat of the opinion, in those early years, that still prevails to a large extent, namely that those engaging in missionary work among the Spanish people, did not require that degree of native and acquired ability that is required of those engaged in religious work among the more highly cultured classes," pp. iii–iv.

58. *HMM* 19 (Nov. 1904), 9–10. See also Elliot quoted in Blake, "Presbyterian Mission Work," 169; Allison, *HMM* 20 (April 1906), 122; J. C. Ross, *HMM* 29 (Nov. 1914), 16.

59. Fish, "Life in a Mexican Plaza," *HMM* 28 (Nov. 1913), 8.

60. Walker, 105.

61. For example, Kate Hamilton, "Timoteo's Flag," *HMM* 19 (March 1905), 108–109; Blake, "Presbyterian Mission Work," 120. Agnes Smedley, riding alone through Hispanic New Mexico at this time claimed, "I rode safely, as all women rode safely, for it was a land not only where strong men lived, but it was a land where women were strong also." Smedley, 118.

62. For example, Honora DeBusk, "Evening in a New Mexico Mission"; *HMM* 18 (Nov. 1904), 62–63.

63. *HMM* 26 (Nov. 1911), 19. This development eliminated the "need" for a mission school on this site.

64. Roberts, "Difficulties Met . . . ," *NMJE* 3 (April 1907), 10–11.

65. Alice Blake, *HMM* 14 (May 1900), 146; and see "The Great Need," *HMM* 22 (Nov. 1907), 16; Benham, *HMM* 15 (Nov. 1900), 5.

66. *HMM* 19 (Nov. 1904), 10; *HMM* 20 (Nov. 1905), 16; *HMM* 17 (July 1903), 213. Sandra Myres, *Westering Women and the Frontier Experience* (Albuquerque, 1982), 170.

67. *HMM* 21 (Nov. 1906), 6. Contrast with Zuver, *HMM* 23 (Nov. 1908), 15. To Zuver, the greater hardship was watching two of her "bright girls" die because of inadequate medical attention.

68. Myres, 74–75; Myres, "Mexican Americans and Westering Anglos: A Feminine Perspective," *NMHR* 57 (Oct. 1982), 326.

69. Rev. B. McCullough, "The Industries of New Mexico," *HMM* 27 (Nov. 1912), 5; *HMM* 14 (March 1900), 109.

70. Mary Teats, national evangelist, WCTU, iv; Fish, "Land of Poco Tiempo," *HMM* 26 (Nov. 1911), 11; Mary James, *HMM* 18 (Nov. 1903), 5; and see, for example, *HMM* 19 (Nov. 1904), 4.

71. *HMM* 26 (Nov. 1911), 17; see also Angeline Badger, "The 'Chiquitos' or Little Children," *HMM* 31 (Nov. 1916), 21.

72. Barbara Welter, "She Hath Done What She Could: Protestant Women's Missionary Careers in Nineteenth Century America," *American Quarterly* 30 (Winter 1978), 630. Richard Storrs, "The Prospective Advance of Christian Missions" (1885), quoted in *ibid.*; Hunter, xv.

73. Welter, 630; Hunter, 161, 179; Craig, 25–26 on the tyrannical husband/father; *HMM* 16 (Jan. 1902), 14–15; *HMM* 14 (Nov. 1899), 11 on the loveless marriage and the brutality of parents and husbands.

74. Arthur Pettit, *Images of the Mexican American in Fiction and Film* (College Station, Tex., 1980), 3–60. Kirkwood, *HMM* 15 (Nov. 1900), 15; and see Myres, *Westering Women*, 78. Hyson, *HMM* 28 (Nov. 1913), 16, for denial of racial inferiority.

75. Orton, "Tierra Amarilla . . . ," *HMM* 22 (Nov. 1907), 11.

76. Mrs. Granger, *HMM* 16 (May 1903), 161; Clark, *HMM* 16 (Nov. 1901), 12; the fictional summary is from "A New Mexico Incident," Congregational Education Society, n.a, n.d., DeBusk Papers, WHC.

77. Clark, *HMM* 16 (Nov. 1901), 12.

78. *HMM* 14 (Nov. 1899), 10. Blake, "A Glimpse . . . ," *HMM* 27 (Nov. 1912), 18.

79. *HMM* 14 (Nov. 1899), 10; Barber and Agnew, 18.

80. Charles Hayden manuscript, 66, Hayden papers, WHC.

81. Conway in Bernice Martin, *People of the Book* (Monte Vista, 1956), 35–36.

82. One manifestation of this conflict was in concepts of "play." Although a few mission women recognized that Hispanic children played games (Kellogg, 74), most saw children in their leisure hours as dangerously and unwholesomely idle. (H5 Craig, PHS; Hoff, "The Life . . . ," *HMM* 29 (Nov. 1914), 12). The problem was tackled at interdenominational conferences and given voice in such worries as "What can be expected from such a listless childhood but a fruitless maturity?" (Allaben, *HMM* 28 (Nov. 1913), 14; Sawhill, "Play Is the Lev-

eler," *HMM* 29 (Nov. 1914), 6). At the same time, Zoe Ellsworth recalled that parents had requested their children only study in school, and not waste time there in play, but Ellsworth insisted that play helped learning, and reported in 1919 that "a real spirit of play [has] been awakened, and we now feel that our boys and girls are very much what all little Americans should be" ("The Game of Learning and of Living," *HMM* 33 (May 1919), 148). And see "Teaching Spanish-American Beginners," *NMJE* 12 (June 1916), 14. Facundo Valdez, *"Vergüenza,"* in Paul Kutsche, ed., *The Survival of Spanish American Villages,* Colorado College Studies no. 15 (Spring, 1979), 106.

83. Hyson, *HMM* 15 (Nov. 1900), 13; Catherine Wallace, "Santa Fe," *HMM* 15 (March 1901), 107.

84. Sawhill, *HMM* 29 (Nov. 1914), 8.

85. Barber and Agnew, 33, 53; Blake, "Presbyterian Mission Work," 122; Hyson, "Twenty-five Years in New Mexico," *HMM* 22 (Aug. 1908), 242; Zuver, *HMM* 23 (Nov. 1908), 15; Dr. Hubert Johnson, "Need of Medical . . . ," *HMM* 27 (Nov. 1912), 9.

86. Elsasser et al.: Vigil, 13–14; Flora Garcia, "Margarita Ruyball Lucero," *SLVH* 8 (1976), 7.

87. Catherine Wallace, "Santa Fe," 107; Harriet Elliot, at Truchas, *HMM* 33 (May 1919), 162, reported that the children in public school did not learn English, and while boys could learn the language doing seasonal labor in Colorado, girls could only learn it in the mission schools.

88. Allaben, "Allison-James," *HMM* 28 (Nov. 1913), 12; "The Native New Mexican," *ibid.,* 4.

89. Craig, 82; Baker, *HMM* 16 (Nov. 1901), 5; *HMM* 19 (Nov. 1904), 16. Barber and Agnew, 95; Olinda Meeker, "The Evolution of Allison-James School," *HMM* 31 (Nov. 1916), 5. From January 1907 to June 1913, the James School in Santa Fe provided a male counterpart for the Allison School, "with the hope," according to Meeker, "that co-education might solve the problem of establishing future Christian Protestant homes among Mexicans." The experiment was doomed, however, as "conditions did not seem to fulfill the hope," and the James School became a dorm for Allison.

90. *Ibid.,* and Allaben, "Allison-James," *HMM* 28 (Nov. 1913), 12.

91. Brengle, *HMM* 25 (Nov. 1910), 15–16; Allaben, *HMM* 28 (Nov. 1913), 12. N.B.: At Menaul they also taught boys to cook and keep house, and saw themselves not as taking women's tasks from women, but as destroying the men's "possible opinion of themselves as supreme and infallible." *HMM* 31 (Nov. 1916), 12. In particular, Esther Buxton, "The Old Road and the New," *HMM* 32 (May 1918), 151, saw her mission as that of liberating women from roles as "submissive, unthinking, colorless drudges whose very thoughts their husbands direct," and aimed at a time when "a young girl utterly refuses to be disposed of at the convenience and according to the judgment of her father, and marries the man of her choice, even though she must leave home to do so. A

vision has come to her of the free untrammeled womanhood that is our pride and actual possession." Note that this is before woman suffrage. Buxton's experience seems to have been limited to the boarding school; she lacked the intimate exposure to actual village life of some plaza school teachers. Buxton, *HMM* 31 (July 1917), 216–217, saw these free and untrammeled women ideally returning home, advancing the village in cleanliness and comforts, and turning out, "before long . . . our realized vision—a free womanhood, a race of manly men; a God-fearing people, the glory and pride of New Mexico."

92. For example, L. T. Granger, *HMM* 17 (July 1903), 214; George McAfee, "Our Mexican Work," *HMM* 18 (Nov. 1903), 6; "A Symposium," *HMM* 28 (Nov. 1913), 15; Parker, "Sunny Days," *HMM* 29 (Nov. 1914), 3, 17; Brengle, *HMM* 25 (Nov. 1910), 16.

93. For example, Hayden manuscript, 70; Allison, *HMM* 16 (Nov. 1901), 2–3; *HMM* 19 (Nov. 1904), 5.

94. Leadingham, *HMM* 18 (Sept. 1904), 268; *HMM* 23 (Aug. 1909), 244. *The Church at Home and Abroad* (May 1888), 542, cited in R. Douglas Brackenridge and Francisco O. García-Treto, *Iglesia Presbiteriana: A History of Presbyterians and Mexican Americans in the Southwest* (San Antonio, 1974), 50. Hunter, 134; *HMM* 14 (Nov. 1899), 10; Blake, *HMM* 27 (Nov. 1912), 18.

95. Crowell, 88; Hyson, *HMM* 14 (Nov. 1899), 16; *HMM* 19 (Nov. 1904), 5.

96. At the Allison School, girls had their own rooms, to instill more middle-class notions of privacy. Sherman Doyle, *Presbyterian Home Missions* (New York, 1905), 208–209; Craig, 25; *HMM* 23 (Aug. 1909), 244; Allaben, "Allison-James," *HMM* 28 (Nov. 1913), 12.

97. Clements, *HMM* 26 (Nov. 1911), 15; Hyson, *ibid.,* 22; Benham, *HMM* 15 (Nov. 1900), 2; Tait, *HMM* 27 (Aug. 1913), 238.

98. Blake, *HMM* 27 (Nov. 1912), 18. The mission teacher's home was itself considered "one of the most potent evangelizing agencies at work." *HMM* 19 (Nov. 1904), 10; Hyson, *HMM* 21 (Nov. 1906), 12. Built-in closets aroused particular interest. Davis, *HMM* 26 (Nov. 1904), 19; McAfee quoted in Crowell, 82.

99. Rutherford, *HMM* 18 (March 1904), 107; Conklin, *HMM* 16 (Nov. 1902), 12; "The Closed and the Open Door," *HMM* 21 (Nov. 1906), 7. Even the bread had to be Anglo: made with wheat flour and yeast. *HMM* 22 (March 1908), 5; Brengle, *HMM* 25 (Nov. 1910), 16; Annette Thorp, "Chana," WPA 5.5.52, no. 71, NMHL.

100. Walker, 211–212; and see *Old Faith and Old Glory: Story of the Church in New Mexico since the American Occupation* (Santa Fe, 1946), 14 quoted in Marta Weigle, *Brothers of Light, Brothers of Blood* (Albuquerque, 1976), 69.

101. For example, Blake, "Presbyterian Mission Work," 102; Walker, 142. Walker brings out the irony of the Protestants' condemnation of the priests' fees as extortion and later demanding that the local congregation assume the pastor's

salary; and see Clements to Mrs. Bennet, 30 June 1910, H5 Clements, PHS, on trying "to get the people trained into paying the tuition and bringing the school wood."

102. *HMM* 19 (Nov. 1904), 10; Clark, *HMM* 23 (Nov. 1908), 18; Minutes of G. G. Smith Memorial Church, Truchas, 1903–1931, MHL; Atkins, 45; Barber and Agnew, 91–92. Prudence Clark was treasurer of the church at Chimayo in 1903.

103. Olen Leonard, *The Role of the Land Grant in the Social Organization and Social Processes of a Spanish-American Village in New Mexico* (1943, reprint ed., Albuquerque, 1970), 55 on education and access to information as contributing to the status of the priest.

104. Leva Granger, *HMM* 17 (July 1903), 214; Walker, 137; Quintana in Blake, "Presbyterian Mission Work," 114.

105. Barber and Agnew, 55.

106. Wesley Hurt, "Manzano: A Study of Community Disorganization" (Master's thesis, Univ. of New Mexico, 1941), 129.

107. Barber and Agnew, 64; *HMM* 16 (June 1903), 70. *HMM* 16 (Nov. 1901), 12. The ban on smoking seemed aimed particularly at women, as one missionary commented, "[T]he majority of our mothers now realize that we do not approve of smoking, and the cigarette is hid quickly under the apron. Our Protestant women do not smoke—they leave that behind when they take up the new faith." *HMM* 14 (Nov. 1899), 10; *HMM* 24 (Nov. 1909), 1.

108. Donovan Senter and Florence Hawley, "The Grammar School as the Basic Acculturating Influence for Native New Mexicans," *Social Forces* 24 (May 1946), 401–402. On resettlement see Barber and Agnew, 62. Cf. Robert F. Berkhofer, Jr., *Salvation and the Savage: An Analysis of Protestant Missions and American Indian Response, 1787–1862* (New York, 1972).

109. Polita Padilla, *HMM* 20 (Nov. 1905), 15.

110. *HMM* 20 (Nov. 1905), 8; Blake, "Presbyterian Mission Work," 100; for other examples see the following issues of *HMM*: 14 (March 1900), 99; 17 (Feb. 1903), 101; 19 (Nov. 1904), 6, 11; 20 (June 1906), 178; 21 (Nov. 1906), 16; 22 (Aug. 1908), 243; 23 (Nov. 1908), 4; 26 (Nov. 1911), 18. And see Grainger, 96–97; John Lawrence Diary, 16–17 Jan. 1902; Weatherby, 62; Zellers, Oral History, TC93, p. 3, MHL.

111. On village treatment: Zuver, *HMM* 23 (Nov. 1908), 15; *HMM* 19 (Nov. 1904), 5. On a group of Allison graduates' network among villages: Allison, *HMM* 23 (Nov. 1908), 10; *HMM* 14 (Aug. 1900), 227. Cf. Nancy Cott and Carroll Smith-Rosenburg on school-girl relationships creating new peer bonds. On education leading to a certain status in the village, and a dense web of marriages between Hispanic ministers' families: Zuver, *HMM* 21 (Nov. 1905), 13; Grainger, 30, 34, 35, 86. On Protestant Hispanic attitudes toward Hispanic women and their role in the church: *HMM* 20 (Nov. 1905), 9–10; Minutes of the G. G. Smith Memorial Church, MHL; "La Madre en el Hogar," *La Aurora,* 15 July

1910, 2, and "El Hombre y la Mujer," *ibid.*, 1 Nov. 1910, 2: "Aquel es la mas elevedad de las criaturas . . . ," etc. Grainger, 30, 33, 35 on a few women preachers; Craig, *HMM* 24 (Nov. 1909), 15; Crowell, 88–89; Blake, "Presbyterian Mission Work," 96; *Menaul Historical Review,* 7, History File 45: Protestant Churches and Groups, NMSRCA, on Marcelina Sanchez, a missionary teacher in southern Colorado and student at College of the Southwest in the 1890s; Mary Wilson, *HMM* 33 (Aug. 1919), 223–224; *Menaul School Echo* 15 (Fall 1976), 4, History File 45, NMSRCA.

112. Barber, Oral History, TC35C, MHL; Forsythe, *HMM* 24 (Nov. 1909), 10; Allison, "Three Links," *HMM* 20 (Nov. 1905), 11; Barber and Agnew, 95; Esther Buxton, "The Old Road and the New," *HMM* 32 (May 1918), 151: over half the girls graduating from Allison in June 1917 became teachers in plaza public schools. Zellers, Oral History, TC93, 2, MHL. Krohn, *HMM* 18 (Nov. 1903), 14. Bonine to Craig, 23 March 1909, H5 Breckinridge/Bonine, PHS. Pingrey, 19 Nov. 1900, Record Group 51, Box 2, folder 8, PHS; *HMM* 15 (March 1901), 99; Clements, *HMM* 26 (Nov. 1911), 15–16; Barber and Agnew, 34; H5 Zuver, PHS. Zuver left the Board of New Mexico her entire estate, estimated at $20,000.

113. See, for example, Craig to Pingrey, 3 Feb. 1901, folder 16 and Meryberry to Pierson, 24 June 1901, folder 14, Record Group 51, Box 2, PHS.

114. Craig, *HMM* 29 (Nov. 1914), 16.

115. Riley, *HMM* 20 (Nov. 1905), 16, and 22 (Nov. 1907), 11; Blake; *HMM* 20 (Nov. 1905), 4; Jeanette Smith, "Lights and Shadows," *HMM* 34 (May 1920), 164.

116. Clark, *HMM* 16 (Nov. 1902), 10. During the May services for Mary, Clark's Sunday school attendance became almost entirely male. Blake, "Presbyterian Mission Work," 121 on Penitentes attending both Protestant services and Penitente rites. Zoe Ellsworth, "Changes in a Plaza," *HMM* 33 (July 1919), 205, re: "a young people's meeting modeled after the Christian Endeavor Society, though that name is not used since a number of Catholics take active part."

117. Marion LeDuc, *HMM* 23 (Nov. 1908), 16; *HMM* 16 (Nov. 1902), 14; Leadingham, *HMM* 17 (March 1903), 13; Zuver, *HMM* 22 (Nov. 1907), 16. Weigle, 104; New Mexico Baptist Historical Society, Appointment Calendar, 1980, History File 45: Protestant Churches, NMSRCA; Corbin, 31–32, on book burning; Clements, *HMM* 31 (Nov. 1916), 7 and 32 (Nov. 1917), 20 on vandalism. For example, Barber, Oral History TC35C, MHL, on the failure of a Catholic school deliberately erected to rival the mission school in Holman, and Anon., *HMM* 21 (Nov. 1906), 6.

118. *HMM* 19 (April 1905), 123; John Lawrence Diary, 22 July 1900, WHC; Clements, *HMM* 22 (Nov. 1907), 10. J. C. Ross, *HMM* 27 (Aug. 1913), 236; Blake, "Presbyterian Mission Work," 143.

119. Martinez to Catron, 28 April 1915, Catron Papers, Archive 29, Box 502:1, folder 16: "Post Office Appointments, Rio Arriba County," UNM. On

Hispanic women appointees see *ibid.,* folder 15, Gallina and Tusas, at a compensation of $170 and $64. On membership: Alice Reiche, "Spanish American Village Culture: Barrier to Assimilation or Integrative Force?" in Kutsche, 111. Interview with Orlando Romero, Santa Fe, 10 Nov. 1983.

120. See problems surrounding Kate Kennedy's condescending article during her residence at Embudo: *HMM* 15 (Nov. 1900), 14–15. In *HMM* 16 (Nov. 1901), 6; Rev. Gabino Rendon, letter of protest, 2 Jan. 1902; Craig to Pierson, 17 July 1901, Record Group 51, Box 2, folder 10, PHS. Another missionary, Nellie Snyder, wrote a story for an East Las Vegas, New Mexico, paper which roused the Spanish weekly, *La Bandera Americana,* to protest (23 Nov. 1901).

121. Interview with Romero, and see Reiche, 111.

122. Russell, "New Mexico's Needs," *HMM* 21 (July 1907), 217. *HMM* 19 (Nov. 1904), 9.

123. Leadingham, *HMM* 18 (Sept. 1904), 268.

124. Zuver (1895) in Blake, "Presbyterian Mission Work," 121. Occasionally on Saturdays they drew the women out to teach them dressmaking. Leadingham, *HMM* 18 (Sept. 1904), 268; Hyson, "Ranchos de Taos," *HMM* 21 (Nov. 1906), 12.

125. "The Social and Economic Background of State Teachers College Students," citing 1911 study by Coffman; *NMJE* 2 (April 1916), 17.

126. Blake to Fraser, 23 March 1912, on vacations, H5 Blake, PHS. Blake, "Presbyterian Mission Work," 34–35, 145. Louise Conklin to Pearson, 8 Jan. 1902, Record Group 51, Box 2, folder 10, PHS. Martin, and "A New Mexico Incident" (Congregational Education Society, n.d.) in Darley Family Collection, WHC. For examples of donations, see Sarah Sutherland and Alice Hyson, H5 files, PHS.

127. According to Charles Briggs, "a relationship of inequality between two individuals would be effectively eliminated if one were to inaugurate a set of interactions aimed at incorporating a family into his or her unit and the other was to accept." Briggs, "'Our Strength Is in the Land': The Structure of Hierarchy and Equality and the Pragmatics of Discourse in Hispano ('Spanish-American') 'Talk About the Past'" (Ph.D. dissertation, Univ. of Chicago, 1981), 170.

128. Blake, "Presbyterian Mission Work," 145; Conklin to Pearson, 8 Jan. 1902, Record Group 51, Box 2, folder 10, PHS.

129. *HMM* 16 (Nov. 1901), 7; Conklin, *HMM* 16 (Nov. 1902), 12; Padilla, *HMM* 21 (Nov. 1906), 15; Orton, "Do the People . . . ," *HMM* 29 (Jan. 1915), 67; *HMM* 18 (Nov. 1903), 10.

130. *HMM* 24 (Nov. 1909), 16.

131. Melton at La Costilla, *HMM* 16 (Nov. 1901), 8–9. *HMM* 18 (Nov. 1903), 15; *HMM* 23 (Nov. 1908), 18.

132. Clements, *HMM* 30 (May 1916), 6–7; Conklin, *HMM* 16 (Nov. 1902), 12; Barber and Agnew, 91; Blake, *HMM* 18 (Feb. 1904), 106; Clements, H5 file,

PHS. On attitudes toward Anglo doctors, see Fish, "Land of Poco Tiempo," *HMM* 26 (Nov. 1911), 12, and Hoff, "The Life . . . ," *HMM* 29 (Nov. 1914), 13.

133. *HMM* 15 (Nov. 1900), 16.

134. It also eased the potential rivalry when Anglo women respected the knowledge of the parteras as Alice Blake did, learning from them, as well as helping to equip them, signing birth certificates, and sterilizing instruments. Barber and Agnew, 89. There were one or two convent schools north of Santa Fe in this period, but the sources on the nuns, the schools, and their interactions with villagers in this period were not accessible if, in fact, they exist at all. This important facet of Hispanic New Mexico needs further research. The far larger number of Presbyterian schools made them a logical focus for this book. Nonetheless, nuns existed within the Hispanic Catholic tradition as acceptable female roles. No villager with whom I spoke, however, nor any of the literature, mentioned village girls becoming nuns. See Louis Avant, "History of Catholic Education in New Mexcio since American Occupation" (Master's thesis, Univ. of New Mexico, 1940), 16–18, 56, 60, 73, 77–79, on convent schools and Catholic-run public schools in northern New Mexcio. Avant found such schools at Santa Fe, Mora, Las Vegas, and Taos before 1920; later Sisters ran the public school at Taos, Penasco, Santa Cruz, and Ranchos de Taos.

135. *HMM* 21 (April 1906), 5–6. Blake to Scott, 4 Dec. 1928, H5 Blake, PHS.

136. Jaramillo, 32; Clements, "Mexican Appreciation," *HMM* 26 (Nov. 1914), 15. And, for example, Davis, *HMM* 26 (Nov. 1911), 19; Barber and Agnew, 33; Clements, *HMM* 20 (Nov. 1905), 14; and see Sydney Ahlstrom, *A Religious History of the American People* (New York, 1975) II: 336 on Christian Endeavor Societies.

137. Ruth Barber, Oral History TC35C, MHL.

138. Blake, "Presbyterian Mission Work," 140. Scanlund, *HMM* 20 (Nov. 1905), 14; Craig, *HMM* 16 (Nov. 1901), 18; Hyson, *HMM* 26 (Nov. 1911), 22; Clark, "Shall Our New State," *HMM* 27 (Nov. 1912), 4; Barber and Agnew, 33.

139. Blake, *HMM* 17 (March 1903), 114; Clark, *HMM* 22 (Nov. 1907), 2; Galbraith, *HMM* 16 (Nov. 1902), 15; *HMM* 16 (Dec. 1901), 26.

140. Ann Douglas, *The Feminization of American Culture* (New York, 1977), chpt. 2; and see Hunter, 28–29 on the similar background of the China missionaries.

141. Hyson, *HMM* 23 (Nov. 1908), 14.

142. Clements to Voss, 9 March 1922, H5 Clements, PHS. See also Sutherland to Boole, 8 Oct. 1906 and 31 Dec. 1906, and J. C. Ross, "An Influence in New Mexico," service pin series, H5 Sutherland, PHS; and Blake to Scott, 23 Oct. 1905, H5 Blake, PHS. Blake to Scott, 23 Oct. 1905, H5 Blake, PHS.

143. Mary Goodall to Pierson, 28 May 1900, Record Group 51, Box 2, folder 6, PHS; Barber and Agnew, 33; Mollie Clements, "A Service of Joy," *HMM* 31 (Nov. 1916), 7; Leadingham, *HMM* 18 (Sept. 1904), 269.

144. Blake to Scott, 26 Sept. 1929, H5 Blake, PHS.

145. See H5 files, PHS. Prudence Clark Ortega and Pearl English Trujillo were among the nineteen of these mission women known to marry at all, two of whom were Hispanic. Only six of the sixty for whom I have information on why they left the field did so because of marriage.

148. Colin Goodykoontz, *Home Missions on the American Frontier* (Caldwell, Idaho, 1939), 426. Walker, 222 on the difficulty; Douglas, throughout, and Hunter, throughout, on the culture.

149. Blake, *HMM* 22 (Nov. 1904), 4.

146. Hyson to Long, 19 Dec. 1914, H5 Hyson, PHS.

147. Brengle to Boole, 30 April 1906, Record Group 51, Box 3, folder 1, PHS; Blake to Voss, 13 Jan. 1943, H5 Blake PHS.

Chapter 4. Hispanics in the Coal Fields

1. Agnes Smedley, *Daughter of Earth* (1929; reprint ed., Old Westbury, N.Y., 1973), 110.

2. *C&P* 2 (13 Aug. 1902), 130.

3. *Ibid.* 1 (31 May 1902), 461.

4. Ms. Census, RACo, 1910, see Truchas, Cordova, and Chimayo in particular. U.S. Dept. of Commerce, Bureau of the Census, *Thirteenth Census of the United States, 1910: Abstract of the Census* (Washington, D.C., 1913), 184.

5. R. E. McClung Papers, DPL. James B. Allen, *The Company Town in the American West* (Norman, 1966), 52; U.S. Congress, Senate, Commission on Industrial Relations, *Colorado Miners Strike,* 64th Cong., 1st sess., 1916, S.doc.415, 6451: CFI, 40%; Victor American Fuel Company, 15%; Rocky Mountain Fuel Company, 12%.

6. Ms. Census, Las Animas County, 1910: Aguilar had 858 people; on the outskirts were an additional 438 Hispanics and about the same number of Anglos. Only two of the Spanish surnamed on the outskirts were born in Mexico. And see Bennie Garcia, "Mexicans in Las Animas County," Mexican-Americans in Colorado Collection, WHC. Garcia describes Leroy Valdez, 1868–1913, who went to Delagua to get better land, but ended in the mines. Anne Lucero, "Aguilar and Its Western Valley of Trujillo Creek," in Jose de Onís, ed., *The Hispanic Contribution to the State of Colorado* (Boulder, 1976), 163–176.

7. See *C&P* 1 (1902) throughout: in Engle, for example, Hispanics were second to Italians, 140 to 94, of a population of 1000. Hispanics did have a majority in the Fierro Iron Mine and in some of the timber camps.

8. *C&P* 2 (13 Aug. 1902), 130. For housing monopolies, see Senate Journal, 13th Assembly of the State of Colorado, Tues., 26 Feb. 1901: Committee to Investigate Conditions in Relation to Coal Strike in the State of Colorado, Josephine Roche Papers, Box 6, WHC.

9. "How Miners Live," *Immigration* 2 (1910), 128. Colorado Coal Mine Inspector, *Annual Report* (1909–1910).

10. Smedley, 93; *Colorado Latin American Personalities* (Denver, 1959), 41; *Colorado Miners' Strike,* 6730: E. H. Weitzel. Colorado Bureau of Labor Statistics, *Biennial Report* (1911–1912), 57, and (1907–1908), 113, 132. Victor Clark, *Mexican Labor in the United States,* U.S. Labor Bureau Bulletin no. 78 (Sept. 1908), 486. James A. Ownbey Collection, Box 15-4, WHC: in 1913, Hispanics at Wootton earned from one dollar a day (an oiler) to $3.10 for mule drivers. Note that Clark, 488, explains that Mexican immigrants at the coke ovens near Trinidad earned only $1.50 a day.

11. See, for example, Aguilar vicinity and Madrid Plaza, Ms. Census, Las Animas County, 1910; and Colorado Bureau of Labor Statistics, *Biennial Report* (1907–1908), 113.

12. *Colorado Miners' Strike,* 7081: 22 April 1913, for an example of a man working part of the year on a ranch and part in the mines for two to three years; Garcia; Joint Convention Contest Committee (Feb. 1905), 308, DeBusk Papers, WHC. Integrated into the coal system through networks of relatives, these rural Hispanic villages nonetheless had a relatively large renter and boarder population. But whether the men migrated to the mines seasonally, weekly, or even daily, the new labor pattern encouraged in the villages a sexual division of labor more closely resembling that of northern New Mexico than that of the mining camps. See Ms. Census, Las Animas County, Stonewall, Abeyton, Hoehne, El Moro, 1900, and Madrid and the outskirts of Aguilar in 1910.

13. Leonard Arrington, *The Changing Economic Structure of the Mountain West 1850–1950* (Logan, 1963), 30–35: in 1900 there were 5,472, in 1910 there were 12,606. Allen, 52, 156–159. By 1903 there were at least 19 such camps in southern Colorado, at least 15 of which belonged to the CFI.

14. Colorado Coal Project, "Toil and Rage"—Scamehorn segment; Allen, 7, 50, 161. And see similar camp replacements of villages in William Taylor and Elliott West, "Patron Leadership at the Crossroads: Southern Colorado in the Late Nineteenth Century," *PHR* 42 (Aug. 1973), 342. J. M. Madrid, U.S.C.W.A., *Interviews,* UN3, CWA M216 reel 5, 83–84. Ralph Taylor, *Colorado South of the Border* (Denver, 1963), 288–289; Lucas Martinez, 0-200, CHS. Garcia. *TCN,* 13 Oct. 1904. Rouse and Starkville also had "Mexican Plazas," see *C&P* 1 (1902) and census and school census records.

15. John Reps, *Cities of the American West* (Princeton, 1979), 49.

16. *C&P* 1 (5 April 1902), 268–269, and 2 (25 Oct. 1902), 397.

17. *C&P* 3 (11 Feb. 1903), 156–157 contrasting Weston and Jansen, and 5 (9 April 1904), 325–326 contrasting Varos and Segundo, and 1 (1 March 1902), 179.

18. *Colorado Miners' Strike,* 6788: Patterson.

19. U.S. Congress, Senate, Commission on Industrial Relations, *Rockefeller Interests in Colorado,* 64th Cong., 1st sess., 1916, S.doc.415, 8929: Sopris

camp physician's report, 29 June 1914. Italians in particular also invaded other Hispanic localities, entering cattle ranching and mercantile enterprises, see Frederick Bohme, "The Italians in New Mexico," *NMHR* 34 (April 1959), 110, and Ms. Census, Las Animas County, 1900, 1910.

20. Olen Leonard, *The Role of the Land Grant* (1943, reprint ed., Albuquerque, 1970), 75, 133.

21. Corwin to Hearne, CFI, *Annual Report of the Sociological Department* (1904–1905), 11. Colorado Coal Project, "Rage and Toil." "Goats in CF&I Coal Camps," *C&P* 3 (23 May 1903), 465. Some Italians also had goats.

22. *C&P* 5 (26 March 1904), 242–243, and 2 (13 Aug. 1902), 132.

23. Senate Journal, Colorado, 26 Feb. 1901; Allen, 129–130. Ownbey Collection, Box 15-4, WHC; Wootton Land and Fuel Company Collection, 712, CHS. This company, 1906–1911, apparently benefited greatly from its company store. Clark, 486, 496.

24. *C&P* 2 (23 Aug. 1902), and Corwin to Kebler, CFI, *Annual Report of the Sociological Department* (1901–1902), 6. "Rockefeller Welfare Plan in 'Camp' Schools, a Farce," report submitted 15 Jan. 1916 at Valdez, Roche Papers, Box 6. Re: lending money, see, for example, CFI, *Annual Report of the Sociological Department* (1902–1903), 20.

25. Corwin to Hearne, CFI, *Annual Report of the Sociological Department* (1904–1905), 11; (1903–1904), 36; (1904–1905), 9.

26. *Ibid.* (1904–1905), 12.

27. "A Short History of the Troubles . . . ," Colorado Bureau of Labor Statistics, *Biennial Report* (1903–1904), 193. *Colorado Miners' Strike, 7204.*

28. Ms. Census, Las Animas County, 1900, 1910. Even in North Starkville, a mining community since the 1870s, a third of the Hispanics rented housing.

29. Ms. Census, RACo (New Mexico) and Las Animas County, Colorado, 1880, 1900, 1910.

30. *Ibid.* Coyote (RACo) had one boarder in 1880 and two in 1900, and El Rito had one in 1910 after the Spanish American Normal school was established there. See South Starkville, North Starkville, Berwind, and Primero in Ms. Census, Las Animas County, 1910. Boarders were usually Hispanic, but occasionally not, with Italians making up most of the non-Hispanic boarders in Hispanic households.

31. *Ibid.*

32. *Ibid.* In the one move which directly integrated these women into the mining economy and sometimes gave them independent income, some of them brought suit against the companies for which their husbands had died, and many won cash settlements, in particular against Victor American in 1911, and Wootton Land and Fuel Company in 1912, Las Animas County, District Court Indexes, vols. 1–2, Trinidad. Three suits in 1916 against CFI and Ideal Fuel Company awarded compensation for the widow and the minor children, Industrial Commission (Colorado), Commissioners Findings and Awards, Box 19141,

vol. A, 139, 157, 271, CSA. For similar cases, see Dale Wells, "Early Mexican-American Contact with Federal Courts in Southern Colorado 1879–1907" (1974), Mexican-American Collection, WHC.

33. CFI, *Annual Report of the Sociological Department* (1901–1902), 14. *C&P* 2 (23 Aug. 1902), 185. *TCN,* 1 Nov. 1904, p. 5; CFI, *Annual Report of the Sociological Department* (1904–1905), 20. Dorothy Morton, "A History of Quay County, New Mexico" (Master's thesis, Univ. of Colorado, 1938), 39–40. Colorado Coal Project, "Toil and Rage" shows an Anglo woman saying, "But we didn't go to the Mexican dances. We were a little bit afraid of them."

34. For example, Ramon Trujillo, Ludlow testimony, Dec. 1913, 72, CSFL Papers, Box 1, WHC. *C&P* 2 (30 Aug. 1902), 202. Colorado Coal Mine Inspector, *Annual Report* (1909–1910), 148, huge Delagua explosion in which 32 "Mexicans," 12 Italians, 9 Austrians, and 7 Montenegrins died. *Colorado Miners' Strike,* 6916: an Anglo labor politician accompanied by a "Mexican" friend went into the camps "to talk Mexican to the Mexicans down there" in 1913. Colorado Coal Mine Inspector, *Annual Report* (e.g. 1899–1900), 59, working with Anglo; (1901), 63, with Italian, 67–68, with Black. Even after 1911, the Mexican-born never made up a large proportion of these miners in this period, see Vigil and Tapia transcripts, 222, Colorado Coal Project.

35. Census records show most intermarriages occurring among farmers outside the mining towns, and this may have held true for the period before 1900. The marriage register, however, tells a different story. Clark, 512. Ms. Census, Las Animas County, 1880, 1900, 1910. Intermarriages seem to have been declining in Trinidad (19 in 1880 and 10 in 1900), and North and South Starkville had no intermarriage in 1910, Sopris had two and one Mexican-Spanish American marriage. Berwind had one in 1910. Three of these four (total) occurred after 1904. Marriage registers, Las Animas County, County Court House, Trinidad. Other sources for information on intermarriage include *Colorado Latin American Personalities,* 42; Taylor and West, 345; John Lawrence Diary, WHC; Elfido Lopez, Sr. Collection 813, FF1, CHS; and U.S.C.W.A., *Interviews,* reel 5, Las Animas County, 289.

36. Colorado Coal Project, "Toil and Rage."

37. Clark, 513.

38. Clark, 486, 487, 492.

39. Spanish Americans and Mexicans both played both parts. *Ibid.,* 516. David Lavender, *The Southwest* (New York, 1980), 302. Juan Gómez-Quiñones, "The First Steps: Chicano Labor Conflict and Organizing, 1900–1920," in Manuel Servín, ed., *An Awakened Minority: The Mexican Americans* (Beverly Hills, 1974), 90. Though Frances Swadesh contends native-born Hispanics started calling themselves Spanish-American to differentiate themselves from imported Mexican strikebreakers, I've found many different roots for that development, e.g. showing loyalty in the Spanish-American War. JCCC, throughout. Mary Jones, *Autobiography of Mother Jones* (1925, reprint ed., New York,

250 *Notes to Pages 95–97*

1969), 99, 113, 187. John Simpson, "A Short History . . . ," Colorado Bureau of Labor Statistics, *Biennial Report* (1903–1904), 192–197. Bound materials in the Western Federation of Miners Papers, WHC, indicate two Hispanic labor organizers in 1913, but not where they were employed: there were others after 1916.

40. Inspector D-87 Florence Case AAF, 23 May 1910, Roche Papers, Box 6, Reports of Industrial Spies.

41. CFI, *Annual Report of the Sociological Department* (1901–1902), 14–15; and, e.g., Allen, 62.

42. Though not necessarily Protestant, as opposed to the mission women; cf. Chapter 3. See *C&P* 2 (20 Sept. 1902), 277–278. William H. Tolman, *Social Engineering: A Record of Things Done by American Industrialists Employing Upwards of One and One-Half Million of People* (New York, 1909). John Higham, *Strangers in the Land* (New York, 1966), 83. Jane Hunter, *The Gospel of Gentility* (New Haven, 1984), 148. CFI, *Annual Report of the Sociological Department* (1901–1902), 32.

43. *Ibid.,* 16.

44. Corwin to Kebler, *ibid.,* 5.

45. *Ibid.* (1902–1903), 27.

46. Corwin to Hearne, *ibid.* (1903–1904), 10. Corwin found it "gratifying" that attendance at the schools increased during the strike, but the increase could have come from youthful strikers or from children released from household duties by the presence of working adults.

47. Dr. Walter Morritt, quoted in Clark, 487. *C&P* 4 (19 Sept. 1903), 221–223, and 1 (29 March 1902), 253. For a slightly contrasting view of the "Mexican" or "half breed" as "earning an honest living . . . and . . . more peaceable than many of his white neighbours," see *C&P* 1 (1 March 1902), 178; and on women, *C&P* 4 (19 Sept. 1903), 223.

48. CFI, *Annual Report of the Sociological Department* (1903–1904), 31, and Corwin to Kebler, *ibid.* (1901–1902), 5.

49. *Ibid.* (1901–1906).

50. There were thirteen kindergartens in 1905. Corwin to Kebler, CFI, *Annual Report of the Sociological Department* (1901–1902), 5–6. See also Tolman, 259 on the CFI program.

51. *Ibid.* (1903–1904), 32; (1901–1902), 19–20; and (1902–1903), 12. *C&P* 2 (30 Aug. 1902).

52. Corwin to Kebler, CFI, *Annual Report of the Sociological Department* (1902–1903), 5–6, 12.

53. *C&P* 5 (6 Feb. 1904), 79.

54. CFI, *Annual Report of the Sociological Department* (1902–1903), 8, 12, although a caption in the 1903–1904 report mentioned a "cozy corner in the Sociological House at Pictou, Colorado" which in the photo had ruffled pillows (p. 16). Also, Lizabeth Cohen has taken up this issue with regard to women in interclass and intercultural relations in the city in her article, "Embellishing a

Life of Labor: An Interpretation of the Material Culture of American Working Class Homes 1885–1915," *Journal of American Culture* 3 (Winter 1980), 752–775, and Jane Addams also thought overstuffed furniture unsanitary.

55. *Ibid.* (1904–1905), 12, *C&P* 5 (6 Feb. 1904), 93.

56. CFI, *Annual Report of the Sociological Department* (1904–1905), 11–12, 22–24.

57. *C&P* 4 (5 Dec. 1903), 500.

58. CFI, *Annual Report of the Sociological Department* (1902–1903), 7.

59. *Ibid.*, 6.

60. *Ibid.* (1904–1905), 8, 12; (1901–1902), 42; and (1904–1905), 24.

61. *Ibid.* (1903–1904), 10; (1901–1902), 24; (1903–1904), 26; and (1905–1906), 30.

62. Nan Elsasser et al., *Las Mujeres: Conversations from a Hispanic Community* (Old Westbury, N.Y., 1979): Susana Archuleta, 36.

63. CFI, *Annual Report of the Sociological Department* (1902–1903), 14.

64. *Ibid.*, and *C&P* 2 (23 Aug. 1902), 206. See Jane Addams's work for similar patterns of resistance among immigrant mothers with regard to the use of margarine, and Betty Boyd Caroli et al., eds., *The Italian Immigrant Woman in North America* (Toronto, 1978) for similar patterns elsewhere.

65. CFI, *Annual Report of the Sociological Department* (1901–1906).

66. Katharine Crowell, *Our Mexican Mission Schools* (New York, n.d. [c. 1913]), 33.

67. *Colorado State Business Directory* (1906), 952; *TCN,* 1 Oct. 1904; Feliz Cordova, U.S.C.W.A., *Interviews,* reel 5, 1; Ms. Census, Las Animas County, 1900, 1910. Shomburg, 0-155, CHS; McClung, 0-106, CHS. Taylor and West, 349–350.

68. Betty Naster, "Casimiro Barela, Colorado's 'Perpetual Senator' 1847–1920" (Master's thesis, Univ. of Denver, 1974), 14. Vigil Family Collection, Box 1, WHC. C-S Garcia, Publisher of *El Faro,* Trinidad, Paul Taylor Papers, Colorado, Utah, and Wyoming Folder, Bancroft Library, for which I am indebted to Kathy Morrissey. Colorado State Bureau of Child and Animal Protection, Biennial *Report* (1908), CSA.

69. In 1880 only 22% of Hispanic households in Trinidad had been female-headed. Ms. Census, Las Animas County, 1880, 1900, 1910, of 84 households in Trinidad's first ward and 39 in the others, in 1900. In 1910 over one-quarter of the Hispanic-headed households in the first ward were headed by women (27), 14 of whom were widows, 11 married, one divorced, and one single. In the second ward, 10 of 29 such households had female heads, including only one widow, two divorced women, and three single women. In 1900 there were also nearly as many female Anglo heads of households in the city. Cf. Albert Camarillo, *Chicanos in a Changing Society* (Cambridge, Mass., 1979), 137; Richard Griswold del Castillo, *The Los Angeles Barrio, 1850–1890: A Social History* (Berkeley, 1979), 98–99, and *La Familia: Chicano Families in the Urban Southwest, 1848 to the Present* (Notre Dame, 1984), 55.

70. Ms. Census, Las Animas County, 1880, 1900, 1910—cf. southern California and El Paso where many did. See Camarillo, and Mario García, *Desert Immigrants* (New Haven, 1981), and as cited in Maxine Baca Zinn, "Mexican-American Women in the Social Sciences," *Signs* 8 (Winter 1982), 266. More Hispanic women seem to have have servants in 1910 than in 1900 in Trinidad, however.

71. Over a third of the first ward's Hispanic wage workers were women. Colorado Bureau of Labor Statistics, *Biennial Report* (1909–1910), 206. Clark, 495. Ms. Census, Las Animas County. The job of domestic servant in most Hispanic households with servants was usually held by an Indian (usually Navaho) "captivo." By 1909 the laundry workers of Trinidad had had a shortlived union, but it is unclear whether Hispanic women participated. (Helen Sumner, *Equal Suffrage: The Results of an Investigation in Colorado* (New York, 1909), 172–174, 177.) In 1910 among female heads in Trinidad, though not necessarily among married women, more women were laundresses than took in boarders. In the first ward in 1910, 52 women earned an income in approximately 100 Hispanic households, 22 did laundry, 20 took in roomers, 6 were prostitutes, and 5 had miscellaneous occupations. Of 73 Hispanic male heads of households, only 16 owned their housing, including only 3 common laborers.

72. "Arguments of the Woman Suffrage Delegates before the Committee on the Judiciary of the U.S. Senate," 23 Jan. 1880 in U.S. Congress, Senate, Committee on the Judiciary, *Reports and Hearings on Woman Suffrage,* 62nd Cong., 3rd sess., 1913, S.doc. 1035, 39–40. The man to whom Anthony referred was most likely Democrat Agapito Vigil, who submitted a minority report to that effect. He had come to Colorado from Taos, New Mexico, raised stock and farmed and spoke no English.

73. Billie Barnes Jensen, "The Woman Suffrage Movement in Colorado" (Master's thesis, Univ. of Colorado, 1959), 32, 37, 55, 56, 63. Hispanics were voting for prohibition by the 1910s.

74. Meredith to Anthony, 14 June 1893, Ellis Meredith Papers, Box 1, FF5, CHS. Naster, 56.

75. Their accusers believed these women to be not merely befuddled voters, but part of organized corruption within the county. JCCC, 473–475, and re: illegal voting, 138, 373, 378 at Aguilar, Martinez Plaza, and Abeyton. Also see Hispanic women on elected school boards, 1894–1897 (presidents in districts 23, 3, and 4 in different years and several treasurers, for example), School Superintendents' Records, Las Animas County, Boxes 13101, 13099, 13100, CSA.

76. Mrs. Eutimia Mascarenas to J. U. Vigil, 7 Nov. 1906, Vigil Family Collection, Box 1.

77. Hoehne register of Electors, 1910 and 1912, DeBusk Papers, Oversize. Unmarried Hispanic women as well as married women registered and voted. In Hoehne the Hispanics were only very slightly the majority by 1912. Sumner has

figures on the registration of voters in Las Animas County by sex, conjugal status, land tenure, and profession, but not by ethnicity. Though she explains her figures on low female voter turnout in Trinidad with the assertion that "evidently the women of this race ["Mexicans"] did not vote in as large numbers as the men," Anglo women in general also did not vote in as large numbers as the men, and Sumner provides no evidence that Hispanic women voted in lower proportion than Anglo women, p. 106.

78. James Wright, *The Politics of Populism: Dissent in Colorado* (New Haven, 1974), 52. Naster, 22, 24.

79. See Taylor and West on patrons, 350–351; John Lawrence Diary, 9 Nov. 1904; and JCCC to see the number of non-English-speaking yet important political officials, indicating the importance of the Hispanic vote in Las Animas County, and Shomburg, 0-155, CHS, on Frank Donleavy's patronage system and the Hispanics. In Rio Arriba County, New Mexico, the Hispanics did retain considerable political control, though not economic control. See Fernando Padilla and Carlos Ramírez, "Patterns of Chicano Representation in California, Colorado and Nuevo Mexico," *Aztlan* 5 (Spring and Fall 1974), 189–234.

80. Monica Eklund, "Massacre at Ludlow," *Southwest Economy and Society* 4 (Fall 1978), 23. Colorado Adjutant-General's Office, *The Military Occupation of the Coal Strike Zone* (Denver, n.d. [1914]), 7–8. Colorado Coal Project, "Out of the Depths."

81. Colorado Adjutant General's Office, 10–11; Eklund, 23.

82. Mike Livoda transcript, 9, 11, Colorado Coal Project.

83. Minutes of special convention of District 15, United Mine Workers, Trinidad, Colorado, 15–16 Sept. 1913, *Colorado Miner's Strike,* 7025–7039.

84. Clipping, 9 March 1914, about 2 Dec. 1913, Northern Colorado Coal Company Collection 467, Box 2, FF87, CHS. Colorado Coal Project, "Out of the Depths." Colorado Adjutant-General's Office, 39. Ludlow Testimony (Jan. 1914), 426–428, 436, CSFL, Box 1.

85. Livoda, 8, 9, Colorado Coal Project. Colorado Adjutant-General's Office, 45, reports arrest of 141 foreigners, including 43 Mexicans. Ludlow testimony, 16–17, 230–231, CSFL. Brace exhibit no. 2, *Colorado Miners' Strike,* 7418.

86. *Ibid.,* 6451, 6802–6803, 7296–7311. Sisneros, Ludlow testimony, 437, CSFL.

87. *Colorado Miners' Strike,* 6879–6880, 7327.

88. Ludlow testimony, 245–249, CSFL.

89. For example, Ludlow testimony (Dec. 1913), 16–17, CSFL, Box 1, and *RMN,* 14 March 1914.

90. *Colorado Miners' Strike,* 7211.

91. *Ibid.,* 6350–6351, 7363. Gómez-Quiñonez, 96.

92. Robert Kern, "A Century of Labor in New Mexico," in Kern, ed., *Labor in New Mexico* (Albuquerque, 1983), 6–7.

Chapter 5. Impact of World War I and Mexican Migration

1. Victor Clark, *Mexican Labor in the United States,* U.S. Labor Bureau Bulletin no. 78 (Sept. 1908), 468–470. John Martinez, *Mexican Emigration to the United States 1910–1930* (1930; reprint ed., San Francisco, 1971), 2–5. Ms. Census, Weld and Las Animas counties, Colorado, and RACo, 1910. Arthur Corwin and Lawrence Cardoso, "Vamos al Norte: Causes of Mass Mexican Migration to the United States," in Corwin, ed., *Immigrants—and Immigrants* (Westport, Conn.: 1978), 38–43.

2. Martinez, 8–9, 41. Figures of legal emigration show a rise from 46,491 in 1910 to 98,595 in 1912, but then a decline to about 60,000 in 1913 and 15,230 in 1915, probably in response to U.S. economic depression. On heritage of mobility see Corwin and Cardoso, 43, and Rose Mary Koob's article, Clipping File, Greeley Municipal Museum, on the Carbajals, who married in Chihuahua in 1910, left Mexico for New Mexico in 1913, and arrived in Greeley in 1926.

3. *TTL* (Jan. 1913), 29; (July 1913), 30; (April 1913), 10.

4. H. Mendelson, *TTL* (Sept. 1916), 295; USDL, Commissioner-General of Immigration, *Annual Report* (1913), 250–251. Also see Roden Fuller, "Occupations of the Mexican-Born Population of Texas, New Mexico, and Arizona, 1900–1920," *Journal of the American Statistical Association* 23 (March 1928), 66–67; N. R. McReery, "The 1914 Beet Contract," *TTL* (Jan. 1914), 43–44; N. P. Hogerty, "Agricultural Notes," *TTL* (April 1914), 121; "Agricultural Notes," *TTL* (June 1915), 160.

5. H. Mendelson, "Next Year's Labor Supply," *TTL* (Oct. 1916), 294; William May, "The Great Western Sugarlands: History of the Great Western Sugar Company" (Ph.D. dissertation, Univ. of Colorado, 1982), 248, 250, 252; Great Western Sugar Company Statistics, GWSCo Papers, WHC. Joshua Bernhardt, *Government Control of Sugar* (*Quarterly Journal of Economics* reprint, 1921), 672–677, 688–689, 693–694.

6. *TTL* (Sept. 1916), 285. Carey McWilliams, *North from Mexico* (1948, reprint ed., New York, 1968), 181; McWilliams, *Ill Fares the Land* (Boston, 1942), 110: U.S. Congress, House of Representatives, Committee on Immigration and Naturalization, *Hearings: Temporary Admission of Illiterate Mexican Laborers,* 66th Cong., 2nd sess., 1920, 210–212. General Manager to Carey, 5 April 1915, re: American Beet Sugar Labor Difficulties, National Sugar Manufacturing Company Papers, Box 1, FF40, CHS. H. Mendelson, "Notes on Labor," *TTL* (Dec. 1919), 585; C. V. Maddux, "Two Ways of Sizing Up the Beet Labor Market," *TTL* (Jan. 1919), 62; "Notes," *TTL* (June 1918), 273–274.

7. Southern Colorado beet companies and many other companies had always employed at least a few Mexican born-laborers. *Hearings: Temporary Admission,* 26: Mandeville. American Beet Sugar Company, one of four companies in the Arkansas Valley, imported 1,677 Mexicans in 1916 and 2,320 in 1917.

8. USDL, Commissioner-General of Immigration, *Annual Report* (1917), xvii.

9. Mark Reisler, *By the Sweat of Their Brow: Mexican Immigrant Labor in the United States, 1900–1940* (Westport, Conn., 1976), 26–27; USDL, Commissioner-General of Immigration, *Annual Report* (1918), 16; J. B. Gwin, "Back and Forth to Mexico," *Survey* 39 (Oct. 1917), 9; Martinez, 21–22.

10. Martinez, 10, 18.

11. USDL, Commissioner-General of Immigration, *Annual Report,* e.g. (1918), 16, and (1920), 287; *U.S. Bureau of Immigration Service Bulletin* 1 (June 1918), 1; 1 (Aug. 1918), 1, and (Oct. 1918), 2. There had also been a provision that a portion of the wages be held back pending return to Mexico; the amount and the timing of return changed from 1918 to 1921.

12. See Arthur Pettit, *Images of the Mexican American in Fiction and Film* (College Station, Tex., 1980), 85, and Emory Bogardus, *Immigration and Race Attitudes* (Boston, 1928), 20–21, 44–47, 68–70.

13. John Blum, *Woodrow Wilson and the Politics of Morality* (Boston, 1956), 88–93; David Lavender, *The Southwest* (New York, 1980), 295; Joan Moore with Alfredo Cuellar, *Mexican Americans* (Englewood Cliffs, 1970), 23; and Anita Brenner, *The Wind That Swept Mexico* (New York, 1943). Pershing returned with 2,030 Mexican refugees; J. B. Gwin, "Making Friends of Invaders," *Survey* 37 (March 1917), 621. Pershing had about 50,000 National Guardsmen still on duty on the Mexican border in February 1917; USDL, Commissioner-General of Immigration, *Annual Report* (1917), 148.

14. David Kennedy, *Over Here: The First World War and American Society* (New York, 1980), 10; Martinez, 18.

15. Miller to Charles Mayer, Denver, President W.F.M., 15 July 1915 and 23 Aug. 1915, Executive Board Minutes, pp. 20–21, Western Federation of Miners Papers, WHC. Kennedy, 264; Jay Stowell, *The Near Side of the Mexican Question* (New York, 1921), 113; Pollard, Luna County Chairman, Council of Defense, to Governor, 4 Aug. 1917, Gov. Lindsey Papers, "Labor Disputes in Gallup Region: Attempted Deportations," NMSRCA. According to Pollard, the Columbus citizens showed "some disposition. . . to drive these men into the republic of Mexico."

16. Risdon to Lindsey, 7 Aug. 1917, Gov. Lindsey Papers, "Labor Disputes in the Gallup Region," NMSRCA. The strike mainly concerned union recognition. And see 12 March 1917, Misc. Records, Women's Suffrage, NMSRCA. Risdon to Lindsey, 7 Aug. 1917 and 5 Aug. 1917, and a petition apparently from miners against the Council of Defense, 7 Aug. 1917, with about 14 Hispanic names, many Slavic names, and some Anglo ones. Troops were eventually called in for three months. Gov. Lindsey Papers, "Special Reports and Investigations."

17. Martinez, 20. "Mexican Miners Going Back Home," *Survey* 39 (Oct. 1917), 97–98.

18. Alfred White, *The Apperceptive Mass of Foreigners as Applied to Americanization, The Mexican Group* (1923, reprint ed., R&E Research Associates, 1971), 8. John Higham, *Strangers in the Land* (New York, 1966), 204–205; Kennedy, 66–68.

19. Robert McLean, "The Changing Southwest Our Postern Gate," *HMM* 32 (May 1918), 148. The missions joined forces interdenominationally to meet the rising Mexican immigration. Rodney Roundy, *HMM* (May 1921), 148–149.

20. Gregory Mason, "New Mexico and the New Southwest," *HMM* 29 (Nov. 1914), 2; M. Katharine Bennett, "Americanization in New Mexico," *HMM* 33 (May 1919), 149; and other articles in this magazine. See also *NMWN,* 5 March 1918, p. 4, L. Bradford Prince Collection, NMSRCA.

21. Higham, 198; Wilson, at Ludlow, quoted in Kennedy, 87.

22. *HMM* 33 (May 1919), 60; Sara J. Reed, "El Rito Folks," *HMM* 32 (Nov. 1917), 4.

23. Kennedy, 12, 46–47, 64; Emory Bogardus, *Essentials of Americanization,* 3rd rev. ed. (Los Angeles, 1923), 17.

24. *Ibid.,* 61, 64–65. Edgar Dunnington Randolph, "An Outline of the Field of Child Welfare," *Colorado State Teachers College Bulletin,* ser. 18 (May 1918); World War I Collection, WHC; WCTU (Colorado), *Annual Report* (1917–1918 to 1921–1922), WHC; Colorado Federation of Women's Clubs, *Yearbook* (1917–1918 to 1921–1922.); White, 3; Louise Collins, "Report of the Work of Home and Child Welfare Department of the Santa Fe Women's Clubs," *NMJE* 11 (April 1915), 11.

25. *TCN,* 15 July 1918; Harper Donaldson, "Natives of Our Great Southwest," *HMM* 33 (July 1919), 207. New Mexico school officials and teachers adopted a proposal in August 1918: "We believe that the English language should be the first means of Americanization and should be the means of communication between all citizens," New Mexico Dept. of Education, Gov. Lindsey papers, Exp. 1. Florence Kluckhohn and Fred Strodtbeck, *Variations in Value Orientations* (Evanston, Ill., 1961), 247: the first public school to require English for teaching in "Atrisco" was established in 1918. *NMJE* 15 (Sept. 1918), 11–12. Confidential Report of the Spanish American Normal School to Governor, 1917, pp. 8–9, Gov. Lindsey Papers. *HMM* 31 (Nov. 1915), 13; Prize Essay "What Uncle Sam Means to Me," and Rose Scott, "An Americanization Plant," *HMM* 34 (May 1920), 147, 155, 161.

26. For example, Clements, *HMM* 32 (Nov. 1917), 19. They also helped in Liberty Bond and Food Administration drives.

27. Sara Reed, "El Rito Folks," *HMM* 32 (Nov. 1917), 4; Edgar Lee Hewett, "The Cost and the Gain," in *New Mexico in the Great War* (special edition), *NMHR* 2 (Jan. 1927), 22. A. V. Lucero, "The Problem of a Foreign Language in the Southwest," *HMM* 35 (May 1921), 147; Lansing Bloom, "To the Colors," in *New Mexico in the Great War, NMHR* 1 (Oct. 1926), 422. Fred Eastman, *Unfinished Business of the Presbyterian Church in America* (Philadelphia, 1921),

45; Ruth Barker, *Caballeros* (New York, 1931), 84; George Sanchez, *Forgotten People* (Albuquerque, 1940), 26.

28. U.S.C.W.A., *Interviews,* M216, reel 5, p. 299: J. Preston Dunlevy (at CHS). *Roster of Men and Women who Served in the World War from Colorado 1917–1918* (Colorado, 1941). Sporleder Papers, Box 5, ff14, DPL. About one-quarter of those serving from Las Animas and Huerfano Counties were Hispanic.

29. *HMM* 32 (Sept. 1918), 245; *HMM* 33 (May 1919), 158–159. The first two graduates of Embudo were drafted in 1917, for example. See also *HMM* 32 (May 1918), 155, and 33 (May 1919), 160, 163.

30. Fabiola Cabeza de Baca Gilbert, *We Fed Them Cactus* (Albuquerque, 1954), 157; Joan Jensen, "Women Teachers, Class, and Ethnicity: New Mexico, 1900–1950," *Southwest Economy and Society* 4 (Late Winter 1978–1979), 5. Hewett, 24; Bogardus, *Essentials,* 27; *Wireless Messages from Home Mission Stations* (Oct. 1918), 16. In that conscription were 40,000 other men in similar straits.

31. Stowell, 110.

32. Charles Briggs, *The Woodcarvers of Córdova, New Mexico* (Knoxville, 1980), 36.

33. Alice Hyson, *HMM* 32 (Aug. 1918), 231; Zoe Ellsworth, "Patriotism in a New Mexico Plaza," *HMM* 32 (Sept. 1918), 245–246; see also Joan Jensen, "Canning Comes to New Mexico: Women and the Agricultural Extension Service, 1914–1919," *NMHR* 57 (Oct. 1982), 373–374 on Hispanic distrust.

34. Kennedy, 105–106.

35. Annetta Bell, *HMM* 32 (Nov. 1917), 19; Zoe Ellsworth, *HMM* 32 (Sept. 1918), 245; Reed, *HMM* 33 (May 1919), 160 at Agua Negra, Chimayo, and Chacon. *TCN,* 5 May 1918; Madrid to Wood, *Evening Picketwire,* 7 May 1918; *ibid.,* 8 May 1918. In mining camps, Hispanic donations averaged about fifty cents.

36. Walter Danburg, "The State Council of Defense," in *New Mexico in the Great War, NMHR* 1 (Jan. 1926), 104; Fernando Padilla and Carlos Ramirez, "Patterns of Chicano Representation in California, Colorado and Nuevo Mexico," *Aztlan* 5 (Spring and Fall 1974), 211–218 on increased office holding among Hispanics during the war in New Mexico but not in Colorado. County councils in New Mexico were often less balanced than the state council; in Mora and San Miguel Counties Hispanics were underrepresented. Mora County Records, Council of Defense Correspondence, 1917–1918, NMSRCA. Mrs. Hernandez, the wife of a prominent Chicano politician in the state, was in charge of the Public Markets Department of the Women's Committee; *Report of the Council of Defense* (1918), 51. *NMWN,* 29 May 1918. Hispanic women in Taos and Rio Arriba Counties chaired county auxiliaries of the state women's committee. Bibliographical Sketches and Photographs of New Mexico in World War I, and J. P. Martinez to Read, 14 June 1920, Read Collection, NMSRCA.

37. Rupert Asplund, "Civilian Activities," in *New Mexico in the Great*

War, NMHR 1 (April 1926), 123–124. *NMWN* began a Spanish edition in July 1918 (Danburg, 111), and the *Santa Fe New Mexican* had a Spanish weekly supplement George Smith, "New Mexico's Wartime Food Problems, 1917–1918, I," *NMHR* 18 (Oct. 1943), 366). *NMWN,* 5 March 1918, 4; *Report of the Council of Defense* (1918), Gov. Lindsey Papers.

38. *Evening Picketwire* (Trinidad), 6 May 1918, 15 Feb. 1918; *TCN,* 3 Oct. 1918, 24 Jan. 1918. According to *TCN,* 9 May 1918, districts 13 and 19 of the Red Cross had Hispanic female leaders, one of whom was Ysabel Cordova, chair of the district's United War Work Committee and a school teacher. The Women's Council of Defense included Mrs. Chacon in Las Animas County and two Hispanic women in Costilla County, Colorado. For other examples see Colorado in World War I Collection, WHC.

39. Report of U.S. Bureau of Public Health Service on Health Administration in New Mexico, p. 16, Gov. Lindsey Papers, Special Reports and Investigations. Blake, *HMM* 33 (May 1919), 165; "Women's Part in the Great War," *NMWN,* 9 April 1918, 4. *Report of the Council of Defense* (1918), p. 38, Gov. Lindsey Papers. Alice Corbin Henderson, "The Women's Part," in *New Mexico in the Great War, NMHR* 1 (April 1926), 243. Clements, *HMM* 35 (May 1921), 164; Women's Council of Defense (Colorado), *Report* (30 Nov. 1918), 60, Colorado in World War I Collection, Box 47. Erna Fergusson, Women of New Mexico, Archive 303, Box 2, UNM. "Erna Fergusson," *Santa Fe New Mexican,* 6 June 1940; Dorothy Woodward, "The Penitentes of New Mexico" (Ph.D. dissertation, Yale Univ., 1935), 292; Estelle Warner, "Mexican Villages of New Mexico," *HMM* 34 (May 1920), 145; P. A. F. Walter, "Art Drama, and Literature in War Service," in *New Mexico in the Great War, NMHR* 1 (Oct. 1926), 409.

40. Smith, 1 349–351, 358–359; *NMWN,* 31 Jan. 1918, I; Kennedy, 121; Woodward, 287. Jensen, "Canning," 361, 367–370, 373–374. The extension service began in 1914 in cooperation with the federal government under the Smith-Lever Act. Henderson, 237; *HMM* 32 (May 1918), 157. Mary Wilson, *HMM* 33 (Aug. 1919), 224. Elizabeth Craig, *HMM* 32 (Nov. 1917), 18. From the start in 1914, the Agricultural Extension Service had made teaching canning methods a part of government policy, a part of the increased efficiency and economy of modern farm life. But the cost of pressure cookers ($18 in 1921), essential at New Mexico's altitude, the scarcity of water, and the paucity of Spanish language instructors meant that though in some counties teams of girls put on canning demonstrations in Spanish and English, drying prevailed as a preservation method well into the 1930s. There were always fewer home demonstration agents than agricultural agents. Until 1917, there was only one. During the war there were thirteen. Gertrude Espinosa of Santa Fe in 1917 became an assistant in club work, and visited 300 Hispanic homes; an Anglo Spanish-speaking woman was added as home demonstrator in February 1918.

41. Stowell, 110. Briggs, 36.

42. Jack D. Tramar responding to Read's request, Misc. World War I material, Read Collection. Ashley Pond, "At the Front," in *New Mexico in the Great War, NMHR* 2 (Jan. 1927), 17–18, 20; interview with Joseph Byers, Denver, 4 Oct. 1983.

43. *El Palacio* 5 (June 1919), 209. Frank Roberts, "The War Executive," in *New Mexico in the Great War, NMHR* 1 (Jan. 1926), 22. Gov. Lindsey protested to both Camp Kearney and Camp Cody; Gov. Larrazolo's files for 1920 also include among the special reports, "Discrimination against Spanish American Soldiers," at Fort Wingate, NMSRCA.

44. Kennedy, 243; Smith, 360, 384–385, and part 2, *NMHR* 19 (Jan. 1944), 19–20. Kluckhohn and Strodtbeck, 185; Gerald Nash, *The American West in the Twentieth Century* (Englewood Cliffs, 1973), 70. Blake and Craig, *HMM* 32 (Nov. 1917), 18; Gilbert, 12, 171–174; Jensen, "Canning," 380.

45. Olen Leonard, *The Role of the Land Grant* (1943, reprint ed., Albuquerque, 1970), xv, 60, 116; Charles Briggs, "'Our Strength Is in the Land'" (Ph.D. dissertation, Univ. of Chicago, 1981), 307; Briggs, *Woodcarvers,* 85; Joan Jensen, "New Mexico Farm Women, 1900–1940," in Robert Kern, ed., *Labor in New Mexico* (Albuquerque, 1983), 65. Ellsworth, 246.

46. Harry Schwartz, *Seasonal Farm Labor in the United States* (New York, 1945), 111; Stowell, 110; *TTL* (Jan. 1913), 26. Wages in beet labor rose from about $18 to about $25 per acre, with the average worker handling seven to ten acres in a season.

47. In the Cokedale/Boncarbo district in 1920, only 15% of the 142 Hispanic residents between the ages of 6 and 21 had been born in the district, and 47% had been born outside the mining area. District 18, Las Animas County School Census, 1920, CSA. Figures were similar, though less extreme, elsewhere in the county. In Trinidad, less than half the Hispanics of school age had been born in town, and many families had doubled up in living quarters. Approximately 21.7% of the children were born in New Mexico, Las Vegas being the largest contributor, and only 2.7% or fifteen had been born in Mexico. (District 1, *ibid.*). Both census and, even more so, school census records would tend to underrepresent migratory populations, particularly those with a relatively small ratio of children to adults.

48. John Andrews, "History of Rural Spanish Settlement and Land Use in the Upper Culebra Basin of the San Luis Valley, Costilla County, Colorado" (Master's thesis, Univ. of Colorado, 1972), 70–71; Nan Elsasser et al., *Las Mujeres: Conversations from a Hispanic Community* (Old Westbury, N.Y., 1979): Patricia Luna, 87. *HMM* 34 (May 1920), 149; Alice Blake, "Away from Home," *HMM* 32 (May 1918), 16.

49. Ellsworth, 246; Mary Wilson, "The Place and Influence of Mexican Women, *HMM* 33 (Aug. 1919), 222; Jay Stowell, *A Study of Mexican and Spanish Americans in the United States* (New York, 1920), 32, 35, 39; New Mexico, Dept. of Education, *Educational Directory* (1916–1917 to 1918–1919).

50. D. L. Joehnck, "Next Years Labor Contract," papers read at the First Annual Meeting, Rocky Mountain Chapter, American Association of Sugar Beet Agriculturists, Denver, Jan. 1921, pp. 1–2, GWSCo Papers, Box 4, WHC. USDL, CB, *Child Labor and the Work of Mothers in the Beet Fields of Colorado and Michigan,* Bureau Publication No. 115 (Washington, D.C., 1923), 3, 5, 11, 14–15, from data collected in 1920 in Weld and Larimer Counties. May, 406; K. D. Knaus and D. Sigwing, "History of the Great Western Sugar Company," 34–35, GWSCo Papers, Bound Histories of Factory Districts, WHC. At Brighton beet labor was 27% "Mexican" in 1917 and 41% in 1922.

51. Weld County School Census, Box 13373, District 104, Vollmer, CSA. Data for place of birth are unavailable through these records before 1920.

52. Weld County Marriage Register, vol. 2, Clerk and Recorders' Office, Civic Center, Greeley. The number rose and fell, but after 1918, never dipped below 20.

53. See clippings in Colorado in World War I Collection, WHC, arranged by county. Some of these Hispanics listed Taos or Clayton, New Mexico, and Trinidad or Walsenburg in southern Colorado as home, but the majority came from the northern beet and mining towns, mostly the former. Denver seems to have had a smaller percentage of Hispanics than did the beet-growing counties at this date. Of the men who actually served in the war, thirty-two of Weld County's contingent were Hispanic, mostly privates in the infantry. *Roster of Men and Women who Served . . . ;* Chris Romero, Oral History, DPL.

54. Joehnck, 2.

55. Agricultural Notes, *TTL* (June 1915), 160. F. L. Cooper, *TTL* (March 1920), 187; Agricultural Notes, *TTL* (Dec. 1916), 370; USDL, CB, *Child Labor and the Work of Mothers,* 68.

56. John Maier, "Beet Labor Contracts," *TTL* (Jan. 1917), 14–15; Notes; *TTL* (Dec. 1917), 446; H. Mendelson, "Notes on Labor," *TTL* (Dec. 1919), 586; USDL, CB, *Child Labor and the Work of Mothers,* 61.

57. Joehnck, 2.

58. USDL, CB, *Child Labor and the Work of Mothers,* 15, 64. For some reason, despite their own exposé of these conditions, and ironically in light of the implied criticism of German-Russian idleness in the winter, the investigators blamed the need for winter employment on the Mexicans for "lacking the thrift" of the German-Russians. A Chicano beetworker in 1918 might have made $250 in the course of six months from April to October, and most made less than an additional $300 the rest of the year. A resident hired hand would have made over $1000 a year; virtually none of these were Chicanos. *TTL* (May 1918), 250. In Weld County, the number of Chicanos on poor relief ranged from 5 to 10% of the relief load. Poor Reports, Office of the Secretary of State, Boxes 9695A and B, CSA.

59. USDL, CB, *Child Labor and the Work of Mothers,* 15; Ms. Census, Weld County, 1910; Lucas Martinez, OH-200, CHS.

60. Zoe Ellsworth, "The Game of Learning and Living," *HMM* 33 (May 1919), 149; Alice Blake, "New Outlook on an Old Field," *HMM* 34 (May 1920), 165.

61. "Evening Classes at Chimayo," *NMJE* 16 (Nov. 1919), 14; Santa Fe County Superintendent's Report, *NMJE* 16 (June 1920), 14. Minutes, State Board for Vocational Education for New Mexico, 14 Feb. 1920, p. 2, Gov. Larrazolo Papers, Exp. 1, Reports, NMSRCA. Jensen, "Canning," 367, 373. There remained a few Hispanic county agricultural agents after the war, but among the decreased number of home demonstration agents there were no Hispanics until Fabiola Cabeza de Baca became an agent in 1929.

62. Even Hispanic women teachers lost ground. By 1920/21 only 19.35% of all Rio Arriba County teachers and 28.3% of Hispanic teachers were Hispanic women, representing a gain over the prewar figure but a loss from the 1918/19 peak. New Mexico, Dept. of Education, *Educational Directory* (1920–1921). Clements, *HMM* 35 (May 1921), 164; Ruth Barber and Edith Agnew, *Sowers Went Forth* (Albuquerque, 1981), 89; *HMM* 35 (May 1921), 161. Despite the postwar establishment of a state Board of Health in 1919, many of the Hispanic counties did not acquire county nurses or medical personnel until the 1930s, and the rural Hispanic villages of Colorado fared no better.

63. Report of Southeast District, Colorado Federation of Women's Clubs, *Official Yearbook* (1919 and 1920), 31, 32, in Colorado State Federation of Women's Clubs Collection, WHC. WCTU (Colorado), *Annual Report* (1922), 33, also claimed "Americanization of the foreign woman in the home" as its "distinctive work," and at Monte Vista boasted a successful kindergarten with 23 "Mexican" children.

64. Nettie Jacobson, Colorado Federation of Women's Clubs, *Official Yearbook* (1920–1921), 23.

65. *Albuquerque Journal,* 11 March 1917, p. 2. The Congressional Union sent an organizer in 1914 and launched a campaign in 1915; in 1916 NAWSA sent Lola Walker for ten days. Misc. Records, Politics and Political Issues, Women's Suffrage in New Mexico, NMSRCA; Joan Jensen, "'Disenfranchisement Is a Disgrace': Women and Politics in New Mexico," *NMHR* 56 (Jan. 1981), 6–8, 10–11. For examples of differing judgments as to Hispanic blame or suffrage failure see Mrs. W. Lindsey to Dr. Anna H. Shaw on political parties, no. 18 (1918), blaming the Catholicism of Hispanics, and the "Native Vote Is Chief Cause," 10 March 1919, in Misc. Records, Politics and Political Issues, Women's Suffrage in New Mexcio, NMSRCA. A Hispanic and an Anglo introduced the 1917 suffrage resolution in New Mexico's House.

66. Jensen, "Disenfranchisement," 15–16. Note that Hispanic women held office in New Mexico, for example, State Librarian, in 1913. Nina Otero-Warren in 1917 became Supt. of Schools in Santa Fe, an elective position. Among Hispanics, voting and politics had been affairs of family interest, with women going to voting places even without the ballot and filling the ranks of onlookers at the

state legislature. "How a Plucky Women Foiled a Governor," *Albuquerque Journal Magazine,* 10 Feb. 1981, p. 10, Women of New Mexico, Vertical File, UNM; Gilbert, 163–164; Katharine Bennett, "Americanization in New Mexico," *HMM* 33 (May 1919), 150. Woman suffrage did not come to New Mexico until it came to the country as a whole.

67. Council of Defense, *Final Report* (1920), 78, Gov. Larrazolo Papers, Special Reports. Agricultural Extension Agent quoted in Jensen, "Canning," 374.

68. Robert McLean, "Latin and Anglo Saxon Points of Contact and Contrast," *HMM* 33 (May 1919), 146, and see other articles in this magazine; White, 54; J. H. Heald, "The Mexicans in the Southwest," *Missionary Review of the World* 42 (Nov. 1919), 860, 863–864; *Hearings: Temporary Admission,* 73: Jones and Vaile; Higham, 254.

69. Rev. Roundy, "The Mexican in Our Midst," *Missionary Review of the World* 49 (May 1921), 363; Larrazolo, *NMJE* 15 (Jan. 1919), 18.

70. Jensen, "Women Teachers," 7; Stowell, *The Near Side,* 86–87; State Board of Education minutes, 9–10 June 1919 and 25 April 1919, Gov. Larrazolo Papers, Reports, Exp. 1. Bennett, 150. New laws, however, merely reinforced older requirements such as that teachers in Hispanic districts be bilingual, and only required the teaching of Spanish when the majority of the local school board so voted. For reactions to Larrazolo's proposal see: L. P. Martinez, *NMJE* 15 (March 1919), 20; *HMM* 33 (May 1919), 154; Stowell, *A Study,* 9; Bennett, 150; James Slayden, "Some Observations on Mexican Immigration," *Annals of the American Academy of Political and Social Science* 93 (Jan. 1921), 125. See also John Chávez, *The Lost Land: The Chicano Image of the Southwest* (Albuquerque, 1984), 102–103.

71. "The Spanish Americans in Colorado," 12, Milton Callon Papers, Box 8, file 30; Nash, 76; "Time Event Chart," *SLVH* 1 (1969), 20; Editor's page, *TTL* (May 1919), 217; GWSCo Statistics, GWSCo Papers, WHC.

72. C. V. Maddux, "Beet Labor at $20.53," *TTL* (Aug. 1919), 378; "Beet Labor," *TTL* (April 1920), 250.

73. *Hearings: Temporary Admission,* 26. Commissioner-General of Immigration, *Annual Report* (1920), 287; (1917), 7; (1919), 13. U.S. Bureau of Immigration, *U.S. Immigration Service Bulletin* (1 Jan. 1919), 1. "Notes," *TTL* (Nov. 1917), 405. U.S. Congress, Senate, Committee on Finance, *Hearings on the Proposed Tariff Act of 1921,* Schedule 5, "Sugar, Molasses, and Manufactures of" (Washington, D.C., 1922), 2257: Francis King Carey, President of National Sugar Manufacturing Company, Sugar City, Colorado. Martinez, 2; May, throughout.

74. USDL, Commissioner-General of Immigration, *Annual Report* (1919), 401 and (1920), 694–696; "Monthly Movements of Aliens July 1913 to June 1920," *Monthly Labor Review* 11 (Nov. 1920), 225; Martinez, 34–35. *Hearings: Temporary Admission,* 44: David Keane; *ibid.,* 210, 214, 230, 231: Mandeville.

"Mexican Labor Preferred by Utah Beet Growers," *TTL* (Aug. 1920), 540; Reisler, 25, 37; Martinez, 13; Schwartz, 111. Cleon Roberts, *Fort Lupton* (Denver, 1982), 286: Weld County Commercial Club and Weld Division of Farm Bureau also sought New Mexican and Mexican labor during the war and in 1919. According to C. V. Maddux, "Soliciting Beet Labor," *TTL* (Jan. 1921), 26, 28, GWSCo engaged 2000 German Russians and 10,000 "Mexicans" (about half from New Mexico and Colorado) for its farmers in 1920 in addition to the labor that farmers contracted by other means. The recruiting cost was $30 per laborer, or about $360,000 in total, most of which went for transportation.

75. *Hearings: Temporary Admission,* 134: William Clarkson; *ibid.,* 55: Fred Roberts. USDL, Commissioner-General of Immigration, *Annual Report* (1918), 319. Martinez, 20. USDL, Commissioner-General of Immigration, *Annual Report* (1920), 288: 327 had died and 11 had legalized their permanent residence in the United States.

76. Elizabeth Broadbent, *The Distribution of Mexican Populations in the United States* (1941, reprint ed., San Francisco, 1972), 12, 28. In 1910 Colorado had, according to the census, 2,062 residents born in Mexico, and New Mexico had 11,918. Weld County School Census Records show the paucity of Chicano residents before the war.

77. "Mexican Invaders Relieving Our Farm Labor Shortage," *Literary Digest* 66 (17 July 1920), 53; Slayden, 126; Gregory Mason, "Today's Invasion of the Southwest by the Mexican," *HMM* 30 (Nov. 1915), 2; A. V. Lucero, "The Problem of a Foreign Language in the Southwest," *HMM* 35 (May 1921), 147.

78. Robert McLean, *HMM* 33 (May 1919), 146, and see Stowell, *The Near Side,* 42.

79. *HMM* 34 (May 1920), 150; Stowell, *A Study,* 61–62. Marta Weigle, *Brothers of Light, Brothers of Blood* (Albuquerque, 1976), 100. On Santa Fe's fiesta see, for example, "The Santa Fe Fiesta," *El Palacio* 7 (Sept. 1919), 99–132.

80. War Diary of U.S. Troops, Gallup, Gov. Larrazolo Papers, Exp. 2, Reports, NMSRCA. Gerald Breitigam, "'*NYT*' on Mexican Labor," *TTL* (Aug. 1920), 436; Robert McLean, "Mexican Labor in the United States," *HMM* 33 (March 1919), 105; Stowell, *The Near Side,* 47–48, 113, 123; Bogardus, *Essentials,* 268; Larrazolo to "Sir," 11 Dec. 1919, on dictatorship of unions, Gov. Larrazolo Papers, Exp. 2, Reports.

81. Harry Fox, Wyoming Federation of Labor, Resolution 193, and in the same vein J. L. Lewis, Mineworkers, American Federation of Labor, *Report on Proceedings of the Thirty-Ninth Annual Convention* (1919), 247, 336, 368.

82. Slayden, 121; Higham, 271–273, 313; *Hearings: Temporary Admission,* 191: Chairman, Knox, and Vaile; *ibid.,* 86: John Davis (Laredo); *ibid.,* 36: Carlos Bee and Roy Miller (Texas). U.S. Congress, Senate, Committee on Immigration, *Hearings: Admission of Agricultural Laborers,* 66th Cong., 2d sess., 1920, 4: Fred Roberts (Texas); *ibid.,* 23: W. H. Knox (Arizona); *Hearings: Temporary*

Admission, 889: Vaile (Colorado). *Ibid.,* 37: Miller. *Ibid.,* 151: Hudspeth (Texas).

83. "Mexican Labor Preferred by Utah Beet Growers," *TTL* (Aug. 1920), 541. The labor had been on the site for two years. And see Higham, 254–255, 262, 266, 269.

84. Sec. Wilson quoted in Reisler, 28.

85. G. F. Warren, Cornell Univ., "Some After the War Problems in Agriculture," *Journal of Farm Economics* 1 (June 1916) reprinted in *TTL* (Sept. 1919), 433. *Hearings: Temporary Admission,* 299–305: John Box (Texas); William Leonard, "Where Both Bullets and Ballots Are Dangerous," *Survey* 37 (Oct. 1916), 86.

86. *Hearings: Temporary Admission,* 13.

87. *Ibid.,* 221: Mandeville; Ricardo Romo, "Responses to Mexican Immigration, 1910–1930," *Aztlan* 6 (Summer 1975), 187; Colorado State Coal Mine Inspector, *Annual Report* (1918 through 1922); "Results of Admission of Mexican Laborers," *Monthly Labor Review* 11 (Nov. 1920), 1097.

88. *Hearings: Temporary Admission,* 88.

89. Harlan Douglas, *From Survey to Service* (New York, 1912), 154–156.

90. *Hearings on the Proposed Tariff of 1921,* Schedule 5, 2264: Francis Carey.

91. *Hearings: Temporary Admission,* 80–81: John Davis.

92. *Ibid.,* 22: Mandeville; *ibid.,* 226: Raker (California). And see Daniel Thomas Moreno, "Social Equality and Industrialization: A Case Study of Colorado Beet Sugar Industry" (Ph.D. dissertation, Univ. of California, Irvine, 1981), 109.

93. *Hearings: Temporary Admission,* 23, 231: Mandeville.

94. "Brief of Repatriation Mexican Indigents under Harding Administration, 1921," RG85, Immigration and Naturalization Service, 674A, NA. Martinez, 52–53, claims 400,000 sought to return to Mexico.

95. May, 260–263; International News Service, 26 Jan. 1921 in U.S. Congress, House of Representatives, Committee on Immigration and Naturalization, *Hearings: Seasonal Agricultural Laborers from Mexico,* 69th Cong., 1st sess., 1926, 332. Virtually no Chicano labor could find employment in northern Colorado from 1 December 1920 to 1 May 1921, though only 450 Chicano families, at the worst point, were on relief in Denver. C. V. Maddux, "Thrifty Beet Labor," *TTL* (June 1921), 267.

96. USDL, Commissioner-General of Immigration, *Annual Report* (1921), 7. Arthur Corwin, "A Story of Ad Hoc Exemptions: American Immigration Policy Toward Mexico," in Corwin, 141; George Kiser, "Mexican American Labor before World War II," *Journal of Mexican American History* 2 (Spring 1972), 130.

97. USDL, Commissioner-General of Immigration, *Annual Report* (1902), 700; American Federation of Labor, *Report of Proceedings of the Fortieth*

Annual Convention (1920), 104; Martinez, 59–60. Even the appropriation of one million dollars for 450 men to patrol the border in 1925 failed to reduce the number of illegals, which, according to Martinez, rose until 1930, although Albert Camarillo places the peak in the early 1920s.

98. May, 264–265; Martinez, 59.

99. Martinez, 26.

100. For example, Lloyd Levy, "Mexican Americans Have Deep Roots Here," *Fort Collins Coloradan,* 18 May 1975, includes a homesteader family in northern Colorado in 1904 and another farming there in 1906.

101. See Mario Barrera, *Race and Class in the Southwest* (Notre Dame, 1979), 196–197 on internal colony, and Julia Kirk Blackwelder, *Women of the Depression: Caste and Culture in San Antonio, 1929–1939* (College Station, Tex., 1984), xvii–xviii, 187–199 on caste.

102. *Hearings: Temporary Admission,* 160: Vaile.

Chapter 6. Chicanos in Northern Colorado, 1920s

1. Notice posted in Chama, New Mexico, 28 April 1924, Emma Burns Becker to the Governor, 29 April 1924, and Kenneth Heron to the Governor, 24 April 1924, Governor Hinkle Papers, Violence in Rio Arriba County, NMSRCA. Florence Kluckhohn and Fred Strodtbeck, *Variations in Value Orientations* (Evanston, Ill., 1961), 60, 63–64, 176–177, 190. Interview with Arthur Maes, Denver, 12 Sept. 1983, and Orlando Romero, Santa Fe, 10 Nov. 1983. Paul Walter, "A Study of Isolation and Social Change in Three Spanish Speaking Villages of New Mexico" (Ph.D. dissertation, Stanford Univ., 1938), 96. Donald Meinig, *Southwest: Three Peoples in Geographical Change, 1600–1970* (New York, 1971), 69–76. Marc Simmons, *New Mexico* (New York, 1977), 171, 174. Olen Leonard and Charles Loomis, *Culture of a Contemporary Rural Community: El Cerrito, New Mexico* (Washington, D.C., 1941), 4. Clark Knowlton, "Causes of Land Loss Among the Spanish Americans in Northern New Mexico," *Rocky Mountain Social Science Journal* 1 (April 1964), 206. Leonard, 107–110; Nan Elsasser et al., *Las Mujeres: Conversations from a Hispanic Community* (Old Westbury, N.Y., 1979): Josephine Turrietta, 29.

2. Colorado State Coal Mine Inspector, *Annual Report,* 1922; Hazel Glenny, "A History of Labor Disputes in the Northern Colorado Coal Mining Fields with Emphasis on the 1927–1928 Strike" (Master's thesis, Univ. of Colorado, 1938), 7; Robert Kern, "A Century of Labor in New Mexico," in Kern, ed., *Labor in New Mexico* (Albuquerque, 1983), 11. Robert McLean and Charles Thomson, *Spanish and Mexican in Colorado* (New York, 1924), 26. In the southwest as a whole, railroads employed approximately 33,000 to 47,000 Chicanos each summer on maintenance work—see U.S. Congress, Senate, Committee on Immigration, *Hearings: Restriction of Western Hemisphere Immigra-*

tion, 70th Cong., 1st sess., 1928: Alfred Thom, 89–90. Most of these, however, were Mexicans and outside of Colorado and northern New Mexico. U.S. Congress, House of Representatives, Committee on Immigration and Naturalization, *Hearings: Western Hemisphere Immigration,* 71st Cong., 2d session, 1930, 407–408: E. McInnis, Atchison, Topeka and Santa Fe Railroad. B. F. Coen et al., *Children Working on Farms in Certain Sections of Northern Colorado* (Fort Collins, 1926), 22, 160; Paul Taylor, *Mexican Labor in the United States Valley of the South Platte, Colorado,* Univ. of California Publications in Economics, vol. 6 (Los Angeles, 1929), 135; C. V. Maddux, "Non Resident Beet Labor," *TTL* (Oct. 1922), 339, and Maddux, "Permanent Beet Labor," *TTL* (Oct. 1973), 381; J. L. Williams, "Company Has Large Force Seeking Labor for Growers This Season," *TTL* (April 1924), 169–170.

3. GWSCo's 55 recruiters also sought labor in Nebraska, Texas, California, and various cities. Editor's notes, *TTL* (July 1926), 236 (hired 75 Indians and approx. 500 schoolboys); T. J. Crane, "Ten Years of Recruiting Labor," *TTL* (July 1929), 326–327. Sara Brown et al., *Children Working in the Sugar Beet Fields of Certain Districts of the South Platte Valley, Colorado* (New York, 1925), 69–70. Knights of Columbus, Colorado State Council, *Annual Report of the Mexican Welfare Committee* (1927), 7 (at DPL). McLean and Thomson, 31–33. *Hearings: Restriction of Western Hemisphere Immigration,* Harry A. Austin, 127. (U.S. Dept of Agriculture estimated the net loss of farm population to the cities at 1,020,000.). Interviews with Juan Gonzales and his brother-in-law, Greeley, 26 Sept. 1983, and Maria Chavez, Greeley, 12 Oct. 1983, all of whom were children when their parents were recruited in New Mexico by the Great Western Sugar Company in the 1920s. (N.B.: Names of most interviewees have been changed to protect their privacy.) Maria recalled also that the recruiters told her uncle, "They used to shovel the money here"; it must have been a standard line. And see "Beet Cultivation Manual for the Workers," in English and Spanish, in U.S. Congress, House of Representatives, Committee on Immigration and Naturalization, *Hearings: Immigration From Countries of the Western Hemisphere,* 70th Cong., 1st sess., 1928, 488–490.

4. Charles E. Gibbons assisted by Howard Bell, *Children Working on Farms in Certain Sections of the Western Slope of Colorado* (New York, 1925), 70–75; Taylor, 107, 162, 165; Theodore Rice, "Some Contributing Factors in the Determining of the Social Adjustment of the Spanish-Speaking People in Denver and Vicinity" (Master's thesis, Univ. of Denver, 1932), vi. Taylor estimated that there were over 14,000 "Mexican" laborers in northeast Colorado alone in 1927, and Rice claimed that 17,000 of 26,000 beetworkers in Northern Colorado in 1929 were Spanish American or Mexican. Alfred White, *The Apperceptive Mass of Foreigners as Applied to Americanization, the Mexican Group* (1923: Ph.D. dissertation, R & E Research Associates reprint, 1971), 52.

5. Brown et al., 94, 95, 97, 100; Bertram Mautner and W. Lewis Abbott, *Child Labor in Agriculture and Farm Life in the Arkansas Valley of Colorado* (New York, 1929), 101; Coen et al., 89, 90, 92; Rice, 116. Interviews with Rose

Lopez and Juan Gonzales, Greeley, 26 Sept. 1983, and Maria Chavez, Greeley, 12 Oct. 1983; Rebecca Cantwell, "Sugar Beet Brought . . . ," *Times-Call* (Longmont) 1981, p. 11 H, Clipping File, WHC. In New Mexico the village households tended to be slightly smaller and the houses to have more rooms. See, for example, Olen Leonard, *The Role of the Land Grant* (1943, reprint ed., Albuquerque, 1970), 87, and the *Tewa Basin Study* (1935), in Marta Weigle, ed., *Hispanic Villages of Northern New Mexico* (Santa Fe, 1975). From 1924, growers agreed to provide a stove for heating and cooking when the sugar company fieldmen requested one on behalf of the labor (Taylor, 162). Emory Bogardus, *The Mexican in the United States* (Los Angeles, 1934), 22.

6. Cantwell; Taylor, 120; Rice, 120; McGinnis to Pershing, 3 Dec. 1921, and Pershing to Lathrop, 10 Dec. 1921, RG102, Children's Bureau, Materials Relating to Bulletin 115, NA. C. V. Maddux testimony 1926, quoted in Robert Lipshultz, "American Attitudes Towards Mexican Immigration, 1924–1952" (Master's thesis, Univ. of Chicago, 1962), 8–9.

7. In 1926. Rice, 50.

8. Taylor, 145–146; Rice, 48–52; interview with Arthur Maes, Denver, 12 Sept. 1983.

9. Brown et al., 10, 73, 84; Coen et al., 81.

10. Of Arkansas Valley families, half earned less than $400 and two-thirds less than $500. On the Western slope they averaged $441 for nuclear and $628 for extended families. Coen et al., 81; Mautner and Abbott, 84; Gibbons and Bell, 68. Harry Austin's testimony using the Labor Department survey in *Hearings: Restriction of Western Hemisphere Immigration,* 132, was more optimistic, but his posited family of four adults still earned only $960 from beets and $150 from other sources.

11. Mautner and Abbott, 29.

12. *Hearings: Immigration from Countries of the Western Hemisphere,* 338: Jess Crosby and the Chairman.

13. U.S. Congress, House of Representatives, Committee on Immigration and Naturalization, *Hearings: Seasonal Agricultural Laborers from Mexico,* 69th Cong., 1st sess., 1926, 100: Tomlinson, Secretary of American National Livestock Association, see also p. 235: Maddux, and pp. 64, 70, 75: Fred Cummings, a Fort Collins grower. Paul Schorenberg, Secretary Treasurer, California State Federation of Labor, at the National Conference of Social Work, quoted by Paul Kellogg and Mary Ross, "Social Work at the Golden Gate," *Survey* 62 (15 Aug. 1929), 521. *Hearings: Restriction of Western Hemisphere Immigration,* 131: Harry Austin, Secretary, U.S. Beet Sugar Association, on the homing instinct. Gibbons and Bell, 83 on responsibility.

14. Gibbons and Bell, 66. *Hearings: Immigration from Countries of Western Hemisphere,* 784: H. H. Maris, President, Humanitarian Heart Mission, Denver, 1 March 1928. Interviews with Juan Gonzales, Rose Lopez, and Arthur Maes.

15. Ramon P. DeNegri, "The Agrarian Problem," *Survey* 52 (1 May 1924),

150. Roden Fuller, "Occupation of the Mexican-Born Population of Texas, New Mexico and Arizona, 1900–1920," *Journal of the American Statistical Association* 23 (March 1928), 64. Mexican industry was depressed since 1920. U.S. Dept. of Labor, Commissioner-General of Immigration, *Annual Report* (Washington, 1927), 3–6. Mexican legal immigration peaked in fiscal 1924 at 105,787.

16. Robert McLean, *The Northern Mexican* (1929, R & E Research Associates reprint, 1970), 15, and McLean, "Mexican Workers in the United States," *Proceedings of the National Conference of Social Work* (San Francisco, 1929), 535. Flora Leavitt, Executive Secretary of the Garfield Welfare Association, was in a community with 42 Spanish-speaking families in 1921, and 178 in 1928, 46 of which were Mexican, and the rest from Colorado and New Mexico; Mrs. Clara Gard, president of the Fairview School, began to have Spanish-speaking students in 1925 and in 1928 had 188 families, 148 of which left each spring; and Miss Francis Doull reported that her 24th Street School had an enrollment in 1928 of 550, with 200 Spanish speakers who all came late and left early. *Report of the First City Conference on Denver's Social Problems,* June 6–8, 1928, under the auspices of the Denver Community Chest, Denver Community Chest Collection, DPL. Miss Cummings, Colfax Community Church Community Work, reporting to Committee on the Foreign Born, 31 July 1922, YWCA Records, Denver YWCA. DPS, Adeline Jesse, "Report on Children from Spanish-Speaking Homes." Bulletin no. 49, May 1935.

17. Taylor, 109, 110, 139. Weld County had the largest percentage of Chicanos of the counties in the area. See also Weld County School Census records, CSA. Colorado State Coal Mine Inspector, *Annual Report* (1920 through 1930). Rice, 64. Insurance Records of Miners, Columbine, 1920s, RMFCo Papers, WHC. This was actually a slightly higher percent than the proportion of Chicanos in the state's coal mines.

18. Taylor, 136, 209. Another town ordered Mexicans to vacate railroad property.

19. Quoted in Taylor, 189.

20. Brown et al., 64. German Russian families averaged over 7.8 members and Spanish-speaking approximately 6.7 members in her study. The average household size in the United States at the time was 4.5. *Hearings: Immigration from Countries of the Western Hemisphere,* 701: Congressman Charles Timberlake. Very few Chicanos became farm owners before World War II in southern Colorado's Arkansas Valley. Virtually no Chicanos became farm owners in the South Platte Valley. Ruby Buhrmester, "A History of the Spanish-Speaking People in Southern Colorado" (Master's thesis, Western State College of Colorado, 1935), 33; "Tenant Farming Shows Huge Increase in Colorado and the Nation," *CLA,* 31 March 1927; Dena Markoff, "Beat Hand Laborers of Sugar City, Colorado, 1900–1920," in Sidney Heitman, ed., *Germans from Russia in Colorado* (Ann Arbor, 1978), 95 on prejudice, land values, and company incentives. Mautner and Abbott, 81; Taylor, 54, 117–118, 171, 185; Gibbons and Bell, 52–

53; Coen et al., 72–73. From 1920–1925, the percentage of farm tenancy (as compared to ownership) in Colorado increased from 23 to 30.9%; in Weld County it went from 35.4 to 50.3%. In Rio Arriba County in 1925 it was 5%, and a quarter of these were relatives of the owners. U.S. Dept. of Commerce, Bur. of the Census, *U.S. Census of Agriculture 1925, Reports for States,* part 3, "The Western States" (Washington, D.C., 1932), 340.

    21. Taylor, 191; and see McLean and Thomson, 34. Displacement was a common concern, see *Hearings: Immigration from Countries of the Western Hemisphere,* particularly p. 423, A. S. Robertson of Las Cruces, who reassured the Committee that, on the contrary, in southern New Mexico the Anglos were displacing the Mexicans. J. T. Woofter, "The Status of Racial and Ethnic Groups," in the President's Research Committee on Social Trends, *Recent Social Trends* (New York, 1933), 566: "Fresh accessions to the Mexican population have been welcomed as the Mexicans have not begun to purchase lands, but have continued as laborers."

    22. See Cantwell. Mary Vela's father left Trinidad because, as she put it, "there were too many strikes in Trinidad. My dad couldn't work." And see anonymous interviews.

    23. Taylor, 209. Only 6% of beetworking families had members who worked in the mines.

    24. Taylor, 138, 186. Great Western Sugar Company Property Records, GWSCo Sugar Building, Denver. *Hearings: Immigration from Countries of the Western Hemisphere,* 61: Maddux. "Colonizing Mexican Beet Workers," *TTL* (Oct. 1923), 393–396, with plans for six towns, houses with two rooms each, and colonists paying in four years. Also see other articles in *TTL,* for example, (June 1924), 323; (July 1923), 291; (Nov. 1924), 562, by which time ten colonies in Northern Colorado had been built; and C. V. Maddux, "Permanent Beet Labor" (Oct. 1923), 380—there is no suggestion of agricultural ladders in the discussion of permanent beet labor. James Mills, "A History of Brush, Colorado" (Master's thesis, Univ. of Colorado, 1965), 70–71 (map including the colony).

    25. Taylor, 185–186, 209; Lina Bresette, *Mexicans in the United States* (Washington, D.C., 1929), 20. Frequently there were seven to eight in one room in Denver. Rice, 94–105.

    26. Mary Ehrmantraut, "They Wanted To Get Rid of the Mexicans," *Greeley Tribune,* 7 Sept. 1980, clipping file, Greeley Municipal Museum; Mills, 74; "A Klan Album," *Colorado Magazine* 42 (Spring 1965), 79. Interview with Arthur Maes; Rice, 107. Brighton apparently also had a segregated park. Mautner and Abbott, 92, 113. On the discriminatory signs: "The Mexican Is Winning Out," *TTL* (Nov. 1927), 484; Mexican Welfare Committee, *Report* (1929); Taylor, 224; Ehrmantraut; and interview with Margarita Garcia, Windsor, 12 Oct. 1983. The signs stayed up in northeastern Colorado until after World War II. Southern Colorado, California, and even Santa Fe, New Mexico, also had similar signs in the 1920s. See Gibbons and Bell, 83; Donald Howard, "A Study of

the Mexican, Mexican-American and Spanish-American Population in Pueblo, Colorado, 1929–1930" (Master's thesis, Univ. of Denver, 1930), 80; McLean and Thomson, 16–17; Manuel Gamio, *Mexican Immigration to the United States* (Chicago, 1930), 213; and Albert Camarillo, *Chicanos in a Changing Society* (Cambridge, Mass., 1979), 192–194.

27. Latter quoted in Taylor, 221. Former from interview with Juan Gonzales, confirmed in *Hearings: Immigration from Countries of the Western Hemisphere,* 611–612: Maddux. Of 203 people, only five tests were even doubtful; and see Rice, 121. Ronald Wyse, "The Position of Mexicans in the Immigration and Nationality Laws," in Leo Grebler, *Mexican Immigration to the United States* (Los Angeles, 1966), Appendix, D, D-10. Raymond Mohl, "The Saturday Evening Post and the 'Mexican Invasion,'" *Journal of Mexican American History* 3 (1973), 132–135. Mark Reisler, *By the Sweat of Their Brow: Mexican Immigrant Labor in the United States, 1900–1940* (Westport, Conn., 1976)155–156, 167, 173. Ricardo Romo, "Responses to Mexican Immigration, 1910–1930," *Aztlan* 6 (Summer 1975), 189–190. Charles Thomson, "Restriction of Mexican Immigration," *Journal of Applied Sociology* 11 (July–Aug. 1927), 577–578. *Hearings: Immigration from Countries of the Western Hemisphere,* 776: Arthur Campbell, Denver.

28. Maddux, "Is Our Present Immigration Restriction Policy Sound," *TTL* (Nov. 1929), 503. *Hearings: Immigration from Countries of the Western Hemisphere,* 679–699. On protests, see, for example, *GDT,* 8 Dec. 1927.

29. McLean, 22. Interview with Fred Holmes, Denver, 4 Sept. 1983. *Hearings: Restriction of Western Hemisphere Immigration,* 137: J. C. Bailey.

30. Interview with Arthur Maes.

31. Taylor, 210; Mautner and Abbott, 74.

32. Brown et al., 83; Mautner and Abbott, 86, 89; Sara Brown, "Denver and Farm Labor Families" (New York, 1925), 4; Gibbons and Bell, 69.

33. E. S. Willis, "Mexicans Meeting Demand for General Farm Workers," *TTL* (April 1928), 175; Taylor, 123.

34. Brown et al., 83. Mario García. *Desert Immigrants: The Mexicans of El Paso, 1880–1920* (New Haven, 1981), 85 for comparison and the lack of an industrial sector as a factor in racial dualism in the labor market. Interview with Juan Gonzales, and with Arthur Maes. Knights of Columbus, Colorado State Council, *Annual Report of the Mexican Welfare Committee* (1928), 4. *Coloradan* (Fort Collins), 18 May 1975.

35. Taylor, 123, 146; Mautner and Abbott, 86–87. Chicanos did sometimes obtain farm work and railroad work for brief periods in the early spring. GWSCo claimed to have placed about 1000 of its hand laborers on the spring railroad work in 1929, see *TTL* (Dec. 1929), 548; Mautner and Abbott, 86. Also note that while miners earned relatively high wages, they suffered deductions from their pay and tended to clear only between zero and twenty dollars twice a month, see Victor American Fuel Company, Payroll Colorado Mines, 1929,

in Colorado Dept. of Natural Resources, Division of Mines, Chief Coal Mine Inspector, box 19141, vol. 18269, book 193, CSA.

36. GWSCo, Statistics, GWSCo Papers, WHC. In northern Colorado as a whole, acreage in beets declined by 49% in the 1924–1925 season, rose 51% the next season, and declined 20% in the following year. The number of beetgrowers shifted in northern Colorado, down 35.4% and up 59.9% respectively from 1924 to 1926.

37. *Hearings: Immigration from Countries of the Western Hemisphere,* 625: J. C. Bailey and Box. Taylor, 129, 131–132.

38. Taylor, 124.

39. Rice, 124.

40. Quoted in Taylor, 213–215; Coen et al., 159; William Bundy, "The Mexican Minority Problem in Otero County, Colorado" (Master's thesis, Univ. of Colorado, 1940), 47, 79. McWilliams, 114; John Burma, *Spanish-Speaking Groups in the United States* (Durham, 1954), 4; and see Camarillo, 183, 189, 190, for similarities in California. Lopez quoted in John R. Chávez, *The Lost Land: The Chicano Image of the Southwest* (Albuquerque, 1984), 93.

41. Buhrmester, 23, 35, 44; Taylor, 220; McLean and Thomson, 13–17; Rice, 55.

42. Taylor, 212–214.

43. Coen et al., 53–54; Taylor, 214–215; Howard, 78; Gamio, 129. According to Gamio, Mexican American citizens called the immigrants "cholos" or "chicanos" and Taylor claimed the Mexicans said, "Santa Ana sold the Spanish Americans for some chewing tobacco," and called them the "manitos" or "little brothers"; other authors claim that the latter is the term Spanish Americans use for each other. Sr. Vasquez, the Mexican consul in Colorado, according to Theodore Rice (p. 70), disparaged Spanish Americans as "spoiled" and "demoralized by the system of charity."

44. Taylor, 213; Ruth Barker, *Caballeros* (New York, 1931), 295.

45. McLean, "Reaching Spanish Americans with the Gospel," *The Missionary Review of the World* 48 (Nov. 1925), 89; Vernon McCombs, *From over the Border* (New York, 1925), 29; Coen et al., 59–60.

46. Mautner and Abbott, 64–65.

47. Gibbons and Bell, 83; and see Max Handman, "Economic Reasons for the Coming of the Mexican Immigrant," *American Journal of Sociology* 35 (Jan. 1930), 610. Long after "nationality" became the more common term in describing Italians, Germans, and other groups, "race" dominated the description of "Mexicans." By 1930, the trend reached its zenith as Albert Johnson, chairman of the House Immigration and Naturalization Committee, persuaded the Secretary of Commerce to classify Mexicans as a separate racial category in the census. Spanish-Americans, both in Colorado and New Mexico, resisted and labeled themselves as "native white" on census returns. Reisler, 137; Anne Reynolds, *The Education of Spanish-Speaking Children in Five Southwestern States*

(Washington, D.C., 1933), 5; Howard, 2; and compare census figures with other contemporary estimates and with school census forms.

48. Bundy, 27.

49. Rice, 52.

50. Taylor, 178.

51. Bundy, 27–29. Taylor, 176–177, 180, 182; Taylor denied that this was debt peonage, as the debt was not specifically and contractually made the means to hold labor on the land. Rice, 60, 82, 90, 97.

52. First City Conference on Denver's Social Problems, *Report,* June 1928. Rice, 70–71, 104.

53. Taylor, 169, 171. In Weld County, about 8% Chicano, the amount spent on Chicano relief hovered around only 3% of relief expenditures in the 1920s, and in Denver, although surveys placed needy Chicanos at 13% of the population surveyed, they constituted only about 7.4% of the city's private relief cases. Rice, 77–78.

54. Colorado Board of Charities and Corrections, Box 66924, CSA; T. Wilson Longmore and Homer Hitt, "A Demographic Analysis of First and Second Generation Mexican Population in the United States: 1930," *Southwestern Social Science Quarterly* 24 (Sept. 1943), 138. "Committee on Foreign Born," (31 July 1922), 2–3, Denver YWCA Records.

55. Mary Coughlin, "Values in Dollars and Cents of Peons to U.S. Shown by Expert," *Denver Catholic Register,* 27 Jan. 1927, Clipping File, Denver Public Library.

56. Rice, 83, and see 78 citing Ainsworth Lee, "Rich Denver Fears Poor Mexicans," *Labor's News,* 11 Jan. 1930, on charity as subsidy and the threat of disorder among the poor. Note that according to Rice, many agencies did not discriminate.

57. Editor's notes, *TTL* (Nov. 1924), 542.

58. Taylor, 203.

59. Charles Brown, "Some Phases of Rural Education in New Mexico" (Master's thesis, Univ. of New Mexico, 1929), 33. The average school year in Rio Arriba County was 7.3 months, the second shortest in New Mexico. Taos County had the shortest. Average daily attendance in Rio Arriba County was only 68% of the enrollment. In the indices of good schools (pp. 20–23), Taos ranked lowest and Rio Arriba County next, and then Mora; all three were heavily Hispanic. Mora and Rio Arriba Counties had the lowest teachers' salaries of the state (p. 33).

60. Mautner and Abbott, 74.

61. Quoted in Taylor, 205–206; Brown et al., 67.

62. Anonymous interview; Mautner and Abbott, 157.

63. Quoted in Taylor, 232.

64. *Ibid.,* 216.

65. *Ibid.,* 205; interview with Margarita Garcia, Windsor.

66. Taylor, 209, 217. "Vacation schools" and separate school rooms for late

arrivals served, at times, both German Russian and Chicano beetworking children. For example, at Hudson, and later at Greeley (interview with Juan Gonzales), and at the rock quarry at Ingleside in a two room school house one room was opened for all the Mexican Americans in mid-November each year. Interview with Arthur Maes. Teachers were divided in their estimates of how helpful or harmful these schools were. Pro: Black to Matthews, Blackwood to Valentine, 7 March 1921, and Lauck to Valentine, 13 Jan. 1921, and con: Ema T. Wilkins, Supt., Fort Collins, 31 July 1920, RG102, Children's Bureau, Materials Relating to Bulletin 115, NA. Coen et al., 149, 151; A. C. Cohagan, "School for Beet-Working Children," *TTL* (May 1925), 235.

67. Bogardus, 40–41; Brown et al., 53.

68. Interview with Juan Gonzales and his brother-in-law. Only one boy from the colony at Greeley made it through high school in the 1920s and 1930s.

69. Interview with Margarita Garcia. Juan Gonzales's parents, like a few others, made brief attempts to send him to a local Catholic school, St. Peter's, which was about 2% Hispanic, but the fees and cost of good shoes defeated them.

70. Gibbons and Bell, 89–90, 94, 101, 105; Coen et al., 112–113, 146; and Reynolds, 36. Miss Francis R. Doull, 24th Street School, "The Schools and Our Spanish Speaking Neighbours," First City Conference on Denver's Social Problems; Rice, 137.

71. At its 1920s' peak, the number of Chicanos enrolled in Denver's high schools, in all four grades, was 30. There were 105 Chicanos in fifth grade alone. DPS, *Annual School Superintendent's Report,* 1925–1930. Weld County School Census, CSA. Denver Area Welfare Council, Inc., "The Spanish American Population of Denver" (July 1950), 149 (at DPL) includes a table listing the percentage of Spanish American dropouts between grades one and four from 1926 to 1933. Weld County School Records, Box 13361, 7th- and 8th-grade exam scores, 1920–1927, CSA, show that approximately three each year were Hispanic. Taylor, 204. The school attendance was similar in San Antonio, Los Angeles, and Arizona; all were centers of regionally migrant Chicanos. Reynolds, 39, 40–44, 45.

72. Quoted in Taylor, 195.

73. Quoted in Taylor, 197, and see pages 152, 195, 196, 198; Brown et al., 152, 162; Coen et al., 126. For the Arkansas Valley see Mautner and Abbott, 154, 156, 157; for the Western Slope see Gibbons and Bell, 111.

74. Roger Babson, "Shall Farm Children Be Denied Work?" *TTL* (June 1923), 224; C. W. Doherty, "The Field Labor Problem," *TTL* (Aug. 1925), 353.

75. Brown et al., 112; Mautner and Abbott, 155.

76. *Hearings: Seasonal Agricultural Laborers from Mexico,* 246. Brown et al., 113. Other contemporary references to caste include McLean, *Northern Mexican,* 12. "A Mexican," one grower informed Taylor, "is the best damn' dog any white man ever had." Taylor, 155.

77. For example, interview with Lucy Romero, Greeley, 12 Oct. 1983, on

gender roles and decision making. And see F. A. Armijo, Rio Arriba County, pp. 28, 31, NMAES, *Annual Reports* (microfilm) T876-10-1928, NA.

78. Warranty Deed Record, vol. 17, Rio Arriba County Courthouse, Tierra Amarilla, New Mexico. For example, Maria Trujillo, widow, sold lots for $738.95 in 1923; another Hispanic woman in 1926 bought 160 acres for $300, and in 1920 Celina Gallegos sold land her parents had deeded her seven years earlier. On occupations see Victor American Fuel Company, Payroll; Las Animas County School Records, Box 13104, District Secretary Book, District 4, CSA; Walter, 117; interviews.

79. F. A. Armijo, Rio Arriba County, p. 13, NMAES, *Annual Reports,* T876-11-1929.

80. Interview with Arthur Maes; interview with John Trujillo, Chimayo, 12 Nov. 1983. On Anglos, see Joan Jensen, "New Mexico Farm Women," in Kern, 69.

81. "Home Economics Evening School Classes for Spanish American Women," *NMSR* 4 (April 1925), 15. Fran Leeper Buss, *La Partera: Story of a Midwife* (Ann Arbor, 1980), 32. Ruth Barber, "Financial Independence Increasing," *W&M* 40 (May 1924), 68. Twenty of the school girls at Allison-James had worked all or part of the previous summer for wages. Interview with Rose Lopez and Maria Torres who both did "baby-sitting" in New Mexico.

82. Interview with Trujillo, who also claimed that "families accepted it because they were working and earning." Charles Briggs, "'Our Strength Is in the Land'" (Ph.D. dissertation, Univ. of Chicago, 1981), 312.

83. Buss, 50. N. Howard Thorp, "Rio Arriba County History," 3, WPA files, 220, NMSRCA. Mary A. Steer, "A Journey Abroad at Home," *W&M* 2 (May 1925), 48.

84. Ivie Jones, Home Demonstration Agent, San Miguel County, p. 13, NMAES, T876-10-1928. Dora Ortiz Vasquez, *The Enchanted Dialogue of Loma Parda and Canada Bonita* (n.p., 1983), 10. Saunders, "The Social History of Spanish-speaking People in Southwestern United States since 1846," read at First Conference of Historians of the United States and Mexico at Monterrey, 1949, p. 8, Community Relations Papers, Box 2, DPL. Buss, 29; Elsasser et al.: Ida Gutierrez, 67; Barker, 303. Joan Jensen, "Canning Comes to New Mexico: Women and the Agricultural Extension Service, 1914–1919," *NMHR* 57 (Oct. 1982), 362.

85. Burma, 22. From 1921 to 1938 the death rate per 1000 for the U.S. was 10.3, for New Mexico, 16.2, and was highest in Spanish American areas. Of the births, 85 to 90% were attended by midwives. McLean and Thomson, 10–11 indicates that southern Colorado was much the same.

86. Eleanor Tilford, "Presenting Chacon," *W&M* 2 (May 1925), 50, and other articles in that magazine. Also see Evelyn Fisher Frisbie, M.D., Women of New Mexico, Archive 303, UNM. New Mexico Bureau of Public Health, *Report* (1927–1928), 15, 19. McLean and Thomson, 19. Dr. Forbes, "Maternity

and Infancy Welfare Work in the Nation and in Colorado," *Proceedings of the Colorado Conference of Social Welfare* (Denver, 8–11 Oct. 1924), 24. Mission schools also still provided many of the village teachers, see: Ruth K. Barber, "All Interpreters," *W&M* 6 (May 1929), 51, and "Their Alma Mater—Allison James," *W&M* 4 (May 1927), 68. Fifty percent of the Allison-James graduates were teaching, 20% were in college.

87. Interview with Rose Lopez, who had a vegetable garden and did not work beets, and with Juan Gonzales, whose mother had one and did canning as did "lots of families" in the colony. Bundy, 54; Mautner and Abbott, 105–106; *TTL* (Nov. 1924), 571; Buhrmester, 38.

88. Coen et al., 99; interview with Margarita Garcia. For property owning, see for example, GWSCo Property records, Sugar Building, Denver.

89. Brown et al., 102–104; Coen et al., 95–100; and see Gibbons and Bell, 77 for Western Slope. Margaret Mead, ed., *Cultural Patterns and Technical Change* (Paris, 1953), 213.

90. Interview with Juan Gonzales, with Alfonso Esquibel, Santa Fe, 9 Nov. 1983, with Arthur Maes, and with Charles Vigil, Denver, 13 Sept. 1983. Coen et al., 108; Mautner and Abbott, 110.

91. Interview with Margarita Garcia. Weld County marriage licenses and registers, County Courthouse, Greeley. In 1920 there were 8 Catholic and 15 Justice of the Peace Hispanic marriages; in 1922, 6 and 12; in 1926, 28 and 15. Compare to Rio Arriba County, New Mexico, where at least three-quarters of the Hispanic marriages were by Catholic priests; and Las Animas County, Colorado, with 57.3% Catholic and 41.8% civil marriages among Hispanic marriages in 1926. Rio Arriba County marriage licenses and registers, County Courthouse, Tierra Amarilla, Las Animas County marriage licenses and registers, County Courthouse, Trinidad.

92. Carlos Jimenez, OH72, DPL. His sister-in-law converted as soon as she arrived in Denver; the reaction was, "one religion's as good as another, it's only hope." Interview with Arthur Maes, whose father also became a Presbyterian in Denver, and with Alfonso Esquibel, who met former acquaintances from Trementina, New Mexico, when he became a Presbyterian minister to a Spanish-speaking congregation in Denver. Interview with Juan Gonzales.

93. McLean and Thomson, 50; interview with Arthur Maes. Minutes (7 Aug. 1926), Young People's Work, Colorado Council of Churches Papers, Box 2, WHC. Taylor, 226; interview with Juan Gonzales. Greeley's Hispanic Catholic youth group met in the Colony.

94. Coen et al., 105; Mautner and Abbott, 111; Gibbons and Bell, 78. Interview with Juan Gonzales on difficulty of registering to vote, and Brown et al., 109. All of the interviewees had mothers who were keen on politics. Record of the District Secretary, District 4, Las Animas County Schools, Box 13104, CSA. Interview with Charles Vigil. Joan Jensen, "'Disenfranchisement Is a Disgrace': Women and Politics in New Mexico, 1900–1940," *NMHR* 56 (Jan. 1981), 25–

30. Interview with Margaret McKenzie whose Hispanic aunt was active in New Mexico politics and whose grandmother was a strong Democrat, which led to disputes with her Republican son-in-law. History file 76, Women, NMSRCA on Adelina Otero-Warren, congressional candidate in 1922. And see Women in New Mexico, vertical files, UNM and Women of New Mexico, Archive 303, UNM.

95. Barker, 90–91.

96. Coen et al., 69–71. On the Western Slope Hispanic mothers had lost nearly one-quarter of their children. Gibbons and Bell, 58–59; Howard, 14–15. Hispanic babes contributed 15.2% to births in Pueblo and 31.5% to infant deaths. Only 2% of Anglos had no physician attending birth, whereas over 20% of the town's "Mexicans" had none and usually lacked hygienic precautions. There are some indications that by the early 1930s some Chicanas in Colorado and New Mexico were, as Bogardus found generally, becoming interested in birth control. See Bogardus, 26; Elsasser et al.: Esperanza Salcida, 64.

97. Interviews with Arthur Maes, Rose Lopez, Juan Gonzales, Margarita Garcia, and Lucy Romero.

98. Interview with Maria Chavez; Taylor, 228, revealed that in smaller rural communities in the eastern part of the South Platte Valley where there were fewest Mexicans, there was occasional social mingling at dances; and Margarita Garcia's father learned German from his association with the German-Russian beet families, and gave German square dancing calls.

99. Interview with Margarita Garcia. One owner's wife, a Swede, was friendly, the other did not want much to do with them. Taylor, 155. Weld County Marriage registers. There were three intermarriages in 1920 and one in 1922. Compare to 17 in 1926 in Las Animas County (13.9% of Hispanic and 3.8% of all registered marriages) and 7 in Rio Arriba County (10% of all marriages). Howard, 56, found only 0.68% of his sample of 735 families in Pueblo to be intermarriages.

100. Interview with Lucy Romero; Coen et al., 131–134.

101. Interview with Amelia Cordova. Rice, 62. Coen et al., 107–108, 135–136; Brown et al., 60–61, 109; on the Western slope, see Gibbons and Bell, 82; on the Arkansas Valley, Mautner and Abbott, 108–109. Language was a factor; in 1920, only 17% of Mexican and just over half Spanish American mothers knew enough English to make themselves understood, whereas 42% of the Mexican and almost all of the Spanish American fathers did, a legacy of dealing with external affairs. But even within groups, many families had no visiting contacts at all. USDL, CB, *Child Labor and the Work of Mothers,* 17–18.

102. Taylor, 228, 230. One Spanish American girl mentioned to Taylor that her science teacher advised against intermarriage on "scientific" grounds.

103. Interview with Margarita Garcia. Taylor, 234. Hispanic mother and superintendent quoted in Taylor, 220. Coen et al., 104–105, 158.

104. Note that, as family labor, the labor of Chicanas in the beetfields tended not to be recorded by the Anglo census takers, so that, for example, only approx-

imately 9.5% of Chicanas in Colorado were recorded as gainfully occupied in 1930, the lowest proportion of any racial or ethnic group listed, whereas beet labor studies showed that 60% of Chicana mothers worked in beets. (*Fifteenth Census of the United States,* vol. 4, *Population,* 238.) Also note that Hispanic men were recorded as gainfully employed at 74.1%, only slightly higher than the native Anglo (73.8%) and lower than black and foreign-born, which may have been due to the time of year when the census was taken, to the reluctance of census takers to enter the barrios, or to their inability to communicate once they did. Interview with Arthur Maes. See Mario Barrera, *Race and Class in the Southwest* (Notre Dame, 1979), 98 on agricultural *wage* as new to Chicanas.

105. Mautner and Abbott, 86; Brown et al., 83. Rice, 76, from Greeley Salvation Army report, Jan.–March, 1930.

106. "Survey of Employed Women in Denver, Colorado," (Aug. 1920), 7, Denver YWCA Records. Colorado Industrial Commission, *Annual Report* (1930), 29, on women's wages. Interview with Maria Chavez, born in 1913 in New Mexico, only went as far as the third grade because she "topped" or harvested beets in December and cleaned houses in winter. She learned English through her contact with Anglos as a domestic worker.

107. Quoted in Taylor, 225.

108. "Survey of Employed Women in Denver, Colorado," 3. Howard, 76; *Denver Catholic Register,* 27 Jan. 1927, 1. For numbers, see *Fifteenth Census,* vol. 4, *Population,* 235. Lyle Dorsett, *The Queen City: A History of Denver* (Boulder, 1977), 175. Various "Foreign Born Surveys," c. 1922.

109. Despite the tendency of the men I interviewed to be unable at first to recall many Hispanic domestic workers, at least one had a mother who had taken in laundry, and over half the women interviewees said either themselves or their mothers or sisters had done domestic work of some kind in northern Colorado. Margarita Garcia's mother took in laundry, as did Arthur Maes's mother (a widow). Maes commented, "that was how they made extra . . . not a lot of women, those who had to do it, had to because of the kids." Maes also remembered girls who went out and did day work in Denver. Rose Lopez continued to do domestic work, principally child care (live-in) after she was married. And see *Hearings: Immigration from Countries of the Western Hemisphere: Timberlake,* 699. In the 1930 census, 41.6% of gainfully employed "Mexicans" were listed under domestic service and 41.5% under farm labor. Barrera, 97; Howard, 24.

110. "Mexican Girl of 13 Years Makes Eloquent Plea for Child Labor Amendment," *CLA,* 28 Feb. 1929, 1.

111. DPS, *Annual Report-Education and Financial Statistics* (1925–1930). Weld County School Records, 7th- and 8th-grade exam scores, 1920 to 1927, Box 13361, CSA. In contrast, only about half to four-fifths as many Chicanas as Chicanos enrolled in Denver's public evening and daytime vocational training facilities. DPS, *Educational Statistics* (1925–1931).

112. Colorado Bureau of Labor Statistics, *Biennial Report* (1928), 51. Col-

orado Industrial Commission, *Annual Report* (1928–1930), 29. See, for example, Feliciano Rivera, *A Mexican American Sourcebook* (Menlo Park, 1970), 141, and *Colorado Latin American Personalities* (n.p., 1959), and interviews with Aurelia Aragon, telephone, 10 Nov. 1983, and with Charles Vigil. Walter, App. B, 318. Cf., for example, Miriam Cohen "Italian American Women in New York City, 1900–1950: Work and School," in Milton Cantor and Bruce Laurie, eds., *Class, Sex and the Woman Worker* (Westport, Conn., 1977), 120–143, and Judith E. Smith, "Italian Mothers, American Daughters: Changes in Work and Family Roles," in Betty Boyd Caroli et al., eds., *The Italian Immigrant Woman in North America* (Toronto, 1978), 206–221.

113. DPS, *Annual Reports.* Barrera, 97, 133–134. Marcela Trujillo, "The Colorado Spanish Surnamed Woman of Yesteryear," in Evelio Echevarría and José Otero, eds., *Hispanic Colorado* (Fort Collins, 1976), 93 on aspirations in the 1920s. Interview with Margaret McKenzie.

114. Quarterly Examination of Teachers, 1920s, Weld County School Records, Box 13361, CSA. Taylor, 225.

115. Case of Helen Salazar, clerk at Penney's in Monte Vista, Colorado Board of Charities and Corrections, Box 66927, CSA. *TNC,* 3 Sept. 1925, 5. Interviews with Alfonso Esquibel and with Juan Gonzales. Sue Zuver, H5, PHS. Weld County School Records, Box 13361, CSA. Reyes Gutierrez began teaching there in 1926.

116. The boys got such useful industrial training as weaving. Mrs. Clara Gard, "The Schools and Our Spanish Speaking Neighbours," First City Conference on Denver's Social Problems. For New Mexico, see, for example, Ruth Barber, "The Girlhood of New Mexico," *HMM* 35 (May 1921), 155–156; Harriet Carson, "Playtime at Allison-James," *HMM* 37 (Aug. 1923), 227; "Torches of Enlightenment," *HMM* 36 (May 1922), 161; and Glen O. Ream, "A Study of Spanish Speaking Pupils in Albuquerque High School" (Master's thesis, Yale Univ., 1930).

117. Merton Hill, "The Development of an Americanization Program" (1928), reprinted in *Aspects of the Mexican American Experience* (New York, 1976), 93, 103. Reynolds, 17.

118. Barker, 268; Estelle Hynes Warner, "Mountain Villages of New Mexico," *HMM* 34 (May 1920), 145; James Gaither, "A Return to the Village: A Study of Santa Fe and Taos, New Mexico, as Cultural Centers, 1900–1934" (Ph.D. dissertation, Univ. of Minnesota, 1957), 139; San Miguel County, pp. 25–26, NMAES, T876-10-1928. Jean McConn, "A Desert Flower," *HMM* 37 (Sept. 1923), 241; Francis Noble, "At the Sunset Hour," *W&M* 2 (May 1925), 73; Jane Atkins Grainger, *El Centenario de la Palabra: El Rito Presbyterian Church, 1879–1979* (Albuquerque, 1980) 38; Dorothy Spencer, letters, 1928–1930, MHL.

119. Coughlin, "Values in Dollars and Cents." Taylor, 124, also mentioned suggestions by social workers in the South Platte area involving "the development of a handicraft industry among the Mexicans."

120. Flora Leavitt, "Our Spanish-Speaking Neighbours," First City Conference on Denver's Social Problems.

121. See, for example, Camarillo, 177–179, 221; Garcia, 77, 253; and Julia Kirk Blackwelder, *Women of the Depression* (College Station, 1984).

122. Alice Kessler-Harris, "Stratifying by Sex: Understanding the History of Working Women," in Richard Edwards et al., *Labor Market Segmentation* (Lexington, Mass., 1975), 231.

123. W. H. Slingerland, *Child Welfare Work in Colorado* (Boulder, 1920), throughout, on training for domestic labor as a solution. Report of Industrial Committee, Colorado State Federation of Woman's Clubs, *Yearbook* (1914), 54. Dorothy Overstreet, "Problems and Progress Among Mexicans of Our Own Southwest," *HMM* 32 (Nov. 1917), 6. Grace Farrell, "Homemaking with the 'Other Half' Along Our International Border," *Journal of Home Economics* 21 (June 1929), 418.

124. Sarah B. Sutherland, *HMM* 35 (May 1921), 68. And see Maxine Seller, "Beyond the Stereotype—A New Look at the Immigrant Woman, 1880–1924," *Journal of Ethnic Studies* 3 (Spring 1975), 59; Seller, "The Education of the Immigrant Woman 1900–1945," *Journal of Urban History* 4 (May 1978), 307–330; Seller, "Protestant Evangelism and the Italian Immigrant Woman," in Caroli et al., 128–129; Rudolf Glanz, *The Jewish Woman in America* (New York, 1976), 20; Emory Bogardus, *Essentials of Americanization,* 3rd rev. ed. (Los Angeles, 1923), 354.

125. Bogardus, *The Mexican in the United States,* 43.

126. Mrs. Bacon and Miss Cummings (connected with Colfax Community Church, in community work), "Committee on Foreign Born," 31 July 1922.

127. McLean, "Reaching Spanish Americans," 870–871; Fred Eastman, *Unfinished Business of the Presbyterian Church in America* (Philadelphia, 1921), 53. Some of these missionaries were Hispanic products of village missions. Taylor, 225. The Greeley House of Neighbourly Service closed in 1927 and has reopened by the 1930s; Brighton opened in 1924, Denver in 1925. R. Douglas Brackenridge and Francisco García-Treto, *Iglesia Presbiteriana* (San Antonio, 1974), 154. McLean and Thomson, 24–35, 46. Denver Area Welfare Council, Inc., "A Report on the House of Neighbourly Service at Brighton, Colo." (July 1953), 2 (at DPL). And see WTCU, *Annual Convention Report* (1927), 54 (at WHC).

128. Knights of Columbus (Colorado), *Annual Report of the Mexican Welfare Committee* (1927), 2–3. *Ibid.* (1928), 6.

129. The Catholic Charities of the Diocese of Denver, Inc., *Annual Reports* (1927–1929). Knights of Columbus (Colorado), (1928), 4; "New Social Center of National Council of Catholic Women Has Splendid Corps of Workers," *Denver Catholic Register,* 15 April 1928. Knights of Columbus (Colorado), (1928), 6; Catholic Charities of the Diocese of Denver, Inc., *Annual Report* (1928), 41; *ibid* (1930), 22. In 1930, the Catholic church sponsored social worker Miss L. Fernandez who spent $650 on relief, visited 500 sick in their homes, and 12 in

hospitals, gave food or clothing to 300, and instructed 50 adults in towns surrounding Ft. Collins. Rice, 75.

130. Florence Means and Harriet Fullen, *Rafael and Consuelo* (New York, 1929); Robert McLean and Mabel Crawford, *Jumping Beans* (New York, 1929); both are stories of Chicano beetworking families in Colorado.

131. McLean, "Getting God Counted among the Mexicans," *Missionary Review of the World* 46 (May 1923), 362.

132. *Ibid.,* 362.

133. McLean and Thomson, 4; *Colorado Latin American Personalities,* 32.

134. Alice Schlegel, "An Overview," in Schlegel, ed., *Sexual Stratification: A Cross-Cultural View* (New York, 1977), 353.

135. Cf. Laila Shukry Hamamsy, "The Role of Women in a Changing Navaho Society," *American Anthropologist* 59 (1957), 109.

136. Cf. Schlegel, 350.

137. Interview with Arthur Maes; Roland Tharp et al., "Changes in Marriage Roles Accompanying the Acculturation of the Mexican-American Wife," *Journal of Marriage and the Family* 30 (Aug. 1968), 409.

138. See Miguel Montiel, "The Chicano Family: A Review of Research," *Social Work* 18 (March 1973), 25 on the erection of "the hypothetical traditional family," something evident in masters' theses of the 1930s and 1940s at the University of New Mexico, and in Alfred White's 1923 master's thesis, p. 31: "Mexican men like to refer to their wives as having influence and wisdom although they know such has never been the case."

139. On decision making: interviews with Margarita Garcia, Maria Chavez, and others; Reyes Ramos, "Movidas: The Methodological and Theoretical Relevance of Interactional Strategies," *Studies in Symbolic Interaction* 2 (1979), 141–165; Ramos, "Discovering the Production of Mexican American Family Structure," *De Colores* 6 (1982), 1–19 (typescript version); Helen Walker, "Mexican Immigrant and American Citizenship," *Sociology and Social Research* 13 (May–June 1929), 469; Tharp et al., 409; and Miguel Montiel, "The Social Science Myth of the Mexican American Family," *El Grito* 3 (Summer 1970), 56, 61–62. On marriage ages: Weld and Rio Arriba counties, marriage registers and licenses; Irma Johnson, "A Study of Certain Changes in the Spanish American Family in Bernalillo County, 1915–1946" (Master's thesis, Univ. of New Mexico, 1948), 37. Both men and women continued to marry at younger ages than Anglos did. William Ogburn, "The Family and Its Functions," in President's Research Committee on Social Trends, *Recent Social Trends,* 680.

140. U.S. Industrial Commission, *Report,* part 1, vol. 11, 79, quoted in Stuart Jamieson, *Labor Unionism in American Agriculture* (Washington, D.C., 1945), 11. *GDT,* 29 May 1919, quoted in George Sanchez, ed., "First Regional Conference on the Education of Spanish Speaking People in the Southwest" (March 1946), Community Relations Commission Papers, Box 2, DPL.

141. Taylor, 166.

142. McCombs, 86; and see Mautner and Abbott, 74–75, 102, 113.

143. See, for example, *GDT,* 4 Feb. 1924, 5 Feb. 1925, 28 July 1924, 26 Aug. 1924, 20 Sept. 1924, 27 Oct. 1924, etc., and see Markoff for Arkansas Valley.

144. Paul Taylor et al., "The Mexican Immigrant and the Problem of Crime and Criminal Justice," in National Commission on Law Observance and Enforcement, *Report on Crime and the Foreign Born* (Washington, D.C., 1931), 216. *Hearings: Immigration from Countries of the Western Hemisphere,* 610: Maddux. State Penitentiary, New Admissions, 1926, Colorado Board of Charities and Corrections, Box 66924. Applications for Clemency, including three violations of the Volstead Act of seven Hispanics listed (among 40 names), Docket no. 9, July 1926, *ibid.,* Box 66919. In New Mexico one Hispanic ex-villager revealed that it was with capital from moonshining that investors underwrote his grandfather's baler, as only "moonshiners had *cash*" in the villages; and see Frances Swadesh, *Los Primeros Pobladores* (Notre Dame, 1974), 123–124, who claims that most subsistence farmers in the San Juan Basin supplemented their income with bootlegging. Special Reports, Gallup Coal Strike, Gov. Mechem Papers, Adjutant General Reports to Governor, 1922, list several Hispanic men and two Hispanic women arrested for selling liquor. In Las Animas County, Mrs. E. G. Martinez pled not guilty to charges relating to intoxicating liquors in 1925, case 7296, Las Animas County Courthouse.

145. *GDT,* 29 May 1919, cited by Sanchez, 5; *Hearings Immigration from Countries of the Western Hemisphere,* 610: Maddux. Rice, 126, for data on Adams, Larimer, Morgan, Boulder, Logan, and Weld counties' courts in 1924; and see Howard, 44.

146. Taylor et al., 216, 238; Howard, 49; Knights of Columbus (Colorado) *Annual Report of the Committee on Mexican Welfare* (1927 and 1928); Jamieson, 234.

147. Measured against percentage of each group in the population and as a ratio to marriages. County and District Court Indexes, Las Animas and Weld counties; Johnson, 60, 64–65. In 1926 Weld County had 49 Hispanic marriages and 4 Hispanic divorces; in that year Las Animas County had 122 Hispanic marriages and 17 Hispanic divorces. There were 47 Hispanic divorces from 1920 to 1930 in Weld County and 209 in Las Animas County; Bernalillo County, New Mexico, had 91 during the 1925–26 year alone. In Weld County, divorcées tended to have been married for a shorter period, in many cases only one year. Note that there was a residence requirement to obtain a divorce.

148. Colorado Board of Charities and Corrections, Box 66924.

149. *Hearings: Immigration from Countries of the Western Hemisphere,* 610: Maddux. Rice, 88.

150. Derived from a sample of over 450 RMFCo Chicano miners at Columbine in the 1920s, Insurance Records of Miners, RMFCo Papers, WHC. Of miners with living parents, 57 of 125 miners born in Mexico sent money, 43 of 118 of those born in Colorado, and 26 of 66 of those born in New Mexico.

151. *Ibid.,* 69.8% of Mexican wives lived in northern Colorado, 82.1% of New Mexican wives, and 65.5% of Coloradan wives.

152. Taylor, *Mexican Labor,* 113.

153. RMFCo Papers. More Chicano miners than beetworkers were single males, but about half were married, and many single miners had parents in the area.

154. Interview with Arthur Maes. Subcommittee, "Report on Racial, Social and Economic Conditions in Denver," p. 2, First City Conference on Denver's Social Problems.

155. Interview with Arthur Maes; Taylor, *Mexican Labor,* 191.

156. McLean and Thomson, 24.

157. Sanchez, and "The Spanish American Population in Denver: A Supplementary Report" (June 1952), 127–129, Community Relations Commission Papers, Box 6. The Spanish Methodist Church had 456 active members in 1925, 943 in 1931. And see File on Institute of Ethnic Affairs—Citizens' Service Organizations (Latin American), untitled report, p. 9, *ibid.,* Box 2. McLean and Thomson, 24; Spanish-American Club Holds Meeting," *Denver Post,* 11 Jan. 1928; "Spanish-American Citizens Organize," *ibid.,* 29 March 1931.

158. Woofter, 564.

159. Coen et al., 83.

160. Interview with Margarita Garcia; Chris Romero, uncatalogued oral history, DPL. Taylor, *Mexican Labor,* 210. Lloyd Levy, "Economics, Culture; The Forming of the Barrio," *Coloradan* (Fort Collins), 19 May 1975. "Ingenuity and Perseverance Shown by Mexicans in Constructing Adobe Houses," *TTL* (Nov. 1924), 571; "Juan, Home Builder and Ingenious Mechanic," *TTL* (Dec. 1925), 495. As the Hispanic community grew, non-company clusters also held dances, etc., for Spanish-speaking friends and relatives. Mautner and Abbott, 113; Buhrmester, 43–44; Taylor et al., "The Mexican Immigrant," 217; "'Con Auxilio o Ayuda del Ranchero' Written by a Spanish-Speaking Beet Worker," *TTL* (Nov. 1924), 568. In 1925 GWSCo sponsored distinctly "American" flag day exercises in two of the colonies, complete with boy scouts, almost as if to prove to the colonists and the townspeople both that this was United States soil. "Flag Day Exercises at Fort Morgan Mexican Colony," *TTL* (July 1925), 323; "Flag Raising at Johnstown-Milliken Colony," *TTL* (Nov. 1925), 474.

161. Interview with Juan Gonzales; "Church Dedicated at Spanish Colony," *Greeley Tribune,* 12 Jan. 1930, clipping file, Greeley Municipal Museum; Buhrmester, 39; "Neighbours," *Survey* 50 (April 1923), 46.

162. In 1924, northern Colorado contract families averaged 6.58 years at contract labor in Colorado, but only 1.5 years on their present farm. Coen et al., 84, 87; Gibbons and Bell, 67; Mautner and Abbott, 83; McLean and Thomson, 23 (on Chicano turnover at the Pueblo steel mills; even the personnel manager recognized the reason as "industrial rather than racial"); Bogardus, *The Mexican in the United States,* 50, claimed that railroad turnover reached 300% in a single year.

163. Quoted in Taylor, *Mexican Labor,* 183; Walker, 468.

164. Chris Aragon vs. E. L. Trollope et al., signed 11 May 1927, case 7176, Colorado District Court, County Courthouse, Greeley, claiming $500. Chicanos and Chicanas in both northern and southern Colorado continued to sue companies for injury or death of a relative, Colorado Industrial Commission, for example, *Annual Reports* (1924–1926), CSFL Papers, Box 22, WHC.

165. Mary Ehrmantrout, "They Wanted To Get Rid of the Colony," *Greeley Tribune,* 7 Sept. 1980, clipping file Greeley Municipal Museum; interview with Juan Gonzales; Taylor, *Mexican Labor,* 213, 227.

166. Taylor, *Mexican Labor,* 219, 222, 223.

167. *Ibid.,* 184–185. For example, the Sociedad Vicente Guerrero at Gilcrest and Frederick, Club Numero Uno at Johnstown, Commisiones Honorificas at Brighton and Longmont.

168. "Spanish Colony Organized," *Greeley Tribune,* 3 April 1970, clipping file, Greeley Municipal Museum; "Curfew Bell Will Ring at Spanish-America Village," 3 May 1928, *ibid.* And see "Flag Raising at Johnstown," *TTL* (Nov. 1925), 474.

169. McLean and Thomson, 6; Colorado Coal Mine Inspector, *Annual Reports* (1921–1928). For occupation mobility see Victor American Fuel Company, Payroll Records; McLean and Thomson, 7; Colorado Coal Mine Inspector, *Annual Reports* (1923), 93; (1926), 79; (1928), 67; and (1930), 85 on fire boss and first-class foremen certificates; only two Hispanics were listed throughout the decade, both in southern Colorado. Ray Redmond, "A Study of Industrial Relations within the Colorado Fuel and Iron Company" (Master's thesis, Univ. of Denver, 1923), App. A, 2–4, and App. C, 42, giving jobs and names of employee representatives for CFI. RMFCo records show that whatever the Chicano's prior experience, he almost always became a loader at Columbine. Note also, however, that at Delagua, in southern Colorado, Chicanos earned less than Anglos on average, more than $500 less per year; *Colorado Industrial Hearings: Miner's Wage and Working Conditions—1927 Strike* (6 Feb. 1928), 3423: A. B. W. Snodgrass, President, Victor American Fuel Company, Josephine Roche Papers, Box 7, WHC.

170. "Great Western Sugar Co. Imports 3000 Mexican Families," *CLA,* 21 April 1927. Claude and Laurence Amicarella, transcripts, 96–97, Colorado Coal Project, Boulder. AFL, *Report of the Proceedings of the Annual Convention,* for example, (1924), 146. Leo Grebler et al., *The Mexican American People* (New York, 1970), 91–92.

171. Amicarella, transcript, 96–97.

172. Henry Lawson, "The Colorado Coal Strike of 1927–1928" (Master's thesis, Univ. of Colorado, 1950), 156; Department of Research and Education, Federal Council of Churches of Christ in America, "Industrial Relations in the Coal Industry in Colorado," 38, Roche Papers, Box 7. Miners' wages in Colorado had fluctuated during the 1920s, but never returned to a high of approximately $7.75 per day for a company man in Sept. 1922, and had been further

cut in early 1927 (Lawson, 35). *Colorado Industrial Hearings,* 3692: Welborn, President, CFI.

173. James H. Buchanan, "Disturbances in the Colorado Coal Industry 1903–1928," 43, Roche Papers, Box 6.

174. Lawson, 36, 56, 64.

175. Charles Friday, "Government Interference in the Settlement of Industrial Disputes in Colorado" (Master's thesis, Univ. of Colorado, 1947), 61. The state's Industrial Commission virtually washed its hands of the strike, declaring it "illegal" largely because of the procedures used to select its strike committee and the employment status of these representatives, some of whom had been fired by CFI between the August and October strikes but continued to represent the miners. NDV to Industrial Commission, 4 Nov. 1927, Roche papers, Box 7. Other estimates for turnout earlier in the strike were, in October, five to six thousand. Josephine Roche, "Mines and Men," *Survey* 61 (Dec. 1928), 343.

176. "350 Raid IWW Hall; Arrest 42," *GDT,* 28 Dec. 1927; American Civil Liberties Union, "The War on the Colorado Miners," 9, Roche Papers, Box 7. *Hearings: Immigration from Countries of the Western Hemisphere,* 652, 662–666, 668. A list of the 698 most active persons in the strike by a rabid anti-radical of Colorado, included among 25 different "nationalities," 343 "Mexicans," at least 77 of whom were Spanish Americans.

177. On the strike, see: *Colorado Industrial Hearings* (10 Feb. 1928), 3: RMFCo response to Weitzell testimony; (19–22 Dec. 1927), 92, 94, 102: Manuel Duran, age 20, re: getting out to see his wife who lived at Erie, building a "shack" for $200 on company land, being dispossessed, and the failure of the company doctor to come when called; (20 Dec. 1927), 166–172: Ortega, age 32, on conditions in the camp. Lawson, 77, 119, 148. Most northern miners lived in open towns, but Columbine, like so many of the southern camps, was a closed camp. Dept. of Research and Education, "Industrial Relations," 45; Erwin Meyer, "Six Killed, Twenty Wounded: A Case Study of Industrial Conflict," *Survey* 59 (Feb. 1928), 644, 646; "Weld Picketing Attempt Broken by 4 Arrests," *GDT,* 5 Jan. 1928. Memos re: 1927 Columbine Strike, 17 Oct. 1927, at Columbine camp, Roche Papers, Box 7; *GDT,* 22 Nov. 1927. Roche, 341–344; Dorsett, 155, 157; biographical information on Roche, WHC.

178. Lawson, 157 on wages.

179. Taylor, *Mexican Labor,* 123, 146, 153; *GDT,* 11 Nov. 1927.

180. Taylor, *Mexican Labor,* 211; "Fourteen IWW Beet Laborers' Groups Formed," *GDT,* 31 Jan. 1928.

181. "Beet Labor To Meet Saturday at Brighton," *GDT,* 20 Jan. 1928; "Beet Laborers of Northern Weld Organized but Having Nothing To Do with IWW, Leader Claims," *GDT,* 24 Jan. 1928; "Beet Laborers Modify Original Strict Demands," *GDT,* 27 Jan. 1928; Jamieson, 236. The IWW was centered in southern Weld and Boulder counties, around the mines and the beet fields adjacent to them, according to "Beet Laborers Request Better Working Conditions," *GDT,* 12 Jan. 1928.

182. The IWW also claimed 42% of the beet laborers of southern Colorado, see "Fourteen IWW Beet Laborers' Groups Formed." "Newlon Says 1700 Beet Laborers Join IWW," *GDT,* 23 Jan. 1928; "42 Percent of Beet Laborers Said Organized," *GDT,* 23 Feb. 1928.

183. Taylor, *Mexican Labor,* 159; Jamieson, 237–238; "Drive to Organize Beet Workers in State Is Launched," *CLA,* 18 July 1929, regarding an A.F.L. attempt and describing a meeting of 500 "Mexican" beet workers at Fort Lupton who had incorporated under state law but remained unaffiliated. Rice, 2, 13. Farmers made about what beetworkers made from each acre of beets, averaging $25.50 per acre, 1922–27. Hand labor was approximately one-quarter of the total cost of production in northeastern Colorado in the 1920s, Taylor, *Mexican Labor,* 125. Jamieson, 236–237; "Weld Beet Labor Association Not an IWW Local," *GDT,* 3 Feb. 1928. Note that Mexicans in California migrant labor were simultaneously starting to organize, see Sam Kushner, *Long Road to Delano* (New York, 1975), 56.

184. See Meinig, 125.

185. McCombs, 70.

186. *Ibid.,* 23; Coen et al., 21.

187. Cf. Edwards et al., "Introduction," xii. Labor market segmentation theory had yet to be invented, but the dynamics of the actuality existed, and the choice between blaming economics or cultural forces for inequality was understood, as were its ramifications, at the time.

188. Taylor, *Mexican Labor,* 191.

189. Rice, 67, and see White, 11.

190. Cf. John Bodnar, *Immigration and Industrialization: Ethnicity in an American Mill Town, 1870–1940* (Pittsburgh, 1977); Rudolph Vecoli, "Contadini in Chicago: A Critique of *The Uprooted,*" *Journal of American History* 51 (Dec. 1964), 404–417.

191. Elsasser et al.: Patricia Luna, 87–88.

Chapter 7. Depression, Government, and Regional Community

1. W. S. Brummett, "Will 1929's Bitter Experience Help Us in 1930?" *TTL* (March 1930), 105. Olaf Larson, "Beet Workers on Relief in Weld County, Colorado," Cooperative Plan of Rural Research between Colorado State Agricultural Experiment Station, Fort Collins, Colorado, and Rural Section, Division of Social Research, Federal W.P.A., Bulletin no. 4 (March 1937), 1, 28.

2. J.C. Bailey, vice president of Holly Sugar Corp., to Costigan, 7 July 1931, Edward Costigan Collection, Box 48, WHC. "Drought Depression and the Farm Programs," 1, 17, in Baer Collection, WHC.

3. The Sedgwick Beet Workers Group to Gov. Johnson, May 1935, Gov. Rec., Box 26903, FF 236 CSA. SCS, "Village Dependency on Migratory Labor in the Upper Rio Grande Area," RB 47 (July 1937), 29; *GDT,* 5 May 1932;

Bound Factory Histories, Sterling, 81, GWSCo, WHC. Daniel Valdes, *Th⟨* *Spanish Speaking People of the Southwest* (Denver, June 1983); William Bundy "The Mexican Minority Problem in Otero County, Colorado" (Master's thesis Univ. of Colorado, 1940), 24; Carey McWilliams, *Ill Fares the Land: Migrant* *and Migratory Labor in the United States* (Boston, 1942), 114–115; *Colorad⟨* *Springs Gazette,* 20 May 1938.

4. Harry Schwartz, *Seasonal Farm Labor in the United States* (New York 1945), 127. W. Lewis Abbott, "Report for the Committee on Labor Condition⟨ in the Growing of Sugar Beets" (March 1934), 35, Costigan Collection, Box 49 Re: growers defaulting on labor contracts after work was completed, see Indus- trial Commission of Colorado, *Thirteenth Report* (1932–1934), 29, CSFL Papers, Box 22; and McWilliams, 112 cites a Mexican consul in Denver wh⟨ never had fewer than 500 wage claims pending for Mexican sugar-beet worker⟨ from 1933 to 1935. Settlement frequently took two or three years. See also Per- kins to Secretary of Agriculture, 18 Aug. 1933, RG145, AAA, Subject correspon- dence, Sugar, NA; Edwin Miller to Costigan, 2 Oct. 1934, Box 34; Albert Dakar to Costigan, 15 Nov. 1935, and W. D. Hoover to Costigan, 22 May 1934, Box 48, Costigan Collection.

5. Elizabeth S. Johnson, *Welfare of Families of Sugar-Beet Laborers* USDL, CB Publication no. 247 (Washington, D.C., 1939), 59, 64; Theodore D Rice, "Some Contributing Factors in the Determining of the Social Adjustmen⟨ of the Spanish Speaking People in Denver and Vicinity" (Master's thesis, Univ of Denver, 1932), 42. From 1930 to 1932 wages fell 21%, while the cost of livinℊ fell only 8 to 12%.

6. Stuart Jamieson, *Labor Unionism in American Agriculture,* USDL Bureau of Labor Statistics Bulletin no. 836 (Washington, D.C., 1945), 239. Min- utes of the Regional Sugar Beet Conference (March 1937), 39, RG69, WPA, Col- orado, 640, NA.

7. John Gross, "The Present Status of Emergency Unemployment Relie⟨ in Colorado" 24 March 1933, Memoranda of the Committee Representinℊ Industry, Organized Labor, and Agriculture, CSFL Collection, Box 10. Jean Sin- nock et al., *The Denver Relief Study* (Denver 1940), 10; Catholic Charities of th⟨ Diocese of Denver, *Annual Reports* (Denver, 1929–31); DPS, *The Education o⟨* *Spanish-Speaking American Children* (Denver, 1937), 3. In some school dis- tricts the number of Spanish-speaking families on relief was as high as 97% *RMN,* 26 Oct. 1937. Larson, 2. Committee to Hopkins, 14 Aug. 1933, and Jessi⟨ Lummis to Hopkins, 8 Aug. 1933, CSFL Papers, Box 10.

8. State Inspector of Coal Mines (Colorado), *Annual Reports* (1931–1937) See also statement of the Northern Coal Producers Association, National Indus- trial Relations Administration hearing on the bituminous coal industry, modi- fication proposal, vol. 3, day session, 11 April 1934, 535, Roche Papers, Box 9 WHC. Milan W. Gadd, "Significant Problems of Spanish-Speaking Persons and a Study of Their Registrations in the Denver Office of the Colorado State

Employment Service" (Master's thesis, Univ. of Denver, 1941), 10, 53–54. Ruberson to Industrial Commission, Sept. 1931, Costigan Collection, Box 49. Colorado F.E.R.A. and Colorado T.B. Association, *History of Public Health Nursing in Colorado,* 254, Colorado Nurses Association Collection 146, CHS.

9. Olaf Larson and John E. Wilson, "Survey of Applicants for WPA Aid, Weld County, Colorado, 9/1936–3.1.1936," Confidential Research Bulletin no. 1, p. 3, RG102, CB, Records of the Central Files Relating to Child Labor, 20-164-6, NA. Gadd, 24, 55–56, 87. Ora Gjerde Ethell, "A Study of Fifty Spanish-Speaking and Mexican Families in Denver County Granted Aid to Dependent Children April to October 1936 and Receiving Grants Continuously to June 1942" (Master's thesis, Univ. of Denver, 1943).

10. Interviews with Margarita Garcia, Windsor, Colo., 12 Oct. 1983, and Maria Chavez, Greeley, Colo., 12 Oct. 1983.

11. Johnson, 85; Larson and Wilson, 3; Bundy, 6. While not even all farm-dwelling Hispanics had gardens, fewer than 4% of Denver's Hispanics did. Bundy, 67; Johnson, 73–74. M. Pijoan and R. W. Roskelley, "Nutrition and Certain Related Factors of Spanish-Americans in Northern Colorado" (Denver, 1943). Charles E. Gibbons, "Statement on Conditions . . . ," Costigan Collection, Box 49; Larson, 14. DPS, *The Education of Spanish-Speaking American Children,* 9; Glenn W. Stewart to F. D. Roosevelt, 1 Feb. 1937 with clipping, RG69 WPA Colorado-692; Mrs. Isham of Adams County, minutes of official meeting, Colorado State Relief Committee and Boards of County Commissioners (9 Aug. 1932), 7, CSFL, Box 10, WHC.

12. Johnson, 72; Rice, 71, 74; Ethell, 41; *RMN,* 26 Oct. 1937; Charles Lundien, Weld County Justice of the Peace, April 1932, CSFL Papers, Box 10; Sinnock et al., 4, 13.

13. Bundy, 20. See USDL, CB, Carl Heisterman, "Memorandum on State Statutory Provision Relating to Settlement for Purposes of Obtaining Relief . . ." (Washington, D.C., Jan. 1931), 6, Costigan Collection, Box 48.

14. "Ever Greater Opportunities," *W&M* 10 (May 1933), 43; Frances Smith diary, 1936–1937, *San Jose News,* Teachers' Diaries, Univ. of New Mexico, Dept. of Education, Archive 306, UNM.

15. "Notes from Alice Hyson Mission," *W&M* 10 (May 1933), 56.

16. "Village Dependence on Migratory Labor," 5–7; Allan G. Harper et al., *Man and Resources in the Middle Rio Grande Valley* (Albuquerque, 1943), 77; U.S. Bureau of the Census, *Sixteenth Census of the United States, 1940, Internal Migration* (Washington, D.C., 1943), 116–117; 5,742 went from Colorado to New Mexico, 3,197 from New Mexico to Colorado from 1935–1940.

17. Matt Meier and Feliciano Rivera, *Readings on La Raza* (New York, 1974), 34–35; Arthur F. Corwin, "A Story of Ad Hoc Exemptions: American Immigration Policy Toward Mexico," in Corwin, ed., *Immigrants—and Immigrants* (Westport, Conn., 1978), 145–146; Abraham Hoffman, *Unwanted Mexican Americans in the Great Depression: Repatriation Pressures 1929–1939,*

(Tucson, 1974), 31; Paul S. Taylor, "More Bars Against Mexicans?" *The Surve* 64 (April 1930), 26–27.

18. Estimates of repatriations from Colorado usually placed at 10,000 t 15,000 are almost certainly too low, based on local newspaper reports. See Ric 146–147; *GDT,* 31 May 1932, 10 June 1932, 28 May 1932, 5 May 1932, 10 Ma 1932; *CLA,* 8 Oct. 1931, 12 May 1932. J. R. Ruberson to Industrial Commi sion, 12 May 1933, Costigan Papers, Box 48; Mahoney; Hoffman, ix; Wayn Moquin with Charles van Doren, eds., *A Documentary History of the Mexica Americans* (New York, 1971), 253; Robert McLean, "Goodbye Vicente, *Graphic Survey* 66 (May 1931), 182–183; R. Douglas Brackenridge and Frar cisco O. García-Treto, *Iglesia Presbiteriana: A History of Presbyterians an Mexican Americans in the Southwest* (San Antonio, 1974), 158; Emory S. Boga dus, *The Mexican in the United States* (Los Angeles, 1934), 90; Valdes.

19. Weld County Board of County Commissioners to Commissioner-Ger eral of Immigration, 11 April 1933, RG85, Records of the Naturalization Serv ice 55639-616A, NA.

20. James Frederick Wickens, *Colorado in the Great Depression* (New Yor 1979), 104; *Denver Post,* 3 May 1935. Johnson to Cordell Hull, 10 May 193! and Hull to Johnson, 10 May 1935, Gov. Rec., Box 26903, FF236, CSA; Abra ham Hoffman, "The Trinidad Incident," *Journal of Mexican American Histor* 2 (Spring 1972), 143–146; Ruby Buhrmester, "A History of the Spanish-Speal ing People in Southern Colorado, Especially Those in Otero County" (Master thesis, Western State College of Colorado, 1935), 64–65. *GDT,* 20 April 193 21 April 1936, 24 April 1936, 29 April 1936, 30 April 1936. Johnson Statemer ending blockade, Gov. Rec., Box 26916, FF236, CSA. Tom Jenkins, Chic Inspector, Port of Entry at Tres Piedras, NM, on phone, 2 April 1936, Go Tingley Papers, Special Issue: Colorado Embargo, NMSRCA. *Alb. Trib.,* 2 April 1936, 22 April 1936.

21. Abraham Hoffman, "Mexican Repatriation During the Great Depres sion: A Reappraisal," in Corwin, 240; for letters from both sides, see Colorad Gov. Rec., 1936, Box 26916, FF236, CSA; other Anglos opposed the action o constitutional grounds, see the same file and *GDT,* 23 April 1936. *RMN,* 2 April 1936.

22. For Hispanics in favor of Johnson's policies from 1935 to 1936, se Colorado Gov. Rec. 1935 and 1936, Box 26903, FF236 Aliens, including th Liga Cooperative and Educational of Prowers County, the Spanish America League of Greeley, and Box 26916, FF236, CSA.

23. *TCN,* 27 April 1936; *GDT,* 24 April 1936; interview with Arthur Mae Denver, 12 Sept. 1983. Local 20, 190, Greeley, to Governor, 20 April 1936, an Secretary, Beet Worker Union, no. 20, 105, Longmont to Governor, and othe in Colorado Gov. Rec., 1936, Box 26916, FF236, CSA. *CLA,* 20 Oct. 1932.

24. Santa Fe District Attorney David Chavez, New Mexico State Comp troller Juan Vigil, the Las Vegas Chamber of Commerce and the Alianza Hi

pana-Americana of Walsenburg and Denver also voice opposition. *TCN,* 27 April 1936; *The Boulder Daily Camera,* 20 April 1936, saw the blockade as part of an attempt by the A.F.L. beet unions to keep out the Communist beet unions, but the about-face of the A.F.L. Greeley union belies this (see WHC clipping file); Gov. Rec., Box 26916, FF236, CSA, includes a letter from Aida Vigil, 20 May 1936, who saw the anti-blockade sentiment in Southern Colorado as arising from political manipulation. *El Annunciador* (Trinidad), 24 April 1936; *GDT,* 23 April 1936; C. C. Buhrman, ex-secretary, Policy Committee of Colorado to Shriver claimed a minimum of 50,000 Spanish American voters felt discriminated against by the Democratic state machine because of the use of the National Guard on the border, in RG69 WPA Colorado, 641 O-P, July 1936; *Alb. Trib.,* 27 April 1936, *TCN,* 22 April 1936. It is worth noting that in April 1939, three years later, the headline "'Foreign' Beet Workers Are Turned Back" once again graced the front page of the *Pueblo Chieftain,* 26 April 1939. For population figures see school census records, Weld County, at CSA, for example Columbine, Galeton, Vollmer, and Eaton; DPS, *Education of Spanish Speaking American Children,* 5; Gadd, 32, 105.

25. Olen Leonard and Charles Loomis, *Culture of a Contemporary Rural Community: El Cerrito, New Mexico* (Washington, 1941), 6.

26. Eleanor Daggett, *Chama New Mexico* (Chama, 1973), 29–30; Relief Administration in Taos and Rio Arriba Counties, 1932 and Emergency Relief Committee, Margaret Reeves, Director, Gov. Seligman Papers, NMSRCA; J. C. McConvery to Governor, 13 July 1934, Gov. Hockenhull Papers, General Correspondence re: Relief Administration, NMSRCA. Fabiola Cabeza de Baca Gilbert, *We Fed Them Cactus* (Albuquerque, 1954), 177; FA Armijo, Rio Arriba County, 1, NMAES T876-16-1934. Albertano C. de Baca, Mora County, 29, NMAES T876-18-1935/1936.

27. Fabiola Gilbert, Santa Fe County, 34, NMAES, T876-20-1937. Alvar Carlson, "El Rancho and Vadito: Spanish Settlements on Indian Lands," *El Palacio* 85 (Spring 1979), 32, 34, 38; *Tewa Basin Study,* vol. 2. *The Spanish American Villages* (Washington, 1935), reprinted in Marta Weigle, ed., *Hispanic Villages of Northern New Mexico* (Santa Fe, 1975), 52.

28. They needed to make up a loss of more than $750,000 formerly sent back by migrants. Leonard and Loomis, 6; *Tewa Basin Study,* 81, 178, 190; U.S.D.A., Soil Conservation Service, "Handling of a Cash Crop (Chili)," regional bulletin 46 (July 1937), reprinted in Weigle; F. A. Armijo, 18, NMAES T876-12-1930.

29. Quoted in Joan Jensen, "New Mexico Farm Women, 1900–1940," in Robert Kern, ed., *Labor in New Mexico* (Albuquerque, 1983), 72; and see Vernita Conley, San Miguel County, 14, NMAES T876-20-1937. Ruth K. Barber, "Pressing on Despite Depression," *W&M* 9 (May 1932), 46. Julian Duran, "The Hopefulness of Trementina," *W&M* 9 (May 1932), 53.

30. Harper et al., 77; Dr. Sarah Bowen, 9 Nov. 1935, Embudo Hospital,

Vertical Files, MHL; Duran, 54. Note that conditions did improve between 1935 and 1937, though in this decade never returned to the 1920s position. In 1937, 4500 migrants earned one million dollars, according to Harper et al., and according to Paul Walter's 1938 Stanford University dissertation, "A Study of Isolation and Social Change in Three Spanish Speaking Villages of New Mexico," in Sandoval County a cash income of $100 a year was considered comfortable for a Hispanic small farmer (p. 82).

31. Carolyn Zeleny, *Relations between the Spanish-Americans and Anglo-Americans in New Mexico* (Ph.D. dissertation, Yale Univ., 1944, reprinted and revised, New York, 1974), 181; *Tewa Basin Study:* "Handling of a Cash Crop," 225.

32. Callaway, 19, NMAES T876-19-1936.

33. *Tewa Basin Study;* Leonard and Loomis, 1; Robert Coles, *The Old Ones of New Mexico* (Albuquerque, 1973), 30–31; Olen Leonard, *The Role of the Land Grant in the Social Organization and Social Processes of a Spanish-American Village in New Mexico* (1943, reprint ed., Albuquerque, 1970), 17–18, 125.

34. "Memorandum to Miss Margaret Reeves Regarding the Relief Situation in Tierra Amarilla," 4 April 1932, Gov. Seligman Papers, 1932 Relief Administration in Taos and Rio Arriba Counties, NMSRCA; *Tewa Basin Study,* 41, 48, 92, 120; Wesley Robert Hurt, Jr., "Manzano: A Study of Community Disorganization" (Master's thesis, Univ. of New Mexico, 1941), 103; interviews with Gabino Rendon, Jr., Las Vegas, New Mexico, 25 Oct. 1983, and Tom Chaves, Santa Fe, 9 Nov. 1983, on successful family survival strategies.

35. Margaret Reeves to Gov. Seligman, 4 March 1933, To All Representatives and Subcommittee Members, 29 March 1933, and To All Local Relief Agencies, 29 March 1933, Gov. Seligman Papers, Relief Administration of Federally Assisted Public Welfare in New Mexico, 1933, NMSRCA. Lydia Richer Haystead, Field Representative, to Miss Reeves, 3 April 1932, Gov. Seligman Papers, 1932 Relief Administration in Taos and Rio Arriba Counties, NMSRCA. Spanish Americans on Relief (petition), Clovis, to Governor, 26 June 1933, Governor Seligman Papers, NMSRCA. Lillian Franzen to Governor, 28 June 1934, Conway to Governor, 20 July 1934, and Arthur Gallup to Reeves, 1 Aug. 1934, Gov. Hockenhull Papers, General Correspondence re: Relief Administration. New Mexico Dept. of Public Welfare, *Activities* 1 (March 1937) 3, 10. Leonard and Loomis, 6; New Mexico Emergency Relief Administration, *The Bulletin* 2 (26 Feb. 1935), 2, estimates of employables for four northern New Mexico counties almost make up the difference between the two thousand migrating in 1935 and the seven to ten thousand migrating in 1929. James Swayne, "A Survey of the Economic, Political and Legal Aspects of the Labor Problem in New Mexico" (Master's thesis, Univ. of New Mexico, 1936), 79.

36. *Tewa Basin Study;* Leonard and Loomis, 1; Coles, 30–31; Leonard, 17–18, 125.

37. Mayme Sweet, "Specific Racial and Social Groups within the 'Dark' Areas," 27, in Denver Council of Social Agencies, *Social Welfare in Denver Yesterday Today—Tomorrow* (May 1939); interview with Arthur Maes on Fort Collins; Weld County school census records, 1925–1940.

38. DPS, "Report on Children from Spanish-Speaking Homes," Dept. of Research and Curriculum, Bulletin 49 (17 May 1935), 1, 3. Denver Unity Council, "The Spanish-Speaking Population of Denver—Housing Employment Health Recreation Education" (April 1946), 4; Brackenridge and García-Treto, 160; Larson, 16; Denver Area Welfare Council, Inc., "The Spanish American Population in Denver, A Supplementary Report" (June 1952), 129, Community Relations Papers, Box 6, DPL; Paul Kutsche and John R. Van Ness, *Cañones* (Albuquerque, 1981), 80, 84; Donald S. Howard, "A Study of the Mexican, Mexican-American and Spanish-American Population in Pueblo, Colorado, 1929–1930" (Master's thesis, Univ. of Denver, 1930), 79; Gallup Defense Bulletin, "Special Brighton Boys Issue," 1 (July 1933), 16, Radical Organizations, IDL, file 11, CHS.

39. George I. Sanchez, "The Education of Bilinguals in a State School System" (1934, reprinted in *Education and the Mexican American,* New York, 1974), 22, 79ff; Gerald Nash, *The American West in the Twentieth Century* (Englewood Cliffs, 1973), 142. Frances Smith, 27 Jan. 1937, 17 Feb. 1937, 22 April 1937, in Box 1, Vera Cornelius 1936–1937 in Box 2, Vera Cutler, 1936–1937 in Box 3, Teachers Diaries, Archive 306, UNM. Leah Thompson, "On Top of the World," *W&M* 9 (May 1932), and "The New Church at Chimayo," *W&M* 10 (May 1933); Maria Girard Vincent, "Ritual Kinship in an Urban Setting: Martineztown, New Mexico" (Master's thesis, Univ. of New Mexico, 1966), 20; Juliet Warwick, Greeley House of Neighborly Service to E. Johnson, 1 Jan. 1937 in RG102, CB, Central Files Relating to Child Labor, 1916–40, 20-164-6, NA. Gadd, 43. DPS, *Education of Spanish Speaking American Children,* 2; DPS, *Educational Statistics for the School Year* (1930–31, 1936–37, 1937–38), from 2.5% in 1927 to 4% in 1930/31 to 8.09% in 1937/1938. Johnson, 52. Weld County school census records, District 6. The Hispanic proportion of Greeley's school census rose from 5.4% in 1925 to 13% in 1935, reflecting the move to urban centers. In 1925 there were approximately 77 Chicano families listed; in 1930, 83; and in 1935, 188; Las Animas County school census records. *New Mexico School Review* 15 (Oct. 1935), 37, and (Nov. 1935), 19; Nan Elsasser et al., *Las Mujeres: Conversations from a Hispanic Community* (Old Westbury, N.Y., 1980), 50; *Tewa Basin Study.*

40. *Denver Post,* 29 March 1931; George Sanchez, ed., "First Regional Conference on the Education of Spanish Speaking People in the Southwest" (March 1946), and "Institute of Ethnic Affairs—Citizens' Service Organizations (Latin American)" (1946), 9, Community Relations Papers, Box 2, DPL; *RMN,* 9 Sept. 1938; RG69 WPA Colorado, 641, Denver Correspondence and 693; and RG145 AAA, Subject Correspondence, Sugar; all contain correspondence with branches

of Hispanic organizations in Colorado. Rice, 141 cites *El Imparcial* of Denve:
2 June 1932, as listing 6 Hispanic clubs or mutualistas in Denver, 2 in Brightoi
and 11 others in Colorado. The trend was not, however, limited to norther
Colorado. See, also, Donald McNaughton, "A Social Study of Mexican ani
Spanish-American Wage-Earners in Delta, Colorado" (Master's thesis, Univ. c
Colorado, 1942), 69, 70–71; New Mexico State Corporation Commissioi
Annual Report (1930–1937); Leonard, 86; Radical Organizations, file 3; Henr
Hough, ed., "Americans with Spanish Names" (Colorado WPA, 1942), 4, 7, 1(
Observers differed as to the rise or decline of the Penitentes in the 1930s; se
Walter, 64–65; Dorothy Woodward, "The Penitentes of New Mexico" (Ph.I
dissertation, Yale Univ., 1935), 220; Paul Kutsche and Dennis Gallegos, "Con
munity Functions of the *Cofradía de Nuestro Padre Jesús Nazareno,*" in Pai
Kutsche, ed., *The Survival of Spanish American Villages,* Colorado Colleg
Studies no. 15 (Spring 1979), 43.

41. Although it experienced difficulty in persuading the district attorneys i
file, the anti-discrimination group won a suit regarding a swimming pool i
Lafayette, Colorado, built with public funds but closed to "Mexicans." Intei
view with Arthur Maes. Re: the Spanish American Citizens Association, se
CLA, 20 Oct. 1932, 4 May 1933, 20 April 1934, 8 Aug. 1934, 6 Sept. 1934. Lit
Gallegos to Josephine Roche, 4 Aug. 1934, and E. M. Quintana, President, Span
ish American Citizens Association, Denver, to Roche n.d. (1934), and Roche t
Montoya, 28 July 1934 (under Denver) in Roche Papers, Box 10; Buhrmeste
68–70.

42. Harry Schwartz, "Organization of Agricultural Labor in the Unite
States 1930–1940" (Master's thesis, Columbia Univ., 1941), 37–38; Jamiesoi
18, 20–25.

43. Magdalena Velasquez to Costigan, 9 June 1934, Costigan Collectioi
Box 48; *GDT,* 20 May 1932, 25 May 1932. "Save the Gallup Workers" bulletii
18 May 1935, Correspondence and Minutes of meetings, 1935, Radical Orga
nizations Collections, files, 1, 4, 11. Mrs. Mauricio Trujillo to F. D. R., 5 Oc
1936, and Mrs. Joe H. Martinez, Workers Alliance, to Board of County Con
missioners, 19 Oct. 1936, RG69 WPA Colorado, 641, NA. Ben Whitehurst i
Mrs. Aurelia Sanchez, 22 April 1936, RG69 WPA Colorado 693, NA. Marcel
Trujillo, "The Colorado Spanish Surnamed Women of Yesteryear," in Eveli
Echevarría and José Otero, eds., *Hispanic Colorado: Four Centuries' Histor
and Heritage* (Fort Collins, 1976), 120; Bundy, 64 citing *Denver Post,* 14 Jul
1940, article by Anna Mestas protesting discrimination against Spanish Amer
cans in Denver. For Chicanas active in other states, see, for example, Dougla
Monroy, "La Costura en Los Angeles, 1933–1939: The ILGWU and the Politic
of Domination," in Magdalena Mora and Adelaida R. Del Castillo, eds., *Me:
ican Women in the United States: Struggles Past and Present* (Los Angele:
1980), and Julia Kirk Blackwelder, *Women of the Depression: Caste and Cultur
in San Antonio, 1929–1939* (College Station, Tex., 1984).

44. Gross to Wallace, 21 May 1934, Nick Medina of Vale and Walsenburg to Costigan, 5 July 1934, 1 Jan. 1935, Costigan Papers, Box 48. Denver Interracial Commission, 2 May 1934 meeting, Denver YWCA records. Rebecca Cantwell, "Sugar Beets Brought . . . ," *Longmont Daily Times-Call* 1981 Clipping File, WHC. *CLA,* 10 July 1930. Alice E. vonDiest to Costigan, 7 May 1934, Al Litel, President, Mountain States Beet Growers Association, to Costigan, 24 March 1936 and Albert Dakan to Costigan, 5 June 1935, Costigan Papers, Box 48. Paul S. Taylor, *Mexican Labor in the United States Valley of the South Platte, Colorado,* Univ. of California Publications in Economics vol. 6 (1929), 115–116; *GDT,* 25 April 1936. On ethnicity: William Hamm to Bill Morison, 1 Feb. 1935, Henry Schnechterle to Henderson, 27 Dec. 1934, RG145 AAA, Alphabetical correspondence, Rocky Mountain Beet Laborers Association, NA. Agricultural Workers Union no. 20190, 13 April 1936, had an Anglo secretary and a Hispanic president, which may explain the shift in policy of the border closing mentioned earlier, RG69 WPA Colorado, 641A, NA.

45. *CLA,* 6 Feb. 1930, 17 April 1930, 28 Sept. 1933, 17 Jan. 1935, 19 March 1936, 26 March 1936, 3 Sept. 1936. Rice, 141–142; Index of Correspondence, Roche-Costigan, 1934, includes letters from beetworkers' associations in Platteville, Ft. Lupton, Greeley, Walsenburg, Fountain, Colorado, and South Dakota, Roche Papers, Box 12. Jamieson, 27, 244–246, 249, 425–426. J. J. Rios to Costigan, 15 May 1934, Henry Ruiz to Costigan, 24 Sept. 1934, E. R. Kielgass to Costigan, 20 April 1935, J. M. Lopez to Costigan, 6 March 1934, Alfred Crandall to Costigan, 4 March 1934, Costigan Papers, Box 48. Schwartz, 54, 56, 67–68. Ninth Labor Political Convention, Canon City, Colorado, 5 June 1936, included eight agricultural and beetworker unions and four Hispanic representatives of those unions sat on the Labor State Central Committee, CSFL papers, Box 4. *GDT,* 10 March 1936, 21 March 1936, 23 March 1936, 3 April 1936, 4 April 1936. Daniel Vigil to F. D. R., 28 March 1936, John Gross to Rev. Francis Haas, 1 May 1936, National Beetworkers Conference Secretary Paul Arias to Hopkins, 20 Jan. 1936, Fred Borrego, chair, Longmont to Hopkins, 1 March 1937, and other letters, RG69 WPA Colorado 641, 1936, and see 641 files 1937 and 1938 from UCAPAWA and unaffiliated locals including Borrego at Longmont, Gavino Gamboa at Crowley, Eduard Gonzales at Denver, Ben Martinez at Julesberg, Fidel Herrera at Granada, M. V. Martinez at Wiley, and Manuel Dominguez at Ft. Collins. Austin Beasley was president of the Colorado UCAPAWA in 1938. Wickens, 106; Edith Lowry, comp., *They Starve That We May Eat: Migrants of the Crops* (New York, 1938), 30–31; U.S. Office of War Information Washington, D.C., Microfilm ser. 457 (June 1943) taken by U.S. Farm Security Administration: *Agriculture Farm and Mining at the End of the Depression: (1938–1940):* 15799E, 15801E, and 15806E by Allison depict a union meeting of sugar-beet workers in Colorado, 1938.

46. Other demands included an end to forcing contracted labor to pay for extra labor hired at the growers' discretion, the right to trade at any store, credit,

and transportation. Minutes of Conference of Beet Field and Agricultural Workers Unions, Greeley, 22 March 1936, RG69 WPA Colorado 641.

47. In regard to other beet strikes: Nebraska beetworkers threatened to strike in 1934 (*CLA,* 1 Oct. 1934 and 17 Oct. 1934), in Fremont, Ohio, beetworkers struck in 1938, while they called off a strike in Colorado. RG16, Secretary of Agriculture, General Correspondence, Sugar 4, "Wage Rates," NA; and see *RMN,* 13 April 1938, and other clippings in the DPL clipping file; and Jamieson, 30–38.

48. In regard to the 1932 strike in Colorado: *CLA,* 19 May 1932, 26 May 1932; *GDT* (daily), 11 May 1932 through 30 May 1932.

49. The sugar company refused to recognize the union on the grounds that it was communist, and some leaders were threatened with deportation on the same grounds. Harry Schwartz, *Seasonal Farm Labor in the United States* (New York, 1945), 135; Schwartz, "Organization of Agricultural Labor," 39–40; Rice 142–143. Strike leader Paul Arias, a Mexican, was threatened with deportation as a result of this role, according to J. Austin Beasley, President of UCAPAWA, Dist. 3, Beasley to Perkins, 25 Oct. 1938, RG280, Federal Mediation and Concilation Service, file 195–705, NA, and "Special Brighton Boys Issue," 12. Radical Organizations Collection, file 11. See also Jamieson, 239–240. *GDT,* 11 May 1932, 17 May 1932.

50. Harry Rubenstein, "The Great Gallup Coal Strike of 1933," *NMHR* 52 (April 1977), 174; Harry Rubenstein, "Political Repression in New Mexico: The Destruction of the National Miner's Union in Gallup," in Kern, 116; Clyde Johnson, Dist. 3 President, UCAPAWA to Elizabeth Johnson, 30 March 1940, RG102, CB, 20-164-8; J. Edwin Sharp, "The Spanish Speaking People and Organized Labor," in Hough, 6; Jamieson, 241; Radical Organizations, file 3 (pledge cards and delegate cards, Gallup Defense conferences, 1935–36, Denver). Dalton to Rafael Benevidez, Spanish Speaking Workers League, Denver, 21 May 1934, RG145 AAA, Subject Correspondence, Sugarbeet, 1934, NA. E. E. Maes, "The Labor Movement in New Mexico," *New Mexico Business Review* 4 (1935), 139; Swayne, 30–32. A Mexican and a Spanish leader of La Liga in New Mexico were arrested and held for deportation, 1934–36, see Radical Organizations, Gallup Defense Bulletin (July 1936), 11–12, and D. H. Dinwoodie, "Deportation: The Immigration Service and the Chicano Labor Movement in the 1930s," *NMHR* 52 (April 1977), 193; Kern, 14; Schwartz, "Organization of Agricultural Labor," 83; Liga Petition from a 30 Jan. 1938, Las Vegas, New Mexico, meeting (Mrs. Petra Sisneros, secretary), RG69 New Mexico WPA 640L, 1938, NA. Walter, 225; *Tewa Basin Study.*

51. *CLA,* 17 Aug. 1933. J. J. Rios to Costigan, 10 May 1934, Costigan Papers, Box 48; Schwartz, "Organization of Agricultural Labor," 74–75; RG59 State Department, 311.1215/87. Regional Sugar Beet Conference (March 1937), 2, 43, 47, 57, RG69 WPA Colorado, 640, NA. Daniel Vigil, chairman, federal labor union 20153, to F. D. R., 28 March 1936, RG69 WPA Colorado, 641, NA.

52. Rubenstein in Kern, 116—the investigation came in the wake of INS investigations at Gallup in April 1935, and the Liga may have begun to decline in power, though it did not disappear, as it became tied to communism in the public mind. See Nancie González, *The Spanish Americans of New Mexico: A Distinctive Heritage* (Los Angeles, 1967), 67.

53. Bundy, 60; Johnson, 80; Gadd, 21; Buhrmester, 45.

54. Denver Interracial Commission, for example, 21 March 1935 minutes in YWCA records; and see NMAES, T876-15-1933, Ivie Jones, San Miguel County, 49 re: Romeroville. Some Denver and Albuquerque public school teachers and officials also tried to ease tensions, see DPS, "Report on Children from Spanish Speaking Homes," 6, and Teachers' Diaries, 1936–1938, Archive 306, UNM.

55. Gadd, 23, 69–70; Hough, 17; R. W. Roskelley, "Beet Labor Problems in Colorado," *Proceedings of the Western Farm Economics Association* (Colorado, July 1940), 7–9; Ten women's representatives to Hull, 13 May 1935, RG59 State Department, 311.1215/83, NA; re: the Lafayette, CWA-built, segregated swimming pool, RG69 Colorado WPA 651.363, State Reports, 4, NA; Denver Interracial Commission, 23 May 1934 meeting; DPS, "Status of Spanish-Speaking Children . . . ," 4, 6–7; Radical Organizations, file 11, "ILD No Legal Aid Society," 10 Jan. 1933, 18; *GDT,* 25 April 1936, 1 May 1936, re: handbills, which were also distributed to Rocky Ford in the Arkansas Valley.

56. Roskelley, 9.

57. San Luis Valley: Daniel Valdez, ed., *History of the San Luis Valley,* 1936; interview with Mrs. Moeny, Adams State College; Robert Parham, "The Civilian Conservation Corps in Colorado, 1933–1942" (Master's thesis, Univ. of Colorado, 1981), 140, 142, 144. Eugen Archuleta, "Hispanic Villagers, the CCC and the Beginning of Social Mobility in the San Luis Valley," 16, Mexican Americans in Colorado Collection, WHC. New Mexico: Hearings on Racial Prejudice, Univ. of New Mexico, May 1933, Gov. Seligman Papers, NMSRCA. The mere suggestion of a survey of interracial relations in New Mexico aroused a gale of Hispanic resentment. Carlos Jimenez, oral history, 31 March 1969, DPL. *La Voz del Rio Grande,* 20 Sept. 1935, 10 Sept. 1937. Zeleny, 301, 316.

58. NYA (Colorado), Annual Report, 1939–40, Denver Occupational Adjustment Service, 19, RG119, NYA, 330, NA.

59. Bundy, 61; "Gov. Johnson Exposed" (bilingual), Radical Organizations Collection. Rice, 79.

60. Anon. to Johnson, 11 Sept. 1935, Gov. Rec., Box 26903, FF236, CSA.

61. Albert Straight to Johnson, 3 May 1935, Gov. Rec., Box 26903, FF236, CSA, and see many other letters, same file and in Box 26916, FF236 for 1936; also in RG69 Colorado WPA 662, NA (Mrs. Georgia Wallace, Denver, to Mrs. Roosevelt); W. Wiley Dumm, Denver, to Gov. Tingley, 24 April 1936, Gov. Tingley Papers, NMSRCA. Gadd, 31.

62. Falogrady to Costigan, 6 March 1934, Costigan Collection, Box 47.

63. Carl Jensen, "A Study of the Spanish-American Normal School at E Rito" (Master's thesis, Univ. of New Mexico, 1939), 6. Sporleder to Swann, 1. Nov. 1937, Sporleder Papers, Box 1, DPL. Ann Jones diary and Frances Smith diary, Teachers Diaries, Archive 306, Box 1, UNM. See also Buhrmester, 21 Bundy, 62; Pijoan and Roskelley, 4–6; Roskelley, 5. Valdez; Hurt, 156, 159, 162 Florence Kluckhohn and Fred Strodtbeck, *Variations in Value Orientation.* (Evanston, 1961), 227; J. C. Davidson, Las Animas County, to Johnson, 4 Ma 1936, Gov. Rec., Box 26916, FF236, CSA.

64. Many of these same complaints were made by white employers in the south regarding blacks. H. L. Robertson to Governor, 29 April 1936, Gov. Rec. Box 26916, FF236, CSA.

65. Hopkins to Johnson, 5 Nov. 1934, Gov. Rec., Box 26888, FF212, Suga Beet Production, CSA.

66. J. C. Davidson to Governor Johnson, 28 April 1936, 4 May 1936, Gov Rec., *ibid.; GDT,* 28 April 1936; Gadd, 23–24, 31, 65, 90. Petition with 96 sig natures from Albuquerque to Congressman J. J. Dempsey against being forced through relief policies, to take beet and sheep work at low wages in areas o prejudice against Spanish-Americans, RG69 WPA New Mexico 690, NA McWilliams, 120–121. Leonard and Loomis, 36; "Keeping on at Truchas,' *W&M* 10 (May 1933), 52; Sinnock et al., 40; Minutes of Sugar Beet Conference Denver, March 1937, Summary RG69 WPA Colorado, 640, NA. Case of Man uel Cruz, RG69 WPA Colorado 641, NA.

67. *GDT,* 25 March 1936; AFL Statement, Denver, 5 March 1936, Costigar Collection, Box 48.

68. Shriver to Nels Anderson, 31 March 1936, 4 April 1936, RG69 WPA Colorado, 641F, NA. Letters from Anglos protesting reductions, and Terry Owens to G. M. Macmillan, 23 June 1936, RG69 WPA Colorado, 693, NA Minutes of Sugar Beet Conference, and Shriver to Anderson, 4 March 1937 RG69 WPA Colorado, 640, NA.

69. Shriver to Anderson, 30 April 1937, RG69 WPA Colorado, 640, NA Jamieson, 254. SCS, "Village Dependence on Migratory Labor," 8; Minutes o Regional Sugar Beet Conference, 26, op. cit.

70. Petition to Hopkins with 17 signatures from Salida, Colorado, Hispan ics who refused beetwork, not being accustomed to it, in file 641(T–Z); Antonio Martinez, Del Norte, Colorado, World War I Veteran, to F. D. R., 9 Aug. 1935 in file 693; Regional Sugar Beet Conference, March 1937, 57–58 in file 640 RG69 WPA Colorado, NA. Hispanic beet organizations from Longmont, Boul der, Ft. Lupton, and Ft. Collins to Wallace, Secretary of Agriculture, 22 Aug 1934, and American Federated Beetworkers, Denver to Johnson, 7 May 1934 in Gov. Rec., Box 26888, FF212, Sugar Beet Production, CSA.

71. *CLA* 17 Aug. 1933, 3 Oct. 1935. *GDT,* 26 Sept. 1934, 19 Sept. 1934, 2. Sept. 1934, 4 April 1936. RG16, Secretary of Agriculture, General Correspon dence, Sugar, "Hearings," NA. Colorado State Federation of Agricultura

Unions, Vicente Vigil, Ft. Collins to Wallace, 3 May 1935, RG145, AAA General Correspondence, Alphabetical, NA. Johnson, 1. Leonard Arrington, *Beet Sugar in the West: A History of the Utah-Idaho Sugar Company 1891–1966* (Seattle, 1966), 129–132. Joshua Bernhardt to James Patten, 20 March 1939, RG16, Secretary of Agriculture, General Correspondence, Sugar (5), 1938, NA.

72. Johnson, 12, 29; McWilliams, 119; Juliet G. Warwick, Greeley House of Neighbourly Service, to Elizabeth Johnson, 27 Nov. 1938, RG102 CB, 20-164-6, NA.

73. Schwartz, *Seasonal Farm Labor,* 128; Roskelley, 5; Johnson, 69–71.

74. Many married Hispanic women taught, some alongside their husbands. Hispanic women also stayed in teaching longer than they previously had. *La Voz del Rio Grande,* e.g., 10 Sept. 1937 and 5 Nov. 1937. Senator J. M. Madrid and Eusebio Chacon, U.S.C.W.A., *Interviews Collected During 1933–1934 for State Historical Society of Colorado,* UN3, CWA M216, reel 5, 86, 174, CSA. Valdez, 2; Adams State College, *El Conquistador* (College Annual, 1931–37). New Mexico Department of Education, *Annual Report,* and *Educational Directory* (1918–1938). Mrs. Crucita Ballegos to Governor, 8 March 1935, and Mrs. Isabella Gutierez, 11 May 1938, Governor Tingley Papers, State Board of Education, 1935–1938, NMSRCA; Lydia Zellers, OH-TC93, 12, MHL; Antonio Goubaud-Carrera, "Food Patterns and Nutrition in Two Spanish American Communities" (Master's thesis, Univ. of Chicago, 1943), 9.

75. Interview with Margaret McKenzie, Denver, 14 Sept. 1983. Eusebio Chacon, U.S.C.W.A., *Interviews,* reel 5, 174; *TCN,* 12 Feb. 1935; History file 69, legislative members, NMSRCA; *New Mexico Blue Book,* e.g. (1931), 58, 84; Concha Ortiz y Pino de Kleven, Women of New Mexico, Archive 303, Box 1, UNM. Cleo Fernandez, lawyer and legislator, and Ernestine Griego Evans, Women in New Mexico, vertical files, UNM. Vigil Papers, Box 2, WHC. *La Voz Del Rio Grande,* 1 Sept. 1933, 10 Dec. 1937, 21 Oct. 1932.

76. Walter, 84–85; Mrs. Faustino Santillanos, Postmaster, Alameda to Howard Hunter, 22 July 1941, RG69 WPA New Mexico 690A–Z, NA. Ruth K. Barber, "One of the Unknown Heroines," *W&M* 13 (Sept. 1936); Fabiola Gilbert, Santa Fe County, 22, NMAES T876-21-1938. *El Faro,* 19 Sept. 1934, Roche Papers. Mary Little diary, 1937–38, Teachers Diaries, Archive 306, Box 4, UNM. "Handling of a Cash Crop," 229; Joan Jensen, "'I've Worked, I'm Not Afraid to Work': Farm Women in New Mexico," *NMHR* 61:1 (Jan. 1986), 37.

77. Laura Whiteman, "Economic and Social Status of Wards in the State Welfare Homes for Girls, Albuquerque, New Mexico" (Master's thesis, Univ. of New Mexico, 1941), 49. A. J. Chapman, NRA, Denver to John Gross, 13 Nov. 1934, CSFL Papers, Box 2; N. W. Bolling to Secretary, CSFL, re: Rocky Ford waitress, 9 Aug. 1934, *ibid.,* Elsasser et al.: Esperanza Salcido, 63.

78. Most Chicanas throughout the region continued to marry at 18 or 19. Weld County and Rio Arriba County marriage licenses and certificates, and Leonard, 78; Hurt, 109. U.S. Bureau of the Census, *Fifteenth Census of the*

United States, Population, vol. 4, 243, 246–247, *General Report on Occupations,* vol. 5, 86–91. Irma Yarbrough Johnson, "A Study of Certain Changes in the Spanish American Family in Bernalillo County, 1915–1946" (Master's thesis, Univ. of New Mexico, 1948), 67. For other mention of the prevalence of Hispanic women working see Zeleny, 188–190; Goubaud-Carrera, 29, 33–34; Elsasser et al., 29–31, 45, 67; Fran Leeper Buss, *La Partera: Story of a Midwife* (Ann Arbor, 1980), 49; Ivie Jones, San Miguel County, 37, NMAES, T876-17-1935; Fabiola Gilbert, Santa Fe County, 15, T876-20-1937. Santa Fe County Relief Office Reports, 1935, E. Boyd Collection, NMSRCA; SCS, "Village Dependency on Migratory Labor," 10–11; Walter, 85, 219; Larson, 4; Gadd, 17, 39–41, 56–57, 64; YWCA Employment Bureau, Annual Report, Denver, 1931, Denver YWCA records. The drop in the number of Hispanic divorces in Las Animas County from an average of 21.2 per year 1926–30 to 9.4 per year 1931–35 may also be attributable to the inability of women to make a living on their own during the Depression (Las Animas County and District Court Records).

79. "Special Reports: Depression and New Deal—NRA and Relief: lists of workers on Federal Aid Projects," Seligman Papers, NMSRCA; Walter, 108 on the increasing centralization of patronage hurting village politicians, but note that it also freed them to organize on an other than party-line basis, for example, the rise of La Liga could be seen in this context, as well as the small political clubs and the "mass" protest meetings. RG69 WPA New Mexico, 640, NA, has political complaints, including many against Senator Dennis Chavez. See RG119, NYA New Mexico, 51, NA, for correspondence re: the appointment of *one* Spanish American assistant for the six person Advisory Committee. Lorin Brown et al., *Hispanic Folklife of New Mexico* (Albuquerque, 1978), appendix, 248.

80. Cf. Blackwelder on Hispanic needlewomen. Thomas believed "some splendid supervisors" would "overcome this difficulty." Petition from workers on a shoe-repair project in Trinidad, Colorado, including many Hispanics, male and female, to Hopkins, 14 Nov. 1938, re: hours, RG69 WPA Colorado, 641T, NA. Walsenburg, Colorado petition from WPA employees on a clerical project to Gov. Johnson, seven of the fourteen signers were Hispanic, including one woman; there were four Anglo women, Jan. 1938, *ibid.,* 663. Mary Stephenson, Assistant State Director, Employment Division, to David Niles, Washington, 19 March 1937, re: Della Aranda, employed on a WPA sewing project in Denver at $55 per month, *ibid.,* 641A. *Ibid.,* 662 contains several letters of complaint from women, including Loccria Flores, Raton, 5 Aug. 1936 on a sewing project. Miss Delphine Serrano and Miss Felice Herrera, WPA clericals, to Hopkins, 14 June 1938, re: wages, hours, vacation, RG69 WPA, New Mexico, 641, NA. I am indebted to Suzanne de Bourgheyi-Forrest for the following citations: NA RG69 CWA New Mexico, Review of the State CWA Activities in New Mexico, HD3890, N6AS, 1934, "New Mexico Relief Before Nov. 15, 1933," 9; NA RG69 WPA New Mexico 661 May–July 1936, Mary Perry, WPA New Mexico Direc-

tor Women's Activities and Public Service Projects to Ellen Woodward, 19 Dec. 1935, re: women plastering, employing two women in Rio Arriba County; NA RG69 FERA state files 1933–1936 New Mexico Relief Administration, 453.1, Director of Women's Work, Helen Dail Thomas to Woodward, 14 Nov. 1934, "New Mexico Relief Bulletin," 20 Dec. 1934, Helen Thomas to Woodward, 24 Sept. 1934.

81. Margaret Reeves to Ellen Woodward, 18 Sept. 1934, 20 Oct. 1933. Suzanne Forrest, "Federal Relief Comes to New Mexico" (unpublished manuscript, 1986), 27–31.

82. Ellen Woodward memo to Thad Holt, 28 Oct. 1936; Woodward to Mary Isham, Regional Director, WPA, Salt Lake City, 20 Nov. 1936; Andrews to Woodward, 6 Aug. 1936, and complaints in this file from several counties, RG69 WPA New Mexico, 660, NA. Forrest found that 700 unemployed Taos farmers, on the other hand, petitioned for part-time rather than full employment, to spread the wages further. Forrest, 32–33.

83. Archuleta, 16. Lela Weatherby, "Adult Education," *W&M* 17 (May 1940), 46 mentioning Mrs. Amalia Maes, WPA Adult Homemaking Division. H. G. Sandoval, Taos County, 49, NMAES T876-20-1937, mentioning Mrs. Julia Martinez, Home Supervisor, Farm Security Administration. NM ERA, *The Bulletin* 1 (18 Aug. 1934), 1. Mary Jean Simpson memo to Mrs. Mason, 14 June 1937, and *Denver Post* clipping, 18 Dec. 1938, "Rugs Woven by Colorado Women To Be Part of National Exhibit," RG69 WPA Colorado, 663, July–Aug. 1937, April–June 1937, 1939.

84. Sinnock et al., 38; Mary Isham to Ellen Woodward, 20 Nov. 1935, Feb. 1936 approval of plan, and March 1936, Mary Patton, Denver Director, to Anna Marie Driscoll, National Supervisor of WPA Household Training Program in RG69 WPA Colorado, 661, NA. Patton considered the distaste "little short of amazing." George Sanchez claimed in 1946 that "a group of church women in one Colorado town attempted a small project to assist the Spanish-speaking citizens; one of the activities was to teach the girls homemaking—a noble enough purpose, but some of the women were still 'teaching' the girls homemaking long after they had learned, and for this postgraduate internship in housework, the girls received ten cents an hour." (Sanchez, ed., "First Regional Conference." For a Santa Fe, New Mexico, "vocational training project for household workers" employing 58 women, see WPA, *The Reporter* (April 1936), 6, E. Boyd Collection, NMSRCA. For other programs, see: Candalaria Chavez to Mrs. Roosevelt, 5 Dec. 1938, Mrs. Senaida Garcia to Mrs. Roosevelt, 6 Dec. 1938 (both laid off), RG69 WPA New Mexico, 662; Phyllis Mayne, "Scope of Operations for Housekeeping Aide Projects," 16 Jan. 1941, RG69 WPA New Mexico, 651.3.

85. Sanchez, "First Regional Conference," 6; Zeleny, 289; Elsasser et al.: Susanna Archuleta, 37; Vernita Conley, San Miguel County, 40, NMAES T876-18-1936; *New Mexico Youthograms* (March 1937), 7; (July 1937), 4; and (Aug. 1937), 2 mention Hispanic women in domestic training, sewing, and weaving

as instructors of NYA girls, RG119, NYA New Mexico, 330 (NYA State Publications), NA. Bundy, 95; George Bickel to Hal Blue, 20 March 1937, RG119 NYA Colorado, 52, NA.

86. Religion: see, for example, Religious Directory for New Mexico, 1940, WPA files, no. 267, NMSRCA. Education: "Suggestions to Teachers" and Taos County, "The Bilingual Method and the Improvement of Instruction," Feb. 1938, A. M. Bergere Collection, Santa Fe County Superintendent of Schools, Bilingual Education, 1938–41, Taos County Rural Schools, 1938–39, NMSRCA; Conference on the Problems of Education Among Spanish Speaking Populations of Our Southwest, "Recent Educational and Community Experiments in New Mexico Affecting the Spanish-Speaking Population," Aug. 1943, 3–5; "Nambe . . . A Community School," n.d. (1939), Dorothy Woodward Collection, Public Education, NMSRCA; Victoria Davis de Sanchez diary, and Frances Watson diary, 1938, Teachers Diaries, Archive 306 Box 4, UNM; "San Jose Training School," UNM *Bulletin* 1 (Oct. 1930), 3–4, 8; Anne Reynolds, *The Education of Spanish-Speaking Children in Five Southwestern States,* Department of Interior, Office of Education, Bulletin no. 1 (Washington, D.C., 1933), 26–28; San Jose Experimental School, "We Learn English: A Preliminary Report of the Achievement of Spanish Speaking Pupils in New Mexico" (Albuquerque, July 1936), 5–7, 31–32. Recreation: State Reports, Division of Professional and Service Projects as of 1 Feb. 1939, p. 3 mentions Spanish American recreation centers at Eaton, Ft. Collins, Las Mesitas, Del Carbon, and Lamar, RG69 WPA Colorado, 651.363, NA. Literacy: D. W. Rockey, "Illiteracy, Its Recognition and Corrections," in minutes of Rio Arriba Sub District Educational Advisors Association, 25 Aug. 1936, WPA files, Rio Arriba County History, NMSRCA; Comparative Table Showing Improvement in Grade Classification: 23 teachers (7 Anglo, 16 Hispanic), 501 rural enrollees, ages approximately 18 to 65, WPA files, Education NMSRCA; Mrs. Otero Warren, "Experiences and Human Interest Stories," Literacy Division, WPA, 12 July 1939, RG69 WPA New Mexico, 661-1/1939; Workers' Education (Colorado WPA), "Forms for Workers' English Among Spanish Speaking," June 1937, mimeo, DPL. Other Services: *Workers Service in Colorado: First Six Months 1940–1941,* p. 16, 18 including work translating material on labor problems in beet sugar for UCAPAWA and Workers' Alliance, and (p. 10) nursery schools; Betty Johnson, "Nursery Schools and the Spanish Speaking People," in Hough; Writers Project no. 18, "Los Senadores," 149–152, WPA files, NMSRCA; *Denver Junior Consultation Center,* 4, WPA Collection 689, CHS; Leonard and Loomis, 17; Helen Shoecraft and Sherley Scotts, "Spanish Speaking People and the Cooperative Movement," in Hough; and Daniel Valdes, introduction.

87. Leonard and Loomis, 30–31; Kluckhohn and Strodtbeck, 60, 217; note also that the continuing disputation of land titles made it impossible for some landholders to get federal loans based on their land, see, for example, John Hinkle to H. H. Kramer, Gov. Hockenhull Papers, General Correspondence re:

Relief Administration, NMSRCA. Walter, 156–157; Harper et al., 53, 63; *Tewa Basin Study,* 87, 94, 96; SCS, Section of Human Surveys, "The Santa Cruz Irrigation District, A Brief History" (July 1937), 2, 4–10, Eastburn Smith Papers, NMSRCA.

88. Andrew Cordova, "The Taylor Grazing Act," *New Mexico Business Review* 4 (1935), 197–198; Leon Schingledecker to Niles, 24 Feb. 1938, RG69 WPA New Mexico, 641S, NA. D. S. Spencer letters, 6 Aug. 1936, MHL; Rev. Julian Cordova, "A Survey of Cordova," in *Spanish Speaking Work in the Southwest* (1937), MHL; Charles Loomis and Glen Grisham, "The New Mexican Experiment in Village Rehabilitation," *Applied Anthropology* 2 (June 1943), 23, 26, 30. Forrest, "From Indian New Deal to Hispanic New Deal," 11, and "The Final Years and Later," 29, 36 (unpublished ms.s, 1986).

89. Interview with Rose Lopez, Greeley, 26 Sept. 1983. Ivie Jones, San Miguel County, 11–12, NMAES T876-13-1931; Vernita Conley, San Miguel County, 3, T876-20-1937; Ivie Jones, 45, T876-15-1933; Conley and Apodaca, San Miguel County, 45, T876-21-1938.

90. Shoecraft and Scotts in Hough, 13. Conley, 31, NMAES T876-18-1936. Fabiola Gilbert, Santa Fe County, 40, T876-21-1938. On the Greeley House of Neighbourly Service's unique Spanish American NYA program: Juliet Warwick to Elizabeth Johnson, 1 Jan. 1937, RG102 CB, 20-164-6, NA. *Youth at Work under the NYA in Colorado* (1936), 7, RG119 NYA Colorado 51, NA. Hal Blue to Brown, 20 April 1936, RG119, NYA Colorado, 52, NA. 1 May 1936 report, RG119 NYA Colorado 249, NA. On intermediaries see Leonard, 72; D. S. Spencer letters, 1 Dec. 1932, 9–10; Albert Dakan to Costigan, 5 June 1935, Costigan Collection, Box 48.

91. P. A. F. Walter, "Population Trends in New Mexico," in *The Population of New Mexico* (Albuquerque, 1947), 17. Roskelley, 7–8. "Addenda to Report on Expansion of the Federal-State Cooperative Programs for Maternal and Child Health," in Roche Papers, Box 16. Edwin Miller to Costigan, 2 Oct. 1934, containing "Brief of Joint Labor Committee of Larimer County, Fort Collins," 6, Costigan Collection, Box 34. Larson, 23–24; Harper et al., 110–111. On midwife programs see Sister M. Lucia Van der Eerden, *Maternity Care in a Spanish-American Community of New Mexico* (Washington, D.C., 1948), 21–25, 32; Buss, 116, 118; New Mexico Bureau of Public Health, *Biennial Reports* (1929–30, 1933–34), and *New Mexico Health Officer* 12 (Dec. 1944), 22–30, 36; Florence Webbert, "A Study of the Effect of State and National Legislation on Child Welfare during the Years 1929 to 1940" (Master's thesis, Univ. of Colorado, 1940), 87.

92. The Ranchos de Taos midwife averaged 75 deliveries a year. Elsasser et al.: Susana Archuleta, 39; Van der Eerden, 26–29, 32, 34–35, 37.

93. Minutes of Regional Sugar Beet Conference, summary and throughout (March 1937).

94. Ramirez, Santa Fe County, 73, NMAES, T876-10-1929; Joan Jensen,

"Canning Comes to New Mexico: Women and the Agricultural Extension Service, 1914–1919," *NMHR* 57 (Oct. 1982), 369, 381–382.

95. Reynolds, 17; Austin to Zimmerman, 25 Nov. 1930, Mary Austin Letters, Archive 255, T. M. Pearce Collection, Box 5, no. 26, UNM.

96. DPS, *Education of Spanish Speaking American Children*, 7–8; Manuel Gamio, *Mexican Immigration to the United States* (Chicago, 1930), 69; McNaughton, 86; *TTL* (June 1926), 279; Katherine Flenroot, Assistant Chief Children's Bureau, "Statement of Economic Conditions and Child Labor in Families Employed in the Beet Fields of Colorado" (11 Aug. 1933), 6, Costigan Collection, Box 49; Rice, 63; Bundy, 30; Bertram Mautner and W. Lewis Abbott, *Child Labor in Agriculture and Farm Life in the Arkansas Valley of Colorado* (New York, 1929), 107–108.

97. Fabiola Gilbert, Santa Fe County, 32, NMAES T876-18-1936, and see Conley and Apodaca, San Miguel County, 12, T876-21-1938; Larson, 15. DPS, *Education of Spanish Speaking American Children*, 8; Alice L. Thompson, "Winter in Truchas," *W&M* 12 (May 1935), 45; Leonard and Loomis, 31; Buhrmester, 37.

98. Alice Corbin Henderson, *Brothers of Light: The Penitentes of the Southwest* (1937, reprint ed., Santa Fe, 1977) 40, 43; Walter, 128, 133, 196–197; V. A Voorhies, M.D., Letters Home and Diary, Dixon, New Mexico, Feb. 1939–Sept 1941, MHL; Lorin Brown, "The Deep Village," 5–6, WPA files no. 220, Rio Arriba County History, NMSRCA; Johnson, "A Study of Certain Changes," 68 Leonard and Loomis, 49; Hurt, 110.

99. Jensen, "Canning," 365; Project 3B Food and Nutrition Specialist, 18 24, 27, NMAES T876-13-1932; Fabiola Gilbert, Rio Arriba and Santa Fe counties, 7–8, 13, T876-14-1932; Fabiola Gilbert, Santa Fe County, 3, 8, and R. F Gonzales, Mora County, 13, T876-17-1935; Vernita Conley, San Miguel County, 4, 15–16, T876-18-1936; Gilbert, 12–13, T876-20-1937. Goubaud-Carrera, 44–45; *Tewa Basin Study;* Leonard and Loomis, 28; Henderica Van Hine "Chacon Day School and Community Center," (1937), 2, in D. S. Spencer letters, MHL; Victoria Sanchez diary, 14 Nov. 1938, Teachers Diaries, Archive 306, Box 4, UNM; Watson diary, *ibid.,* Box 5.

100. Erna Fergusson, *Our Southwest* (New York, 1940), 248; Leonard, 134 Walter, 8, 248.

101. Hurt, 183; Ruth Laughlin Barker, *Caballeros* (New York, 1931), 367 John Sloan, 1925, quoted in James Mann Gaither, "A Return to the Village: A Study of Santa Fe and Taos, New Mexico, as Cultural Centers, 1900–1934" (Ph.D. dissertation, Univ. of Minnesota, 1957), 163; Mary Austin, "Rural Education in New Mexico," *Univ. of New Mexico Bulletin,* Training School Ser., 2 (Dec. 1931), 29; Mary Austin, quoted in Kern, 144–145.

102. Gaither, 1; Charles Briggs, *The Woodcarvers of Córdova, New Mexico Social Dimensions of An Artistic "Revival"* (Knoxville, 1980), 44; Spanish American Normal School, Sophomore English Class, "In the Land of Manana,"

mimeo (at UNM), including Jake Herrera, "Our Primitiveness," 32; Barker, 300; Arthur Campa, "Spanish Folklore in New Mexico," *NMSR* 9 (Nov. 1929), 23; Valdes, "Spanish Speaking People," chart II: "The Conflict of Cultures."

103. Societies (and their founding dates) involved in Hispanic arts include: Taos Society of Artists, 1915; Santa Fe Arts Club, 1920; Santa Fe Fiesta, 1919; Spanish Colonial Arts Society, 1926; Native Market, 1934. See Gaither, 110, 117; Briggs, 47, 48; Marta Weigle, "The First Twenty-five Years of the Spanish Colonial Arts Society," in Weigle, ed., *Hispanic Arts and Ethnohistory in the Southwest* (Santa Fe, 1983), 181–182; Alice Corbin Henderson quoted in P. A. F. Walter, "Art, Drama, and Literature in War Service," *NMHR* 1 (1926), 410.

104. E. Dana Johnson, *New Mexican* (Santa Fe), 29 July 1924, quoted in Gaither, 82; Austin quoted in Briggs, 46.

105. Alice Bullock, *Mountain Villages* (Santa Fe, 1981), 13; Goubaud-Carrera on Cundiyo; Armijo, Rio Arriba County, 25, NMAES T876-11-1928, and Armijo, Rio Arriba County, 33, T876-12-1929. Sarah Nestor, *The Native Market of the Spanish New Mexican Craftsmen, Santa Fe 1933–1940* (Santa Fe, 1978), 25; and see particularly Briggs, xiii, 51.

106. Helen Cramp McCrossen, "Native Crafts in New Mexico," *School Arts Magazine* 30 (March 1931), 458; Shop correspondence, death of Mary Austin, 1934, Data Blank vol. 31 American Art Annual, NMSRCA, for which I am indebted to Esther Stineman; Briggs, 52, 53, 64; Mary Austin, "Mexicans and New Mexico," *Graphic Survey* 66 (May 1931), 189–190; Mary Austin to Zimmerman, 25 Nov. 1930, folder 13, no. 26, Cyrus McCormick to Mary Austin, 4 Nov. 1930, no. 1; McCormick to Austin, 15 Oct. 1931, no. 3; and McCormick to Austin, 1932 re: unemployed CFI coal miners' rug weaving, no. 4 folder 21, Mary Austin Letters, Archive 255, Box 5, UNM.

107. See Donovan Senter, "Acculturation among New Mexican Villagers in Comparison to Adjustment Patterns of Other Spanish-Speaking Americans," *Rural Sociology* 10 (March 1945), 46 for one analysis of Spanish American classes in New Mexico. Weigle, "First Twenty Five Years," 194; Women of New Mexico, Archive 303, Box 1, biographical information; Gilbert, 85, 148–151, 158–161; Nina Otero, *Old Spain in Our Southwest* (New York, 1936), 39, 47, 110–111; Fabiola Gilbert, Santa Fe County, 19, NMAES T876-14-1932.

108. For example of innovations and "revivals" see Nestor, 8, 27–28, e.g., padded seats, beds, portable desks. Mary Wheelwright informed Mary Austin in 1927 of pitfalls in Austin's plans, as Chimayo weavers never had made their own dyes, and that spinning their own yarns would make the blankets too expensive, which leads one to question who was more "naive" in their selection of cross-cultural traits, the Anglos or the Hispanics. See Mary C. Wheelwright to Mary Austin, 22 Feb. 1927, Mary Austin Letters, Archive 255, Box 5, folder 21, no. 41, UNM.

109. Sewell to Austin, 12 Sept. 1933, Archive 255, Box 5, folder 23, no. 31, UNM. Trade and Industrial Education Teachers, Dept. of Vocational Educa-

tion, 1935–38, 1937–38, Gov. Tingley Papers, NMSRCA. Most were Hispanic. Richard Brown memo to Whory, 8 April 1937, RG119, NYA New Mexico 51, NA. Brice Sewell, "Problems of Vocational Education in New Mexico," Dept of Vocational Education 1931–33, and NM Extension Service, Report (1932), 238, Gov. Seligman Papers, NMSRCA. Fabiola Gilbert, 13, 15, NMAES, T876-14-1932, Ivie Jones, San Miguel County, 45, 48, T876-15-1933; Vernita Conley, San Miguel County, 26, 28, and Gilbert, 25, T876-20-1937. John Friedmann and Clyde Weaver, *Territory and Function: The Evolution of Regional Planning* (Berkeley, 1979), 4–5, 30–31, 35–37.

110. Weigle, 93; Brown et al., 19–29, 241–246; NM ERA, *The Bulletin* 2 (20 March 1935), 1; Briggs, 86; Nestor, 1, 12; F. A. Armijo, Rio Arriba County, 69, NMAES T876-21-1938; Fabiola Gilbert, 24, and A. S. Sandoval, Taos County, 15, T867-18-1936.

111. Tom Popejoy, Assistant State Director, NYA, to Aubrey Williams, Executive Director, NYA, Washington, 10 Oct. 1935, RG119 NYA New Mexico, 51, NA. A. G. Sandoval, Taos County, 28, NMAES T876-17-1935. Mildred Andrews, Director, Division of Women's and Professional Projects to Woodward, 2 July 1936, RG69 WPA, 661, NA. Brice H. Sewell, State Director of Vocational Education and Training, "A New Type of School," *NMSR* 15 (Oct. 1935), 49; NM ERA, *The Bulletin* 2 (May 1935), 18. Armijo, Rio Arriba County, 67, NMAES T876-21-1938.

112. Nestor, 17; Brown et al., 255. "A Renaissance of Dobe Construction," *WPA Worker* 1 (Aug. 1936), 7, and Alberta Redenbaugh, Marketing Specialist, Professional and Service Division, to Paul Shriver, 9 Aug. 1939, RG69 WPA Colorado 661, NA. *Youth Work under the NYA in Colorado* (March–June 1936), 5, RG119 NYA Colorado, 57, NA. Brown to Hal Blue, 8 Aug. 1936, and Blue, *An Analysis of the Work Project-Program* (Nov. 1936), RG119 NYA Colorado, 52, NA. Colorado Emergency Relief Administration, *Bulletin* 2 (April 1935); Charles Mulford, State Supervisor, "Contributions of the WPA Adult Education Program," in Hough, 14.

113. See, for example, SANS, which like other schools took advantage of the new funding sources and switched its focus to "the type of instruction in manual arts which will enable the young people to avail themselves of their native genius," i.e. rugweaving, wrought-iron work, agriculture, and home-making. SANS did offer courses in stenography and business administration. Catalogue of the Spanish American Normal School, 1938–39, Clara Olsen Papers, NMSRCA; Sewell to Seligman, 2 Aug. 1933, Dept. of Vocational Education 1931–33, Gov. Seligman Papers, NMSRCA. Mary Austin to Seligman, 6 Feb. 1931, Sewell to John De Huff, 1 Aug. 1933 (both brought to my notice by Esther Stineman) in L.R. and L.D. SANS file, *ibid.* Philip Larson, "State Educational Institutions," WPA Collection, 5.5.57 no. 16, NMHL.

114. Roskelley, 10.

115. Mr. Angel diary, Feb. 1938, Teachers Diaries, Archive 306, Box 5, UNM.

116. NM ERA, *Bulletin* 2 (May 1935), 16.

117. Bundy, 97; *Christian Science Monitor* cited by Nestor, 31; Armijo, 43, NMAES, T876-17-1935; 34, T876-18-1936; and 60, T876-19-1937. Goubaud-Carrera, 35.

118. Mary Austin, "Rural Education," 27; Conference on Educational Problems in the Southwest with Special Reference to the Educational Problems in Spanish Speaking Communities, *Committee Reports* (Santa Fe, 1943), 2 (at UNM).

119. *Tewa Basin Study,* 71, 87, 91, 112, 131; "WPA Art . . .", *El Palacio* (March–April, 1936), 93; Mela Sedillo Brewster, "A Practical Study of the Use of the Natural Vegetable Dyes in New Mexico," *Univ. of New Mexico Bulletin,* Training School Series, 2 (5 May 1937), 3.

120. Ivie Jones, 46, NMAES T876-15-1933. Grace Russell, "Summer Activities at a Plaza Station," *W&M* 16 (May 1939), 58; and see note 121.

121. Nestor, 5, 34, 39; Fabiola Gilbert, 32, NMAES T876-18-1936, Gilbert, 12, T876-20-1938. Fredrik Rummell to Mrs. McCrossen, 16 March 1931, Spanish Colonial Arts Society, Shop Correspondence, death of Frank Applegate—1931, at NMSRCA, for which I am indebted to Esther Stineman, and Correspondence, Crafts People, 1930–1931, in the same collection. Briggs, 50.

122. Maud A. Kinniburgh, "A School on the Tourist Trail," *W&M* 7 (May 1930), 53; Minnie Cook, "Summer in a Plaza Station," *W&M* 14 (May 1937), 52; Briggs, 90, 93; Goubaud-Carrera, 35; Kluckhohn and Strodtbeck, 193; Leonard and Loomis, 60.

123. Jamieson, 250, 253; Schwartz, *Seasonal Farm Labor,* 133; Denver Area Welfare Council, Inc., "The Spanish American Population in Denver, A Supplementary Report" (June 1952), 9, 25–26, 28. Gadd, 26; Pijoan and Roskelley, 3.

124. Kalervo Oberg, "Cultural Factors and Land-Use Planning in Cuba Valley, New Mexico," *Rural Sociology* 5 (Dec. 1940), 445.

125. Leonard and Loomis, 4, 6.

126. Nestor, 53; Leonard, 51; Kutsche, introduction, 12. John Burma, *Spanish-Speaking Groups in the United States* (Durham, 1954), 18.

Conclusion

1. David Snow, "Rural Hispanic Community Organization in New Mexico: An Historical Perspective," in Paul Kutsche, ed., *The Survival of Spanish American Villages,* Colorado College Studies no. 15 (Spring 1979), 52; see also Alice Reiche, "Spanish American Village Culture: Barrier to Assimilation or Integrative Force?" in Kutsche, 107–108.

2. On the migration of other peoples, see, for example, Tamara Hareven, "The Laborers of Manchester, New Hampshire 1912–1922: The Role of Family and Ethnicity in Adjustments to Industrial Life," *Labor History* 16 (Spring

1975), 249–265; William Thomas and Florian Znaniecki, *The Polish Peasant in Europe and America* (New York, 1927); Frank Thistlethwaite, "Migration from Europe Overseas in the Nineteenth and Twentieth Centuries," in Herbert Moller, ed., *Population Movements in Modern European History* (New York, 1964), 73–91; E. A. Wilkening et al., "Role of the Extended Family in Migration and Adaptation in Brazil," *Journal of Marriage and the Family* 30 (Nov. 1968), 689–695. On similar family economy strategies see Jean Quataert, "The Changing Nature of Family Work in Nineteenth Century: A Case of German Textiles," paper at the German Historical Institute, London, 1984.

3. Elizabeth Johnson, *Welfare of Families of Sugar Beet Laborers,* U.S. Dept. of Labor, Children's Bureau Publication no. 247 (Washington, D.C., 1939), 53.

4. See Maxine Baca Zinn, "Mexican-American Women in the Social Sciences," *Signs* 8 (Winter 1982), 259–272 for a review of this literature.

Bibliography

Dissatisfied with one-site studies of migratory people and with the tendency of written histories of immigrants to focus on ethnic minorities as "uprooted," I embarked somewhat naively on a regional study of a people who in a historical sense were virtually invisible. I quickly discovered both the vastness and the limits of material, and the importance of interviews. The sources on which community studies rely, such as newspapers, marriage records, deed records, manuscript and school censuses, and criminal records, multiplied alarmingly, so I chose three counties—Weld, Las Animas, and Rio Arriba—and focused on them. In addition, many studies of Hispanic beetworkers and urban dwellers were undertaken in the 1920s and 1930s both for government and private agencies and for advanced degrees, and these provided as much data as the more typical community records. More qualitative archival evidence, with the exception of the extraordinary missionary records, was found an item or two at a time, by digging through various collections and court cases. On the other hand, I found modern secondary sources almost totally lacking. It quickly became apparent that I would have to uncover the history not simply of the women, but of the whole group, and as I conducted my research, the impossibility of making sense of one sex's history without that of the other also became apparent. As I revised my views on village women and the dynamic of this intercultural arena, I turned to sociological studies of women from similar economies across the globe and across history for confirmation. Community studies of Chicanos in other locations also provided useful comparisons as well as occasional methodological guides.

307

Archival Sources

Allison School. Santa Fe, NM. Scholarship List and Student Lists 1900–1904. MHL.

American Red Cross, Santa Fe Chapter. Annual Reports 1932–67; Chapter Reports 1923–52. NMSRCA.

Baer Collection, WHC.

Barber, Ruth, compiler. "Presbyterian Medical Work in New Mexico." MHL.

————. Vertical Files. MHL.

Bear Canyon Coal Company. Collection 44. Boxes 10 and 11. CHS.

Bent and St. Vrain Collection. WHC.

Bergere, Family Collection. Nina Otero-Warren Papers. NMSRCA.

E. Boyd Collection. NMSRCA.

Brandt, Lucas. Collection 991. CHS.

C. de Baca, Fabiola. Scrapbook. NMSRCA.

Callon, Milton W. Papers. Boxes 4–8. DPL.

Catron, Thomas Benton. Archive 29. Boxes 210: 4, 5, 7, 8, 10; 408: 1, 4; 502: 1; and 901: 1. UNM.

Colorado Board of Charities and Corrections. Boxes 26922, 66918, 66919, 66922–924, 66927, 66936, 66945. CSA.

Colorado Coal Project. Two films and numerous transcripts. Boulder, Colo.

Colorado Council of Churches. Boxes 1, 2. WHC.

Colorado Governor's Papers. Governor Johnson. Boxes 26888, 26901, 26903, 26915, 26916, CSA.

Colorado in World War One. Boxes 1, 2, 12, 13, 17–20, 47. WHC.

Colorado Industrial Commission. Referees' Findings and Awards, Boxes 19168, 19173, and Commissioners' Findings and Awards, Boxes 19141, 19149. CSA.

Colorado Nurses Association. Collection 146. CHS.

Colorado State Federation of Labor Collection. Boxes 1, 4, 19–22. WHC.

Colorado State Federation of Women's Clubs Collection. WHC.

Community Relations Commission Papers. Boxes 2, 6. DPL.

Cook, Miss Minnie. "Loma Verde Camp." 25 May 1979. MHL.

Costigan, Edward. Collection. Boxes 36, 37, 48, 49, 53. WHC.

Darley Family Collections. Boxes 3, 7. WHC.

DeBusk, Samuel. Papers. Boxes 1, 5. WHC.

Denver Public Library. Clipping Files. DPL.

Dickey, Louretta, compiler. "The Presbyterian Church in New Mexico." MHL.

Dillon, Governor Richard C. Papers. NMSRCA.

Duran, J. *Libro de la Escuela Dominical.* Las Notas de la Sesion de la Iglesia Segunda Presbiteriana (Hispanola) de Santa Fe. MHL.

East, J. H. Collection. 219. CHS.

Eastburn Smith Papers. NMSRCA.

Embudo Hospital. Vertical File. MHL.

Fergusson, Erna. Archive 45. Boxes 1, 2, 7. UNM.

G. G. Smith Memorial Presbyterian Church. Truchas, NM. Minitas y Registro de los Miembros de la Iglesia Presbiteriana 1903–1931. MHL.

Great Western Sugar Company Papers. Boxes 4, 16A, and uncatalogued material. WHC.

————. Property Records. Denver Office, Great Western Sugar Company. Sugar Building. Denver, Colo.

Hall's Peak. Vertical Files, MHL.

Hannett, Governor Arthur T. Papers. NMSRCA.

Hayden, Charles. Papers. WHC.

Hinkle, Governor James F. Papers. NMSRCA.

History Files: 45, 69, 76, 120. NMSRCA.

Hockenhull, Governor. Papers. NMSRCA.

Johnson, J. G. Papers. WHC.

Larrazolo, Governor Octaviano A. Papers. NMSRCA.

Las Animas County. County Court Indexes. District Court Office, Trinidad, Colo.

————. District Court Indexes. Civil and Criminal, vols. 1–4. District Court Office, Trinidad, Colo.

————. Marriage Registers. Las Animas County Courthouse, Trinidad, Colo.

————. School Records. Boxes 13066, 13067, 13099–13104, 13106, and others for school census. CSA.

Lawrence, John. Diary. WHC.

Lindsey, Benjamin. Collection 389. CHS.

Lindsey, Governor Washington E. Papers. NMSRCA.

Long, Dr. Margaret. Collection 730. CHS.

Lopez, Elfido, Sr. Collection 813. CHS.

McDonald, Governor Wm. C. Papers. NMSRCA.

McGrath, Maria Davies. Papers. DPL.

McKittrick, Margaret. Collection. NMSRCA.

Mechem, Governor Merritt C. Papers. NMSRCA.

Meredith, Ellis. Collecton 427. Boxes 1, 2. CHS.

Mexican-Americans in Colorado Colletion. WHC.

Meyer, Erwin. Collection. Smss. WHC.

Misc. Records, Politics, and Political Issues. NMSRCA.

Moloney, A. I. (Mrs.). Collection. WHC.

Mora County Records. 1917–18, Council of Defense. Correspondence. NMSRCA.

National Sugar Manufacturing Company Collection. Box 1. CHS.

New Mexico. Department of Education Records. County Reports, Rio Arriba County, 1924–37; and Annual Report of the County Superintendents, vol. 4. NMSRCA.

New Mexico Penitentiary Records. Reels 1, 3. NMSRCA.

Northern Colorado Coal Company, Inc. Collection 467. Boxes 1, 2. CHS.

Norton, Leonard S. Collection. WHC.

Olsen, Clara. Papers. NMSRCA.

Ortiz y Pino Collection. Archive 336. UNM.

Otero Collection. Archive 21. Boxes 1, 2, 4.UNM.

Ownbey, James A. Collection. Boxes 15, 26. WHC.

Paramount Literary Society. Minutes. El Rito (Chacon), NM. 1922–29. MHL.

Pearce, T. M. Collector. Archive 255. Box 5 (Mary Austin letters). UNM.

Poor Reports. Office of the Secretary of State. Boxes 9694A, 9695A, B. CSA.

Presbyterian Historical Society. H5 Files (Personal). PHS.

Prince, L. Bradford. Collection. NMSRCA.

Radical Organizations: International Labor Defense. Collection 512. CHS.

Read Collection. NMSRCA.

Renehan Gilbert Papers. NMSRCA.

Rio Arriba County. Board of County Commissioners: Teachers Contracts, School Census, and Reports. NMSRCA.

Rio Arriba County Educational Association. Archive 73. UNM.

Rio Arriba County Marriage Records: Licenses and Certificates. Index. Rio Arriba County Courthouse, Tierra Amarilla, N.M.

Rio Arriba County Records. Applications for Licenses, 1884–1925. NMSRCA.

———. Criminal and Civil Docket. Vols. D, E; Cases 488, 649, 650, 662, 705; Reception Book 1887–1912; and Property Transfers 1899–1900. NMSRCA.

———. Juez de Paz Record Book, Abiquiu (Judge J. Duran). NMSRCA.

———. Jury Lists. 1904–21. NMSRCA.

———. List of Marriages. 1902–04. NMSRCA.

———. Partido Contracts. NMSRCA.

Rio Arriba County Warranty Deed Record. Vol. 17. Rio Arriba County Courthouse, Tierra Amarilla, N.M.

El Rito Presbyterian Church, Chacon, N.M. El Rito Treasury 1917–22, and 1922–40. MHL.

———. Missionary Society of Women of Chacon, N.M. Minutes. MHL.

———. Sunday School. 1927–52. MHL.

Roche, Josephine. Papers. Boxes 7–10, 12, 15–17. WHC.

Rocky Mountain Fuel Company. Papers. Boxes 2, 4, 7, 9, 13. WHC.

Rose, Dr. Edward. Collection. Box 1. WHC.

Ross, Calvin. Archive 218. Box 4. UNM.

Ruibal, Joe. Collection. Greeley Municipal Museum. Greeley, Colo.

St. Mary's School. Collection 553. CHS.

Sants Fe Public Library. Clipping and pamphlet file. Santa Fe, NM.

Seligman, Governor Arthur. Papers. NMSRCA.

Shellabarger Papers. DPL.

Spanish Colonial Arts Society Collection. NMSRCA.

Spencer, Dorothy Sherwin. "Letters from Chacon, N.M." MHL.

Sporleder, Lousi Bernhardt. Papers. Boxes 1–5. DPL.

Stewart, Omer. Collection. Box 26. WHC.

Taylor, Paul. Papers. Colorado, Utah, and Wyoming Folder. C-S Garcia. Publisher of El Faro, Trinidad. Bancroft Library.

Territorial Archives of New Mexico. NMSRCA.

Tingley, Govr. C. Papers. NMSRCA.

U.S. Census. Manuscript Schedules. Rio Arriba County, N.M., and Las Animas County, Colo., 1880, 1900, and 1910; and Weld County, Colo., 1910.

U.S. Children's Bureau. Correspondence and Survey Materials relating to Bulletins nos. 115, 247. Record Group 102. NA.

U.S. Department of Agriculture. Agricultural Adjustment Administration. Subject Correspondence. Sugar. 1933–38 and General Correspondence, Alphabetical. Record Group 145. NA.

————. Soil Conservation Service, Region 8, Albuquerque, NM. Hugh C. Calkins, Regional Conservator. "Rural Rehabilitation in New Mexico." RB no. 50, C.E.S. no. 23. Dec. 1935. NMSRCA.

————. ————. "San Miguel County Villages." RB no. 51, C.E.S. 24 Feb. 1938. NMSRCA.

————. ————. "Village Dependence on Migratory Labor in the Upper Rio Grande Area." RB no. 47, C.E.S. 20 July 1937. NMSRCA.

(For U.S.D.A. 1930s surveys of northern New Mexico see the Eastburn Smith Papers, NMSCRA.)

U.S. Federal Mediation and Conciliation Service. Record Group 280. File 195-705. NA.

U.S. Immigration and Naturalization Service. Record Group 85. 55739/674, Movement of Mexican Indigents across U.S. Border 1931–32; 55639/616, Comments from the Public for and against Mexican 1929–32. NA.

U.S. National Youth Administration. Administrative Correspondence with State and Territorial Directors; Adminsitration Projects File; and Misc. Publications. Record Group 119. Files 51, 52, 330. NA.

U.S. Office of War Information, Washington, D.C. Microfilm Ser. 457–458, 461, 463, 472. filmed 6/1943 from Farm Security Administration photos taken 1938–40. WHC.

U.S. Secretary of Agriculture. General Correspondence. Sugar. 1935–38. Record Group 16. NA.

U.S. State Department. Correspondence. Record Group 59. File 311.1215/79 to /88. NA.

U.S. Works Progress Administration. State Series for New Mexico and Colorado. Record Group 69. NA.

University of New Mexico. Department of Education. Archive 306. Teachers' "Diaries" from San Jose Experiment and Nambé Community Schools. 1935–41. Boxes 1–5. UNM.

Victor American Fuel Company. Payroll Colorado Mines, 1929. In Colorado

Department of Natural Resources, Division of Mines. Chief Coal Mine Inspector. Box 19141 vol. 18269. Book 193. CSA.

Vigil Family Collection. Boxes 1, 2. WHC.

Voorhies, V. A. Letters Home from Dixon, N.M., and Diary. Feb. 1939–Sept. 1941. MHL.

Weld County. County Court Records, 1915–44. Index. District Court and County Court, 1911–23. Index. County Clerk's Office. Greeley, Colo.

———. County Court Records, 1917–37. Weld County courthouse. Greeley, Colo.

———. District Court Records, 1927–31. CSA.

———. Marriage Register, vol. 2, 1912–40; and Marriage Certificate. Clerk and Recorder's Office, Civic Center. Greeley, Colo.

———. School Census, Superintendent's Records, Educational Directories, School District Officers, Record Cards, and other school records. CSA.

Western Federation of Miners Papers (and International Mine Mill and Smelters Union). Organizers' Accounts and Executive Board Minutes. WHC.

Wilson, Francis. Papers. NMSRCA.

Women in New Mexico. Vertical Files. UNM.

Women of New Mexico. 1598–1976. Archive 303. Boxes 1, 2. UNM.

Women's Board of Home Missions. Inbound Correspondence. Record Group 51. Boxes 2, 3. PHS.

Women's Christian Temperance Union. Box 6. WHC.

Women's Christian Union. Silverton, Colo. Minutes. 1914–29. DPL.

Woodward, Dorothy. Collection. NMSRCA.

Wootton Land and Fuel Company. Collection 712. CHS.

Works Progress Administration. Colorado. Collection 689. CHS.

———. New Mexico. *The Reporter.* April 1936. in the E. Boyd Collection. NMSRCA.

———. Writers' Project. New Mexico. NMNL.

———. Writers' Project. New Mexico. NMSRCA.

Y.W.C.A. Records, Basement, Y.W.C.A., Denver, Colo.

Printed Sources

Abkemeier, Maryann, and Laura Robertson. *Stand against the Wind. A Biographical Sketchbook of New Mexico Women.* Albuquerque: Wahili Enterprises, 1977.

Acuña, Rodolfo. *Occupied America: The Chicano's Struggle Toward Liberation.* San Francisco: Canfield Press, 1972.

———. *Occupied America: A History of Chicanos.* 2d. ed. New York: Harper & Row, 1981.

Adams State Normal School. *Record of the First Year of Adams State Normal*

School, and Annuals 1925–37. (From 1931–37 the yearbook's title was *El Conquistador.*) (Adams State College Archives)

Agnew, Edith, et al., "Spanish Speaking Work in the Southwest." Albuquerque: Menaul Historical Library, n.d.

Agnew, Edith J., and Ruth K. Barber, "The Unique Presbyterian School System of New Mexico." *Journal of Presbyterian History* 49 (Fall 1971): 197–221.

Ahlstrom, Sydney E. *A Religious History of the American People.* vol. 2. Garden City, N.Y.: Image Books, 1975.

Allen, James B. *The Company Town in the American West.* Norman, Okla.: Univ. of Oklahoma Press, 1966.

Alvarado, Ernestine. "Mexican Immigration to the United States." *Proceedings of the National Conference of Social Work.* New Orleans. April 1920: 479–480.

Álvarez, Jose Hernandez. "A Demographic Profile of the Mexican Immigration to the United States, 1910–1950." *Journal of Inter-American Studies* 7 (July 1966): 471–496.

Alvarez, Salvador. "Mexican American Community Organizations." *El Grito* 4 (Spring 1971): 68–77.

American Civil Liberties Union. "The War on the Colorado Miners." New York: n.d. [1928] (in Roche Collection, WHC)

American Federation of Labor. *Report of Proceedings of the Annual Convention.* Washington, D.C.: Law Reporter Printing Co., 1919–39.

Anderson, Robert A. "A Study of Vocational Opportunities in Albuquerque, New Mexico." *Research* 2 (June 1938): 59–63.

Arellano, Anselmo F., ed. *La Tierra Amarilla: The People of the Chama Valley.* Tierra Amarilla: Chama Valley Independent Schools, District 19, 1978.

Arrington, Leonard J. *Beet Sugar in the West: A History of the Utah-Idaho Sugar Company, 1891–1966.* Seattle: Univ. of Washington Press, 1966.

————. *The Changing Economic Structure of the Mountain West 1850–1950.* Logan: Utah State Univ. Press, 1963.

Aspects of the Mexican Experience. New York: Arno Press, 1976.

Atkins, Carolyn. *The Allison-James Picture Book 1866–1959.* Albuquerque: Menaul Historical Library of the Southwest, 1983.

————, ed. *Los Tres Campos—The Three Fields: A History of Protestant Evangelists and Presbyterians in Chimayó, Córdova and Truchas, New Mexico.* Albuquerque: Menaul Historical Library of the Southwest, 1978.

Atkins, James. *Human Relations in Colorado—A Historical Record.* Denver: Colorado Department of Education, Division of Elementary and Secondary Education, Office of Instructional Services, 1968. (at the Greeley Municipal Museum)

Austin, Mary. "Rural Education in New Mexico." *Univ. of New Mexico Bulletin,* Training School Series, 2 (Dec. 1931).

Baca, Emilie M. "Pachita." *The Family* 8 (Feb. 1942): 178–187.

Bamford, Edwin F. "The Mexican Casual Problem in the Southwest." *Journal of Applied Sociology.* 8 (May–June 1924): 363–371.

Banner, Roy, and Arthur Maes. "The Justice of Peace Courts of New Mexico with Particular Emphasis on Those of Bernalillo County." *Research* (Univ. of New Mexico) 1 (April 1937): 99–112.

Barber, Ruth K., and Edith J. Agnew. *Sowers Went Forth: The Story of Presbyterian Missions in New Mexico and Southern Colorado.* Albuquerque: Menaul Historical Library, 1981.

Barker, Ruth Laughlin. *Caballeros.* New York: D. Appleton, 1931.

Berrera, Mario. *Race and Class in the Southwest.* Notre Dame: Univ. of Notre Dame, 1979.

————, Carlos Muñoz, and Charles Ornelas, "The Barrio as an Internal Colony." In F. Chris Garcia, ed., *La Causa Política: A Chicano Politics Reader,* pp. 281–301. Notre Dame: Univ. of Notre Dame Press, 1974.

Barton, Josef J. *Peasants and Strangers: Italians, Rumanians and Slovaks in an American City, 1890–1950.* Cambridge, Mass.: Harvard Univ. Press, 1975.

Batchen, Lou Sage. "La Curandera." *El Palacio* 18 (Spring 1975): 20–25.

Beck, Warren A., and Ynez D. Haase. *Historical Atlas of New Mexico.* Norman: Univ. of Oklahoma Press, 1969.

Beecher, Catharine. *The Duty of American Women to Their Country.* New York: Harper and Brothers, 1845.

————. *Educational Reminiscences and Suggestions.* New York: J. B. Ford and Company, 1847.

Bell, Colin, and Howard Newby. *Community Studies: An Introduction to the Sociology of the Local Community.* New York: Praeger, 1972.

Berkhofer, Robert F. *Salvation and the Savage: An Analysis of Protestant Missions and American Indian Response, 1787–1862.* New York: Atheneum, 1972.

Bernhardt, Joshua. *Government Control of Sugar in the United States during the War of 1917–1918 and the Transition to Competitive Conditions.* 1921. Reprinted from *Quarterly Journal of Economics* 33 (Aug. 1919) and 34 (Aug. 1920).

Blackwelder, Julia Kirk. "Women in the Workforce: Atlanta, New Orleans, and San Antonio, 1920–1940." *Journal of Urban History* 4 (May 1978): 331–358.

————. *Women of the Depression: Caste and Culture in San Antonio, 1929–1939.* College Station: Texas A & M Univ. Press, 1984.

Blum, John Morton. *Woodrow Wilson and the Politics of Morality.* Boston: Little, Brown, 1956.

Bodnar, John. *Immigration and Industrialization: Ethnicity in an American Mill Town, 1970–1940.* Pittsburgh: Univ. of Pittsgurgh Press, 1977.

————. *The Transplanted: A History of Immigrants in Urban America.* Bloomington: Indiana Univ. Press, 1985.

Bogardus, Emory S. *Essentials of Americanization.* 3rd rev. ed. Los Angeles: Univ. of Southern California Press, 1923.

————. *Immigration and Race Attitudes.* Boston: D.C. Heath, 1928.

————. "The Mexican Immigrant." *Journal of Applied Sociology* 11 (May–June 1928): 470–488.

————. *The Mexican in the United States.* School of Research Studies no. 5. Los Angeles: Univ. of Southern California Press, 1934.

————. "Second Generation Mexicans." *Sociology and Social Research* 13 (Jan.–Feb. 1929): 276–283.

Bohme, Frederick G. "The Italians in New Mexico." *NMHR* 34 (April 1959): 98–116.

Bond, Frank, "Memoirs of Forty Years in New Mexico." *NMHR* 21 (Oct. 1946): 341–349.

Brackenridge, R. Douglas, and Francisco O. Garcia-Treto. *Iglesia Presbiteriana: A History of Presbyterians and Mexican Americans in the Southwest.* San Antonio: Trinity Univ. Press, 1974.

Brenner, Anita, *The Wind That Swept Mexico.* New York: Harper and Brothers, 1943.

Bresette, Linna E. *Mexicans in the United States: A Report of a Brief Survey.* Washington, D.C.: National Catholic Welfare Conference, n.d. [1929]. Reprinted in *Church Views of the Mexican American.* New York: Arno Press, 1974.

Brewster, Mela Sedillo. "A Practical Study of the Use of the Natural Vegetable Dyes in New Mexico." *The Univ. of New Mexico Bulletin,* Training School Series, 2 (May 1937).

Briggs, Charles L. *The Woodcarvers of Córdova, New Mexico: Social Dimensions of an Artistic 'Revival'.* Knoxville: Univ. of Tennessee Press, 1980.

Broadbent, Elizabeth. *The Distribution of Mexican Populations in the United States.* 1941. Reprint ed. San Francisco: R & E Research Associates, 1972.

Brown, Rev. Edwin R. "The Challenge of Mexican Immigration." *The Missionary Review of the World* 49 (March 1926): 192–196.

Brown, Lorin. (Lorenzo de Cordova). *Echoes of the Flute.* Santa Fe: Ancient City Press, 1972.

————, with Charles L. Briggs and Marta Weigle. *Hispanic Folklife of New Mexico.* Lorin W. Brown Federal Writers' Project Manuscripts. Albuquerque: Univ. of New Mexico Press, 1978.

Brown, Sara A., assisted by Robie O. Sargent and Clara B. Armentrout. *Children Working the Sugar Beet Fields of Certain Districts of the South Platte Valley, Colorado.* New York: National Child Labor Committee, 1925.

————. "Denver and Farm Labor Families." New York: National Child Labor Committee Publication no. 328 [1925].

Bryant, Keith L, Jr. "The Atchison, Topeka and Santa Fe Railway and the Development of the Taos and Santa Fe Art Colonies." *WHQ* 9 (1978): 437–453.

Buck, Carl E. *Health Survey of the State of New Mexico.* Santa Fe: New Mexican Publishing, n.d [c. 1938].

Bullock, Alice. *Mountain Villages.* Rev. ed. Santa Fe: Sunstone Press, 1981.

Burma, John H., ed. *Mexican Americans in the United States: A Reader.* Cambridge, Mass.: Schenkman Publishing, 1970.

————. *Spanish-Speaking Groups in the United States.* Durham: Duke Univ. Press, 1954.

Burnett, Hugh, and Evelyn Burnett. "Madrid Plaza." *Colorado Magazine* 42 (Summer 1965): 224–237.

Burran, James A. "Prohibition in New Mexico, 1917." *NMHR* 48 (April 1973); 133–149.

Buss, Fran Leeper. *La Partera: Story of a Midwife.* Ann Arbor: Univ. of Michigan Press, 1980.

Cabello-Argandoña, Roberto, and Juan Gómez-Quiñones. *The Chicana: A Comprehensive Bibliographic Study.* Los Angeles: Chicano Studies Center. Univ. of California, 1975.

Callaway, R. P., and P. W. Cockerill. "Tax Delinquency of Rural Real Estate in New Mexico." Las Cruces: Agricultural Experiment Station of the New Mexico College of Agriculture and Mechanic Arts Bulletin no. 234, Dec. 1935.

Calvin, Ross. "The People of New Mexico." In *The Population of New Mexico,* pp. 20–38. Albuquerque: Division of Research, Department of Government, Univ. of New Mexico, June 1947.

Camarillo, Albert. *Chicanos in a Changing Society: From Mexican Pueblos to American Barrios in Santa Barbara and Southern California, 1848–1930.* Cambridge, Mass.: Harvard Univ. Press, 1979.

————. "Observations on the 'New' Chicano History: Historiography of the 1970s." Working Paper Ser. no. 1. Stanford Univ.: Stanford Center for Chicano Research, Jan. 1984.

Camp and Plant (Colorado Fuel and Iron Company). vols. 1–5.

Campa, Arthur L. *Hispanic Culture in the Southwest.* Norman: Univ. of Oklahoma Press, 1979.

————. "Piñon as an Economic and Social Factor." *New Mexico Business Review* 1 (1932): 144–147.

Cantor, Milton, and Bruce Laurie, eds. *Class, Sex and the Woman Worker.* Westport, Conn.: Greenwood Press, 1977.

Carlson, Alvar. "El Rancho and Vadito: Spanish Settlements on Indian Lands." *El Palacio* 85 (Spring 1979): 29–39.

————. "New Mexico's Sheep Industry, 1850–1900: Its Role in the History of the Territory." *NMHR* 44 (Jan. 1969); 25–50.

Caroli, Betty Boyd, et al., eds. *The Italian Immigrant Woman in North America.* Toronto: Proceedings of the Tenth Annual Conference of the American Italian Historical Association, 1978.

Carter, Genevieve Wiley. "Juvenile Delinquency in Bernalillo County." *Research* (Univ. of New Mexico) 1 (Dec. 1936): 45–69.

Casillas, Mike. "Mexican Labor Militancy in the United States: 1896–1915." *Southwest Economy and Society* 4 (Fall 1978): 31–42.

Catholic Charities of the Diocese of Denver. *Annual Report.* Denver, 1927–37. (at DPL)

Chávez, John R. *The Lost Land: The Chicano Image of the Southwest.* Albuquerque: Univ. of New Mexico Press, 1984.

The Church at Home and Abroad. 1895.

Church Views of the Mexican American. New York: Arno Press, 1974.

Clark, Victor, S. *Mexican Labor in the United States.* United States Labor Bureau Bulletin no. 78, Sept. 1908.

Clopper, Edward N., and Lewis W. Hine. *Chile Labor in the Sugar Beet Fields of Colorado.* New York: National Child Labor Committee Pamphlet no. 259, March 1916.

Cockerill, P. W., and R. P. Callaway. "Economics of the Production and Marketing of Apples in New Mexico." Las Cruces: Agricultural Experiment Station, New Mexico College of Agriculture and Mechanic Arts, Bulletin no. 242, June 1936.

Coen, B. F., Wilbur E. Skinner, and Dorothy Leach. *Children Working on Farms in Certain Sections of Northern Colorado.* Fort Collins: Colorado Agricultural College Bulletin no. 2, Nov. 1926.

Cohen, Lizabeth A. "Embellishing a Life of Labor: An Interpretation of the Material Culture of American Working Class Homes 1885–1915." *Journal of American Culture* 3 (Winter 1980): 752–775.

Coles, Robert. *The Old Ones of New Mexico.* Albuquerque: Univ. of New Mexico Press, 1973.

Colorado Adjutant-General's Office. *The Military Occupation of the Coal Strike Zone of Colorado by the Colorado National Guard 1913–1914.* Denver: Smith-Brooks Printing, n.d. [1914].

Colorado. Bureau of Labor Statistics. *Biennial Report.* 1901–37.

————. Bureau of Mines. *Report.* 1901–13.

————. Industrial Commission. *Report.* 1919–38. (in CSFL Papers)

————. *Social Welfare in Colorado. Bulletin on Social Statistics* 2 (July–Sept. 1935): 19–20.

————. State Bureau of Child and Animal Protection. *Biennial Report.* 1901–30.

————. State Inspector of Coal Mines. *Annual Report.* 1884–1937.

Colorado Emergency Relief Administration. *Bulletin* 2 (April 1935).

Colorado Fuel and Iron Company. *Annual Report of the Sociological Department.* Denver. 1901–6.

————. Medical and Sociological Departments. *Bulletin, Sanitary and Sociological* 2 (1904).

————. *Report of the Medical and Sociological Departments of the Colorado Fuel and Iron Company.* 1904–6, 1909–10.

Colorado Latin American Personalities. Denver: n.p., 1959.

Colorado State Business Directory. vols. 31, 46, 53, 62.

Conference on Educational Problems in the Southwest with Special Reference to the Educational Problems in Spanish Speaking Communities. *Committee Reports.* Santa Fe, Aug. 1943. (at UNM)

————. *Recent Educational and Community Experiments and Projects in New Mexico Affecting the Spanish-Speaking Population.* Santa Fe, Aug. 1943. (UNM)

Cordova, Andrew R. "The Taylor Grazing Act." *New Mexico Business Review* 4 (1935): 193–201.

Corwin, Arthur F., ed. *Immigrants—and Immigrants.* Westport, Conn.: Greenwood Press, 1978.

————. "Mexican-American History: An Assessment." *PHR* 42 (Aug. 1973): 269–308.

Cott, Nancy F., and Elizabeth Pleck, eds. *A Heritage of Her Own: Toward a New Social History of American Women.* New York: Simon and Schuster, 1979.

Craig, Rev. Robert M. *Our Mexicans.* New York: Home Missions of the Presbyterian Church in the U.S.A., 1904.

Crowell, Katharine R. *Our Mexican Mission Schools.* New York: Woman's Board of Home Missions of the Presbyterian Church in the U.S.A., n.d. [1913 or 1914].

Daggett, Eleanor. *Chama New Mexico.* Chama: A Nature Trek Publication, 1973.

Davis, James. "Colorado under the Klan." *Colorado Magazine* 42 (Spring 1965): 93–108.

Dawley, Alan. *Class and Community: The Industrial Revolution in Lynn.* Cambridge, Mass.: Harvard Univ. Press, 1976.

deBuys, William. *Enchantment and Exploitation: The Life and Hard Times of a New Mexico Mountain Range.* Albuquerque: Univ. of New Mexico Press, 1985.

————. "Fractions of Justice: A Legal and Social History of the Las Trampas Land Grant, New Mexico." *NMHR* 56 (Jan. 1981): 71–97.

Decker, Peter. *Fortunes and Failures: White Collar Mobility in Nineteenth-Century San Francisco.* Cambridge, Mass.: Harvard Univ. Press, 1978.

DeHuff, Elizabeth Willis. "People of the Soil." *New Mexico* 18 (June 1940): 26–27, 44, 46, 48.

De León, Arnoldo. *The Tejano Community, 1836–1900.* Albuquerque: Univ. of New Mexico Press, 1982.

Denver Area Welfare Council, Inc. "A Report on the House of Neighborly Service of Brighton, Colorado." July 1953. (at DPL)

————. "The Spanish American Population of Denver." July, 1950. (at DPL)

Denver Council of Social Agencies. *Social Welfare in Denver Yesterday Today—Tomorrow. Second City-Wide Conference on Denver's Social Problems.* May 1939.

Denver Public Schools. *Annual School Superintendent's Report;* and *Annual Statistical Report.* 1898–1932, 1935–38.

————. Course of Study Monograph. *The Education of Spanish-Speaking American Children.* Denver: Department of Research and Curriculum, April 1937, (at the Denver Public Schools Professional Library)

————. Adeline Jesse, "Report on Children from Spanish-Speaking Homes." Denver Public Schools Bulletin no. 49, May 1935. (bound with above)

Denver Unity Council. "The Spanish-Speaking Population of Denver—Housing Employment Health Recreation Education." Denver, April 1946. (at DPL)

Dickerson, Roy E. "Some Suggestive Problems in the Americanization of Mexicans." *Pedagogical Seminary* 26 (Sept. 1919): 288–297.

Dinwoodie, D.H. "Deportation: the Immigration Service and the Chicano Labor Movement in the 1930s." *NMHR* 52 (April 1977): 193–206.

————. "Indians, Hispanos, and Land Reform: A New Deal Struggle in New Mexico." *WHQ* 17 (July 1986): 291–323.

Dorsett, Lyle W. *The Queen City: A History of Denver.* Boulder: Pruett Publishing, 1977.

Douglas, Ann. *The Feminization of American Culture.* New York: Avon Books, 1977.

Douglas, Harlan Paul. *From Survey to Service.* New York: Council of Women for Home Missions and Missionary Education Movement, 1921.

Doyle, Sherman H. *Presbyterian Home Missions.* New York: Presbyterian Board of Home Missions, 1905.

Dupré, Georges, and Pierre Philippe Rey. "Reflections on the Relevance of a Theory of the History of Exchange." In David Seddon, ed., *Relations of Production: Marxist Approaches to Anthropology.* Helen Lackner, trans. Pp. 171–208. London: Frank Cass and Company, 1978.

Eastman, Clyde. "Assessing Cultural Change in North Central New Mexico." Agricultural Experiment Station Bulletin no. 592, Jan. 1971.

Eastman, Fred. *Unfinished Business of the Presbyterian Church in America.* Philadelphia: Westminster Press, 1921.

Echevarría, Evelio, and José Otero, eds. *Hispanic Colorado: Four Centuries' History and Heritage.* Fort Collins: Centennial Publications, 1976.

Edwards, Richard C., Michael Reich, and David M. Gordon, eds. *Labor Market Segmentation.* Lexington, Mass.: D. C. Heath, 1975.

Eklund, Monica. "Massacre at Ludlow." *Southwest Economy and Society* 4 (Fall 1978): 21–29.

Elsasser, Nan, Kyle Mackenzie, and Yvonne Tixier y Vigil. *Las Mujeres: Con-*

versations from a Hispanic Community. Old Westbury, N.Y.: Feminist Press, 1979.

Esquibel, Alfonso. *Vaquero to Dominic: The Nine Lives of Alfonso Esquibel* (as told to J. A. Schufle). Santa Fe: Rydal Press, 1978.

Ewen, Elizabeth. "City Lights: Immigrant Women and the Rise of the Movies." *Signs* 5 (Spring Supplement 1980): S45–66.

Fairbank, John K., ed. *The Missionary Enterprise in China and America.* Cambridge, Mass.: Harvard Univ. Press, 1974.

Farrell, Grace A. "Homemaking with the 'Other Half' Along Our International Border." *Journal of Home Economics* 21 (June 1929): 413–418.

Fergusson, Erna. *Our Southwest.* New York: Knopf, 1940.

Fergusson, Harvey. "Out Where the Bureaucracy Begins." *Nation* 121 (22 July 1925): 112–114.

First City Conference on Denver's Social Problems. *Report.* June 1928. (at DPL)

Folks, Homer. *Changes and Trends in Child Labor and Its Control.* New York: National Child Labor Committee Publication no. 375, 1938.

Friedman, John and Clyde Weaver. *Territory and Function: The Evolution of Regional Planning.* Berkeley: Univ. of California Press, 1979.

Fuller, Roden. "Occupations of the Mexican-Born Population of Texas, New Mexico and Arizona, 1900–1920." *Journal of the American Statistical Association* 23 (March 1928): 64–67.

Galarza, Ernest. "Life in the United States for Mexican People: Out of the Experience of a Mexican." *Proceedings of the National Conference of Social Work.* San Francisco, June–July 1929: 531–538.

Gallegos y Chavez, Ester. "The Northern New Mexican Woman: A Changing Silhouette." In Arnulfo D. Trejo, ed., *The Chicanos As We See Ourselves,* pp. 67–80. Tucson: Univ. of Arizona Press, 1979.

Gamio, Manuel, collector. *The Life Story of the Mexican Immigrant.* 1931. Reprint ed. New York: Dover, 1971.

———. *Mexican Immigration to the United States: A Study of Human Migration and Adjustment.* Chicago: Univ. of Chicago Press, 1930.

García, Mario T. "The Chicana in American History: The Mexican Women of El Paso, 1880–1920—A Case Study." *PHR* 49 (May 1980): 315–337.

———. *Desert Immigrants: The Mexicans of El Paso, 1880–1920.* New Haven: Yale Univ. Press, 1981.

Gibbons, Charles E., assisted by Howard M. Bell. *Children Working on Farms in Certain Sections of the Western Slope of Colorado.* New York: National Child Labor Committee, 1925.

Gilbert, Fabiola Cabeza de Baca. *We Fed Them Cactus.* Albuquerque: Univ. of New Mexico Press, 1954.

Glanz, Rudolf. *The Jewish Woman in America.* New York: Ktav Publishing House, 1976.

Godelier, Maurice. *Perspectives in Marxist Anthropology.* Robert Brain, trans. Cambridge: Cambridge Univ. Press, 1977.

Gonzales, Sylvia Alicia. "The Chicana Perspective: A Design for Self-Awareness." In Arnulfo D. Trejo, ed., *The Chicanos As We See Ourselves,* pp. 81–99. Tucson: Univ. of Arizona Press, 1979.

González, Nancie L. *The Spanish Americans of New Mexico: A Distinctive Heritage.* Los Angeles: Univ. of California Press, 1967.

————. *The Spanish-Americans of New Mexico: A Heritage of Pride.* Albuquerque: Univ. of New Mexico Press, 1969.

Gonzales, Rosalinda M. "Chicanas and Mexican Immigrant Families 1920–1940: Women's Subordination and Family Exploitation." In Joan M. Jensen, and Lois Scharf, eds., *Decades of Discontent: The Women's Movement 1920–1940,* pp. 59–84. Westport, Conn.: Greenwood Press, 1983.

Goodykoontz, Colin. *Home Missions of the American Frontier.* Caldwell, Idaho: Caxton Printers, 1939.

Gorrell, Donald K. "'A New Impulse': Lay Leadership and Service by Women of the United Brethren in Christ and the Evangelical Association, 1870–1910." In Hilah F. Thomas and Rosemary Skinner Keller, eds. *Women in New Worlds,* pp. 233–245. Nashville: Abingdon Press, 1981.

Graham, Mabel S. "The Trend of Employment in New Mexico from July, 1937, to July, 1938." *New Mexico Business Review* 7 (1938): 214–220.

Grainger, Jane Atkins. *El Centenario de la Palabra: El Rito Presbyterian Church, 1879–1979.* Albuquerque: Menaul Historical Library of the Southwest, 1980.

Grant, Blanche C. *Taos Today.* Taos: n.p., 1925.

Grebler, Leo. *Mexican Immigration to the United States: The Record and its Implications.* Los Angeles: Mexican-American Study Project, Univ. of California, Advanced Report 2, Jan. 1966.

————, Joan W. Moore, Ralph Buzman et al. *The Mexican-American People: The Nation's Second Largest Minority.* New York: Free Press, 1970.

Green, James R. *Grass-Roots Socialism. Radical Movements in the Southwest 1895–1943.* Baton Rouge: Louisiana State Univ. Press, 1978.

Griffith, Beatrice. *American Me.* 1948. Reprint ed. Westport, Conn.: Greenwood Press, 1973.

Griswold del Castillo, Richard. *The Los Angeles Barrio, 1850–1890: A Social History.* Berkeley: Univ. of California Press, 1979.

————. *La Familia: Chicano Families in the Urban Southwest, 1848 to the Present.* Notre Dame: Univ. of Notre Dame Press, 1984.

————. "Quantitative History in the American Southwest: A Survey and Critique." *WHQ* 15 (1984): 407–426.

Grubbs, Frank H. "Frank Bond: Gentleman Sheepherder of Northern New Mexico 1883–1915." *NMHR* 35 (July and Oct. 1960): 199, 293–308; 36 (April, July and Oct. 1961): 138–158, 230–243, 274–345; 37 (Jan. 1962): 43–71.

Gutman, Herbert. *Work, Culture and Society in Industrializing America.* 1966. Reprint ed. New York: Vintage Books, 1977.

Gwin, J. B. "Immigration Along Our Southwest Border." *Annals of the American Academy of Political and Social Science* 93 (Jan. 1921): 126–130.

————. "Social Problems of Our Mexican Population." In *Proceedings of the National Conference of Social Work.* Cleveland, Ohio. May 1926: 327–332.

Hamamsy, Laila Shukry. "The Role of Women in a Changing Navaho Society." *American Anthropologist* 59 (1957): 101–111.

Handman, Max Sylvius. "Economic Reasons for the Coming of the Mexican Immigrant." *American Journal of Sociology* 35 (Jan. 1930): 601–611.

Hansen, William. "Pioneer Life in the San Luis Valley." *The Colorado Magazine* 17 (July 1940): 146–155.

Hareven, Tamara K. "Family Time and Industrial Time: Family Work in a Planned Corporation Town, 1900–1924." *Journal of Urban History* 1 (May 1975): 365–389.

————. "The Laborers of Manchester, New Hampshire 1912–1922: The Role of Family and Ethnicity in Adjustments to Industrial Life." *Labor History* 16 (Spring 1975): 249–265.

Harper, Allan G., Andrew R. Cordova, and Kalervo Oberg. *Man and Resources in the Middle Rio Grande Valley.* Albuquerque: Univ. of New Mexico Press, 1943.

Harwood, Rev. Thomas. *History of New Mexico Spanish and English Missions of the Methodist Episcopal Church from 1850 to 1910 in Decades.* 2 vols. Albuquerque: El Abogado Press, 1910.

Heald, Josiah H. "The Mexicans in the Southwest." *Missionary Review of the World* 42 (Nov. 1919): 860–865.

Heitman, Sidney, ed. *Germans from Russia in Colorado.* Ann Arbor: Western Science Association, 1978.

Henderson, Alice Corbin. *Brothers of Light: The Penitentes of the Southwest.* 1937. Reprint ed. Santa Fe: W. M. Gannon, 1977.

Hernandez, Jose Amaro. *Mutual Aid for Survival: The Case of the Mexican American.* Malabar, Fla.: Robert E. Krieger Publishing, 1983.

Higham, John. "The Reorientation of American Culture in the 1890s." In John Higham, *Writing American History Essays on Modern Scholarship,* pp. 73–102. Bloomington: Indiana Univ. Press, 1970.

————. *Strangers in the Land: Patterns of American Nativism 1860–1925.* New York: Atheneum, 1966.

Hill, Emma Shepard. *An Authorized and Complete History of the Central Presbyterian Church of Denver, Colorado 1860–1930.* Denver: Eames Brothers, 1930.

Hill, Lillian B., and George B. Mangold. *Migratory Child Workers.* New York: National Child Labor Committee Publication 354, June 1924.

Hoffman, Abraham, "The Trinidad Incident." *Journal of Mexican American History* 2 (Spring 1972): 143–151.

————. *Unwanted Mexican Americans in the Great Depression: Repatriation Pressures 1929–1938.* Tucson: Univ. of Arizona Press, 1974.

Hough, Henry, ed. "Americans with Spanish Names." Colorado WPA, 1942.

Home Mission Monthly. vols. 14–38. 1899–1923.

Hunter, Jane. *The Gospel of Gentility: American Women Missionaries in Turn-of-the-Century China.* New Haven: Yale Univ. Press, 1984.

Hutchinson, Charles E. "The Albuquerque Housing Survey." *New Mexico Business Review* 9 (Jan. 1940): 137–142.

Hutchinson, William R. "Modernism and Missions: The Liberal Search for an Exportable Christianity, 1875–1935." In John K. Fairbank, ed., *The Missionary Enterprise in China and America,* pp. 110–131. Cambridge, Mass.: Harvard Univ. Press, 1974.

Immigration. vols. 1, 2. 1909–11.

Jamieson, Stuart. *Labor Unionism in American Agriculture.* U.S. Dept. of Labor, Bureau of Labor Statistics Bulletin no. 836. Washington, D.C.: Government Printing Office, 1945.

Jaramillo, Cleofas. *Romance of a Little Village Girl.* San Antonio: Naylor, 1955.

————. *Shadows of the Past.* Santa Fe: Seton Village Press, 1941.

Jeffrey, Julie Roy. "Women on the Trans-Mississippi Frontier: A Review Essay." *NMHR* 57 (Oct. 1982): 395–400.

Jensen, Joan M. "Canning Comes to New Mexico: Women and the Agricultural Extension Service, 1914–1919." *NMHR* 57 (Oct. 1982): 361–386.

————. "'Disenfranchisement Is a Disgrace': Women and Politics in New Mexico, 1900–1940." *NMHR* 56 (Jan. 1981): 5–35.

————. "'I've Worked, I'm Not Afraid to Work': Farm Women in New Mexico, 1920–1940." *NMHR* 61 (Jan. 1986); 27–52.

————. "Women Teachers, Class, and Ethnicity: New Mexico, 1900–1950." *Southwest Economy and Society* 4 (Later Winter 1978–1979); 3–13.

————, and Lois Scharf, eds. *Decades of Discontent: The Woman's Movement 1920–1940.* Westport, Conn.: Greenwood Press, 1983.

Johansen, Sigurd. *Rural Social Organization in a Spanish-American Culture Area.* Univ. of New Mexico Publications in Social Science and Philosophy no. 1. Albuquerque: Univ. of New Mexico Press, 1948.

Johnson, Elizabeth, S. *Welfare of Families of Sugar-Beet Laborers: A Study of Child Labor and Its Relation to Family Work, Income, and Living Conditions in 1935.* U.S. Dept. of Labor, Children's Bureau Publication no. 247. Washington, D.C.: Government Printing Office, 1939.

Jones, Mary. *Autobiography of Mother Jones,* 1925. Reprint ed. New York: Arno Press, 1969.

Jones, William H. *The History of Catholic Education in the State of Colorado.* Washington, D.C.: Catholic Univ. of America Press, 1955.

Justis, Guy. T. *Twenty-five Years of Social Welfare.* Denver: Community Chest, n.d. (in Colorado State Federation of Labor Papers, Box 21, WHC)

Kaplan, David, and Robert A. Manners. *Culture Theory.* Englewood Cliffs, N.J.: Prentice-Hall, 1972.

Katzman, David. *Seven Days a Week: Women and Domestic Service in Industrializing America.* New York: Oxford Univ. Press, 1978.

Kaufman, Polly Welts. *Women Teachers on the Frontier.* New Haven: Yale Univ. Press, 1984.

Keleher, William A. "Law of the New Mexico Land Grant." *NMHR* 4 (Oct. 1929): 350–371.

————. *Memoirs: 1892–1969 A New Mexico Item.* Santa Fe: Rydal Press, 1969.

Kellogg, Mrs. Harriet S. *Life of Mrs. Emily J. Harwood,* Albuquerque: El Abogado Press, 1903.

Kennedy, David. *Over Here: The First World War and American Society.* New York: Oxford Univ. Press, 1980.

Kern, Robert, ed. *Labor in New Mexico: Unions, Strikes, and Social History since 1881.* Albuquerque: Univ. of New Mexico Press, 1983.

Kiser, George C. "Mexican American Labor before World War II." *Journal of Mexican American History* 2 (Spring 1972): 122–142.

————, and David Silverman. "Mexican Repatriation during the Great Depression." *Journal of Mexican American History* 3 (1973): 139–164.

Kiwanis International. *Child Welfare Survey Colorado-Wyoming District.* 1925.

Klaczynska, Barbara. "Why Women Work: A Comparison of Various Groups— Philadelphia, 1910–1930." *Labor History* 7 (Winter 1976): 73–87.

"A Klan Album: From the Collection of Fred and Jo Mazulla." *Colorado Magazine* 42 (Spring 1965): 109–114.

Kluckhohn, Florence Rockwood, and Fred L. Strodtbeck. *Variations in Value Orientations.* Evanston, Ill: Row, Peterson, 1961.

Knights of Columbus, Colorado State Council, *Annual Report of the Mexican Welfare Committee.* 4th: Denver, May 1927; 5th: Pueblo, May 1928. (at DPL)

Knowlton, Clark S. "Causes of Land Loss among the Spanish Americans in Northern New Mexico." *Rocky Mountain Social Science Journal* 1 (April 1964): 201–211.

Krause, Corinne Azen. "Urbanization without Breakdown: Italian, Jewish and Slavic Women in Pittsburgh, 1900 to 1945." *Journal of Urban History* 4 (May 1978): 291–306.

Kushner, Sam. *Long Road to Delano.* New York: International Publishers, 1975.

Kutsche, Paul, ed. *The Survival of Spanish American Villages.* Colorado College Studies no. 15. Colorado Springs, Spring 1979.

Kutsche, Paul, and John R. Van Ness. *Cañones: Values, Crisis and Survival in a Northern New Mexico Village.* Albuquerque: Univ. of New Mexico Press, 1981.

LaFont, John. *The Homesteaders of the Upper Rio Grande.* Birmingham, Ala.: Oxmoor Press, 1971.

Lamar, Howard Roberts. *The Far Southwest 1846–1912: A Territorial History.* New York: W. W. Norton, 1970.

Larson, Olaf, F. "Beet Workers on Relief in Weld County, Colorado," Cooperative Plan of Rural Research Between Colorado State Agricultural Experiment Station, Fort Collins, Colo., and Rural Section, Division of Social Research, Federal Works Progress Administration Bulletin no. 4, May 1937. (at WHC)

————. "Rural Households and Dependency: A Comparative Study of Composition and Behavior of Relief and Non-Relief Households in Three Colorado Counties." Colorado State College Experiment Station, Fort Collins, and Rural Section, Division of Social Research, Federal Works Progress Administration. Bulletin no. 444. May 1938.

Larson, Robert W. *New Mexico Populism: A Study of Radical Protest in a Western Territory.* Boulder: Colorado Associated Univ. Press, 1974.

Lavender, David. *The Southwest.* New York: Harper and Row, 1980.

Lawrence, Una Roberts. *Winning the Border: Baptist Missions among the Spanish-Speaking Peoples of the Border.* Atlanta: Home Mission Board, Southern Baptist Convention, 1935.

Leacock, Eleanor Burke. *Myths of Male Dominance: Collected Articles on Women Cross-Culturally.* New York: Monthly Review Press, 1981.

Lecompte, Janet. "The Independent Women of Hispanic New Mexico, 1821–1846." *WHQ* 12 (Jan. 1981): 17–35.

Lee, Joseph Walter. "Problems of a Rural Juvenile Court: A Description of the Work of the Juvenile Department of the County Clerk of Weld County Colorado." *Colorado State Teachers College Bulletin* no. 7. Oct. 1919.

Leonard, Olen, E. *The Role of the Land Grant in the Social Organization and Social Processes of a Spanish-American Village in New Mexico.* 1943, Reprint ed. Albuquerque: Calvin Horn Publisher, 1970.

Leonard, Olen, and Charles P. Loomis. *Culture of a Contemporary Rural Community: El Cerrito, New Mexico.* U.S.D.A., Bureau of Agricultural Economics, Rural Life Studies no. 1. Washington, D.C.: Government Printing Office, 1941.

Lerner, Elinor. "Into the Melting-Pot." *Women's Review of Books.* 3 (June 1986): 12.

Lescohier, Don H. "The Vital Problem in Mexican Immigration." *Proceedings of the National Conference of Social Work.* Des Moines, Iowa, May 1927: 547–554.

Longmore, T. Wilson, and Homer L. Hitt. "A Demographic Analysis of First and Second Generation Mexican Population of the United States: 1930." *Southwestern Social Science Quarterly* 24 (Sept. 1943): 138–149.

Loomis, Charles, and Glen Grisham. "The New Mexican Experiment in Village Rehabilitation." *Applied Anthropology* 2 (June 1943): 13–37.

Loomis, Charles P. "Systemic Linkage of El Cerrito." *Rural Sociology* 24 (March 1959); 54–57.

————. "Wartime Migration from the Rural Spanish Speaking Villages of New Mexico." *Rural Sociology* 7 (Dec. 1942): 384–395.

López, José Timoteo. *La Historia de la Sociedad Protección Mutua de Trabajadores Unidos.* New York: Comet Press, 1958.

Lotchin, Roger W., and David J. Weber. "The New Chicano Urban History." *History Teacher* 16 (1983): 219–247.

Lowry, Edith E., compiler. *They Starve That We May Eat: Migrants of the Crops.* New York: Council of Women for Home Missions and Missionary Education Movement, 1938.

Luhan, Mabel Dodge. *Intimate Memories.* vol. 4. *Edge of Taos Desert: An Escape to Reality.* New York: Harcourt, Brace, 1937.

McCombs, Vernon Monroe. *From over the Border. A Study of the Mexicans in the United States.* New York: Council of Women for Home Missions and Missionary Education Movement, 1925. Reprinted in *Church Views of the Mexican American.* New York: Arno Press, 1974.

————. "Rescuing Mexican Children in the Southwest." *The Missionary Review of the World* 46 (July 1923): 529–532.

McCrossen, Helen Cramp. "Native Crafts in New Mexico." *School Arts Magazine* 30 (March 1931): 456–458.

McLean, Robert N. "Getting God Counted among the Mexicans." *Missionary Review of the World* 46 (May 1923): 359–363.

————. "Mexican Workers in the United States." *Proceedings of the National Conference of Social Work.* San Francisco, June–July 1929: 531–538.

————. *The Northern Mexican.* n.d. Reprint ed. San Francisco: R & E Research Associates, 1971.

————. "Reaching Spanish-Americans with the Gospel." *Missionary Review of the World* 48 (Nov. 1925): 869–874.

————, and Mabel Little Crawford. *Jumping Beans: Stories and Studies about Mexicans in the United States for Junior Boys and Girls.* New York: Friendship Press, 1929.

————, and Charles A. Thomson. *Spanish and Mexican in Colorado.* New York: Department of the City, Immigrant, and Industrial Work, Board of National Missions of the Presbyterian Church in the U.S.A., Aug. 1924. Reprinted in *Church Views of the Mexican American.* New York: Arno Press, 1974.

McWilliams, Carey. *Ill Fares the Land: Migrants and Migratory Labor in the United States.* Boston: Little, Brown, 1942.

————. *North from Mexico: The Spanish-Speaking People of the United States.* 1948. Reprint ed. New York: Greenwood Press, 1968.

Maes, E. E. "The Labor Movement in New Mexico." *New Mexico Business Review* 4 (1935): 137–140.

Mahoney, Thomas F. "Industrial Relations in the Beet Fields of Colorado." Address at the Third Catholic Conference on Industrial Problems. Denver, April 1931. (at DPL)

————. "Problem of the Mexican Wage Earner." Address at the Second Catholic Conference on Industrial Problems. Denver, May 1930. (at DPL)

Markoff, Dena. "Beet Hand Laborers of Sugar City, Colorado, 1900–1920." In Sidney Heitman, ed. *Germans from Russia in Colorado,* pp. 81–103. Ann Arbor: Western Science Association, 1978.

Marriner, Gerald Lynn. "Klan Politics in Colorado." *Journal of the West* 15 (Jan. 1976): 76–101.

Martin, Bernice. *"People of the Book" A History of the First Presbyterian Church.* Monte Vista: n.p., 1956. (in Darley Family Collection, Box 3, WHC)

Martinez, John. *Mexican Emigration to the United States 1910–1930.* 1930. Reprint ed. San Francisco: R & E Associates, 1971.

Mautner, Bertram H., and W. Lewis Abbott et al. *Child Labor in Agriculture and Farm Life in the Arkansas Valley of Colorado.* New York: National Child Labor Committee, 1929.

Mayor's Interim Survey Committee on Human Relations. *A Report on Minorities in Denver.* 1948. (in Colorado State Federation of Labor Papers, Box 19, WHC).

Mead, Margaret, ed. *Cultural Patterns and Technical Change.* Paris: UNESCO, 1953.

Means, Florence Crannell, and Harriet Louise Fullen. *Rafael and Consuelo: Stories and Studies about Mexicans in the United States for Primary Children.* New York: Friendship Press, 1929.

Meier, Matt S., and Feliciano Rivera. *Readings on La Raza: The Twentieth Century.* New York: Hill & Wang, 1974.

Meillassoux, Claude. "The Social Organisation of the Peasantry: The Economic Basis of Kinship." In David Seddon, ed., *Relations of Production: Marxist Approaches to Anthropology.* Helen Lackner, trans. Pp. 159–169. London: Frank Cass and Company, 1978.

Meinig, Donald W. *Southwest: Three Peoples in Geographical Change, 1600–1970.* New York: Oxford Univ. Press, 1971.

Melzer, Richard. *Madrid Revisited: Life and Labor in a New Mexican Mining Camp in the Years of the Great Depression.* Santa Fe: Lightning Tree, 1976.

Menaul Historical Library. *The Living Word.* Albuquerque, 1957.

Menefee, Selden C. *Mexican Migratory Workers of South Texas.* Division of Research, Social Research Section, Works Progress Administration. Washington, D.C.: Government-Printing Office, 1941.

"Mexican Invaders Relieving Our Farm-Labor Shortage." *Literary Digest* 66 (17 July 1920): 53–54.

Miller, Darlis A. "Cross-Cultural Marriages in the Southwest: The New Mexico Experience, 1846–1900." *NMHR* 57 (Oct. 1982): 335–360.

Mirandé, Alfredo, and Evangelina Enríquez. *La Chicana: The Mexican American Woman.* Chicago: Univ. of Chicago Press, 1979.

Mohl, Raymond A. "The Saturday Evening Post and the 'Mexican Invasion.'" *Journal of Mexican American History* 3 (1973): 131–138.

Montgomery, David. *Workers' Control in America.* Cambridge: Cambridge Univ. Press, 1979.

"Monthly Movement of Aliens, January, 1913, to June, 1920." *Monthly Labor Review* 11 (Nov. and Dec. 1920): 225–227, 217.

Montiel, Miguel. "The Chicano Family: A Review of Research." *Social Work* 18 (March 1973): 22–31.

———. "The Social Science Myth of the Mexican American Family." *El Grito* 3 (Summer 1970): 56–63.

Moore, Joan W., with Alfredo Cuéllar. *Mexican Americans.* Englewood Cliffs: Prentice Hall, 1970.

Moorehouse, L. A., et al. "Farm Practice in Growing Sugar Beets for Three Districts in Colorado 1914–1915." U.S. Dept. of Agriculture Bulletin no. 726, Dec. 1918.

Moquin, Wayne, with Charles van Doren, eds. *A Documentary History of the Mexican Americans.* New York: Praeger, 1971.

Mora, Magdalena, and Adelaida R. Del Castillo, eds. *Mexican Women in the United States: Struggles Past and Present.* Occasional Paper no. 2. Los Angeles: Chicano Studies Research Center, Univ. of California, 1980.

Motto, Sytha. *Madrid and Christmas in New Mexico.* n.p., 1973.

Murray, Andrew E. *The Skyline Synod: Presbyterianism in Colorado and Utah.* Denver: Golden Bell Press, n.d. (in Darley Family Collection, Box 3, WHC)

Myres, Sandra L. "Mexican Americans and Westering Anglos: A Feminine Perspective." *NMHR* 57 (Oct. 1982): 317–334.

———. *Westering Women and the Frontier Experience 1800–1915.* Albuquerque: Univ. of New Mexico Press, 1982.

Náñez, Clotide Falcon. "Hispanic Clergy Wives: Their Contribution to United Methodism in the Southwest, Later Nineteenth Century to the Present." In Hilah F. Thomas and Rosemary Skinner Keller, eds., *Women in New Worlds,* pp. 161–177. Nashville: Abingdon, 1981.

Nash, Gerald D. *The American West in the Twentieth Century: A Short History of an Urban Oasis.* Englewood Cliffs: Prentice-Hall, 1973.

National Association for the Advancement of Colored People. Albuquerque Branch and Albuquerque Civil Rights Committee. *New Mexico's Segregated Schools.* Albuquerque: n.p., n.d. [1949] (mimeograph at UNM)

National Child Labor Committee. Pamphlets 237, 248, 249, 344 on child labor in the United States.

———. *Child Labor Facts.* vols. 306, 357. 1922, 1930.

————. "The Farmer and the Federal Child Labor Amendment." 1937.

Neighborhood House Association. *Annual Report.* Denver, 1907.

Nestor, Sarah. *The Native Market of the Spanish New Mexican Craftsmen, Santa Fe 1933–1940.* Santa Fe: Colonial New Mexico Historical Foundation, 1978.

New Mexico Agricultural Extension Service. *Annual Reports of County Agents.* National Archives Microcopy no. T876, rolls 10–20, 1927–38.

New Mexico Blue Book. 1931.

New Mexico. Bureau of Public Health. *Biennial Reports.* Third to eighth. 1923/24–1933/34.

————. Common Schools. *Annual Statistical Report of the Superintendent of Public Instruction.* 1930–31.

————. Department of Education. *Educational Directory.* 1913–38.

————. Department of Public Health. *New Mexico Health Officer* 10 (July 1942) and 12 (Dec. 1944).

————. Department of Public Welfare. *Activities: Relief Statistics.* vol. 1, March through Dec. 1937.

————. Emergency Relief Administration. *The Bulletin.* Jan. 1934–July/Aug. 1935.

————. State Corporation Commission. *Annual Reports.* 1912–20, 1923–31, 1932–35.

————. Superintendent of Public Instruction. *Biennial Report of the Governor of New Mexico.* 1910/11–1911/12; 1917/1918.

The New Mexico Hispano. New York: Arno Press, 1974.

New Mexico in the Great War. Special issue of *NMHR* 1 (1926) and 2 (Jan. 1927).

New Mexico Journal of Education. vols. 1–16. 1905–20.

New Mexico Normal University. *Southwest Wind.* (Yearbook) Las Vegas, N.M., 1930. (at NMSRCA)

New Mexico School Review. vols. 1–16. 1921–37.

New Mexico State University. *Agricultural Research at New Mexico State University Since 1889.* Las Cruces, March 1969.

Nostrand, Richard L. "'Mexican American' and 'Chicano': Emerging Terms for a People Coming of Age." *PHR* 42 (Aug. 1973): 389–406.

Oberg, Kalervo, "Cultural Factors and Land-Use Planning in Cuba Valley, New Mexico." *Rural Sociology* 5 (Dec. 1940): 438–448.

de Onís, José, ed. *The Hispanic Contribution to the State of Colorado.* Boulder: Univ. of Colorado Centennial Commission, Waterview Press, 1976.

Ortiz, Roxanne Dunbar. *Roots of Resistance: Land Tenure in New Mexico, 1680–1980.* Los Angeles: Chicano Studies Center and American Indian Studies Center, Univ. of California, 1980.

Otero(-Warren), Nina. *Old Spain in Our Southwest.* New York: Harcourt, Brace, 1936.

Overpeck, J. C. "Corn Production in New Mexico." Agricultural Experiment

Station of the College of Agriculture and Mechanic Arts Bulletin no. 166, Feb. 1928.

Padilla, Fernando V., and Carlos B. Ramírez. "Patterns of Chicano Representation in California, Colorado and Nuevo Mexico." *Aztlan* 5 (Spring and Fall 1974): 189–234.

El Palacio. vols. 6–47. 1919–40.

Parish, William J., ed. "Sheep Husbandry in New Mexico, 1902–1903." *NMHR* 37 (July and Oct. 1962): 201–213, 260–308.

Peñalosa, Fernando. "Mexican Family Roles." *Journal of Marriage and the Family* 30 (Nov. 1968): 680–689.

Pettit, Arthur G. *Images of the Mexican American in Fiction and Film.* College Station: Texas A&M Univ. Press, 1980.

Pijoan, M., and R. W. Roskelley. "Nutrition and Certain Related Factors of Spanish-Americans in Northern Colorado." Denver: Rocky Mountain Council on Inter-American Affairs, 1943.

Pinckert, Leta. *True Stories of Early Days in the San Juan Basin.* Farmington, N.M.: Hustler Press, 1964.

Pletcher, David M. *Rails, Mines and Progress: Seven American Promoters in Mexico, 1867–1911.* Ithaca: Cornell Univ. Press, 1958.

Potter, Jack M., Mary N. Diaz, and George M. Foster, eds. *Peasant Society: A Reader.* Boston: Little, Brown, 1967.

President's Research Committee on Social Trends. *Recent Social Trends in the United States.* vol. 1. New York: McGraw-Hill, 1933.

Proceedings of the Colorado Conference of Social Work. Denver, 1924, 1927. (at DPL)

Proceedings of the National Conference of Social Work. Denver, June 1925.

Rabe, Valentin H. "Evangelical Logistics: Mission Support and Resources to 1920." In John K. Fairbank, ed., *The Missionary Enterprise in China and America,* pp. 56–60. Cambridge: Harvard Univ. Press, 1974.

Rael, Juan B., Reyes Martinez, and excerpts from WPA files. "Arroyo Hondo: Penitentes, Weddings, Wakes." *El Palacio* 81 (Spring 1975): 4–19.

Ramos, Reyes. "Discovering the Production of Mexican American Family Structure." *De Colores* 6 (1982): 1–19. (typescript copy)

———. "Movidas: The Methodological and Theoretical Relevance of Interactional Strategies." *Studies in Symbolic Interaction* 2 (1979): 141–165.

Randolph, Edgar Dunnington. "An Outline of the Field of Child Welfare." *Colorado State Teachers College Bulletin.* Ser. 18, no. 2 (May 1918).

Rebolledo, Antonio. "Objective of the New Mexico Spanish Research Project." *New Mexico Quarterly Review* 12 (Feb. 1942): 25–30.

Redfield, Robert (for M. Gamio). "The Antecedents of Mexican Immigration to the United States." *American Journal of Sociology* 35 (Nov. 1929): 433–438.

Reisler, Mark. *By the Sweat of Their Brow: Mexican Immigrant Labor in the United States 1900–1940.* Westport, Conn.: Greenwood Press, 1976.

Reps, John W. *Cities of the American West: A History of Urban Planning.* Princeton, N.J.: Princeton Univ. Press, 1979.

"Results of Admission of Mexican Laborers, Under Departmental Orders, for Employment in Agricultural Pursuits." *Monthly Labor Review* 11 (Nov. 1920): 221–223.

Reynolds, Anne. *The Education of Spanish-Speaking Children in Five Southwestern States.* U.S. Dept. of Interior, Office of Education Bulletin no. 1. Washington, D.C.: Government Printing Office, 1933.

Rice, Ruth Kessler. *Letters from New Mexico 1899–1904.* Albuquerque: Adobe Press, 1981.

Rincon, Bernice. "La Chicana Her Role in the Past and Her Search for a New Role in the Future." *Regeneracion* 1 (1971): 15–18.

Rivera, Feliciano. *A Mexican American Source Book.* Menlo Park, Calif.: Education Consulting Associates, 1970.

Roberts, Cleon. *Fort Lupton, Colorado: The First Hundred and Forty Years.* Denver: n.p., 1982.

Romo, Ricardo. *East Los Angeles: History of a Barrio.* Austin: Univ. of Texas Press, 1983.

―――. "Responses to Mexican Immigration, 1910–1930." *Aztlan* 6 (Summer 1975): 173–194.

―――. "Work and Restlessness: Occupational and Spatial Mobility Among Mexicanos in Los Angeles, 1918–1928." *PHR* 46 (May 1977): 157–180.

―――, and Raymund Paredes, eds. *New Directions in Chicano Scholarship.* La Jolla, Calif.: Chicano Studies Monograph Series, Univ. of California, San Diego, 1978.

Rosaldo, Renato. "Chicano Studies, 1970–1984," *Annual Review of Anthropology* 14 (1985): 405–427.

―――, et al., eds. *Chicano: The Evolution of a People.* Minneapolis: Winston Press, 1973.

Rosenbaum, Robert. *Mexicano Resistance in the Southwest "The Sacred Right of Self Preservation."* Austin: Univ. of Texas Press, 1981.

Roskelley, R. W. "Beet Labor Problems in Colorado." *Proceedings of the Western Farm Economics Association.* July 1940.

―――. "Population Trends in Colorado." Cooperative Plan of Rural Research: Colorado Agricultural Experiment Station, Colorado State College, Fort Collins, and Rural Section, Division of Research, Federal WPA, Bulletin 462, Sept. 1940.

Roster of Men and Women Who Served in the World War from Colorado 1917–1918. Colorado: Adjutant General's Department, Colorado National Guard, 1941.

Roundy, Rev. Rodney. "The Mexican in Our Midst." *Missionary Review of the World* 44 (May 1921): 361–367.

Rubenstein, Harry R. "The Great Gallup Coal Strike of 1933." *NMHR* 52 (April 1977): 173–192.

San Jose Experimental School. *We Learn English: A Preliminary Report of the Achievement of Spanish Speaking Pupils in New Mexico.* Albuquerque: Univ. of New Mexico, July 1936.

"San Jose Training School." *Univ. of New Mexico Bulletin.* Training School Series 1 (Oct. 1930 and March 1931).

San Luis Valley Historian. vols. 1–8. 1969–77.

Sanchez, George. "'Go After the Women': Americanization and the Mexican Immigrant Woman 1915–1929." Working Paper Ser. no. 6. Stanford Univ.: Stanford Center for Chicano Research, n.d.

Sanchez, George Isidore. "The Education of Bilinguals in a State School System." 1934. Reprinted in *Education and the Mexican American.* New York: Arno Press, 1974.

————, ed. "First Regional Conference on the Education of Spanish Speaking People in the Southwest." March 1946. (in Community Relations Papers, Box 2)

————. *Forgotten People. A Study of New Mexicans.* Albuquerque: Univ. of New Mexico Press, 1940.

Schlegel, Alice. "An Overview." In Alice Schlegel, ed., *Sexual Stratification: A Cross-Cultural View,* pp. 344–357. New York: Columbia Univ. Press, 1977.

Schlesinger, Andrew Bancroft. "Las Gorras Blancas, 1889–1891." *Journal of Mexican American History* 1 (Spring 1971): 87–143.

Schwartz, Harry. "Agricultural Labor in the First World War." *Journal of Farm Economics* 24 (Feb. 1942): 178–187.

————. *Seasonal Farm Labor in the United States with Special Reference to Hired Workers in Fruit and Vegetable and Sugar-Beet Production.* New York: Columbia Univ. Press, 1945.

Scruggs, Otey M. "The First Mexican Farm Labor Program." *Arizona and the West* 2 (Winter 1960): 319–326.

Seller, Maxine. "Beyond the Stereotype—A New Look at the Immigrant Woman, 1880–1924." *Journal of Ethnic Studies* 3 (Spring 1975): 59–70.

————. "The Education of the Immigrant Woman 1900–1935." *Journal of Urban History* 4 (May 1978): 307–330.

Senter, Donovan. "Acculturation among New Mexican Villagers in Comparison to Adjustment Patterns of Other Spanish-Speaking Americans." *Rural Sociology* 10 (March 1945): 31–47.

————, and Florence Hawley. "The Grammar School as the Basic Acculturating Influence for Native New Mexicans." *Social Forces* 24 (May 1946): 398–407.

Servín, Manuel P., ed. *An Awakened Minority: The Mexican Americans.* 2d ed. Beverly Hills: Glencoe Press, 1974.

Shontz, Orfa. "The Land of Poco Tiempo: A Study of Mexican Family Relations in a Changing Social Environment." *The Family* 8 (May 1927): 74–79.

Simmons, Marc. *New Mexico: A Bicentennial History.* New York: W. W. Norton, 1977.

———. *Witchcraft in the Southwest: Spanish and Indian Supernaturalism on the Rio Grande.* Flagstaff: Northland Press, 1974.

Simpson, Thomas K. "The 'Anglo' Revolution in New Mexico." *La Confluencia* 2 (Dec. 1976): 2–12; 3 (March 1979): 32–39; 3 (June 1979): 38–48.

Sinnock, Jean, et al. *The Denver Relief Study.* Colorado State Department of Public Welfare, 1940. (at DPL)

Skinner, G. William. "Chinese Peasants and the Closed Community: An Open and Shut Case." *Comparative Studies in Society and History* 13 (July 1971): 270–281.

———. "Mobility Strategies in Late Imperial China: A Regional Systems Analysis." In Carol A. Smith, ed., *Regional Analysis.* vol. 1. *Economic Systems,* pp. 327–364. New York: Academic Press, 1976.

Slayden, James L. "Some Observations on Mexican Immigration." *Annals of the American Academy of Political and Social Science* 93 (Jan. 1921): 121–126.

Slingerland, W. H. *Child Welfare Work in Colorado.* Univ. of Colorado Bulletin vol. 20, no. 10. Boulder, 1920.

Smedley, Agnes. *Daughter of Earth.* 1929. Reprint ed. Old Westbury, N.Y.: Feminist Press, 1973.

Smith, Carol A., ed. *Regional Analysis.* Vols. 1 and 2. New York: Academic Press, 1976.

Smith, George Winston. "New Mexico's Wartime Food Problems, 1917–1918." *NMHR* 18 (Oct. 1943): 349–385; 19 (Jan. 1944): 1–54.

"The Social and Economic Background of State Teachers College Students." *Colorado State Teachers College Bulletin* 6 (Sept. 1925).

Spanish American Normal School. Sophomore English Class. "In the Land of Mañana." n.d. [1934] (mimeograph at UNM)

Spicer, Edward, and Raymond H. Thomas, eds. *Plural Society in the Southwest.* New York: Interbook, 1972.

Sporleder, Louis B. *The Romance of the Spanish Peaks.* n.p.: O'Brien Printing and Stationery, 1960.

Sprague, Marshall. *Colorado: A Bicentennial History.* New York: W. W. Norton, 1976.

Stooker, Wilhelmina. *Adverturing with Rafael and Consuelo: How a Sand Pile Helped Some Primary Children to an Intimate Feeling of Friendship for a Mexican Laborer's Family.* Boston: Pilgrim Press, 1935.

Stowell, Jay S. *The Near Side of the Mexican Question.* New York: George H. Doran, 1921.

———. *A Study of Mexicans and Spanish Americans in the United States.*

New York: Home Missions Council and the Council of Women for Home Missions, 1920.

Sturges, Vera L. "The Progress of Adjustment in Mexican and United States Life." *Proceedings of the National Conference of Social Work.* New Orleans, April 1920: 481–485.

Sugg, Redding S. "The Pedagogy of Love." *Virginia Quarterly* 54 (Summer 1978): 411–426.

Sumner, Helen. *Equal Suffrage: The Results of an Investigation in Colorado Made for the Collegiate Equal Suffrage League of New York State.* New York: Harper and Brothers, 1909.

The Survey. vols. 27–75. 1912–39.

Swadesh, Frances Leon. *Los Primeros Pobladores: Hispanic Americans of the Ute Frontier.* Notre Dame: Univ. of Notre Dame Press, 1974.

Taylor, Paul S. "The Mexican Immigrant and the Problem of Crime and Criminal Justice." In National Commission on Law Observance and Enforcement, *Report on Crime and the Foreign Born.* 1931. Reprinted in *The Mexican American and the Law.* New York: Arno Press, 1974.

―――. *Mexican Labor in the United States Valley of the South Platte, Colorado.* Los Angeles: Univ. of California Publications in Economics, vol. 6, 1929.

Taylor, Paul Schuster and Dorothea Lange. *An American Exodus: A Record of Human Erosion.* 1939. Reprint ed. New York: Arno Press, 1975.

Taylor, Ralph C. *Colorado South of the Border.* Denver: Sage Books, 1963.

Taylor, William B., and Elliott West. "Patron Leadership at the Crossroads: Southern Colorado in the Late Nineteenth Century." *PHR* 42 (Aug. 1973): 335–357.

Tharp, Roland G., et al. "Changes in Marriage Roles Accompanying the Acculturation of the Mexican-American Wife." *Journal of Marriage and the Family* 30 (Aug. 1968): 404–412.

Thistlethwaite, Frank. "Migration from Europe Overseas in the Nineteenth and Twentieth Centuries." In Herbert Moller, ed. *Population Movements in Modern European History,* pp. 73–91. New York: Macmillan, 1964.

Thomson, Charles A. "Cooperative Broadcasting to the Mexicans in the United States." *Missionary Review of the World* 48 (Dec. 1925): 937–943.

―――. "Restriction of Mexican Immigration." *Journal of Applied Sociology* 11 (July–Aug. 1927): 574–578.

Through the Leaves, 1913–1935. (in Great Western Sugar Company Papers, WHC)

Tilly, Louise A. "Comments on the Yans-McLaughlin and Davidoff Papers." *Journal of Social History* 7 (Summer 1974): 452–459.

Tireman, Lloyd. "Reading in the Elementary Schools of New Mexico." *Elementary School Journal* 30 (April 1930): 621–626.

Tolman, William H. *Social Engineering: A Record of Things Done by American*

Industrialists Employing Upwards of One and One-Half Million of People. New York: McGraw Publishing, 1909.

Torres, Luisa. "Palabras de Una Viejita/The Words of an Old One." *El Palacio* 84 (Fall 1978): 8–18.

Torrez, Robert J. "'El Bornes': La Tierra Amarilla and T. D. Burns." *NMHR* 56 (April 1981): 161–175.

Trejo, Arnulfo D., ed. *The Chicanos as We See Ourselves.* Tucson: Univ. of Arizona Press, 1979.

Ulrich, Laurel Thatcher. *Goodwives: Image and Reality in the Lives of Women in Northern New England 1650–1750.* New York: Knopf, 1982.

United States Bureau of Immigration. *United States Immigration Service Bulletin* 1 (1918–19).

United States. Civil Works Administration. *Interviews Collected During 1933–1934 for State Historical Society of Colorado.* UN3CWA, M216, 6 reels. (at CHS)

United States Congress. House of Representatives. Committee on Immigration and Naturalization. *Hearings: Immigration from Countries of the Western Hemisphere.* 70th Cong., 1st sess. Washington, D.C.: Government Printing Office, 1928.

————. *Hearings: Seasonal Agricultural Laborers from Mexico.* 69th Cong., 1st sess. Washington, D.C.: Government Printing Office, 1926.

————. *Hearings: Temporary Admission of Illiterate Mexican Laborers.* 66th Cong., 2d sess. Washington, D.C.: Government Printing Office, 1920.

————. *Hearings: Western Hemisphere Immigration.* 71st Cong., 2d sess. Washington, D.C.: Government Printing Office, 1930.

United States Congress. House of Representatives. Select Committee to Investigate. *The Interstate Migration of Destitute Citizens.* 77th Cong., 1st sess. H. Rep. 369. Washington, D.C.: Government Printing Office, 1941.

United States Congress. Senate. Commission on Industrial Relations. *The Colorado Miners' Strike and Rockefeller Interests in Colorado.* In *Industrial Relations: Final Report and Testimony Submitted to Congress.* 64th Cong., 1st sess. S.doc. 415. Washington, D.C.: Government Printing Office, 1916.

United States Congress. Senate. Committee on Finance. *Hearings on the Proposed Tariff Act of 1921.* Schedule 5, "Sugar Molasses, and Manufactures of." 67th Cong., 2d sess. S.doc. 108. Washington, D.C.: Government Printing Office, 1922.

United States Congress. Senate. Committee on Immigration. *Hearings: Admission of Agricultural Laborers.* 66th Cong., 2d sess. Washington, D.C.: Government Printing Office, 1920.

————. *Hearings: Restriction of Western Hemisphere Immigration.* 70th Cong., 1st sess. Washington D. C.: Government Printing Office, 1928.

United States Congress. Senate. Committee on the Judiciary. "Arguments of the

Woman Suffrage Delegates before the Committee on the Judiciary of the United States Senate, January 23, 1880." In *Reports and Hearings on Woman Suffrage*. 62d Cong., 3d sess. Washington, D.C.: Government Printing Office, 1913.

United States Congress. Senate. *Report of the Immigration Commission*. 61st Cong., 2d sess. S.doc. 85, part 25, vol. 2. Washington, D.C.: Government Printing Office, 1911.

United States. Department of Commerce. Bureau of the Census. *Twelfth Census of the United States, 1900: Abstract*. Washington, D.C.: Government Printing Office, 1900.

————. *Thirteenth Census of the United States, 1910: Population*. vol. 2. Washington, D.C.: Government Printing Office, 1910.

————. ————. *Abstract of the Census*. Washington, D.C.: Government Printing Office, 1913.

————. ————. *Fourteenth Census of the United States, 1920: Abstract and Population*. vol. 3. Washington, D.C.: Government Printing Office, 1923.

————*Fifteenth Census of the United States, 1930: Population* vol. 3, part 1; *Unemployment Bulletin* vols. 1, 2; and *Agriculture* vol. 2, part 3. Washington, D.C.: Government Printing Office, 1932.

————. ————. *Population* vols. 4, 5. "Occupations, by States"; "Families." Washington, D.C.: Government Printing Office, 1933.

————. *Sixteenth Census of the United States, 1940: Population*. 3d ser. "The Labor Force Occupation, Industry, Employment, and Income." Washington, D.C.: Government Printing Office, 1941.

————. ————. *Population: Internal Migration, 1935–1940*. Washington, D.C.: Government Printing Office, 1943.

————. ————. *Population: Nativity and Parentage of the White Population: Mother Tongue*. Washington, D.C.: Government Printing Office, 1943.

————. *United States Census of Agriculture. 1925. Reports for States*. Part 3, "The Western States." Washington, D.C.: Government Printing Office, 1927.

United States. Department of Labor. Children's Bureau. *Child Labor and the Work of Mothers in the Beet Fields of Colorado and Michigan*. Bureau Publication no. 115. Washington, D.C.: Government Printing Office, 1923.

United States. Department of Labor. Commissioner-General of Immigration. *Annual Report*. Washington, D.C.: Government Printing Office, 1913–30.

University of Colorado. University Extension Division and Mountain Division, American Red Cross. *Boulder County Studies 1919–1921*. Univ. of Colorado Bulletin. General Series, vol. 21, Boulder, 1921.

University of New Mexico Library. "A Checklist of New Mexico Newspapers." *Univ. of New Mexico Bulletin Sociological Series,* vol. 2, Dec. 1935.

Vaca, Nick C. "The Mexican-American in the Social Sciences: 1912–1970, Part I: 1912–1935." *El Grito* 3 (Spring 1970): 3–24.

Valdes, Daniel T. *The Spanish-Speaking People of the Southwest.* Denver: WPA Program of Education and Recreation of the Colorado State Department of Education, Bulletin WE-4, June 1938.

Valdez, Daniel, ed. *A History of the San Luis Valley.* Alamosa: Adams State College, 1936. Mimeograph.

Van Arsdale, Jonathan. "Railroads in New Mexico." *Research* (Univ. of New Mexico) 2 (Dec. 1939): 3–16.

Van der Eerden, Sister M. Lucia. *Maternity Care in a Spanish-American Community of New Mexico.* Washington, D.C.: Catholic Univ. of America Press, 1948.

Vasquez, Dora Ortiz. *The Enchanted Dialogue of Loma Parda and Canada Bonita.* N.p., 1983. (at MHL)

Vecoli, Rudolph J. "Contadini in Chicago: A Critique of *The Uprooted.*" *Journal of American History* 51 (Dec. 1964): 404–417.

Vigil, Maurilio E. *Los Patrones: Profiles of Hispanic Political Leaders.* Washington, D.C.: Univ. Press of America, 1980.

Walker, A. L., J. L. Lantow, and K. P. Pickrell. "Economics of Sheep Production in Western New Mexico." Agricultural Experiment Station of the New Mexico College of Agricultural and Mechanic Arts. Bulletin no. 204. May 1932.

Walker, Helen M. "Mexican Immigrants and American Citizenship." *Sociology and Social Research* 13 (May–June 1929): 465–471.

———. "Mexican Immigrants as Laborers." *Sociology and Social Research* 13 (Sept.–Oct. 1928): 55–62.

Wallrich, William. "Auxiliadoras de la Morada." *Southwestern Lore* 16 (June 1950): 4–10.

Walmsley, Myrtle. *I Remember, I Remember Truchas the Way It Was 1935–1956.* Albuquerque: Menaul Historical Library of the Southwest, 1981.

Walter, Paul A. F. "Octaviano Larrazolo." *NMHR* 7 (April 1932): 97–104.

———. "Population Trends in New Mexico." In *Population of New Mexico.* Albuquerque: Division of Research, Dept. of Government, Univ. of New Mexico, June 1947.

Weber, David J. "Turner, the Boltonians, and the Borderlands." *American Historical Review* 91 (Feb. 1986): 66–81.

Weeks, O. Douglas. "The League of United Latin-American Citizens: A Texas-Mexican Civic Organization." *Southwestern Political and Social Science Quarterly* 10 (Dec. 1929): 257–278.

Weigle, Marta. *Brothers of Light, Brothers of Blood: The Penitentes of the Southwest.* Albuquerque: Univ. of New Mexico Press, 1976.

————, ed. *Hispanic Arts and Ethnohistory in the Southwest.* Santa Fe: Ancient City Press, 1983.

————, ed. *Hispanic Villages of Northern New Mexico: A Reprint of Vol. II of the 1935 Tewa Basin Study, with Supplementary Materials.* Santa Fe: Lightning Tree Press, 1975.

————. *Spiders and Spinsters: Women and Mythology.* Albuquerque: Univ. of New Mexico Press, 1982.

Weiss, Lawrence D. "Industrial Reserve Armies of the Southwest: Navajo and Mexican," *Southwest Economy and Society* 3 (Fall 1977): 19–29.

Welter, Barbara. "She Hath Done What She Could: Protestant Women's Missionary Careers in Nineteenth Century America." *American Quarterly* 30 (Winter 1978): 624–638.

White, Alfred. *The Apperceptive Mass of Foreigners as Applied to Americanization, The Mexican Group.* 1923. Reprint ed. San Francisco: R & E Research Associates, 1971.

White, Owen P. "A Glance at the Mexicans." *American Mercury* 4 (Feb. 1925): 180–187.

Wickens, James Frederick. *Colorado in the Great Depression.* New York: Garland Publishing, 1979.

Widdison, Jerold Gwayn. "Historical Geography of the Middle Rio Puerco Valley, New Mexico." *NMHR* 34 (Oct. 1959): 248–284.

Wilkening, E. A., et al. "Role of the Extended Family in Migration and Adaptation in Brazil." *Journal of Marriage and the Family* 30 (Nov. 1968): 689–695.

Wilson, Elizabeth. "The American Situation." In Charles Raven, ed., *Women and the Ministry.* Garden City, N.Y.: Doubleday, Doran, 1929.

Wireless Messages from Home Mission Stations. 1918–1923. (at MHL)

Woll, Allen L. "Latin Images in American Films 1929–1939." *Journal of Mexican American History* 4 (1974): 28–40.

Women and Missions. vols. 1–12, 1924–40.

Workers Service in Colorado. Works Progress Administration of Federal Works Administration, 1940. (at DPL)

Wright, James Edward. *The Politics of Populism: Dissent in Colorado.* New Haven: Yale Univ. Press, 1974.

Yans-McLaughlin, Virginia. *Family and Community: Italian Immigrants in Buffalo 1880–1930.* Ithaca: Cornell Univ. Press, 1977.

Zeleny, Carolyn. *Relations Between the Spanish-Americans and Anglo-Americans in New Mexico: A Study of Conflict and Accommodation in a Dual Ethnic Situation.* Ph.D. dissertation, Yale Univ., 1944. Reprint ed. New York: Arno Press, 1974.

Zinn, Maxine Baca. "Gender and Ethnic Identity among Chicanos." *Frontiers* 5 (Summer 1980): 18–24.

————. "Mexican-American Women in the Social Sciences." *Signs* 8 (Winter 1982): 259–272.

Master's Theses, Dissertations, and Unpublished Papers

Anderson, Karen. "The Chicana in Transition: Mexican and Mexican-American Women, 1910–1950." Paper delivered at Sixth Berkshire Conference on the History of Women. June, 1984.

Andrews, John Philip. "History of Rural Spanish Settlement and Land Use in the Upper Culebra Basin of the San Luis Valley, Costilla County, Colorado." Master's thesis, Univ. of Colorado, 1972.

Avant, Louis. "History of Catholic Education in New Mexico Since American Occupation." Master's thesis, Univ. of New Mexico, 1940.

Barela, Fred. "The Relation Between Scholastic Achievement and Economic Status as Shown by Parental Occupation." Master's thesis, Univ. of New Mexico, 1936.

Blake, Alice. "Presbyterian Mission Work in New Mexico." Unpublished manuscript. 1935. (at MHL)

Briggs, Charles Leslie. "'Our Strength Is in the Land': The Structure of Hierarchy and Equality and the Pragmatics of Discourse in Hispano ('Spanish-American') 'Talk About the Past.'" Ph.D. dissertation, Univ. of Chicago, 1981.

Brown, Charles E. "Some Phases of Rural Education in New Mexico." Master's thesis, Univ. of New Mexico, 1929.

Buhrmester, Ruby. "A History of the Spanish-Speaking People in Southern Colorado, Especially Those in Otero County." Master's thesis, Western State College of Colorado, 1935.

Bundy, William Wilson. "The Mexican Minority Problem in Otero County, Colorado." Master's thesis, Univ. of Colorado, 1940.

Christiansen, H. George. "Teacher-Community Relationships in the Small Communities of Colorado." Master's thesis, Univ. of Colorado, 1939.

Coan, Mary Wright. "The Language Difficulty in Measuring the Intelligence of Spanish-American Students." Master's thesis, Univ. of New Mexico, 1927.

Corbin, Leland Wayne. "The Educational Activities of the Evangelical United Brethren Church in New Mexico." Master's thesis, Univ. of New Mexico, 1949.

Cummins, Densil Highfill. "Social and Economic History of Southwestern Colorado, 1860–1948." Ph.D. dissertation, Univ. of Texas, Austin, 1951.

Ethell, Ora Gjerde. "A Study of 50 Spanish-Speaking and Mexican Families in Denver County Granted Aid to Dependent Children April to October 1936 and Receiving Grants Continuously to June 1942." Master's thesis, Univ. of Denver, 1943.

Forrest, Suzanne. "Federal Relief Comes to New Mexico." "The Final Years and Later." "From Indian New Deal to Hispanic New Deal." "Implementing the Cultural Agenda." Unpublished manuscripts. 1986.

Friday, Charles Bostwick. "Government Interference in the Settlement of Industrial Disputes in Colorado." Master's thesis, Univ. of Colorado, 1947.

Gadd, Milan W. "Significant Problems of Spanish-Speaking Persons and a Study of Their Registrations in the Denver Office of the Colorado State Employment Service." Master's thesis, Univ. of Denver, 1941.

Gaither, James Mann. "A Return to the Village: A Study of Santa Fe and Taos, New Mexico, as Cultural Centers, 1900–1934." Ph.D. dissertation, Univ. of Minnesota, 1957.

Glenny, Hazel Alice. "A History of Labor Disputes in the Northern Colorado Coal Mining Fields with Emphasis on the 1927–1928 Strike." Master's thesis, Univ. of Colorado, 1938.

Goubaud-Carrera, Antonio. "Food Patterns and Nutrition in Two Spanish-American Communities." Master's thesis, Univ. of Chicago, 1943.

Gutierrez, Ramon. "Marriage, Sex, and the Family: Social Change in Colonial New Mexico, 1660–1846." Ph.D. dissertation, Univ. of Wisconsin, Madison, 1980.

Howard, Donald S. "A Study of the Mexican, Mexican-American and Spanish-American Population in Pueblo, Colorado, 1929–1930." Master's thesis, Univ. of Denver, 1930.

Huebert, Lois Edith. "A History of Presbyterian Church Schools in New Mexico." Master's thesis, Univ. of New Mexico, 1964.

Hurt, Wesley Robert, Jr. "Manzano: A Study of Community Disorganization." Master's thesis, Univ. of New Mexico, 1941.

Jensen, Billie Barnes. "The Woman Suffrage Movement in Colorado." Master's thesis, Univ. of Colorado, 1959.

Jensen, Carl Robert. "A Study of the Spanish-American Normal School at El Rito." Master's thesis, Univ. of New Mexico, 1939.

Johnson, Irma Yarbrough. "A Study of Certain Changes in the Spanish American Family in Bernalillo County, 1915–1946." Master's thesis, Univ. of New Mexico, 1948.

Lawlor, Sister Catherine Miriam. "History of the Sisters of Charity in New Mexico (1865–1900)." Master's thesis, Creighton Univ., 1938.

Lawson, Harry O. "The Colorado Coal Strike of 1927–1928." Master's thesis, Univ. of Colorado, 1950.

Leathers, Mabel Wheeler. "Differential Factors in Cases before the Domestic Relations Department of the Denver Juvenile Court." Master's thesis, Univ. of Colorado, 1946.

Lipshultz, Robert J. "American Attitudes toward Mexican Immigration, 1924–1952." Master's thesis, Univ. of Chicago, 1962.

McCullough, Edith Lenore. "A Brief History of the Great Western Sugar Company in Colorado and the Effect of Its Business Policies and Practices upon the Economy of Certain Regions of Northern Colorado." Master's thesis, Univ. of Colorado, 1954.

McNaughton, Donald Alexander. "A Social Study of Mexican and Spanish-American Wage-Earners in Delta, Colorado." Master's thesis, Univ. of Colorado, 1942.

Markoff, Dena Sabin. "The Beet Sugar Industry in Microcosm: The National Sugar Manufacturing Company, 1899–1967." Ph.D. dissertation, Univ. of Colorado, 1980.

May, William John, Jr. "The Great Western Sugarlands: History of the Great Western Sugar Company." Ph.D. dissertation, Univ. of Colorado, 1982.

Mills, James Eugene. "A History of Brush, Colorado." Master's thesis, Univ. of Colorado, 1965.

Moore, Frank C. "San José, 1946: A Study in Urbanization." Master's thesis, Univ. of New Mexico, 1947.

Moreno, Daniel Thomas. "Social Equality and Industrialization: A Case Study of Colorado Beet Sugar Industry." Ph.D dissertation, Univ. of California, Irvine, 1981.

Morton, Dorothy Virginia. "A History of Quay County, New Mexico." Master's thesis, Univ. of Colorado, 1938.

Moyers, Robert Arthur. "A History of Education in New Mexico." Ph.D. dissertation, George Peabody College for Teachers, 1941.

Naster, Betty Roth. "Casimiro Barela, Colorado's 'Perpetual Senator' 1847–1920." Master's thesis, Univ. of Denver, 1974.

Nieweg, Frances Elizabeth. "Beetworkers of Colorado." Master's thesis, Univ. of Colorado, 1941.

Nuckles, Reuben Aieleen. "The Decorating and Furnishing of a Typical Spanish-American House." Master's thesis, Univ. of Chicago, 1927.

Osterud, Nancy Grey. "Strategies of Mutuality: Relations Among Women and Men in an Agricultural Community." Ph.D. dissertation, Brown Univ., 1984.

Parham, Robert Bruce. "The Civilian Conservation Corps in Colorado, 1933–1942." Master's thesis, Univ. of Colorado, 1981.

Quataert, Jean. "The Changing Nature of Family Work in the Nineteenth Century: A Case of German Textiles." Paper at German Historical Institute, London, 1984.

Ream, Glen O. "A Study of Spanish Speaking Pupils in Albuquerque High School." Master's thesis, Yale Univ., 1930.

Redmond, Ray E. "A Study of Industrial Relations within the Colorado Fuel and Iron Company." Master's thesis, Univ. of Denver, 1928.

Rice, Theodore D. "Some Contributing Factors in the Determining of the Social Adjustment of the Spanish Speaking People in Denver and Vicinity." Master's thesis, Univ. of Denver, 1932.

Rohde, Joyce Alberta. "The Employment Status of Spanish-American Office Workers in Selected Firms of the Northern Rio Grande Valley." Master's thesis, Univ. of Colorado, 1957.

Rose, Yancey Lamar. "Cultural Assimilation in Process: A Descriptive Study of a Community in New Mexico." Ph.D. dissertation, Leland Stanford Jr. Univ., 1932.

Rosen, Bernard. "Social Welfare in the History of Denver." Ph.D. dissertation, Univ. of Colorado, 1976.

Samora, Julian. "The Acculturation of the Spanish Speaking People of Fort Collins, Colorado in Selected Culture Areas." Master's thesis, Colorado Agricultural and Mechanical College, 1947.

Schulte, Regina. "Life and Work in Peasant Households in Nineteenth Century Bavaria." Paper at German Historical Institute, London, 1984.

Schwartz, Harry. "Organization of Agricultural Labor in the United States 1930–1940." Master's thesis, Columbia Univ., 1941.

Sherman, Doris Bledsoe. "Business Education in the High Schools of New Mexico." Master's thesis, Univ. of New Mexico, 1948.

Sininger, Harlan. "New Mexico Reading Survey." Master's thesis, Univ. of New Mexico, 1930.

Sjoberg, Gideon. "Culture Change as Revealed by a Study of Relief Clients of a Suburban New Mexico Community." Master's thesis, Univ. of New Mexico, 1947.

Stephenson, Richard B. "The Use of Troops in Labor Disputes in New Mexico." Master's thesis, Univ. of New Mexico, 1952.

Swayne, James B. "A Survey of the Economic, Political and Legal Aspects of the Labor Problem in New Mexico." Master's thesis, Univ. of New Mexico, 1936.

Taylor, Hazel Elizabeth. "An Evaluation of the NYA Student Work Program in High Schools of Colorado." Ph.D. dissertation, Univ. of Colorado, 1942.

Vincent, Maria Girard. "Ritual Kinship in an Urban Setting: Martineztown, New Mexico." Master's thesis, Univ. of New Mexico, 1966.

Walker, Randi Jones. "Protestantism in the Sangre de Cristos: Factors in the Growth and Decline of the Hispanic Protestant Churches in New Mexico and Southern Colorado, 1850–1920." Ph.D. dissertation, Claremont, Graduate School, 1983.

Walter, Paul Jr. "The Press as a Source in the Study of Social Problems." Master's thesis, Univ. of New Mexico, 1933.

————. "A Study of Isolation and Social Change in Three Spanish Speaking Villages of New Mexico." Ph.D. dissertation, Stanford Univ., 1938.

Weatherby, Lela. "A Study of the Early Years of the Presbyterian Work with the Spanish Speaking People of New Mexico and Colorado and Its Development from 1850–1920." Master's thesis, Presbyterian College of Christian Education, 1942.

Webbert, Florence Mae. "A Study of the Effect of State and National Legislation on Child Welfare during the Years 1929 to 1940." Master's thesis, Univ. of Colorado, 1940.

Whiteman, Laura Mary. "Economic and Social Status of Wards in the State

Welfare Home for Girls, Albuquerque, New Mexico." Master's thesis, Univ. of New Mexico, 1941.

Wilson, Owen Meredith. "A History of the Denver and Rio Grande Project, 1870–1901." Ph.D. dissertation, Univ. of California, Berkeley, 1942.

Woodward, Dorothy. "The Penitentes of New Mexico." Ph.D. dissertation, Yale Univ., 1935.

Newspapers

Albuquerque Tribune (daily), April–May 1936.
La Aurora, 1902–14, selected issues at MHL.
La Bandera Americana (Albuquerque weekly), 1917, 1925, 1932, 1935–36.
Catholic Register (Denver), 1916–28, selected issues.
The Chronicle News (Trinidad, Colorado), 1904, 1913–14, 1925, 1934–36.
Colorado Labor Advocate, 1926–36.
Denver Post, 1928–43, selected issues.
Greeley Daily Tribune, 1924–36.
Rocky Mountain News, 1936–38, selected issues.
La Voz del Rio Grande (Española weekly), 1926, 1930–37.

Oral Histories Available in Depositories

Archuleta, Ruth, "Presbyterian Life in Dixon," TC91C, MHL.
Badger, Angelina. "Missionary Service," TC35C, MHL.
Barber, Ruth. TC139C, and "Missionary Service," TC35C, MHL.
Candelaria, Rev. José. "Records of Placitas Church." TC62, MHL.
Cook, Minnie. TC154, MHL.
Jimenez, Carlos. Oral History 72, DPL.
Kelly, Mr. and Mrs. William. 0–96, CHS.
Lobato, Emilio, Sr. 0–104, CHS.
Martinez, Lucas. 0–200, CHS.
McLung, Mrs. Lilian Hughes. 0–106, CHS.
Romero, Chris. Uncatalogued, DPL.
Romero, Rev. Epifanio. "History of Truchas Church." TC36C, MHL.
Sanchez, Mrs. Justa Tafoya. 0–151. CHS.
Shomburg, Thomas W. 0–155, CHS.
Storey, Lucile Dunlavey. 0–49, CHS.
Trujillo, Mrs. Albino and Mrs. Alice Romero. TC24C, MHL.
Velasquez, Meliton. 0–185, CHS.
Walmsley, Myrtle. TC100C, MHL.
Zellers, Lydia. TC93, MHL.

Interviews by the Author

(N.B.: Many of the names have been changed to protect the interviewees' privacy.)

Agnew, Edith. Santa Fe, 8 Nov. 1983.

Aragon, Aurelia. Santa Fe, 10 Nov. 1983.

Byers, Joseph. Denver, 4 Oct. 1983.

C. de Baca, Tita. Denver, 14 Sept. 1983.

Chaves, Maria. Greeley, 12 Oct. 1983.

Chaves, Tom. Santa Fe, 9 Nov. 1983.

Cordova, Amelia. Evans, Colorado, 12 Oct. 1983.

Esquibel, Rev. Alfonso. Santa Fe, 9 Nov. 1983.

García, Margarita. Windsor, Colorado, 12 Oct. 1983.

Gomez, Lydia. Greeley, by telephone, 12 Oct. 1983.

Gonzales, Juan, et al., Española, Greeley, 26 Sept. 1983 (with the aid of Prof. Reyes Ramos, Univ. of Colorado).

Holmes, Fred. Denver, 4 Sept. 1983.

Lopez, Rose. Española, Greeley, 26 Sept. 1983 (with the aid of Prof. Reyes Ramos).

MacKenzie, Margaret. Denver, 14 Sept. 1983.

Maes, Arthur. Denver, 12 Sept. 1983.

Rendon, Gabino Jr. Las Vegas, N.M., 25 Oct. 1983.

Romero, Lucy. Greeley, 12 Oct. 1983.

Romero, Orlando. Santa Fe, 10 Nov. 1983.

Torres, Maria. Greeley, 13 Oct. 1983.

Trujillo, John. Chimayo, 12 Nov. 1983.

Vigil, Charles. Denver, 13 Sept. 1983.

Index

Abiquiu (N.M.), 17, 166
adultery, 57, 59
Agricultural Administration Act, 173
Agricultural Workers Unions, 170
agriculture: *see also* gardens; sugar-beet
    industry
    in communal villages, 14–15, 19–20;
    drought and harvest failure, 114, 128,
        162, 167;
    effect of World War I, 108–109;
    and homesteading, 31, 115;
    leasing of farms, 133;
    and migration from farms to cities,
        123;
    role of women in, 15, 45, 55, 115;
    Spanish Americans in farming, 89,
        114;
    and suspicion of federal programs,
        184–185;
    wage labor in, and status of women,
        146
Aguilar (Col.), 104
Albuquerque (N.M.), 31, 180
alcohol, 98, 152
Allison, Matilda, 67
Allison school, 67, 74, 75, 78
American Beet Sugar Company, 116–
    117
American Federation of Labor, 121,
    122, 156, 158
Americanism, and patriotic fervor, 111,
    121

Americanization: *see also* cultural
        interactions
    and Anglo club women, 118;
    in barrio, 7;
    differing goals of, 148–149, 198, 207;
    feminized version of, 85–86;
    of gender roles, 76–77;
    of homes and homemaking, 77, 86,
        99, 207;
    of Indians, 19;
    and mining companies, 95–96;
    and Protestant missions, 27–28, 64–
        65, 74;
    rejection of assimilation, 119, 122,
        156;
    and selective acculturation, 38–39, 202;
    and stereotypes of Spanish American
        culture, 5;
    support of under Wilson's presidency,
        111–112;
    and women's role, 160
Anglo, term defined, vii
arts, Spanish, revival of, 188–196;
    criticism of, 194–195
Austin, Mary, 189, 190, 191
automobiles, ownership of, 188

Barker, Ruth, 37, 58
Barrera, Mario, 8
barrio, as American colony, 8; spatial
        mobility in, 7

345

beetworkers. *See* sugar-beet industry

Beet Workers Association, 158

Beet Workers Union, 166

birth control, interest of Chicanas in, 276 n 96

Black Hands (Manos Negras), 26, 128

Blake, Alice, 73

boarding, 92–93, 100, 247 n 12

Bond, Frank, 22

Briggs, Charles, 59

Brown, Lorin, 55

brujas. *See* witches

Camarillo, Albert, 8

capitalism

  and expansion of credit, 23, 30;

  and village communalism, 17

cash economy

  in depression, 167;

  and income of missionaries, 81;

  increased dependence on, 21, 55–56, 119, 138, 168, 182

Catholic church, 144; *see also* churches; converts, to Protestantism; Mary, devotion to; Penitentes

  Anglo domination of, 17;

  convent schools, 245 n 134;

  missions of, 184;

  and Protestant mission schools, 27–28, 67;

  rivalry of Presbyterians with Catholic clergy, 78;

  role of women in, 50–51

Catron, Senator Thomas, 20, 80

Chicano, term defined, vii

childbirth. *See* midwives

children: *see also* education

  attitude of missionaries about, 74;

  and child care, 92;

  fostering of, 74, 93;

  and play, 239–240 n 82;

  training in homemaking, 98;

  as wage earners, 93, 130, 140–141, 169, 178–179

Chimayo (N.M.), 32, 54–55, 67;

  and Anglo economy, 113;

  and conscription, 112;

  weavers in, 190

churches: *see also* Catholic church; missionaries; Protestants; religion

  and absence of community spirit, 144;

  discrimination in, 28, 144;

  increased membership in, during Depression, 168;

  and involvement of women, 149;

  subsidy of, in company towns, 91

cigarette smoking, Protestant ban on, 242 n 107

C.I.O. (Congress of Industrial Organizations), 171

cities: *see also* barrio; *and specific city*

  Chicanos in, 9;

  during Depression, 163–164

Clark, Prudence, 35, 55, 85

Clark, Victor, 32, 35, 36, 37, 94

Clements, Mollie, 69, 70, 84

clerks, wages for, 147

coal mining: *see also* mining camps and towns

  heterogeneity of labor force, 88–89, 106;

  labor needs in, 32, 129;

  and migration, 115;

  and strikes, 94–95, 103–105, 110, 156–157, 203;

  suits against companies, 248 n 32;

  and unions, 94, 172

  wages for, 157

colonization theory, 213 n 2

Colorado Fuel and Iron (CFI) Co., 5, 30, 87;

  attempt of, to encourage patriotism, 95–96;

  creation of company towns by, 89–90, 202;

  destruction of plaza structure, 90, 105–106;

  employment of Spanish Americans by, 32;

  and kindergartens, 95, 97;

  Sociological Department of, 95–97

Colorado Supply Company, 91

Columbine Mine, 156

comadre relationships, 49

Communist Party, 172

company towns, 206. *See also* mining camps and towns; sugar-beet colonies
converts, to Protestantism, 27–28, 144; church programs for, 83 marginality of, 78–79 and village ties, 80
Conway, Melinda, 74
cooking, 52; and stoves, 38, 55, 188; teaching of, 75–76
Costigan, Senator Edward P., 92
Councils of Defense, 111, 113
Country Life Commission, 123
Court of Private Land Claims, 20
courtship, 43
crafts
    Anglo sponsorship of, 189–190; increased professionalism in, 56; low wages from, 195; and New Deal jobs programs, 182, 192–193; and Spanish colonial arts revival, 187–196; stereotype of Spanish American aptitude for, 148
Craig, Elizabeth, 79, 85
credit, dependence on, 137; in company towns, 91, 138; during the Depression, 179; and village economy, 22, 23, 30
crime, stereotypes and reality of, 152
cultural interactions: *see also* Americanization; gender roles; regional community
    and acculturation by Spanish Americans, 38, 189–190; and Anglo-Spanish American frontier, 159; and Anglo sense of superiority, 72; conflict of Anglo and Spanish American cultures, 37–38, 209; effects of Depression, 183; and ethnic groups in tent colonies, 104–105; and intermarriage, 24; and migration patterns, 6–7; and pluralism rather than assimilation, 119, 199, 207;

and response to inadequate economic base, 200–201; role of missionaries in, 83–85; and social mixing, 94, 118–119, 145; Spanish colonial arts revival, 187–196; women's involvement in, 64; and World War I, 107
culture, Anglo. *See* Americanization
Cundiyo (N.M.), weaving in, 190, 194
curanderas (herbal healers), 41, 47, 82, 83

De León, Arnoldo, 7, 8
Denver (Col.), 169, 180, 197; and beetworkers' strike, 172; domestic service in, 146–147; Chicanos and Chicanas in, 132, 153–154, 168, 180; cost of living in, 130; education in, 147, 148; organization against police brutality in, 170; social service efforts in, 149; unemployed Mexicans in, 124
Denver Interracial Commission, 174
Depression
    agricultural development programs in, 184–185; agricultural failures in, 162, 167; and government intervention in community, 179, 198; and hostility to Spanish Americans, 166, 174–175; labor organization and strikes during, 169–173, 197, 198; migration patterns in, 164–165, 169; relief efforts in, 175–178; and Spanish colonial arts revival, 187–196; and work programs for women, 179–182
discrimination, 24, 134; *see also* prejudice; stereotypes
    attempt to mobilize against, 26; by churches, 144; in company towns, 94, 116; during the Depression, 166, 169;

discrimination (*continued*)
  income differential between Spanish
    Americans and Anglos, 32;
  myths justifying, 135, 178;
  protests against, 155;
  in schools, 140;
  and segmentation of labor market,
    148–149;
  as strategy of Anglo community, 204–
    205
divorce, 44, 57, 58, 152, 298 n 78
domestic service: *see also* homemaking
  and goals of Americanizers, 149;
  in mining town, 100;
  proportion of women employed in,
    146–147, 180;
  in railroad town, 33;
  training for, 182
draft, for World War I, 112–113
drought, 114–115, 162, 167
Duran, Rev. Julian, 167

economy: *see also* cash economy;
    Depression; labor; trade
  Anglo domination of, 8;
  of communal villages, 15, 58;
  multi-source income, 30–32, 163,
    203;
  role of credit in, 22, 30;
  unemployment, 124, 163, 164, 194;
  and women's work, 54, 205–206
education: *see also* mission schools;
    teachers
  boarding schools, 27, 74;
  of children of beetworkers, 34, 140–
    141;
  in company towns, 91;
  effect of poverty on, 27;
  experiments in, 184;
  of girls, 75–76, 147;
  and hope for a better future, 139;
  irregular attendance in schools, 140–
    141;
  kindergartens, 95, 97, 99;
  and increased enrollment during
    Depression, 169, 179;
  public schools, 65–66, 139;

of ricos, 16;
segregation and racism in, 140;
Spanish American Normal School,
    66–67
electoral politics
  Spanish American participation in,
    26–27, 144;
  and prominent families, 29;
  and women, 118, 179
El Rito (N.M.), 17, 66
Embudo (N.M.), 112, 164; women
    workers in, 33, 54
English language, promotion of, 111,
    149
ethnic relations. *See* cultural
    interactions

families
  changes in, 38–39, 92;
  and child-rearing, 44, 49;
  comadres and parenting networks,49;
  in communal villages, 14–15, 42–43;
  in company towns, 34, 202–203;
  effect of Depression on, 168;
  and fostering, 74;
  income of, 130–131;
  and missionaries, 80, 84;
  and regional community, 153;
  stereotypes of women's role in, 42;
  strength of, 152;
  and sugar-beet labor, 127, 131
fence cutting, 128. *See also* Gorras
    Blancas
Fergusson, Erna, 189
fiestas, 78, 83–84
flagellation. *See* Penitentes
food: *see also* cooking; gardens
  communal production of, 52, 53, 78;
  preservation of, 189, 258 n 40;
  purchase of, 114, 143;
  sharing of, 52–53, 81–82;
  trade in, 53–54
Forgotten People (G. Sanchez), 5
fostering, attitude of missionaries
    toward, 74
Fort Collins (Col.), 132; segregation in,
    135

frontier
  Anglo dominance of, 19;
  concepts of, 10;
  expansion of, 13

gardens, 79;
  in company towns, 91, 117, 143, 203;
  in Depression, 163, 167, 189;
  training of boys in management of, 76;
  in villages, 142;
  women's control of, 51–52, 55, 93, 182
gender roles: *see also* cultural interactions
  Americanization of, 76–77, 151;
  Anglo impressions of, 61;
  and autonomy of women, 48, 205;
  in children, 42;
  in communal villages, 15, 42–43;
  concepts of, 10;
  and devotion to Mary, 50;
  and education for girls, 75;
  interdependence of men and women, 60;
  and marriage, 43–44, 151;
  and reduced opportunities in north, 150–151;
  and work, 33, 54–56, 115, 146, 179, 205–206
German-Russians, 124, 133, 139
Gilbert, Fabiola Cabeza de Baca, 188, 191
godmothers (madrinas), 43, 49
Gorras Blancas, 6; attacks on railroads by, 25–26
Great Western Sugar Company, 34, 116, 162;
  and education of children, 139, 141;
  and Mexican workers, 120;
  recruitment of labor by, 109, 119, 129, 130;
  and sugar-beet colonies, 133–134, 154–155
Greeley (Col.), 166;
  autonomous community in, 156;

and beetworker strike, 172;
  discrimination in, 134, 174
Griswold del Castillo, Richard, 7
Gutman, Herbert, 37

healers, certification of, 117. *See also* curanderas; midwives; missionaries, as healers
health care and services, inadequacy of, 143, 145, 187; increased government attention to, 113–114
Henderson, Alice Corbin, 118, 190
Hispanic, term defined, vii
Holly Sugar Company, 135
Holmes, Jack, 5, 29
Holy Week, 50, 52, 70–71
homemaking: *see also* domestic service
  attitude of missionaries toward, 69, 76–77;
  and kindergarten teachers in company towns, 97;
  teaching of, 75–76, 98, 185
homesteading, 18, 31, 115. *See also* land ownership
Hopkins, Harry, 176, 177
housing: *see also* land ownership
  adobe, 90, 203;
  Americanization of, 77;
  changes in style of, 188;
  in company towns, 90, 203;
  construction of, 54;
  inadequacy of, 128–129, 197;
  and land, 3;
  for missionaries, 68–69;
  and property ownership, 100;
  rented, 56, 100;
  in sugar-beet colonies, 116, 127;
  union demands for, 171
Huerfano County (Col.), 12, 92
"hyphenate issue," 111
Hyson, Alice, 75, 78, 81, 84, 85

illegitimacy, 43, 58
illiteracy, 139, 153. *See also* education
illness, in villages, 68

immigration: *see also* migration
   and alien labor, 136, 166;
   fear of, 121, 174;
   from Mexico, 108, 120, 123, 124–126,
      164–165;
   restrictions on, 164–165
Immigration Act of 1917, 109
Immigration and Naturalization
      Service, 174; and border patrol,
      164
income, multiple sources of, in
      communal village, 14, 30–32. *See
      also* coal mining; sugar-beet
      industry
Indians, American. *See* Native
      Americans
Industrial Workers of the World, 110;
      and mining strike, 156–158
inflation, and food prices, 115
inheritance, equality in, 15, 45
intermarriage, 24, 35, 94, 145;
      condemnation of, 122
irrigation projects, 184

Johnson, Governor (Col.), 165
Jones-Costigan Act (1934), 173

Kearney, Col. Stephen Watts, 13
Kern, Robert, 106
kindergartens, 95, 97, 99
kinship networks, 48–49, 153
Knights of Labor, 25
Ku Klux Klan, 134, 174
Kutsche, Paul, 54, 198

labor: *see also* unionization *and
      particular type of work, e.g.,* coal
      mining
   and Anglo domination of economy,
      8;
   attitudes toward, 31;
   and blockade against aliens, 166;
   child, 93, 130, 169, 178–179;
   in communal villages, 14, 15;
   competition for, during World War I,
      108–109;

by families, 34, 45;
   marginalization of, and crafts revival,
      193;
   and migratory patterns, 36, 39–40,
      164–165;
   need for cheap, 108, 119, 123, 131;
   and New Deal jobs programs, 179,
      182, 185;
   in mines, 21, 31;
   and multi-source income, 30–31, 163,
      203;
   occupational choices of young people,
      196;
   in railroad, 18, 31;
   regional community as source of,
      201;
   and role of men in family, 38–39, 55;
   segmentation of market for, 148–149;
   in sugar-beet industry, 33–35, 170–
      173;
   unemployment during Depression,
      163;
   wage, dependence on, 31, 38–39, 101,
      142, 146, 160, 203;
   women's, 11, 15, 38–39, 54–57, 60–
      61, 93, 101, 142, 146–151, 179–183
land grants
   losses by Hispanics, 20, 27;
   to railroads, 22, 24;
   and subsidy of settlement, 14
land ownership: *see also* homesteading;
      housing
   by Chicanos, 132, 133;
   in communal villages, 14, 16;
   and decreased land base, 23;
   by elite Spanish Americans, 28–29;
   and home ownership in company
      town, 134;
   loss of land used as loan collateral,
      184;
   in mining communities, 92;
   and rising land values, 22
Larimer County (Col.), 12
Larrazolo, Octaviano, Governor
      (N.M.), 119
Las Animas County (Col.), 12, 18, 92,
      94;
   coal mining in, 88, 89;
   and Liberty Bonds, 113;

migration patterns in, 35;
relief in, 175
Las Vegas (N.M.), 25, 26
laundresses, 33, 56, 59, 100, 180;
divorced women as, 57, 58
Lawrence, John, 24, 45
legal system
Anglo dominance of, 20, 24;
and land grant suits, 20;
and women, 44, 45, 58–59
Leonard, Olen, 52, 61
Liberty Bonds, 113
Liga Obrera de Habla Español, 173,
174. *See also* Spanish Speaking
Workers League
Lindsey, Governor (N.M.), 113
livestock, 18; and the Depression, 167.
See also sheep raising
Loomis, Charles, 185
Lopez, José Dolores, 190
Loyalty Leaguers, 111
lumber, and railroads, 24, 26

McAdoo, William, 113
McCormick, Cyrus, 191, 195
McCrossen, Helen, 191
McLean, Robert, 135
Maddux, C. V., 141
madrinas (godmothers), 43, 49
Mandeville, W. B., 124
Manos Negras (Black Hands), 26, 128
marriage, 151; *see also* divorce;
intermarriage
and property rights, 45;
and village society, 45–46;
and women's roles, 43–44
Mary, devotion to, 50;
condemnation of, by missionaries,
78;
as protection against witches, 59
mattress-makers, 56
medical care. *See* curanderas;
midwives; missionaries, as healers
Mexico, 14;
immigration from, 108, 120, 123,
124–126, 164–165;
revolution in, 108, 110;
trade with, 17

midwives, 52, 82, 153;
compensation for, 47;
in northern communities, 143, 144–
145, 206;
place of, in communal villages, 48;
professionalization of work as, 186–
187;
requirement for certification of, 117;
and role of women, 46–47;
training programs for, 186
migration
and agriculture, 123, 125;
of Anglos in Southwest, 7;
effect of Depression on, 164–168,
176–177;
effect of World War I on, 107–110,
115, 126;
government attempts to influence, 14,
187–188;
and kinship webs, 153;
Mexican, 107–109;
and mining camps, 87–88, 93, 115;
patterns of, 4, 19;
seasonal, 35, 39–40, 132, 136, 198,
201, 247 n 12;
stereotypes about, 6;
and sugar-beet labor, 34–35, 131,
170–171, 176;
and village ties, 17
mining, and land acquisition, 21. *See
also* coal mining
mining camps and towns, 87–88, 201–
202;
and child labor, 93;
company control over, 90;
discrimination in, 94;
women's loss of autonomy in, 93, 206
missionaries, Protestant, 63–64, 149;
see also mission schools
attitudes toward, 70;
as bearers of Anglo culture, 64, 72,
86;
cash income of, 81;
and child-rearing methods, 74–75;
fascination about dark side of village
life, 70–71;
as healers, 82;
home visits by, 80–81;
integration of, into village life, 81–86;

missionaries, Protestant (*continued*)
　isolation of, 72, 80, 118, 202;
　living conditions of, 68–69;
　rivalry with Catholic clergy, 78;
　as social directors, 83;
　stereotyped view of Spanish
　　Americans, 70, 71, 73–74, 76;
　view of, as witches, 70, 80
mission schools, 63–65, 67–70; *see also*
　education
　goal of Americanization in, 27–28,
　　64–65, 74;
　organization of, 67;
　and public schools, 65;
　role of women in, 63–64, 68;
　teachers in, 68–69
moonshining, 152
mortality rate, of infants, 143, 145; in
　villages, 113
mutualistas (mutual aid organizations),
　26, 154, 156, 169

Nambé Community School, 183, 184
National Reemployment Service, 175
National Youth Administration (NYA),
　182, 183, 192
National Sugar Co., 33
Native Americans, 4;
　Americanization goals for, 19;
　as slaves, 218 n 9;
　and trade with Spanish Americans, 5;
　transfer of land to Pueblos, 128, 167
nativism, and hostility to Mexicans,
　110, 111, 126. *See also*
　Americanization; prejudice
New Deal, 179, 180, 184. *See also*
　Works Progress Administration
New Mexico, statehood for, 27
New Mexico State Penitentiary, 58–59
New Mexico Writer's Project, 59
nuns, 245 n 134

orphans, 58
Ortiz y Pino, Concha, 191
Otero, Miguel A., 29
Otero-Warren, Adelina, 118, 191

Padilla, Polita, 78
parteras. *See* midwives
"partido" agreements, 22–23, 45
pasture, communal, 14, 18; losses of,
　20, 21, 115, 167
patriarchial society, stereotypes of, 42,
　44
patriotism, during World War I. *see*
　Americanization
patronage, 27
Penitentes
　and Catholic church, 17, 50, 144;
　Holy Week ceremonies of, 70–71;
　political involvement of, 26;
　practices of, 50, 51;
　and Protestant missionaries, 65;
　renaissance of, 121
Pentecostal Assembly of God Church,
　155
People's Party, 25–27
plastering, as women's work, 54, 56,
　142, 180, 186
play, 239–240 n 82
plaza structure, communal orientation
　of, 90; disruption and loss of, 31,
　80, 90, 105–106
prejudice: *see also* discrimination;
　nativism
　against Chicanas by Anglo women,
　　145–146;
　ascendancy of racism, 121–122;
　against Mexicans and other Spanish
　　Americans, 136–137, 174–175;
　and terminology, vii, 137
Presbyterian College of the Southwest,
　28
Presbyterians: *see also* Protestants;
　and mission schools, 67, 68, 75;
　rivalry with Catholic clerics, 78;
　Spanish-speaking churches, 28;
　view of Spanish American culture, 5
pressure cookers, 189
Prince, Governor (N.M.), 25
prison, women in, 58–59
property: *see also* land ownership
　and inheritance, 45;
　and marriage, 44, 45;
　ownership of, 16, 160;

of divorced women, 57;
women's rights to, 15, 44, 45
prostitution, 100
Protestants, 63, 64, 184; *see also*
converts; missionaries,
Presbyterians
and cigarette smoking, 242 n 107;
and goal of Americanization, 27, 77;
and Spanish American majorities, 99
Pueblo Indians, transfer of land to, 128,
167

racism. *See* discrimination; prejudice;
stereotypes
railroads
attacks on, 25–26;
and coal mining, 32;
expansion of, 19, 22, 31;
land grants to, 22, 24;
need for labor in, 18, 31–32, 109,
129;
and transformation of trade, 19, 21
Red Cross, 117, 168
Reeves, Margaret, 181
regional community
beetworker colonies as model of, 203;
and coal miners, 106;
concept of, 12;
as defense against hostile culture, 38,
201–202;
and diminished opportunities for
autonomy, 126;
effect of Depression on, 163, 164,
205;
and government intervention, 198,
208;
people as bonds in, 35–36;
and role of women, 60–61;
and Spanish American identity, 9–10;
as strategy for autonomy, 40;
and ties to villages, 153
relief
Anglo resentment of, 175–176;
cyclical dependence on, 187;
and the Depression, 163, 164, 167,
168, 175, 179;
Mexican aliens on relief rolls, 165,166;

proportion of Spanish Americans
receiving, 152;
protest of relief policies, 178;
reluctance to accept, 138;
stereotypes of recipients, 159, 176,
178, 181;
wages from, 177
religion: *see also* churches; Catholic
church; Missionaries; Penitentes;
Protestants
and Americanization, 149
and popular devotions, 50–51
ricos
relation with villagers, 16;
and social stratification, 28–29;
village vs. plains, 29–30
Rio Arriba County (N.M.), 26, 54, 180;
education in, 27, 65, 66, 169, 179;
handcrafts in, 194;
migration patterns in, 35;
sheep raising in, 21–22
Rio Grande Valley, 12
Robinson, Senator Helen Ring, 105
Rockefeller interests, 87, 88, 91
Rocky Mountain Fuel Company, 156
Romero, Orlando, 80
Romo, Ricardo, 7

Sanchez, George, 5
San Miguel County, and Gorras
Blancas, 25; People's Party in, 25–
27
Santa Claus, 83
Santa Cruz Valley irrigation project,
184
Santa Fe (N.M.), 31, 190; as alien city,
119; conquest of, 13
Santa Fe County, 188
scabs, 94–95, 122
Schlesinger, Andrew, 6
seamstresses, 33, 56, 57, 59; relief
sewing projects, 181
segregation. *See* discrimination
sewing, classes in, 99
sewing machines, 38, 55, 188
sheep raising
boom in, 18, 21;

sheep raising (*continued*)
  in communal villages, 14–15, 17;
  day laborers in, 23;
  by elite Spanish Americans, 28–29;
  role of women in, 45;
  and sharecropping, 22–23
Shriver, Paul, 177, 178
Simmons, Marc, 59
slavery, 218 n 9
Smedley, Agnes, 66, 87
social service workers, 185–186, 206
social status, and patronage of arts, 192;
  of ricos, 28–29
Sociedad Protección Mutua de
    Trabajadores Unidos
    (S.P.M.D.T.U.), 26
Sociological Department, of CFI, 95–
  96; women's role in, 97
Spanish American, term defined, vii,
  137
Spanish American Citizens Association,
  169
Spanish American Normal School, 66–
  67
Spanish language, teaching of, 119
Spanish Speaking Workers League, 166
Spanish Speaking Workers Union, 173
Starkville (Col.), 32
status differences, generational, 15. *See
    also* gender roles
stereotypes
  of criminal tendencies, 151–152;
  cultural, 3, 190;
  of government relief recipients, 159,
    176, 178, 181;
  and handcrafts, 148;
  and justification of low wages, 177–
    178;
  and justification of segregation, 135;
  of Mexicans and Spanish Americans,
    109–111;
  of migrants and migration, 6, 36;
  myth of Spanish American's "homing
    instinct," 131;
  on the part of missionaries, 70, 71,
    73–74;
  of Spanish American children and
    youth, 65–66, 140, 141, 192–193;

  of Spanish American women, 11, 42,
    61, 73–74, 96, 149–150;
  of Spanish American workers, 96,
    122–123, 129–130, 151;
  of villages, 5–6
stoves, 38, 55, 188
strikes
  beetworkers', 171–173;
  mining, 94–95, 103–105, 110, 156–
    158, 203;
  and scabs, 94–95, 122
suffrage, campaign for, 118
Sugar Act (1937), 173, 178
sugar-beet colonies, 34, 117, 129, 203–
  204;
  bad conditions of housing, 116, 127;
  and Great Western Sugar Company,
    133–134, 154–155
sugar-beet industry: *see also* Great
    Western Sugar Company
  alien workers in, 136, 165;
  beetworkers' strike (1932), 171–173;
  conditions for workers in, 116, 129–
    130;
  effect of depression on, 162–163, 167;
  indebtedness of workers, 179;
  and Jones-Costigan Act (1934), 173,
    178;
  labor in, 33–35, 109, 124, 128, 136,
    187, 188, 203;
  and migration, 131, 136;
  and union organization, 158, 166,
    170–171, 197;
  wages in, 115, 120–131;
  and winter work, 135–136
Sugar Trust, 33
syphilis, tests for, 134

Taco Bell restaurants, 185
Taos (N.M.), 190
Taos County (N.M.), 17, 112; education
  in, 27, 67
taxes and taxation
  in company towns, 91;
  and the Depression, 162, 167;
  inequities in, 29;
  and land ownership, 14, 20, 27

Taylor, Paul, 130, 132, 133, 139, 159
Taylor Grazing Act (1934), 185
teachers (maestras), 65–66; *see also*
    education; missionaries
  in mission schools, 68–69;
  role as female models, 82, 83;
  training of, 66–67;
  women as, 68, 115, 147
Tercio (mining camp) (Col.), 87, 89
terminology, vii, 137
Thomas, Helen Dail, 181
Tierra Amarilla (N.M.), 23
Timberlake, Congressman Charles, 135
tourism, income from, 195–196
trade
  and cultural interchange, 5;
  effect of railroad on, 19;
  of food, 53–54;
  in household items, 38;
  with Indians, 19;
  and village economy, 16–17;
  in wool, 22–23
Trinidad (Col.), 99, 154; female-headed
    households in, 100

unemployment
  in Depression, 163, 164;
  and handcrafts programs, 194;
  after World War I boom, 124
unionization
  of beetworkers, 170–173, 197;
  growth of, 169
United Cannery, Agricultural and
    Packing and Allied Workers of
    America (UCAPAWA), 171, 197
United Front Committee, 171–172
United Mine Workers Union, 103, 110
United War Work Campaign, 113

Van Ness, John, 54
villages: *see also* regional community
  and Anglos, 30, 37, 113–114, 119;
  and barrio, images of, 8;
  communal, 14–17, 58;
  and crafts, 196;
  and decreased land base, 23;
  effect of credit on economy of, 22,
    30;
  egalitarianism in, 16;
  flexibility of system in, 18, 30, 32,
    160;
  and government-sponsored
    community organizations, 198;
  health services in, 113–114;
  integrative function of fiestas, 78;
  loss of autonomy in, 199;
  loss of common land in, 20, 21;
  male/female relations in, 15, 42–43,
    60–61;
  marriage in, 43–45;
  and Penitentes, 17;
  preconquest culture of, 9;
  poverty of, 113, 160;
  retreat to, during Depression, 164–
    165, 167, 168;
  rituals and fiestas in, 78, 83–84, 86;
  role of missionaries in, 77–86;
  seasonal migrations from, 35, 39–42,
    198, 200;
  and sharing of food, 52–53, 143;
  and Spanish American identity, 9–10;
  stereotypes of, 5, 11;
  tensions in, 60;
  and trade, 16–17;
  and visiting of homes, 80–81, 90;
  women's community in, 42, 60–61,
    142–143, 179–180
vocational education, and crafts
    training, 193, 196

Walter, Paul, 153, 189
washerwomen. *See* laundresses
weavers, 56, 190
Weld County (Col.), 12, 140, 172;
  Chicanos in, 121, 132;
  intermarriages in, 145;
  labor unrest in, 156, 158
Western Federation of Miners, 110
widows, economic problems of, 93; role
  of, 46
Wilson, Woodrow (President), 111
witches, 59, 82; view of missionaries as,
    70, 80

women. *See* gender roles *and also specific topic, e.g.,* labor, women's
Women's Board of Home Missions (Presbyterian), 67, 68
Woodward, Ellen, 181
wool, trade in, 15, 17, 22
Works Progress Administration (WPA), 164, 171, 183, 192;
  dependence on, 197;
  hostility to, 175, 176;
  and training in domestic service, 182

World War I
  and conscription, 112–113;
  effect on migration patterns, 107–110, 115, 126;
  and nativism, 110–111;
  promotion of war bonds for, 113;
  and veterans' desire for modern facilities, 117

Zeleny, Carolyn, 6, 39